LAND USE
CONTROLS
IN NEW YORK STATE

LAND USE
CONTROLS
IN NEW YORK STATE

A Handbook on
the Legal Rights of Citizens

BY

NATURAL RESOURCES DEFENSE COUNCIL, INC.

ELAINE MOSS, *Editor*

THE DIAL PRESS/JAMES WADE
New York

RECYCLED READING

Library of Congress Cataloging in Publication Data

National Resources Defense Council.
    Land use controls in New York State.

    Includes bibliographical references and index.
    1. Zoning law—New York (State) 2. Land sub-
division—law and Legislation—New York (State)
I. Moss, Elaine. II. Title.
KFN5811.N38   346′.747′045   74–83695
ISBN: 0-8037-4692-X

MANUFACTURED IN THE UNITED STATES OF AMERICA
Designed by Jacques Chazaud

ACKNOWLEDGMENTS

A number of people have participated in the preparation of this book. The NRDC staff members and summer interns who contributed were Phillip Hoose, Robert Stover, Angus Macbeth, Esq., Sarah Chasis, Esq., Cullen Phillips, Robert Meyer, Julie Copeland, Diane Donley, Ronald Outen, J. G. Speth, Esq., David Hawkins, Esq., Richard Ayres, Esq., Frances Beinecke, Laurance Rockefeller, Esq., Paul Glickman, and Anne Davidson. Outside contributors were William R. Ginsberg, Esq., John R. Robinson, Esq., and Judy Stolaroff.

Those who read various chapters and offered invaluable criticisms and suggestions were Albert K. Butzel, Esq., of Berle, Butzel & Kass; Alfred S. Forsyth, Esq., of Forsyth, Decker, Murray & Broderick; Philip Gitlen, Assistant Counsel of the New York State Department of Environmental Conservation; Robert J. Kafin, Esq., of Kafin and Needleman; Langdon Marsh, Esq., Counsel of the New York State Department of Environmental Conservation; Alan Parness, Esq., of Cadwalader, Wickersham & Taft; Diana W. Rivet, Esq., County Attorney of Rockland County; Paul H. Rivet, Esq.; Stuart D. Root, Esq., of Cadwalader, Wickersham & Taft; David Sive, Esq., of Winer, Neuburger & Sive; and Kenneth Toole of the Dutchess County Planning Department.

Much helpful information was provided by Henry G. Williams, Jr., Assistant Director, John Dugan, Esq., Assistant Director, and Sheldon Damsky, Esq., Legal Services, Division of Community Affairs, New York State Department of State, and by various staff members of the New York State Department of Environmental Conservation.

CONTENTS

NRDC

The Natural Resources Defense Council (NRDC) is a nonprofit, tax-exempt, membership organization dedicated to protecting America's endangered natural resources and improving the quality of the human environment. With offices in New York, Washington, D.C., and Palo Alto, California, and a full-time staff of twenty-one lawyers and scientists, NRDC combines scientific research, citizen education, and litigation in a highly effective program of action. NRDC's major involvements have been in the areas of air pollution, water pollution, nuclear safety, land use, noise, mass transit, national forest management, strip mining, and stream channelization. NRDC conducts special projects on specific issues which monitor the performance of key government agencies in carrying out their environmental responsibilities. These include a Land Use Project, a Catskill/Adirondack Project, a Clean Air Project, and a Clean Water Project. NRDC is supported entirely by tax-deductible contributions.

INTRODUCTION

Purpose and Scope of the Book

THIS BOOK IS written primarily for citizens of New York State who are concerned about land development and its impact on natural resources and on people's lives. Some of these citizens may be faced with the immediate problem of trying to find some way of bringing about environmental review of a proposed development project. In some cases, the problems may be so serious that citizens are seeking some way to control or stop a particular project. Other citizens, while not personally engaged in a pressing confrontation, may be committed to the beliefs that land use is one of the most important problems facing our country today and that New York's countryside should be developed in a rational and thoughtful manner.

The great land boom in the United States initially found many Americans unprepared—unaware of the consequences of rapid, uncontrolled growth and unaccustomed to playing active roles in determining how land in their communities would be used. Relishing the prospect of increased tax revenues, many communities eagerly encouraged rapid growth. Today, costs and losses loom much larger in the picture. Subdivisions of prime or second homes have brought new tax payments to localities, but their costs in increased demand for services and in transportation problems, depleted water supply, and sewage pollution have usually proved to be far greater than anticipated. The value of lost natural resources is now much more acutely perceived and appreciated, especially as the interdependence of human and natural activities becomes more and more apparent.

Concern about land use and development has now become a matter of national consciousness. A number of states—such as Vermont, Florida, and Hawaii—have adopted statewide programs of land use control, and many others are seriously studying the problem. Bills which would establish a national land use program have been under active consideration by Congress during the past two years. It is generally recognized that action must be taken. This book addresses itself to the question of what citizens of New York State can do now on the basis of existing laws and circumstances.

New York State has long known the ravages of uncontrolled land development, where big money has been only a subdivision away. In many areas, the character of the land has been permanently transformed. Marshes have been filled and covered with concrete. Pastures have been carved into small pieces, converted into second-home cities, and, ironically enough, sold to buyers seeking respite from urban pressures. Ponds and streams have become receptacles for sewage.

There are many people in the state who want to stop outright abuses and to temper growth with reason, fairness, and a full understanding of consequences. In most cases, citizens do not know what their rights are regarding land development in their communities. They do not know what actions are required of real estate developers or how these requirements are or should be enforced. Most people do not know that there are ways of effectively contesting development proposals without suing the developer. Others may be familiar with local zoning laws, but intimidated by what they perceive to be a jurisdictional morass at the state level. There is little knowledge of existing opportunities for public hearings. Few know what planning tools are available and how they operate. The significance of federal legislation is generally not understood. This book attempts to make this information available to the public in as clear and comprehensive a manner as possible.

The laws and regulations which have an important bearing on land use control in New York State are widely scattered, and many agencies and institutions are involved. Up until the present time, practically no one has had a clear picture of what all the different elements are, what they encompass, and what potential they possess for practical solutions to problems. The task of bringing together such widely dispersed information has not been an easy one, and, no doubt, there is much room for further clarifications and additions.

It is extremely important that citizens not be unduly discouraged or scared off entirely by apparent or real confusion in the workings of government—at local, state, or federal levels. It is equally essential that they realize that specialists, government authorities, and politicians will not solve all their problems for them. In a democracy such as ours, people have the right and the opportunity, though they may have to fight for it, to influence decisions made by those in positions of power, to force government to address itself to the problems of the people, and to compel enforcement of laws. This potential should never be underestimated. Those people who are willing to take action can learn what their specific rights are and how these rights can be most effectively exercised. Through the participation and concern of an active citizenry, government can be obliged to fulfill its responsibilities and to tackle the problems that lie ahead.

Specifically addressed here are the following questions:

How can citizens most effectively exercise their influence? (Chapter 1)

What are the basic constitutional issues that are involved in land use regulation? (Chapter 2)

What land use controls exist at the town, city, or village level of government (Chapter 3), at the county level (Chapter 4), and at the state level? (Chapter 5)

What land use controls have been adopted for the Adirondack Park? (Chapter 6)

What special land development problems exist in the Catskills? (Chapter 7)

How can wetlands in New York State be protected? (Chapter 8)

What impact does federal legislation aimed at environmental protection have on land use control? (Chapters 9, 10, and 11)

How are laws which have been established to protect consumers and investors relevant to land use? (Chapter 12)

What other special controls over land use exist in New York State? (Chapter 13)

How do prevalent property tax myths measure up to reality? (Chapter 14)

What means are there for preserving open space? (Chapter 15)

The following list outlines the major laws and programs, at all levels of government, that are discussed in these chapters.

MAJOR LAWS AND PROGRAMS
DISCUSSED IN THIS BOOK
(See index for page references)

Enabling Legislation for Local Governments

Zoning
Planning Boards
Comprehensive Master Plans
Subdivision Regulations
Official Maps
Capital Improvement Programs
Building Codes
Road Specifications
Historic and Esthetic Preservation
Acquisition of Open Space
Environmental Conservation Commissions or Councils

State Laws and Programs

The Freedom of Information Law
Public Water Supply Permits
The State Pollutant Discharge Elimination System (SPDES)
Stream Protection Permits
The Environmental Analysis Program of the New York State
    Department of Environmental Conservation (DEC)
Subdivision Review and Approval Powers of Health Department
    Officials
The Adirondack Park Agency Act
The Temporary State Commission to Study the Catskills
The Tidal Wetlands Act
Land Subdivision Disclosure Requirements
Registration of Condominiums, Co-ops, and Homeowners' As-
    sociations
Licensing of Real Estate Brokers and Salesmen
Flood Insurance Programs Statute
The Wild, Scenic, and Recreational Rivers System
Siting of Major Steam Electric Generating Facilities
Siting of Major Utility Transmission Facilities

Agricultural Districts Law
Forest Tax Law

Federal Laws and Programs

The Freedom of Information Act
The National Environmental Policy Act (NEPA) —
The Clean Air Act of 1970 —
The Federal Water Pollution Control Act Amendments of 1972 —
The Coastal Zone Management Act —
The Interstate Land Sales Full Disclosure Act
SEC Registration of Investment Contract Condominiums
Mail Fraud Statutes
The National Flood Insurance Program
The Wild and Scenic Rivers Act

Other Laws and Programs

Protection of New York City's Watershed Lands
New York City's Consumer Protection Law

Suggestions for citizen action are set out in each chapter, usually in the concluding section.

The appendix contains the addresses and telephone numbers of federal and state agencies and private organizations discussed in the text. The glossary provides explanations of selected legal terms and procedures. A special note on legal citations, found after the glossary, is provided as an aid for those using the notes at the end of each chapter. This note briefly and simply explains how federal and state court cases, statutes, and regulations are recorded and cited.

Every effort has been made to ensure that the material presented in this book is as up-to-date as possible. In a field like land use, however, such developments as new legislation, regulations, and court decisions are continually taking place. The intent of this book is to set out for citizens the basic structure and procedures of existing land use controls in New York State. It is hoped that this information will aid citizens not only in dealing with present problems, but also in influencing future changes.

Just as this book was going to press the New York State Legislature passed two very important new environmental acts: (1) a state "little NEPA" act,[1] and (2) a fresh water wetlands act.[2] The former, which will become fully effective on June 1, 1976, requires the preparation of environmental impact statements by all state, county, and local agencies for actions that they propose or approve "which may have a significant effect on the environment." Modeled after the National Environmental Policy Act (NEPA), which is discussed in Chapter 9, this state act should provide a vital new means of achieving environmental protection in New York State.

The fresh water wetlands act, which will become effective on September 1, 1975, establishes a rather complicated scheme for the protection of fresh water wetlands. Basic elements of this act include the preparation by the New York State Department of Environmental Conservation (DEC) of a statewide inventory and map of fresh water wetlands; the development and implementation of land use regulations and permit programs by local governments, counties, and DEC; the establishment of a new fresh water wetlands appeals board; considerable agricultural exemptions; and tax abatement provisions. This new law will complement the existing Tidal Wetlands Act, which is discussed in Chapter 8.

NOTES

1. N.Y. Environmental Conservation Law §8-0101 *et seq.*
2. N.Y. Environmental Conservation Law §24-0101 *et seq.*

LAND USE
CONTROLS
IN NEW YORK STATE

CHAPTER 1

The Politics of Citizen Action

T HE MOST IMPORTANT thing a citizen who wants to do something about an environmental problem can do is to find other people who share the problem or who are willing to give support—and organize. One person working alone, no matter how dedicated and persistent, can never hope to be as effective as a well-organized group. A letter written on the letterhead of a group will receive more attention than a letter on plain paper from an individual. Groups may prepare press releases which newspapers will publish. Government officials will be more willing to meet with a representative from a group than with someone who only wants to discuss his own problems. Defending environmental values is often not an easy job, but many more doors will be opened for an organized group than for a single person working alone.

Despite the fact that successful citizen action taken in opposition to powerful industrial, commercial, or real estate interests has received wide publicity, many people still do not fully appreciate the power which an organized citizens' group can wield. The inherent strength of forceful expression of public interests should never be underestimated. Special interests may be heavily financed and sophisticated in organization and technique, but they do not speak for the people. The citizens' group which can serve as an effective vehicle for the expression of the interests and concerns of an aware citizenry can be a very powerful political force.

The number of citizens' groups which have already come into being in New York State is remarkable. They range from such groups as the Scenic Hudson Preservation Conference, whose battles with Consolidated Edison and the Federal Power Commission over the past ten years have gained national recognition, to small local groups formed in response to subdivision problems or threats.

Since many different reasons stimulate the organization of citizens' groups, and actions taken vary greatly according to circumstances, it is not possible to set out a neat explanation of "how it is done." It is possible, however, to suggest some basic strategies and tactics which may prove useful.[1]

Important reasons for organizing have included, among other motivations, the desire to delay, stop, control, or review a particular development; the intent to monitor the actions and decisions of a government agency or agencies to see that they carry out their responsibilities conscientiously and in compliance with the law; the determination to work for better local planning and strong land use controls; and the need to publicize problems or to educate the public on particular issues. Some groups have been formed only to face immediate problems; others have established long-range goals.

Whenever a citizen perceives that group action is needed to address a problem, he should first find out if any established environmental organization or citizens' group is already working on the problem. If so, he can explore the possibility of joining this effort.

If there is no existing organization which focuses effectively on a citizen's concern, then a new group can be formed. Its beginnings can be as simple as a discussion among friends, but a strong core of committed people should materialize to spearhead the work to be done and to provide the continuing motivating force which will be necessary to carry the effort through the difficulties and setbacks it will almost inevitably encounter. Dedication and energy are invaluable assets in the thick of a fight. It is very important, moreover, to recognize the political realities of the situation. If a group is concerned with land use problems, it should assess the political influence of local real estate interests; it should find out where local politicians stand on the issue; and it should work to establish as strong a political base as possible for its own efforts. The support of prominent and influential citizens should be sought.

Once there is a strong, committed, and realistic central group, an appeal can be made to the public for wider membership. Circumstances will dictate how fast all of this must take place. Clearly, if the spur to action is the notice of an imminent public hearing, speed is essential; more deliberation is possible if goals are more long range. Calling a public meeting should not be difficult, though some expenses will probably be incurred. Notices or leaflets can be made or printed to publicize the concern and to announce that an organizing meeting will be held on a specific date at a specific place. A notice can be published in the local newspaper. The meeting place should be large enough to hold the expected crowd and should be in an accessible location. Schools, fire houses, and churches have been used by many groups in the state.

A large part of the initial public meeting should probably be devoted to an elaboration of the problem. Care should be taken to focus as clearly as possible on central issues and to identify possible courses of action which might lead to successful results. Decisions should be made on how available resources can best be used. The need to gather all possible relevant information and evidence on the problems at hand should be recognized and stressed. A preliminary course of action should be charted and specific tasks assigned. Plans should probably be made to try to locate experts, such as environmentally minded scientists, sanitary engineers, teachers, lawyers, or students who would be willing to participate in the work to be done. Local colleges often prove to be extremely fruitful sources of expertise and assistance. In some areas, high school science classes have also made vital contributions to needed research.

A name for the group should be chosen, and, if funds allow, someone should be appointed to have stationery letterhead prepared. Officers may be elected—listing them on the letterhead can make it more effective. Dues will probably be needed to meet expenses. Plans for subsequent meetings should be made.

Groups which envision a long-term existence should consider the possibilities of incorporation and application for tax-exempt status—which, if granted, can enable the organization to solicit contributions which donors may deduct from their income tax. This move increases tremendously the money-raising potential of an organization. A number of different criteria must be met to qualify for exemption; notably, lobbying for legislation is prohibited. A booklet published by the Conservation Foundation, entitled *Law and Taxation: A Guide for Conservation and Other Nonprofit Organizations,* is a helpful introduction to the complexities of incorporation and tax exemption.[2] If an organization wants to pursue these possibilities, the services of a good tax lawyer will be needed.

In general, citizens' groups should be prepared to explore all avenues of possible action. If it is not possible to win review of a development project or projects at the local level, they should be prepared to look for controls at the state or federal level. A setback in one area does not necessarily mean that nothing else can be done. Flexibility and resiliency are essential. All possible courses of action and available controls should be considered.

It should also be pointed out that citizen action is not always directed toward fighting *bad* proposals, plans, and regulations. Many times citizens will be involved in the formulation of good plans and regulations for their communities. Ways in which this can be done are discussed in Chapters 3, 4, and 15. Most frequently, however, the public is aroused to action by the threat of some undesirable activity.

The gathering of information and evidence is a crucial part of the work to be done by a citizens' group.[3] Both in preparing for an immediate confrontation with a developer and in formulating a long-range monitoring plan, it is necessary to find out exactly what the needs of developments are (such as water supply, sewage disposal, roads) and what procedures developers must go through to gain all the necessary approvals—what filings must be made, what permits must be obtained, what agencies must be dealt with. A developer may be subject to laws and regulations at all levels of government. Chapter 3 of this book discusses land use controls at the town, city, or village level in New York State. Using this information as a guide, citizens should find out what controls have been established in their area, what local boards exist and how they operate, and what specific procedures a developer must follow. Chapters 4 and 5 give similar information for county and state levels of government, respectively.

The way in which citizens approach the task of determining what controls a particular developer is subject to is very important. Many complexities and details should be expected, and the impulse to throw up one's hands in despair should be rejected. Developers are willing to combat these complications; so should the citizens whose lives will be affected by their projects. What citizens should be looking for, moreover, are "handles" on the situation—ways in which environmental review can be won and effective action taken. If a developer fails to abide by an existing law or regulation or to follow a specified procedure, it may be possible to challenge an entire project.

Political pressures existing on the local level are often strongly biased toward as much growth as possible. The argument has been traditionally put forth that growth will increase the tax revenues of an area by augmenting the local property tax roll. (As is discussed in Chapter 14, it is now recognized that it is by no means conclusive that growth brings more benefits in tax revenues than it costs in services.) Real estate and commercial interests, moreover, are very deeply entrenched in most areas, and tend to focus on the financial gains they hope to make from land development. The "right" of particular individuals in an area to reap such windfalls was for many years considered sacrosanct. Today it is clear that the profits of individuals are sometimes made at the expense of the community, which must bear the costs of providing services, of losing essential natural resources, and of seeing its way of life destroyed. The citizens' group which is reviewing a particular development should make every effort to see that the full cost of a proposed project to the community is brought out into the open and fully appreciated. This full cost includes not only the expense of providing needed municipal services, but also damage to the environment in terms of polluted streams and groundwater, depleted water supplies, air pollution, and traffic congestion. Only when all these factors are considered can the costs and benefits of a land development project be adequately assessed.[4]

When local politics or lack of controls fails to provide proper review of land development projects, citizens' groups should look for possibilities of achieving this through state programs. As discussed in detail in Chapter 5, particular permits are required by state law for certain kinds of land development. In connection with the issuance of these permits, public notice may be given of the filing of an application, written comment may be invited, and public hearings may be held. Citizens should be completely up-to-date on which of these procedures are or must be practiced with respect to particular applications. In particular, they should take great pains to know when public hearings are possible or required, so that they may press for a hearing when needed, make the necessary arrangements to appear, and prepare testimony. It is particularly important to know exactly what type of public notice is necessary for any public hearing. If public notice is not given exactly as required by law, the transactions of a hearing and any approvals or permits hinging on them may be invalidated. Many actions, especially on the local level, have been successfully challenged by citizens on the grounds that proper hearing notice was not given.

Participation in public hearings is a vital way in which citizens' groups can exert influence. As much care as possible should be taken to be well prepared. All procedural requirements for the particular type of hearing at hand should be determined and carefully followed. The group should find out exactly what its rights will be in the hearing and what will be expected of it. The presentation which the group plans to give should be well organized and non-repetitive. It should include a clear statement of the group's interest in the problem, which should be stated as forcefully and convincingly as possible. Since hearings are quasi-judicial proceedings, the group does not have to be represented by a lawyer, though it may be. If the group does not have a lawyer, it should attempt to choose a spokesman who will have presence of mind and patience in the midst of the formal proceedings and cross-examination of witnesses. Note should probably be made here that some hearing officers have formed a stereotype of the frantic environmentalist who speaks in semi-hysterical tones, impassioned language, and generalities. Hearing officers are often very impatient with such spokesmen. Statements which are calmly presented, objective, and well documented with specific facts will receive far more respect and consideration. Many citizens, appearing for the first time at a hearing, are actually very nervous. Perhaps past exposure to television programs dealing with criminal courts leads them to feel that they are on trial. Careful preparation, reassurance from other group members, and an appreciation that appearance at a public hearing is a citizen's right should help to allay this anxiety.

Objections to the project under consideration which are presented in the group's testimony should reflect all the research the group has done and all consultations with experts. The testimony should focus on basic problems and give clear evidence backing up all arguments. Witnesses should be chosen carefully so that their statements are complementary and not repetitious. Some witnesses —such as a resident, a doctor, or a fisherman—may have personal knowledge of the problems involved. Others may be experts with special expertise: Scientists can discuss the impact of the development on water quality, fish and wildlife, and other aspects of the environment; economists or social scientists can assess the socio-economic effects which can be expected. As far as possible, the impact of the proposed development on all relevant factors—water and air quality, noise, population density, transportation and traffic problems, taxes, municipal services, schools, fish and wildlife, etc.— should be pointed out. In the presentation of complicated or very technical evidence, a determined effort should be made to present information in such a way that the public and hearing officials can understand it.

In the public hearings which are held by the New York State Department of Environmental Conservation, groups which present testimony are also allowed to cross-examine other spokesmen and witnesses. This allows the group's spokesman to pose specific questions to the developer and his witnesses, such as his planner or his engineer, as well as to agency officials who appear. Thus the right to cross-examine is an important one, and citizens should take care to find out whether they will have this right in any hearing.

Since it sometimes happens that not everyone who wishes to speak at a hearing is able to do so, it is wise to prepare written statements. These statements, along with all oral testimony, make up the official record of the hearing. This official record may be invaluable in any subsequent legal action which may be taken to challenge decisions that are made or plans which are approved.

Concurrently with review at local and/or state levels, citizens should explore the possibility that a development might be subject to federal regulation. As discussed in Chapter 9, if any federal funds are involved in a project, it is possible that an environmental impact statement or environmental assessment information may be required under the National Environmental Policy Act (NEPA). Some types of projects are subject to review under the federal Clean Air Act (see Chapter 10). Certain subdivisions must file a registration statement under the Interstate Land Sales Full Disclosure Act and certain condominiums must be registered with the Securities and Exchange Commission (see Chapter 12). All of these possibilities should be explored, and their applicability to the problems at hand determined. If a development is not in full compliance with federal law, citizens should report violations to the proper authorities and press for an investigation and/or enforcement of the law.

In all their activities, citizens' groups should attempt to keep the local press and broadcast news teams well informed. Care should be taken to try to clarify for the media what basic issues are involved and what the specific goals of the group are. The better the problem is defined, the better the story, the wider the coverage, and the clearer the ensuing public understanding. Personal contacts with reporters should be made and maintained. Efforts should be made to know what their needs, interests, and deadlines are and how information can best be supplied to them. Specific procedures for preparing and submitting press releases should be ascertained. In all dealings with the media, it is very important to be as fair and accurate as possible and not to make statements that cannot be supported.

Whether or not a citizens' group needs a lawyer will depend on circumstances. Sometimes it will not be necessary, sometimes simply desirable, and sometimes absolutely essential. When an attorney's services are needed, attempts should be made to find a lawyer who is both sympathetic to the group's position and versed in, or at least familiar with, environmental law. If a law school is located in the vicinity of a group's activities, citizens should find out whether it has an environmental law society or a similar group which might be able to provide assistance on a volunteer basis.

In the course of their work, members of a citizens' group may often be in contact with government officials. It is very important to make these relationships as productive as possible. Efforts should be made to get to know the staff of a local planning board and the personnel of federal agencies who are responsible for important decisions related to land use. A group should seek to gain recognition as a committed organization with serious environmental concerns. Members should try to establish working relationships with agency officials that will facilitate obtaining publications, needed information, and notification of on-going activities.

Government officials may at times be very cautious in dealing with citizen requests. Some officials may find public involvement in their affairs an annoying nuisance; others may actually have something to hide. Citizens should be mindful of the very real stresses and strains involved in a government official's work and should be aware of constraints he or she may face. A self-righteous or threatening approach to agencies should always be avoided. On the other hand, it is equally important that citizens do not settle for anything less than the attention and service they are due. If cooperation cannot be obtained at a lower level in an agency or a field office, contact with a higher administrator may resolve the problem. In general, the higher the echelon, the better informed officials generally are—particularly with respect to regulations or policies pertaining to public involvement. If, however, an impasse is reached on an important question, assistance can also be sought from elected representatives.

Citizens seeking information should try to make their requests as specific as possible. They should also follow up a telephone call with a letter restating any verbal requests. Things usually go much more smoothly for those who are well informed and straightforward in

Each agency must make and publish rules and regulations pertaining to the location and nature of its records.[11] This includes, but is not limited to:

a. The times and places such records are available;
b. The persons from whom such records may be obtained;
c. The fees, to the extent authorized by this article or other statute, for copies of such information; and
d. The procedures to be followed.

Anyone who is denied access to records may appeal such denial to the head or heads of the agency or municipality involved. If *that* person further denies such access, his reasons must be explained fully in writing within seven business days of the time of such appeal. This denial is subject to review under Article 78 of the New York State Civil Practice and Rules.[12]

The establishment of a Committee on Public Access to Records is also provided for under the law. This committee is composed of seven members, three of whom are state government officials and the other four of whom may not be elected or appointed officials or employees of any state or municipal government agency. The latter four members are appointed by the governor and must include two persons who either are or have been representatives of the news media. This committee is responsible for promulgating rules and regulations under the law and for advising agencies and municipalities, and also gives advisory opinions on particular problems.[13]

It is to be hoped that the implementation of the New York State Freedom of Information Law will be carried out in full conformity with the spirit of the legislative intent of this law, which is quoted in in its entirety below:

> The legislature hereby finds that a free society is maintained when government is responsive and responsible to the public, and when the public is aware of government actions. The more open a government is with its citizenry, the greater the understanding and participation of the public in government.
>
> As state and local government services increase and public problems become more sophisticated and complex and therefore harder to solve, and with the resultant increase in revenues and expenditures, it is incumbent on the state and its localities to extend public accountability wherever and whenever feasible.
>
> The people's right to know the process of government decision-making and the documents and statistics leading to determinations is

basic to our society. Access to such information should not be thwarted by shrouding it with the cloak of secrecy or confidentiality.

The legislature therefore declares that government is the public's business and that the public, individually and collectively and represented by a free news media, should have unimpaired access to the records of government.

In summary, organization of citizens' groups is a necessary aspect of environmental protection in this country. Such citizens' groups can provide the means for politically powerful expression of public interests and concerns and for the effective defense of environmental values. Although many variations are possible, important aspects of organizing a citizens' group are the formation of committed and energetic leadership; a realistic appraisal of political factors; identification of basic problems faced and primary goals to be sought; exploration of all possible means of controlling land use on all levels of government; determination of which courses of action are most likely to be successful; solicitation of public support and of needed assistance from experts or willing researchers; effective participation in public hearings; good relationships with the press and other media; a good lawyer, if necessary or possible; and the establishment of productive working relationships with government officials, a task which should be facilitated by recent federal and state laws which provide for public access to government records.

NOTES

1. The U.S. Environmental Protection Agency (EPA) has published a very helpful booklet entitled *Don't Leave It All to the Experts: The Citizen's Role in Environmental Decision Making* (November 1972). This realistic and practical guide is available for 55¢ from the Superintendent of Documents, U.S. Government Printing Office, Washington, D.C. 20402.

2. This booklet, which was published in 1970, can be obtained from the Conservation Foundation, 1717 Massachusetts Avenue, N.W., Washington, D.C. 20036, for $1.

3. Citizens' handbooks published on topics other than land use may offer advice and strategies which can be helpful in this.

4. Chapter 14 deals specifically with the property tax issue and the cost/benefits problem.

5. Wellford v. Hardin, 315 F. Supp. 768, 770 (D.D.C. 1970).

6. 5 U.S.C. §552.

7. 5 U.S.C. §552(b).

8. 33 U.S.C. §1251 *et seq. See* Chapter 11.

9. N.Y. Environmental Conservation Law §17–0801 *et seq. See* Chapter 5.

10. N.Y. Public Officers Law, Article 6, §85 *et seq.* A booklet entitled *Your Right to Know: Guide to the New York State Freedom of Information Law* is available for 25¢ (and a stamped, self-addressed envelope) from New York Public Interest Research Group, Inc., 5 Beekman Street, Room 410, New York, N.Y., 10038.

11. The governing body of a municipality may make and publish uniform rules for any group of or all agencies in that municipality.

12. *See* Glossary for discussion of this article.

13. The address of the committee is as follows: Committee on Public Access to Records (COPAR), Tower Building, Empire State Plaza, Albany, N.Y. 12242.

CHAPTER 2

Basic Constitutional Issues

THE MOST SIGNIFICANT restraint on government control of land use and development is the "takings clause" of the Fifth Amendment to the United States Constitution: ". . . nor shall private property be taken for public use without just compensation."

The New York State Constitution has an analogous provision in Article I, Section 7 (a): "Private property shall not be taken for public use without just compensation."

Government is prohibited by these clauses from taking private property except for a valid public purpose, and if land is so taken, the government must pay a just price for it. A taking may be direct or indirect. Thus the government must provide just compensation not only whenever it takes title to land through condemnation, but also whenever it so regulates the use of land that the restrictions imposed amount to a taking of the property.

Drawing the line between regulation and taking is always difficult. Justice Holmes set out the issue classically in 1922 in his opinion in *Pennsylvania Coal Company* v. *Mahon:*

> The general rule at least, is that while property may be regulated to a certain extent, if regulation goes too far it will be recognized as a taking. . . . We are in danger of forgetting that a strong public desire to improve

the public condition is not enough to warrant achieving the desire by a shorter cut than the constitutional way of paying for the change.[1]

In subsequent years, the Supreme Court has handed down decisions granting communities broad powers to regulate the use of land to promote the general welfare, but the central question has remained: At what point does a regulation become a taking?

Four years after its decision in *Pennsylvania Coal,* the Supreme Court upheld zoning as a legally permissible method of restricting or prohibiting uses of land and types of construction within a community.[2] The Court did not actually reach the takings issue in this case, but stated that future determinations of whether the application of a zoning ordinance amounted to a taking should be made on a case-by-case basis.

Since this ruling, the takings issue has been considered in hundreds of cases involving zoning and other regulations of land use. The right of states, and of local governments when so enabled, to regulate land use is based on the so-called "police power" to legislate for the promotion of public health, safety, morals, or general welfare. The degree to which this power is limited by the takings prohibition depends on particular circumstances. In each case, a court engages in a balancing analysis, weighing the public good involved against the cost imposed on the individual landowner. Since the outcome depends in large part on the facts of the case, it is not possible to formulate a simple set of rules clearly elucidating the line between a taking and a proper exercise of the police power.[3]

In general, although variation exists from state to state, the following four standards are usually applied by state courts in determining whether a particular regulation violates constitutional prohibitions against the taking of property except for a public purpose and with just compensation: The regulation must be reasonably related to the power to legislate for the protection of the public health, safety, morals, or general welfare; it must not unfairly discriminate between similar parcels; it cannot reduce the value of the parcel to the level of confiscation; and it must provide a benefit to the public by preventing harm (such as air pollution or increased traffic) that would be caused by particular uses of the property rather than yielding a benefit (such as recreational land) which is normally acquired by condemnation. If a particular regulation is found to amount to a taking, the regulation will be struck down; however, the government still has the option of taking the property and justly compensating the owner, as long as the taking is for a valid public purpose.

Tough new restrictions on the use of private land, arising from citizens' concern for orderly, non-destructive growth and desire for conservation of limited natural and cultural resources, bring the takings issue to the fore. For example, regulations for the preservation of open spaces or historic sites, regulations to seek elimination of existing uses, regulation of flood-prone areas, estuarine and beach lands, and a variety of deterrents to urban growth are typical regulations which have undergone or will undergo challenge on constitutional grounds. In New York State, such a challenge has already been made to the new Tidal Wetlands Act,[4] which provides for a temporary moratorium on all alterations of tidal wetlands prior to the effective date of land use regulations, unless a special permit has been granted.

While a comprehensive review of the litigation surrounding the takings issue will not be attempted here, some of the critical rulings of New York courts on regulations involving open space, historic preservation, esthetics, and controlled growth will be examined to give readers an appreciation of how some of the newer forms of land use restriction are being viewed.[5] Certain important decisions in other states, as well as a recent Supreme Court decision, will also be discussed.

Regulations and prohibitions of uses harmful to valuable natural resources, such as tidal wetlands, are becoming more and more necessary as scientific data revealing the interdependence of human and natural activities accumulate. Tidal wetlands, as just one example of a key natural resource, perform several invaluable and essential functions: The abundant nutrients of these areas support the marine food chain upon which a majority of commercially valuable fish and shellfish rely; they act as efficient buffers against storms and flooding; they provide pollution control and aid sedimentation. In light of the increasing ability of the scientific community to document the value of such natural resources, coupled with a clearer understanding of how specific uses may negate these values, courts are more and more coming to uphold local, regional, and state land use statutes designed to protect natural resources, conserve open space, and regulate growth since their relationship to the protection of health, safety, and the general welfare is becoming manifest.

Just v. *Marinette County,*[6] a recent Wisconsin case, is a landmark decision in this regard. While the decision of this case is not binding on New York courts, it is significant as an indication of new directions in judicial thought. After finding a public right in the preservation of the natural environment, the Supreme Court of Wisconsin stated the following:

> An owner of land has no absolute and unlimited right to change the essential natural character of his land so as to use it for a purpose for which it was unsuited in its natural state and which injures the rights of others. . . . The changing of wetlands and swamps to the damage of the general public by upsetting the natural environment and the natural relationship is not a reasonable use of that land which is protected from police power regulation . . . [N]othing this court has said or held in prior cases indicate [sic] that destroying the natural character of a swamp or a wetland so as to make that location available for human habitation is a reasonable use of that land when the new use, although of a more economical value to the owner, causes a harm to the general public.[7]

Such a holding makes clear that where a regulation requires that land be left in its natural state, courts will give increasing weight to the importance to the public of such preservation.

The right of governments to regulate land development in the interest of controlling growth was approved by the highest court of New York State in 1972.[8] The town of Ramapo, which is within commuting distance of New York City, extended the concept of zoning to include a permit system for residential development. Under this system no property could be developed for residential purposes until the developer could show that certain capital improvements—whether constructed by the town or by the developer himself —would be available for a project by the time it was completed. The town had developed a comprehensive master plan for its future growth and upon this had based an eighteen-year capital improvement program setting out the town's schedule for construction of municipal facilities. Thus the town's provision of services needed for residential development would not be forthcoming for some land for as long as eighteen years.

In upholding the town's restrictions, the court pointed to the fact that the restrictions were of limited duration and concluded:

> In sum, where it is clear that the existing physical and financial resources of the community are inadequate to furnish the essential services and facilities which a substantial increase in population requires, there is a rational basis for "phased growth" and hence, the challenged ordinance is not violative of the Federal and State Constitutions.[9]

With regard to the taking issue, the court recognized that although the phased growth program would, in effect, preclude development on some land for as long as eighteen years:

> The hardship of holding unproductive property for some time might be compensated for by the ultimate benefit inuring to the individual owner in the form of a substantial increase in valuation; or, for that matter, the landowner might be compelled to chafe under the temporary restriction, without the benefit of such compensation, when that burden serves to promote the public good.[10]

The earlier case of *Westwood Forest Estates, Inc.* v. *Village of South Nyack*,[11] also decided by New York's highest court, reveals how an ordinance which has similar practical consequences for developers can be struck down when it is not properly related to a valid public purpose. In this case, the village of South Nyack had adopted an ordinance barring any new apartment buildings, ostensibly to assure that there would be no further burdening of community sewage facilities. This provision was invalidated on the grounds that it was not limited in time and a direct relationship to sewers was not demonstrated.

The contrasting results in *Ramapo* and *Westwood* are related in large part to the difference in the factual justifications made in the two cases. Unlike the village of South Nyack, the town of Ramapo successfully defended its growth control technique by a thorough presentation of planning data to support its case. Such a factual presentation helped establish the importance of the restrictions to the public, the reasonableness of the regulation, and the non-discriminatory intent of the regulation. Indeed, without such factual support, it is difficult for a community to prove that restrictions are related to a proper public purpose, rather than intended to serve other ends such as excluding lower income groups. Regulations having such a discriminatory purpose may be challenged as a violation of the public purpose requirement of the Fifth Amendment and of the due process and equal protection clauses of the Fourteenth Amendment to the United States Constitution.

A successful constitutional attack on a controlled growth ordinance has recently taken place in a federal court case in California.[12] Ordinances enacted by the city of Petaluma, which lies forty miles north of San Francisco, were struck down on the grounds that they interfered with people's constitutional right to travel and live where they wish. Under the "Petaluma Plan," the city sought to control growth in three basic ways: (1) It limited new housing units to 500 units per year. (2) It created an "urban extension line," i.e., an ultimate boundary intended to mark the outer limits of the city's expansion for twenty years or more. Within this perimeter, the city used density limitations and other techniques to set a maximum population of 55,000 (compared to the projection made in 1962 that the city's population would be 77,000 by 1985). (3) Finally, the city refused, for fifteen years or more, to annex territory or to extend city facilities to land outside the "urban extension line."

In the eyes of the (federal) District Court for Northern California, the plan amounted to an effort to avoid the problems that accompany contemporary trends in population growth by limiting the number of people henceforth permitted to move into the city. The court found that the means employed by the city violated the constitutionally protected right to travel and immigrate to the area. No compelling state interest was found to justify the abridgement of this constitutional right. The financial burden which would be placed on the city if it were to accommodate the greater growth, through provision of sewage treatment facilities and increased water supply, was not found to be adequate justification. Nor was a desire to preserve the city's present character. The court very broadly concluded:

> A zoning regulation which has as its purpose the exclusion of additional residents in any degree is not a compelling governmental interest, nor is it one within the public welfare.

The city of Petaluma is appealing the court's decision.

The United States Supreme Court has made it clear that communities have broad power to regulate land use for public purposes:

> The concept of the public welfare is broad and inclusive. . . . The values it represents are spiritual as well as physical, aesthetic as well as monetary. It is within the power of the legislature to determine that the community should be beautiful as well as healthy, spacious as well as clean, well-balanced as well as carefully patrolled.[13]

Courts, in general, give deference to a locality's determination that particular land use restrictions are needed for public purposes. This principle has been dramatically set out by the United States Supreme Court in a decision handed down in the spring of 1974.[14]

The Court upheld an ordinance of Belle Terre, a village of 700 people located on Long Island's north shore, which restricted land use to one-family dwellings. The word "family" as used in the ordinance means one or more persons related by blood, adoption, or marriage, living and cooking as a single housekeeping unit; or a number of persons, but not exceeding two, living and cooking together as a single housekeeping unit though not related by blood, adoption, or marriage. The ordinance was challenged on the grounds that by prohibiting groups consisting of more than two unrelated people from residing in the community, the ordinance deprived a household of unrelated individuals of the equal protection of the law.

The Supreme Court found the ordinance reasonable since it bore a relationship to such appropriate governmental objectives as low density, reduced traffic flow, clean air, and quiet:

> A quiet place where yards are wide, people few, and motor vehicles restricted are legitimate guidelines in a land-use project addressed to family needs. . . . The police power is not confined to elimination of filth, stench, and unhealthy places. It is ample to lay out zones where family values, youth values, and the blessings of quiet seclusion and clean air make the area a sanctuary for people.[15]

The contrast between this holding and that of the federal district court in the Petaluma case, with respect to low density and the character and values of a community, is notable.

In *Belle Terre*, the Supreme Court found that the ordinance challenged did not interfere with fundamental constitutional rights such as the right to travel, to migrate and settle within a state, or the rights of privacy or association. The case is extremely significant in pointing up the broad judicial reading of the power states and local governments have to institute land use controls, even when serious constitutional questions are raised by such controls.

Other important types of land use regulations that have undergone constitutional challenge in recent years deal with open space, historical landmarks, and esthetic controls.[16] Preservation of open space on private land has been the objective of many zoning provisions which prescribe large lot sizes and deep building setbacks. In a 1971 New York case,[17] a developer brought suit against a town's increase in the minimum lot size while his application for subdivision approval was pending. The developer argued that the value of his land had been so reduced that the regulation amounted to a taking. The highest court of the state enunciated the following guidelines regarding proof: The landowner must first show significant injury; the city must then demonstrate the relationship of the regulation to the health, safety, and welfare of the community; the landowner may still have the regulation found invalid if he shows that the regulation, albeit reasonable, deprives him of "any use of the property to which it is reasonably adapted, or serves to destroy the greater part of its value."[18] In this case, the court upheld the ordinance, finding that the landowner had failed to satisfy the diminution in value test. The evidence suggested that under the old ordinance the proposed subdivision would have been uneconomical and, therefore, the landowner was unable to prove that the new ordinance harmed him in any way.

Historic preservation has been the concern of many local ordinances and state laws. One such law, passed to save the old Metropolitan Opera House in New York City, was struck down because of the uncertainty of compensation.[19] The legislation, which was enacted in 1967, created a corporation with the power to condemn the opera house and appropriate it for public use. A 180-day holding period was established, during which funds to be used for condemnation were to be raised. The court found that the imposition of this holding period amounted to a taking since it materially affected the value of the property without assuring compensation.[20] Even more significantly, the court found the statute not one intended to protect the public health, safety, and welfare. This decision can be understood under a benefit/harm theory: The regulation was for the purpose of obtaining a direct benefit for the public rather than protecting the public from some harm or nuisance. Courts are generally hesitant to impose the cost of providing such a benefit on an individual owner under the guise of regulation.

In other instances, New York courts have upheld regulations to preserve historic landmarks. In one such case, New York City's placement of restrictions on use of historic landmarks and districts was found to be a proper exercise of its regulatory powers:[21]

> We deem certain of the basic questions raised to be no longer arguable. In this category is the right, within proper limitations, of the state to place restrictions on the use to be made by an owner of his own property for the cultural and aesthetic benefit of the community.[22]

Closely related to historic preservation controls are esthetic controls. An ordinance regulating signs, enacted by the village of Ocean

Beach on Fire Island, was upheld by New York's highest court.[23] Adopted pursuant to regulations under the Fire Island National Seashore Act,[24] the ordinance banned signs larger than four feet square in size and required removal of existing nonconforming signs after two years. The court found that, "[i]t is now settled that aesthetics is a valid subject of legislative concern..."[25] The ordinance was judged to be reasonable since it bore a substantial relationship to the economic, social, and cultural patterns of the community, and to be regulatory rather than prohibitory.

In summary, it should again be stressed that the constitutionality of land use regulations is tested by the courts on a case-by-case basis. With respect to the takings prohibition, the most significant constitutional restraint on the control of land use, courts usually apply the following four standards in such tests:

1. The regulation must be reasonably related to the power to legislate for the protection of the public health, safety, morals, or general welfare.

2. The regulation must not unfairly discriminate between similar parcels of land.

3. The regulation must not reduce the value of the parcel of land in question to the level of confiscation.

4. The regulation must prevent harm that would be caused by particular uses of the land rather than yield a benefit that is normally acquired through condemnation.

In determining whether a taking has occurred in the application of a particular regulation, the courts examine all of the facts of the case and engage in a careful balancing analysis, weighing the public interests served by the regulation against the individual's injury which results from the regulation.

Some generalizations can be made about the likely outcome. Where the regulatory objective is one with a strong historic pattern, it is likely to withstand constitutional attack. For example, protection of public safety and prevention of nuisance uses have traditionally been given great weight, whereas protection of esthetic values has not. The likelihood of a court's upholding a particular regulation will also depend on the suitability of the regulation to the nature of the property. Thus, courts look to see whether a regulation permits land to be used in a manner consistent with uses of neighboring parcels. As a corollary to this rule, uses permitted must be those which can be reasonably undertaken on that property.

Finally, the extent of the cost imposed on the landowner plays a part in the court's decision. Eleven years ago, a study revealed that a loss of two-thirds of the property's value represented the average point where a taking occurred.[26] However, other commentators have concluded that there is no basis for precise prediction in dollars and cents and that while financial loss is a relevant consideration, it is not a single or decisive one.[27] Indeed, diminutions of around 75 percent are quite frequent among statutes which have withstood constitutional attack.[28]

One final point should be made. With the growing number of restrictions on land use have come attempts to avert constitutional challenge. Various methods have been developed, including taking windfall profits from landowners benefited by a land use regulation, either by means of advance levies or a capital gains tax, and using the money to compensate those who have suffered or will suffer a loss. Another device which has been used allows higher density development in exchange for provision of public amenities by the developer. One of the more ingenious innovative systems provides for the transfer of development rights.[29] Under this system, a community establishes development rights that are separate from basic land valuation but have monetary value. A landowner restricted from building on his own property may sell his development rights to someone who owns a piece of land where development is permitted. In this way, the constitutional requirement of just compensation may be met.

NOTES

1. 260 U.S. 393, 415–416 (1922).
2. Village of Euclid v. Ambler Realty Co., 272 U.S. 365 (1926).
3. New York State Commission on Eminent Domain. 1971. Report 114.
4. N.Y. Environmental Conservation Law §25–0101 *et seq. See* Chapter 8 for a full discussion of this act.
5. For a comprehensive review of the takings issue see Fred Bosselman, David Callies, and John Banta, *The Taking Issue: An Analysis of the Constitutional Limits of Land Use Control* (Washington, D.C.: U.S. Government Printing Office, 1973), which was prepared for the Council on Environmental Quality. This study is available from the Superintendent of Documents, U.S. Government Printing Office, Washington, D.C. 20402 for $2.35 (domestic postpaid).
6. 201 N.W. 2d 761, 4 ERC 1841 (Wis. 1972).
7. 201 N.W. 2d at 768.
8. Golden v. Planning Board of Town of Ramapo, 30 N.Y. 2d 359, 334 N.Y.S. 2d 138, 285 N.E. 2d 291 (1972).
9. 285 N.E. 2d at 304–305.

10. 285 N.E. at 303.

11. 23 N.Y. 2d 424, 297 N.Y.S. 2d 129, 244 N.E. 2d 700 (1969).

12. Construction Industry Association v. City of Petaluma, 375 F. Supp. 574, 6 ERC 1453 (N.D. Cal. 1974).

13. Berman v. Parker, 348 U.S. 26, 33 (1954).

14. Village of Belle Terre v. Boraas, 416 U.S. 1, 6 ERC 1417 (1974).

15. 416 U.S.

16. *See* Chapter 3 for a discussion of New York State laws enabling local governments to enact measures to protect open space, historic, and esthetic values.

17. Salamar Builders Corp. v. Tuttle, 29 N.Y. 2d 221, 325 N.Y.S. 2d 933, 275 N.E. 2d 585, 3 ERC 1267 (1971).

18. 325 N.Y.S. 2d at 938.

19. Keystone Associates v. Moerdler, 19 N.Y. 2d 78, 278 N.Y.S. 2d 185, 224 N.E. 2d 700 (1966).

20. 278 N.Y.S. 2d at 189.

21. Trustees of Sailors' Snug Harbor v. Platt, 29 App. Div. 2d 376, 288 N.Y.S. 2d 314 (1968).

22. 288 N.Y.S. 2d at 315.

23. People v. Goodman, 31 N.Y. 2d 262, 338 N.Y.S 2d 97, 290 N.E. 2d 139 (1972).

24. 16 U.S.C. §459e.

25. 338 N.Y.S. 2d at 100.

26. Jan Krasnowiecki and Ann Louise Strong, "Compensable Regulations for Open Space," *Journal of the American Institute of Planners* 24 (1963): 89.

27. Robert M. Anderson, *American Law of Zoning: Zoning Planning, Subdivision Control* (Rochester, N.Y.: The Lawyers Co-operative Publishing Co., 1968), §2.23.

28. *See* Jon A. Kusler, "Open Space Zoning: Valid Regulation or Invalid Taking?" 57 *Minn. L. Rev.* 1, 33 (1972).

29. *See* John J. Costonis, "The Chicago Plan: Incentive Zoning and the Preservation of Urban Landmarks," 85 *Harv. L. Rev.* 574 (1972). Development rights are also discussed in Chapter 15 of this book.

CHAPTER 3

Land Use Controls at the Town, City, or Village Level

W HAT CAN BE done on a local level to control the use of land? The answer to this question is not a simple one because a number of different controls are possible in New York State, and different local governments have different mixes. This chapter explains the various existing possibilities. An understanding of these can serve as a guide for concerned citizens in finding out what controls have been established in their particular town, city, or village, and can enable them:

1. To determine what new controls could be instituted in their locality.
2. To monitor implementation of existing controls in terms of statutory requirements, to demand conscientious adherence to the law, and to bring legal actions against abuses.

Local governments in New York State are of four basic types: counties, towns, cities, and villages. Since counties differ significantly from the other three, county land use controls are discussed separately in the next chapter. Towns are subdivisions of counties; they exclude cities but include villages within their boundaries. They are governed by town boards, each of which consists of a town supervisor and other elective members. Cities are specially incorporated by the state legislature to provide governmental services within their boundaries. All cities have elective legislative bodies, but the actual form of administration varies. Villages are incorporated by local action taken in accordance with state law. Each is governed by an elective board of trustees, headed by a mayor. In addition to these basic units of local government, there are also school districts, fire districts, and special districts which often have their own unique boundaries.

The powers that towns, cities, and villages have to establish land use controls are delegated to them by the state. States have what is called the "police power" to enact legislation for the promotion of public health, safety, morals, and general welfare. This power may be delegated by a state to local governments within its boundaries. This has been done in New York State through provisions of Article IX of the State Constitution and the Statute of Local Governments enacted thereunder and through specific enabling legislation passed by the state legislature. The discussion in this chapter is based on the enabling legislation found in the Town Law, General City Law, Village Law, and General Municipal Law,[1] since most land use controls are established on their authority and, as one authority has observed, "[i]t seems doubtful that the Statute of Local Governments added materially to local zoning or planning powers."[2]

It should be noted that the existence of state enabling statutes, empowering local governments to enact and enforce particular types of laws or ordinances (such as a zoning ordinance) pursuant to the police power does not mean that local governments must or will enact them. It simply means that they may do so if they choose. With respect to land use controls, many local governments have not utilized the wide range of powers available to them, despite growing public concern over unsupervised growth.

What types of controls are available to localities? Any of the following institutions, laws, plans, and programs which bear relation to land use control may exist in a town, city, or village:

1. Zoning ordinances and zoning boards of appeals
2. Planning boards
    Comprehensive master plans
    Subdivision controls
3. Official maps
4. Capital improvement programs

5. Building codes
6. Road specifications
7. Protection of historic and esthetic districts, sites, buildings, and objects
8. Acquisition of open spaces
9. Local environmental conservation commissions

In addition to the range of these possible resources, the substance, coordination, and effectiveness of controls adopted vary widely from one local government to another.

A land development project is subject to the controls of the town, city, or village government within whose boundaries it falls, except that, in the case of towns, these controls apply only to those areas which are *outside* the limits of any incorporated village. If, for example, part of a subdivision tract lies within a village and part lies outside, the village's controls would apply to the former portion and the town's to the latter.

Although there are some differences in the state enabling acts for towns, cities, and villages with respect to land use controls, the provisions of the acts are generally similar. For the sake of both clarity and brevity, town controls will serve as the basis of this discussion. Towns were chosen for this illustrative role because they contain the largest proportion of prime land for new development. Where appropriate, attention will be drawn to distinctive features of city and village law.

Ideally local governments should take full advantage of all land use controls available to them. Through careful planning, the future growth and development of a municipality can be approached in a rational manner and the casualities of haphazard, uncontrolled growth can be, if not avoided entirely, at least greatly tempered. Planning permits a community to give consideration to what its values are and what land uses it wants to encourage. Effective implementation of plans allows the preservation of important identified values. For example, irreplaceable natural resources and historic sites which might otherwise fall victim to the profit motive can be preserved for present and future generations.

Local planning boards should be set up to take prime responsibility for planning—which should be based on a comprehensive master plan drawn up by the planning board, with ample opportunity for citizen input. The land use plan of the master plan should set out a long-term plan for the appropriate uses of land within the government's jurisdiction, on an area-by-area basis. This land plan should reflect careful consideration of such factors as population trends, soil conditions, water supply, sewage and solid waste disposal facilities, drainage patterns, transportation, school facilities, and job locations —all against the background of existing land uses. Implementing the recommendations of the plan should be a zoning ordinance, through which land use and population density can actually be controlled. Supplementing the zoning ordinance should be subdivision regulations which insure that projects undertaken meet minimal design standards and criteria. An official map and a capital improvement program should be set up to implement the master plan and its rational approach to future growth. Technically up-to-date, appropriate, and conscientiously enforced building codes and road specifications should further strengthen this system of controls. Protection of historic and esthetic districts, sites, buildings, and objects and the acquisition of open spaces should be considered as ways of preserving the community's historic, esthetic, and natural resources. The possibility of setting up a local environmental conservation commission as a vehicle for the expression of environmental concern and the development of constructive solutions should be explored.

In practice, very few local governments have such fully developed systems of carefully formulated land use controls. What one usually finds is one or more of these controls, often in the very crudest form. All of the possible legal combinations occur. Many towns, for example, have no building codes, yet they have zoning; others have subdivision regulations, but no zoning.

Citizens who want to work to protect land from uncontrolled development must start with the resources at hand, whatever they may be in a given situation. The following discussion explains for these citizens what tools may be available at the local level of government, not only to establish good plans, but also to combat problems which result from bad plans or the complete absence of plans.

Zoning, the most frequently encountered major local control, is discussed first. Then town planning boards are explained, with their right to prepare a comprehensive master plan and, if so empowered, to exercise subdivision control. In both cases, opportunities for citizen action based on these controls are pointed out. Brief descriptions follow of official maps; capital improvement programs; building codes; road specifications; protection of historic and esthetic districts, sites, buildings, and objects; acquisition of open spaces; and local environmental conservation commissions.

ZONING

Zoning is one of the oldest and best known land use controls available to local governments. As has been discussed, zoning and other regulations of land use are founded on the police power to legislate for the promotion of the public health, safety, morals, or general welfare. This power, which resides in the states but may be delegated to local governments, is limited by certain constitutional restraints, notably the prohibition against the "taking" of property except for a public purpose and with just compensation. Local ordinances and regulations also must not violate constitutional provisions under which the states must guarantee to their citizens due process and equal protection of the laws. The courts test particular zoning ordinances and other land use regulations on a case-by-case basis. The standards which are applied to determine whether or not a particular regulation is constitutionally sound are discussed in Chapter 2.

The shortcomings of zoning have been the subject of much debate. Nevertheless, when wisely adopted and enforced, a zoning ordinance may prove invaluable in the protection of land from the ravages of uncontrolled development. Where a zoning ordinance already exists—be it good, bad, or indifferent—it can always be amended and it may provide grounds on which citizens can challenge land development which they believe is detrimental to the general welfare.

Adoption of a Zoning Ordinance

The New York State zoning enabling act for towns states that:

For the purpose of promoting the health, safety, morals, or the general welfare of the community, the town board is hereby empowered by ordinance to regulate and restrict the height, number of stories and size of buildings and other structures, the percentage of lot that may be occupied, the size of yards, courts, and other open spaces, the density of population, and the location and use of buildings, structures and land for trade, industry, residence or other purpose. . . .[3]

The town board may divide the town into districts, and regulate and restrict the type of construction and the use of buildings and land in each. All regulations must be uniform for each class or kind of buildings throughout a district, but the regulations in one district can differ from those in another.

The law expressly states that zoning regulations may be designed to (1) prevent overcrowding; (2) secure safety from fire, flood,[4] panic, and other dangers; (3) provide adequate light and air; (4) avoid undue concentration of population; (5) facilitate adequate provision of transportation, water, sewage, schools, and parks.

According to the law, zoning regulations must be "made in accordance with a comprehensive plan." In cases involving legal challenges on this issue, the courts have traditionally looked not for a separate, written document but for a coherent approach. As will be discussed below, a town may set up a town planning board which may prepare a "comprehensive master plan" for the town. This master plan may provide the rationale for a zoning ordinance, but it is not required. A town may adopt a zoning ordinance without having set up a planning board.

In order to establish in a town the zoning powers that the state makes available, a town board must follow certain procedures prescribed by law.[5] If it does not follow these procedures, the zoning ordinance it enacts is not legally enforceable and may be successfully challenged. In fact, most of the judicial challenges that towns lose on zoning are lost because the town did not follow the exact letter of the law in the adoption of its ordinance.

The town board must first appoint a zoning commission to recommend what the boundaries of the zoning districts should be and to develop appropriate regulations. An existing town planning board may be appointed to serve as the zoning commission.

The zoning commission must make a preliminary report and hold hearings before submitting its final report. "Hearings" has been interpreted to mean that at least two hearings must be held. The town board cannot take any action on the question of zoning until it has received the final report of the zoning commission and has also held a public hearing. The town board is not, however, required to follow the recommendations of the commission. After the submission of its final report, the commission as such goes out of existence.

Before it can adopt a zoning ordinance, a town board must also refer the ordinance in its final form to any county, metropolitan, or regional planning board within whose jurisdiction the town lies. Within thirty days of the receipt of a full statement of such an ordinance, a county, metropolitan, or regional planning board must report its recommendations to the town board. Failure to do so within this time period leaves the town board free to take action without a report. If recommendations are received, the town board may override them by a vote of a majority plus one.

When a town board acts on the proposed zoning ordinance, it must follow specified enactment procedures of voting and entry into official minutes and must see that the ordinance is properly published and posted in the town.

Whenever a town wishes to change a duly adopted ordinance, it is not necessary to appoint a new zoning commission, but it is mandatory that a public hearing with due notice be held and that referral be made to county, metropolitan, or regional planning boards if the modification affects land within 500 feet from the boundary of the town, or of any city or village, or of any existing or proposed county or state park, road, right-of-way, or facility.

The town board may pass an enforcement ordinance imposing penalties for violations of the zoning ordinance.

Implementation of the Zoning Ordinance

If a town board adopts a zoning ordinance, it must appoint a zoning board of appeals to hear and decide (1) appeals from actions taken by the administrative official charged with enforcing the ordinance; (2) all matters referred to it under the ordinance, such as requests for special use permits under conditions specified in the ordinance; and (3) appeals for variances from the requirements of the ordinance.

Either five or seven members must be appointed to the zoning board of appeals, and no one on the town board may be a member. Compensation may be provided, as well as a budget for staff and outside experts.

It is not expressly specified by statute how a municipality can assure that proposed buildings and uses are in compliance with the zoning ordinance. In municipalities which have building codes, the officer charged with reviewing applications for building permits (generally the building inspector) is usually given the responsibility of determining whether a proposed building or use is consistent with zoning regulations. In other municipalities, including both those which have not enacted a building code and those which do not choose to rest zoning responsibilities with the building inspector, a zoning administrator or other official may be specially charged with the enforcement of zoning regulations.[6]

In general, municipalities require compliance with the zoning ordinance for the issuance of (1) building or zoning permits; and (2) certificates of occupancy. The zoning ordinance typically requires that an application for a building or zoning permit contain all the information which the building inspector or zoning administrator needs to determine whether issuing the permit would violate any provision of the zoning ordinance. After completion of construction, the property owner must usually apply for a certificate of occupancy. The building inspector or zoning administrator must then check to see that the building and use are as were proposed and are in full compliance with all regulations.

In principle, determinations by a building inspector or zoning administrator regarding compliance with a zoning ordinance should be strictly based on the zoning regulations and should not be discretionary with respect to relief from these regulations, since this responsibility should rest solely with the zoning board of appeals. In practice, however, building inspectors and zoning administrators often make discretionary decisions which go beyond the scope of their responsibilities. Also, determinations of zoning compliance are sometimes made in an inadequate, cursory manner. Citizens should be on the alert for such irregularities and take action to challenge them, as discussed below.

If a building inspector or zoning administrator decides that a developer's plans would violate the zoning ordinance and denies a permit, the developer can ask the zoning board of appeals to review the decision or he can petition the zoning board of appeals for a variance from the regulations. A variance is a limited exception to the zoning regulations that is allowed on the grounds of "practical difficulties or unnecessary hardships." It can grant relief from specified requirements of the zoning ordinance, such as setback requirements, or it can allow a use of land that is prohibited by the ordinance.

The developer who wishes to build a large project which is clearly not in compliance with the zoning ordinance generally must go a different route. He must petition the town board for a change in the ordinance itself. For example, if a developer wanted to build a residential subdivision on property that was zoned for one-acre minimum lots, he might ask the town board to amend the ordinance to allow one-half-acre lots in that zoning district.

Site Plan Approval

The zoning ordinance should contain provisions for site plan approval in which site plans for commercial, industrial, and multi-family developments must be submitted to the zoning board of appeals for approval.[7] The zoning board of appeals may refer these plans to the town planning board, if one exists, for recommendations. Through this type of required approval, a town can control the location of buildings, parking, access to roads, landscaping, and other features of such developments.

Special Zoning Provisions Which May Affect Subdivisions

Certain provisions of the zoning enabling act for towns pertain particularly to subdivisions of land.

1. Subdivision plats filed prior to adoption of or amendments to a zoning ordinance. State law grants to subdividers limited exemptions from certain crucial zoning restrictions adopted as part of new ordinances or as amendments to existing ordinances.[8] The exemptions apply to regulations establishing a minimum lot size larger than the size of lots on plats which have already been approved by any board or officer of the town vested with such authority and filed in the office of the county clerk or register. The provision is designed to mitigate hardships to the subdivider who has committed funds and would stand to lose his investment because of the new regulations. He is given a limited time to sell his now smaller than regulation lots. If the local jurisdiction previously had no zoning ordinance and no planning board, the developer is exempt for one year. If it had both a zoning ordinance and a planning board, the exemption is for three years. If it had only one or the other, the exemption is for two years.

2. Innovative zoning.
a. *Planning board changes in zoning provisions.* Section 281 of the Town Law is an effort to provide for flexibility in the application of zoning principles to subdivision planning. Under it, a town board may authorize its town planning board (hereafter TPB) to modify provisions of the town's zoning ordinance in certain specified ways upon application by a subdivider and at the discretion of the TPB.

Basically, in order to preserve open space and natural areas, the

TPB can allow reduction in lot sizes in a subdivision while enforcing existing zoning regulations on the number of dwelling units and the population density for the total area of the project. This technique is called "average density zoning," "cluster zoning," or "open space subdivision."

b. *Planned unit developments* (PUDs). This type of innovative zoning requires approval by the local legislative body in addition to planning board approval.

A PUD is usually a large-scale land development project involving mixed uses—residential, commercial, and possibly industrial—and clustering of units in a way that provides open space. It is a concept which lends itself to relatively self-sufficient "new town" type developments. PUDs are becoming increasingly common on the fringes of suburban areas and can be expected to spread into more rural areas as population pressures intensify.

To allow PUDs a municipality must adopt a PUD ordinance as part of its zoning regulations. This prescribes building, density, and design requirements for PUDs and procedures for establishing them, but leaves the actual placement of PUDs on the zoning map indeterminate. When a subdivision developer is interested in carrying out a PUD, he applies to the planning board for approval. (Because the projects are usually large-scale, and extensive planning is involved, a municipality is not likely to have a PUD ordinance unless it also has a planning board authorized to review subdivision plans.)

If a planning board approves a subdivider's PUD project, the local legislative body can still block it by failing to take the necessary legislative action—rezoning of the land involved as a PUD. Unlike the innovative zoning modifications that a planning board can be empowered to make, such as average density zoning, rezoning land as a PUD can involve an increase in the maximum allowable population density for the area of the development.

As a concept, the PUD has a number of appealing features: It encourages a variety of housing—varying in appearance and cost—thus favoring an economic mix of residents, stores can be conveniently located as an integral part of the development, simultaneously reducing highway sprawl and traffic; open space can be preserved; and utilities can be centralized. Some communities, however, have found their PUD ordinances too inviting to developers and too flexible as a corrective to traditional zoning.

Interim or Stop-Gap Zoning

Local governments have employed various stop-gap measures to control land use either prior to the adoption of a zoning ordinance or in anticipation of major amendments to an existing ordinance. The term "interim zoning" has come into use to describe a quickly prepared ordinance, intended to preserve the status quo until more definitive regulations and a zoning map can be drawn up. One such measure that has been used is an ordinance effecting a moratorium on the issuance of all building permits for a specified period of time.

Towns can find themselves suddenly caught up in rapid land development which they are ill prepared to handle. The courts, moreover, have been strict in enforcing the statutory procedure for adopting a zoning ordinance (preliminary report by a zoning commission, public hearings, then a final report and a final public hearing) and for amendments (public hearings on at least ten days' notice). The wording of the enabling acts suggests, and court rulings concur, that zoning regulations must be arrived at by careful deliberation, not by impulsive action, and that there should be ample opportunity for public participation. All this takes time. Interim zoning is an attempt to gain this time while forestalling developments that would be rushed through to escape the effects of measures adopted with due deliberation.

Even towns which are not under severe development pressure have enacted interim zoning measures when it seemed likely that the announced prospect of adopting or changing zoning regulations would cause property owners to initiate hasty changes in land use before the regulations could be adopted.

There have been a number of court challenges to the legality of interim zoning. The results are inconclusive, leaving a split of authority slightly in favor of such ordinances. The possibility of judicial invalidation argues for instituting other control measures if circumstances allow. The New York State Office of Planning Services' legal memorandum on this subject cautiously concluded that stop-gap ordinances could prove beneficial "(1) Where there exists a plan currently under consideration which may precipitate action detrimental to its accomplishment. (2) Where such limitation will be needed for fixed and short-term periods. (3) Where the advantages to be gained outweigh the hardship imposed on property owners in general. Under these circumstances the benefits to be derived are worth the risks, time and effort involved."[9] (As a result of a reorganization within the state government, the Office of Planning Services has now ceased to exist as such and its work dealing with zoning and planning on the local level has been transferred to the Division of Community Affairs of the New York State Department of State.)

Citizen Action

Citizens should be aware of the limitations of zoning ordinances. Zoning does not restrict the sale or rental of land; it controls use. Ordinarily, only when land is being used or is about to be used in contravention of the zoning ordinance can enforcement action be taken by town officials. Thus, where a town has no planning board and no subdivision regulations, the zoning ordinance alone would not prevent the sale of improved subdivided lots or the development of roads to induce sales of such lots. The zoning ordinance would be violated only if construction began without a zoning permit or in contravention of the permit as issued by the zoning administrator. Traditional zoning, standing alone, imposes no requirements on street layout or the provision of basic services (such as water, gas, electricity, and sewage disposal), and may allow subdividers to saddle municipalities with multiple financial burdens. Traditional zoning ordinances also characteristically do not have provisions which allow for the preservation of open space and the protection of natural features.

Zoning ordinances vary in quality, but citizens should always remember that even the best zoning ordinance can be abused in practice. Opportunities for modifying it or escaping its effect are such that the administration of an ordinance and appeals for relief bear close watching. Real estate interests can exert strong influence on official decisions by direct or by devious means. There may be nothing illegal about this; someone simply needs to be constantly abreast of developments, constantly asking whether local administrative and legislative decisions promote the general welfare.

1. Challenging a zoning ordinance or a revision thereof. When a zoning ordinance is adopted that seems to invite land development that does not promote the general welfare, citizens may want to challenge this ordinance and seek stricter controls. If a land developer were challenging a zoning ordinance he might do so either on procedural or constitutional grounds—arguing either that the ordinance was not properly adopted or that it effected a taking of property without due process of law by depriving him of the use value of his land.[10] Citizens challenging zoning ordinances, or modifications thereof, on behalf of stronger land use control must generally use the procedural challenge. The courts have consistently held that the statutory procedural requirements for enacting or amending a zoning ordinance are mandatory. If a town board has not followed all the procedures specified by the enabling act, the zoning ordinance is not legally valid. It is also required that the ordinance not be in conflict with any state law.

The most common legal action for testing the validity of a zoning regulation is an action for a declaratory judgment in which citizens ask the court for a declaration of what their rights are under the law —that is, is the zoning ordinance adopted by the town board legally binding? If a procedural challenge is being attempted, the complaint must allege facts constituting a failure by the town board to meet mandatory procedural requirements. As a requirement for standing as a plaintiff, a person may have to demonstrate that he has suffered or will suffer pecuniary damage as a result of the regulation. He will certainly have to demonstrate that land which he owns or leases will in some way suffer significant adverse effects.

In some cases, it has also been possible for citizens to bring a successful challenge against a zoning ordinance on the grounds that it was not in the best interests of the town. Residents of the town of Wappinger in Dutchess County, for example, challenged a zoning provision allowing apartments in areas where soil was poor, and where sewage and traffic problems already existed. The provision was rescinded.

2. Challenging a decision of the official charged with administering the zoning ordinance. It is possible to appeal before the zoning board of appeals any order, requirement, decision, or determination made by the administrative official responsible for the implementation of the zoning ordinance. Such appeals often charge that a building permit or certificate of occupancy has been issued where a building or use is not in full compliance with the zoning ordinance. A notice of appeal specifying grounds must be filed with the official whose decision is being challenged and with the board of appeals. The form of this notice and the time allowed for appeal are determined by the local zoning board's own rules. Even though this is an administrative rather than a judicial proceeding, if an attorney's assistance can be obtained, it could prove very valuable.

Who can challenge? Any aggrieved person or an officer, department, board, or bureau of the municipality.[11] Court rulings indicate that to qualify as "an aggrieved person" (1) one must be a resident-owner or lessee of zoned property in the municipality in which the official's act is being appealed; and (2) one must have, in addition, "a specific, personal and legal interest" in the action appealed. A general interest in the public welfare is not sufficient. The only persons certain to qualify as aggrieved are a resident-owner whose land may be substantially affected and materially depreciated in value or someone who is leasing such property. Officers, departments, boards, or bureaus of municipalities with adjacent jurisdiction are usually not entitled to initiate appeals.[12]

Most of the procedural details of an appeal before a zoning board of appeals are determined by local regulations, but there *must* be a public hearing after due notice. The Town Law requires that there be a published notice at least five days before the hearing. The procedure at the hearing is usually very informal. Parties may, however, be represented by an agent or attorney. Such a hearing before a zoning board of appeals, regardless of who initiated it, is an excellent opportunity to make public sentiment known by vociferousness and by turnout. A well-organized public complaint and the support of people with influence are assets. Even if the appeal fails, the fact that strong opposition was expressed will be considered in any subsequent judicial review of the zoning board's decision. Under certain circumstances, such as the appearance of new evidence, it may be possible to obtain a new hearing.[13]

3. Opposing an application to the zoning board of appeals for a variance. Here the developer takes the initiative and applies for a variance. Those opposing the variance should express their objections at the required public hearing. Depending on local rules and practice they may or may not need to establish themselves as aggrieved persons in order to be heard. At least one court has ruled that all interested persons should have an opportunity to be heard.[14] If the decision of the board is adverse, it may be possible to obtain a rehearing.

4. Judicial review of decisions made by the zoning board of appeals. Any decision of the zoning board of appeals is subject to judicial review. Among such decisions are those granting a variance, a building permit under any of the special circumstances requiring review or approval by the zoning board of appeals (such as a permit to build in an officially mapped street[15]), or a special use permit.The state zoning enabling statutes specifically provide that any person aggrieved by any decision of a zoning board of appeals may appeal for judicial review under Article 78 of the Civil Practice Law and Rules.[16] State law specifies that such a proceeding must be initiated within thirty days after the decision by the zoning board is filed in the appropriate municipal office.

Who qualifies as an aggrieved person for purposes of judicial review? Judicial precedent indicates that here, too, a person must be a landowner or lessee in the municipality and must be able to show that the decision, if allowed to stand, could have a materially adverse effect on his property.

The greatest obstacle to success in an Article 78 proceeding is the courts' presumption that the zoning board's decision is correct. Since the courts recognize that zoning boards have broad discretion, this presumption is difficult to overcome. The court will not question the board's judgment unless the objector can show abuse of discretionary power or, in other words, can show that the board's decision was arbitrary or capricious.[17]

In addition to situations in which citizens challenge what they consider to be bad decisions by the zoning board of appeals, there may also be times when citizens need to support a wise decision by the zoning board of appeals which is being challenged by a developer. This can be done by intervening on the side of the town in the judicial review proceedings.

5. Preventing land development or improvement that is in violation of a zoning ordinance. State law provides that municipal officials can petition the courts to enjoin activity that is arguably in violation of a zoning regulation if its continuation will result in irreparable damage.[18] Citizens who believe that such an injunction should be issued should press their local officials to take action.

Under certain circumstances citizens themselves can initiate action for injunctive relief. The Town Law is unique in providing that if, after a written request from a resident taxpayer, the proper town official fails or refuses to take appropriate action within ten days, any three taxpayers residing in the district in which an alleged violation exists can institute an action for injunctive relief.[19]

Otherwise, under the Town Law, General City Law, and Village Law, persons who seek to enjoin violations in their private capacity as landowners or lessees must demonstrate that a continuation of the violation will irreparably damage their property interests.[20]

6. Enforcement by criminal proceedings. Only the Town Law makes specific provision for criminal sanctions against violators of zoning regulations: A $50 fine, up to six months imprisonment, or both.[21] City and village ordinances usually include a section on criminal penalties based on the general statutory provision for sanctions against ordinance violations.

In practice, the civil remedy of injunctive relief is much more commonly used.

TOWN PLANNING BOARDS

A town may have a special board set up to deal with planning matters. This town planning board may be given a number of different responsibilities, but the most important of these are the preparation of a "comprehensive master plan" for the town and the right to review and to approve or disapprove subdivision projects.

Establishment of a Town Planning Board

A town planning board (hereafter TPB) may be formed by, and also can be abolished by, action of the town's elected legislative body, the town board. A TPB may have either five or seven members (under certain circumstances, six or eight) appointed for staggered terms by the town board. Compensation may be provided.

The TPB may, and usually does, have a budgetary appropriation which allows it to employ staff members to assist it in carrying out its planning functions. It has full authority to make investigations, maps and reports, and recommendations relating to the planning and development of the town, provided that it does not exceed its appropriation. It should be noted that financing and staffing or obtaining consultant services are difficult problems for many localities. Often local governments find that they do not have the funds to pay for the kind of expertise they need. Sometimes it is possible for several such governments to pool their planning resources.

At its discretion, the town board may refer any matters to the TPB before action by the town board itself or by a town official. Specifically, the town board may authorize the TPB to approve or disapprove (1) changes in the lines of existing streets, highways, or public areas shown on subdivision plats or maps filed in the office of the county clerk; and (2) the laying out, closing off, or abandonment of streets, highways, or public areas under the provisions of town and highway laws. Such approval or disapproval is by way of recommendation only and does not affect the final authority of the town board or town officials.

The TPB may adopt rules and regulations for carrying out its duties which, after public hearing and approval by the town board, have the force of legislative enactments.

Preparation of a Comprehensive Master Plan

The TPB may prepare a comprehensive master plan for the development of the entire area of the town, showing desirable streets, bridges, and tunnels, zoning districts, waterways, and routes of public utilities,

> and such other features existing and proposed as will provide for the improvement of the town and its future growth, protection, and development, and will afford adequate facilities for the public housing, transportation, distribution, comfort, convenience, public health, safety and general welfare of its population.[22]

In developing this plan, the TPB should examine land capabilities (considering such factors as soil, slope, elevation, drainage), natural resources, population, economics, transportation networks, utilities, and community facilities in order to determine the most appropriate pattern of land use for the next ten to twenty years. In addition to a land use plan, a comprehensive plan should include a transportation plan and a plan for the provision of utilities and community facilities. An open space plan is also desirable.

State and federal assistance for the preparation of comprehensive master plans is available through the Division of Community Affairs of the New York Department of State, which now administers U. S. Department of Housing and Urban Development "701" planning grants. Note should be made that environmental assessments are required in all plans prepared under such grants.[23]

In the preparation of the plan, a TPB is entitled by statute to hold public hearings "when it desires." At least ten days' notice must be given for such hearings in a newspaper of general circulation in the town.

It is important to recognize that the comprehensive master plan is not an official town map or a zoning ordinance, both of which are discussed in other sections of this chapter. The master plan is in fact not an official town pronouncement. The state comptroller has ruled that "[u]nless and until the town board officially incorporates the master plan into an ordinance to give it the force of law, the master plan remains only an advisory document or documents and is not capable of enforcement."[24]

In at least two respects, however, the comprehensive master plan can be legally significant:

1. As will be discussed later in this chapter,[25] TPB approval of subdivision plats may require that the road system of the subdivision be "properly related to the proposals shown by the planning board on the master plan."[26]

2. The master plan provides a very strong basis for the zoning ordinance. Basing the zoning map on the land use map of the master plan strengthens the position of the zoning board of appeals or town board which wishes to control development. If a developer challenges a decision of such a board in court on the grounds that the zoning change or variance he seeks has been allowed in the past, the board will most probably be required by the court to give good reasons for the break with precedent. A master plan can often supply these reasons.

The TPB has the authority to change the comprehensive master plan when conditions call for its amendment. Both the plan and all modifications of it must be on file in the office of the TPB and certified copies must be filed in the office of the town engineer or highway superintendent and the town clerk.

Subdivision Control

The Town Law of the State of New York authorizes town boards to vest subdivision control in town planning boards. A town board that wishes to do so must pass a resolution empowering the TPB to approve subdivision plats. The term "subdivision" is not defined in this part of state law. Although a town board could therefore restrict TPB control to larger subdivisions, the state Office of Planning Services has suggested that a broad definition be adopted, extending TPB control over all subdivisions of two or more lots.[27]

When a town board has granted to a TPB the right of subdivision control, subdivision plats may not be accepted for filing by the county clerk or register without an endorsement indicating TPB approval. Thus it becomes unlawful for the subdivider to sell lots or offer them for sale until the project has TPB approval.

The town board may also authorize TPB approval of subdivision plats already filed with the county recording officer when TPB approval is first established, if 20 percent or more of the lots are still "unimproved"—unless existing conditions, such as poor drainage, have prevented development. This provision might prove valuable when redesign or reduction in scope of subdivision plats which have already been filed is needed.

There are no reliable statistics on the number of small, clandestine subdivisions in which TPB approval was required but was never obtained simply because the developer never submitted plans for approval or filing. It is safe to say, however, that as a rule, subdividers go through the formality of obtaining TPB approval where that approval has been authorized by the town board. What is crucial, therefore, are the standards used by a TPB in exercising its power of subdivision approval, and whether the review process effectively serves the public interest.

1. Subdivision regulations. The most stringent control by town governments over subdivision projects exists where the town planning board has adopted a distinct body of subdivision regulations which, after a mandatory public hearing and town board approval, it follows in reviewing plats. Such regulations are enacted under the power granted planning boards under the Town Law to adopt such rules and regulations as they deem necessary to approve subdivision plats.[28] The subdivision regulations which are adopted must follow specific statutory requirements for plat approval and set out procedures for filing and review that are in keeping with statutory provisions. (These statutory bases are discussed in the next two sections.) Local subdivision regulations should also, however, include specific standards based on local needs. Towns may pass an ordinance which imposes penalties for the violation of subdivision regulations.

Model land subdivision regulations have been prepared by the New York State Office of Planning Services and also by the Ulster County Planning Board.[29] The Office of Planning Services urged, however, that:

> While "model" regulations are useful in indicating the material that needs to be included and the procedures that are most effective, it cannot be overemphasized that much needs to be done locally to develop the specific details to be included in a particular set of regulations.[30]

Nevertheless, the existence of model subdivision regulations greatly facilitates the process of instituting this type of subdivision control. Where there is general public sentiment in favor of protecting the town from rapid, unsupervised growth, a town which does not have land use controls can fairly expeditiously establish a planning board, give it the power of subdivision approval, and, after a public hearing, establish subdivision regulations prepared by the planning board. It should be pointed out, however, that subdivision regulations that exist in towns which do not have a zoning ordinance are much weaker than those in towns which do have zoning. Without zoning, it is not possible to control density or use. With regard to streets and traffic flow, moreover, subdivision regulations are strengthened by the adoption by the town board of a carefully conceived official town map.

2. Statutory requirements for TPB approval of subdivision plats. The statutory purposes of TPB subdivision review are comprehensive, warranting a very thorough evaluation of subdivision plans. Aspects to be considered include: Housing, transportation, population distribution, comfort, convenience, safety, health, and welfare. The following requirements that must be met before TPB approval of a subdivision is granted are stated in the law:

> such plat shall . . . show in proper cases and when required by the planning board, a park or parks suitably located for playground or other recreational purposes. . . . the parks shall be of reasonable size for neighborhood playgrounds or other recreational uses . . .

> the streets and highways shall be of sufficient width and suitable grade and shall be suitably located to accommodate the prospective traffic, to afford adequate light and air, to facilitate fire protection, and to provide access of fire-fighting equipment to buildings, and if there be an official map or master plan, they shall be coordinated so as to compose a convenient system conforming to the official map and properly related to the proposals shown by the planning board on the master plan; . . .

> where a zoning ordinance has been adopted by the town the plots shown on said plat shall at least comply with the requirements thereof; . . .

> the land shown on such plats shall be of such character that it can be used safely for building purposes without danger to health or peril from fire, flood, or other menace. . . .[31]

In addition, all the following must be installed in accordance with standards, specifications, and procedures acceptable to the town:

Street signs, sidewalks, street lights, curbs, gutters, street trees, water mains, fire alarm devices, sanitary sewers, and storm drains. The town may require the owner to post a performance bond sufficient to cover the full cost of such installations, as well as the full cost of suitably grading and paving all streets and other public places shown on the plat.

In summary, adequate provision must be made for parks of reasonable size, for a carefully planned and convenient road system, for compliance with an existing zoning ordinance, and for construction of roads and installation of improvements in accordance with standards. Performance bonds may be required to assure that all promised roads and installations are actually provided. The land itself must also be of such a nature that it can sustain the proposed construction without danger to health or safety.

It should be noted, however, that the TPB has the right to waive any of these requirements which

> in its judgment of the special circumstances of a particular plat or plats are not requisite in the interest of the public health, safety and general welfare, or which in its judgment are inappropriate because of inadequacy or lack of connecting facilities adjacent or in proximity to the subdivision.[32]

As the above requirements indicate, whenever a town has a zoning ordinance, a comprehensive master plan, or an official map, they all come into play in TPB approval of subdivision plats. In order to receive TPB approval, subdivision plats must conform to the requirements of a zoning ordinance, although the town board may give the TPB authority to institute innovative zoning measures in connection with subdivision review, as has been discussed in more detail above.

Even though a comprehensive master plan which may have been developed by a TPB is advisory only and not directly enforceable, it does become an effective control in combination with plat approval by the TPB. In the transportation section of the master plan the routes of all existing and proposed roads, as well as proposed improvements, are shown. All subdivision plats must then have a road system that is "properly related" to these proposals of the master plan. Thus a developer must conform his subdivision layout to the projected desirable community road system. This should prevent the town's having to buy up developed land at some future time in order to rectify deficiencies in its road system brought about by uncontrolled subdivision development.[33]

The streets and highways shown on a subdivision plat must also conform to the official town map, if one exists. Coordination with the town's existing and projected road, drainage, and parks systems as shown on this map is required.

If the county in which a town is located has adopted an official county map,[34] the TPB cannot approve a subdivision plat without giving county officials an opportunity for review and recommendation whenever proposed subdivision structures or streets have frontage on, access to, or are directly related to an existing or proposed right-of-way or site shown on the county official map. By a two-thirds vote of all its members, a TPB can approve a subdivision plat contrary to county recommendations if applying these recommendations would deprive the owner of reasonable use of his land.[35]

3. Procedures for TPB review of subdivision plats. In order to monitor subdivision review, it is important to know what procedures a developer and a planning board must follow. Since the revision of Section 276 of Town Law, effective January 1, 1973, there are now significant differences in review procedures set out in the Town Law, the Village Law, and General City Law. Also, procedures set out by statute may be still further developed by local regulations. Consequently, when citizens wish to follow the process of subdivision review, it is always important that they examine the procedures actually specified by their own local government.

The Town Law gives town boards the option of authorizing either of two planning board review procedures, differentiated here as Procedure 1 and Procedure 2.

Procedure 1. This procedure has been generally preferred by the New York State Office of Planning Services.

a. The subdivider submits a preliminary plat to the clerk of the TPB. This plat shows salient features of the proposed subdivision, including road and lot layout, approximate dimensions, topography, and drainage.

b. Within forty-five days of the receipt of this preliminary plat the TPB holds a public hearing after giving at least five days public notice.

c. Within forty-five days after the public hearing (or longer by mutual consent of the TPB and the subdivider), the TPB approves the plat with or without stipulating modifications or the TPB disapproves the plat. Failure of the TPB to make any determination within the prescribed forty-five days is tantamount to preliminary approval.

d. Within five days after approval of a preliminary plat, it is certified by the clerk of the TPB as having been granted preliminary approval.

e. The subdivider then has six months to submit the plat in final form. The TPB can revoke approval of a preliminary plat if this deadline is not met.

f. Within forty-five days of the receipt of the final plat, the TPB may hold a public hearing, again on at least five days' public notice. This second hearing is discretionary with the TPB if it judges that stipulated modifications have been made.

g. A TPB decision on the final plat must be made within forty-five days of the second hearing, if held; otherwise it must be made within forty-five days of the receipt of the final plat (unless a longer period is established by mutual consent).

h. Possible TPB action on the final plat: Approval, disapproval, or conditional approval with or without stipulated modifications. Where approval is conditional, the subdivider has 180 days (a discretionary extension by the TPB of up to 180 additional days is permitted) to meet the conditions.

i. TPB approval, if given, fulfills one of the requirements a developer must meet before filing a plat in the office of the county clerk or register.

Procedure 2. This shorter procedure begins with the submission of a final plat. It consists solely of steps (f) through (i) above, except that the public hearing on the final plat *must* be held, since there was no opportunity for a previous hearing.

4. Fiscal benefits of TPB subdivision control. Planning board approval of subdivision plats can be very advantageous to a town over and above insuring that land is used more wisely. The TPB is also in a position to see that the full costs of a subdivision are borne by the developer, not by the town. When subdivisions are required to conform to prescribed standards, and performance bonds may be required to assure that this is done, towns stand to save significantly on costs related to construction and maintenance of roads, water mains, drains, and other services and utilities, as well as costs of fire protection, school bus operation, and garbage collection. A well-planned and properly constructed subdivision can be serviced much more economically than unregulated subdivision development. Towns without subdivision controls must themselves pay for improvements which could be required of developers under an approval system and may be surprised by any number of unexpected new costs.

Subdivision control by the TPB also makes possible adequate provision of parks and recreational areas. The TPB may require that as much as 10 percent of the total area of a subdivision be allocated for parks. Where the subdivision is relatively small or does not contain suitable land, state law provides that the subdivider can be required to make a cash payment in lieu of park land. The town can use such payments, consolidated in a trust fund, to purchase a single, larger property appropriate for a park sometime in the future.

Another important consequence of requiring developers to pay the full cost of subdivisions is that the more marginal, speculative, and least reliable subdivider may find it impossible to operate in such circumstances.

Citizen Action

If a town does not have a TPB, the first order of business for concerned citizens is to see that one is established, that it is given an adequate budgetary appropriation, and that it is empowered to control subdivisions.

In towns which already have town planning boards, citizens who are concerned about the future of the town should press for: (1) regular meetings of the TPB that are open to the public; (2) announcements of agenda in advance; and (3) opportunities for public participation.

When a TPB is working on a comprehensive master plan, citizens should seek public involvement during the early stages of preparation, not just at later hearings when the plan is basically completed. They should work for early meetings that are open to the public, and might suggest that a questionnaire be distributed to gather the ideas of town residents.

Public interest challenges based on planning board controls can range from efforts to see that subdivision regulations are enforced to appeals for judicial review of a planning board action (administrative) or a town board resolution (legislative). The legal procedures available to citizens are basically the same as those discussed above in connection with zoning.[36]

One additional course of action should be mentioned. Communities whose planning boards are swamped with subdivision applications may want to consider the possibility of adopting local laws establishing a temporary moratorium on application processing. In keeping with what has been said above about interim zoning, such measures may well withstand legal challenge if the moratorium is for a definite, relatively short period of time, if it is to be used for constructive planning, and if the public interest served can be shown. In such cases, citizens may want to press for this kind of action.

Residents of the town of Mamakating in Sullivan County successfully lobbied for the establishment of such a moratorium when their planning board was virtually inundated with subdivision applications. A sixty-day moratorium on the processing of all applications was declared, during which time a study of the development patterns of the town was to be prepared. When, at the end of the sixty days, the study was not yet completed, the moratorium was extended for another thirty days.

The efficacy which TPB subdivision regulations have in protecting environmental values depends, of course, on how well they are formulated and how conscientiously they are applied. Speaking generally, however, citizens who face crisis situations of rapid or speculative development and want to challenge subdivision projects can usually consider themselves very fortunate if they live in towns that have planning boards with subdivision regulations. The procedural and substantive requirements of these regulations offer vastly enlarged opportunities for public scrutiny of a developer's plans and for challenges in the public interest. The public hearings which are mandatory in subdivision review by the TPB provide valuable forums for strong expression of public concern and opposition. In all, planning board subdivision regulations comprise one of the most important land use controls available.

OFFICIAL MAPS

The Town Law authorizes a town board to establish an official map for that part of the town lying outside of any incorporated village or city.[37] When first established, this official map shows the layout of existing streets, highways, and parks that have been duly adopted and established by law. It may also show drainage systems.

Once an official map is adopted, the town board may change it or add to it any proposed new facilities or proposals for improving or abandoning existing facilities. Such changes or additions may be made as often as deemed to be in the public interest, but they must always be preceded by a public hearing. At least ten days' notice of the hearings must be published in a newspaper of general circulation.

If the town has a town planning board, then the town board must refer all proposed changes of or additions to the official map to the planning board before taking action. If the planning board does not make a report on such proposals within thirty days, the town board may proceed without hearing its recommendations.

The above provisions for changing an official town map are set out in a section of the Town Law dealing specifically with official maps.[38] In another section which deals with planning board approval of subdivision plats, another procedure for changing an official map is stated, though a public hearing is still a mandatory part of the process.[39] In this case, streets, highways, and parks shown on a subdivision plat that is approved by a town planning board become a part of the official map of the town. As has been discussed above, a public hearing must always precede a town planning board's decision on a subdivision plat.

The importance of the official map lies in the fact that it is "final and conclusive with respect to the location and width of streets and highways, drainage systems and the location of parks shown thereon." The existence of such an official map may affect land developers in several different ways. A developer who wishes to offer roads for dedication as public roads must present roads that conform to the official system. A developer who prefers to retain private roads must still provide proper access for emergency vehicles, as discussed below, and can be required to conform his private roads to the official map. A subdivider in a town which has a town planning board authorized to control subdivisions must provide on his plat roads which "compose a convenient system conforming to the official map." Even if a town board is prepared to change an official map, adapting it to a developer's scheme, this cannot take place without a public hearing—which gives citizens the opportunity to comment on and to publicize what is happening.

Unless a town board can be persuaded to change an official map, no building permits may be issued to developers who wish to build in the bed of a proposed street or highway on the map. Exceptions to this rule may be made by the town's zoning board of appeals when such a denial prevents a fair return on the value of the property involved. This provision is intended to preclude the "taking of property" without just compensation.[40] Exceptions allowed must cause as little increase as practicable in the cost of opening the proposed road, and "reasonable requirements" which benefit the town may be imposed as a condition of granting permits to build. A public hearing on due notice must be held before such action allowing construction in the bed of a mapped street is taken.

It should be noted again that the official map is distinct from the zoning map and the comprehensive master plan. The official map, however, offers a way of giving legal status to public road, park, and drainage systems proposed by the advisory comprehensive master plan prepared by a town planning board. Once these proposed facilities have become duly adopted parts of an official map, they are accorded the special legal protections due all entries on an official map.

CAPITAL IMPROVEMENT PROGRAMS

Local governments are enabled by state legislation to undertake the planning and execution of capital programs to provide improvements in their jurisdictions.[41] These programs must include a plan of projects to be undertaken during a six-year period, estimated costs, and proposed methods of financing. The improvement projects planned might include, for example, acquisition of land for a park, construction of municipal buildings or sewage disposal facilities, or road improvements. A tentative budget must be prepared each year by a local official and submitted to the local governing body for adoption. This budget must indicate priorities. All legal provisions for public hearings on local tentative budgets and budget adoptions apply to this program, which should be widely discussed in the community.

A capital improvement program can be an excellent long-term means of implementing improvements recommended in a comprehensive master plan prepared by a planning board. Such capital plans and budgets offer to the local government yet another means of approaching its future needs and development in an orderly, responsible manner. The formulation of a long-range program for the provision of improvements can strengthen a community's understanding of its problems and its ability to control the way in which it grows. Once a capital improvement program is established, it becomes much more likely that developers will have to consider the framework of local services, existing and proposed, when they design and propose projects. Pressures for improvements on an *ad hoc* basis—which are often spurred by special interests—can then also be more easily answered and controlled.

It should be pointed out, however, that capital improvement programs can establish a timetable for the provision of improvements which actually attracts or induces new development. This is particularly true when plans appropriate for urban areas are adopted for rural or suburban areas. Citizens should always carefully consider the hypotheses upon which capital improvement programs are based and make sure that established or implicit goals are appropriate for the locality involved.

In the 1960s the town of Ramapo, New York, which is within commuting distance of New York City, developed a capital improvement program which has received national attention. The town planning board of the town first prepared a comprehensive master plan for the town's future growth. The town then enacted a zoning ordinance implementing this plan and established an eighteen-year capital improvement program (involving three six-year capital programs) setting out a schedule for the construction of municipal services. No land in the town could then be developed for residential purposes unless the developer could show that certain capital improvements—whether constructed by the town or by the developer himself—would be available by the time the proposed project was completed. As is discussed in Chapter 2, this program of phased growth was challenged in the courts in *Golden* v. *Planning Board of Town of Ramapo.*[42] The town lost the first court test, but in 1972 New York State's highest court upheld the town.

BUILDING CODES

Local governments are authorized to adopt regulations controlling building construction.[43] These may include building codes (construction specifications), housing codes (minimum standards for utilities, etc.), plumbing, and electrical codes. Again, localities may not have adopted these codes—many have not—but they are entitled to do so if they choose. Such codes are intended to protect health and safety; by themselves they have little or no value as land use controls. For the most part, the developer-builder who can show that he intends to meet the minimum code requirements can proceed to build any number of structures on any property he owns or sells—unless other controls are in effect.

Something approaching land use control, however, is attached as a condition to the issuance of building permits by building inspectors in localities where a building code is in effect. The Town Law requires that proposed structures be accessible to fire trucks, ambulances, police cars, and other emergency vehicles. It stipulates that a building permit must not be granted unless the proposed structure is on a lot with at least 15 feet frontage on a road shown on the official town map or, if not, on one of the following: (1) an existing public road; (2) a street shown on a plat approved by the town planning board; or (3) a street on a plat filed in the office of the county clerk or register.

This provision has some value in bringing under surveillance the small-scale, clandestine developer who is subdividing land and planning to sell homes in the middle of nowhere. When a building lot does not meet the access requirement and this requirement is enforced, the developer must take steps to overcome this deficiency. He may seek to provide access via an approved private road or to dedicate a road to the town. Either way, the law allows the town to impose certain requirements on the road's construction such as width and grading particulars, *if* the town has road specifications. *If* the town has an official map, the layout of the road can also be controlled. And *if* there is a town planning board authorized to approve subdivision plats, the law authorizes additional requirements for access roads. It is not sufficient for the developer to promise to make the requisite improvements. In order to be issued a building permit, he must either make them or furnish the town a performance bond with acceptable security.[44]

ROAD SPECIFICATIONS

The role of controls over road construction and improvements has been discussed in respect to circumstances (1) in which a town planning board exists with authority to approve subdivision plats; (2) in which an official map exists; and (3) in which access roads for emergency vehicles are required for issuance of building permits under a building code. Technically up-to-date and stringent road construction standards strengthen the controls available in such situations. Road standards may, however, also exist in the absence of other controls and may provide one of the few means available to bring a development under public review. Generally speaking, road construction standards alone provide only feeble assistance in land use control and citizens whose local government has only these should in a crisis situation explore possible controls at the state or federal level and over the long run work for the institution of more sophisticated local controls.

Roads may be public—owned, maintained, and improved by a municipality, a county, or the state—or they may be private. Sometimes roads within a development are retained as private roads, at least temporarily; usually, however, subdividers plan to turn over their roads to the local government as soon as possible. Although local governments have the authority under state law to acquire public roads by purchase or condemnation, the usual way in which subdivision roads become public roads is by a process known as dedication: A developer offers a road or roads to the local government and the latter formally accepts them through a resolution by the legislative body. When a developer wishes to make this transfer, the local government may impose conditions; the developer's offer need not be accepted unless certain specifications are met.

In the absence of an official map and planning board controls, the kinds of specifications that can be stipulated deal with construction essentials: Road width, grade, roadbed preparation, surfacing, and drainage. Such specifications for public roads are in effect in most localities. Their importance in a control context results from the facts that (1) they are improvements a developer should be required to make before roads are accepted; and (2) the cost involved may discourage developers operating on a very low budget.

Enforced road specifications can involve costs to a developer whether or not he decides to turn roads over to the local government. If he decides to offer the roads for dedication, he must make the necessary improvements. If he decides to retain them as private roads, he is saddled with the expense of maintenance, which in some areas includes costly snow removal, unless he can pass these expenses on to a homeowners' association. He may also lose sales to potential lot buyers who are apprehensive about the fact that the area is not served by public roads. They may fear that private maintenance will not be reliable. They may know that a town is usually barred from making improvements on private roads.[45] Neither costs of road improvements nor threatened loss of sales is an appealing alternative to a speculator operating on a very narrow margin. Thus the enforcement of even such minimal regulations as these can be significant.

Before a local government agrees to accept roads offered for dedication to the town, it should make sure that necessary improvements have been satisfactorily made or that a performance bond has been posted. Although the formal mode of acceptance of a road is via resolution by the town board, the courts have found acceptance implied by "positive acts of public authorities."[46] Once the dedication process is completed and a road has become a public road, the local government is, of course, no longer in a position to require improvements at the developer's expense. Furthermore, once an offer of dedication is accepted, it cannot be revoked.

Although road specifications may often be beneficial to a community, it is important to realize that these same specifications when adopted or enforced without care and consideration of terrain and local conditions can lead to serious environmental problems. There are areas where the requirement of a fifty-foot wide roadbed and sidewalks can be more damaging than advantageous. Care should be taken to see that road specifications are used wisely and that rural areas do not blindly adopt requirements based on standards used in more densely populated areas.

PROTECTION OF HISTORIC AND ESTHETIC DISTRICTS, SITES, BUILDINGS, AND OBJECTS

In addition to their other planning and zoning powers, local governments have the right to enact regulations "for the protection, enhancement, perpetuation, and use of places, districts, sites, buildings, structures, works of art, and other objects having a special character or special historical or aesthetic interest or value."[47] These regulations may include appropriate and reasonable controls on the use or appearance of neighboring property within public view, though compensation must be paid if these controls constitute a taking of private property.[48]

This provision of state law enables local governments to preserve districts, sites, buildings, and objects of special historic or esthetic value which might otherwise fall victim to expediency. Citizens' groups can play an important role in drawing attention to those things which should be saved and in pressing for action by the local government.

Although New York State does not have an enabling statute specifically authorizing architectural controls in areas of the community wider than those included in the above statute, such ordinances have been enacted by some local governments on the basis of general zoning enabling legislation or of home rule powers. Such ordinances must show a clear relationship between the architectural controls established and the public welfare. Commonly an architectural review board composed mainly of people with special expertise in art, architecture, planning, or other relevant areas administers an architectural control ordinance through approval of building permits.[49]

ACQUISITION OF OPEN SPACES

State law specifically enables local governments to acquire interests or rights in real property for the preservation of open spaces or areas.[50] This may be done expressly to enhance the conservation of natural or scenic resources. The municipality need not actually purchase the land outright; it may acquire any "development rights, easement, covenant, or other contractual right" which makes possible the preservation of open space.[51] This acquistion, which must always be preceded by a public hearing after due notice, may take the form of "purchase, gift, grant, bequest, devise, lease, or otherwise." Agricultural lands actually being used in agricultural production qualify as open lands under this statute.

After a local government acquires a limited interest in an open space, the valuation placed on this land for purposes of real estate taxation must reflect the limitations placed on future use of the land.

LOCAL ENVIRONMENTAL CONSERVATION ADVISORY COMMISSION OR BOARD

New York State law specifically enables any town, village, or city to establish a local environmental conservation advisory council (more frequently called a commission).[52] Such a commission, composed of from three to nine members, can be appointed by the local legislative body "to advise in the development, management, and protection of [the municipality's] natural resources." Among other possible duties and responsibilities of the commission, the following are specified by statute:

1. Research on land areas of the municipality for which it was created.

2. Coordination of the activities of unofficial bodies which are organized for similar purposes and cooperation with other official

municipal bodies which are active in the area of community planning for the municipality.

3. Possibly, the preparation and distribution of materials in connection with its work.

4. Preparation of an inventory and map of all open areas within the municipality with the plan of obtaining information pertinent to proper utilization of such open lands.

5. Preparation of an inventory and map of all open marsh lands, swamps, and all other wetlands and recommendation to the governing body of the municipality of a program for ecologically suitable utilization of all such areas.

6. Maintenance of accurate records of all its activities and submission of an annual report to the local legislative body each year.

A commission may be authorized to accept money or other personal property through gifts, bequests, or other means, to further its work. The local legislative body itself may accept real property in fee, or any lesser interest, for the purposes of this statute. Also, upon written recommendation of the commission, the local legislative body may purchase in fee or any lesser interest, through negotiation or by condemnation, such real or personal property as may be needed to fulfill the purposes of the statute.

The local legislative body may provide for compensation to be paid to the members of the commission and may provide for payment of expenses incurred. Staff employees may be appointed by the commission, if appropriations permit.

No mandated tie with the New York State Department of Environmental Conservation (DEC) is established by the statute, but various types of cooperative activities and requests to DEC for assistance and recommendations are authorized.

The law also provides that if a local environmental conservation commission has prepared and submitted to the local legislative body an open area inventory and map which are accepted and approved by the legislative body as the municipality's open space index, then the local legislative body can redesignate the commission as an environmental conservation board.

Environmental conservation boards are responsible for reviewing all applications received by the local legislative body seeking approval for the use or development of any open area listed in the open space index. Such applications might be made by the building department, the zoning board of appeals, the planning board, or any other administrative body. When such applications are received, the environmental conservation board must, within forty-five days, submit a written report to the body making the application and file a copy of the report with the local legislative body. This report must evaluate the proposed use or development of the open area in terms of the open area planning objectives of the municipality. Further, the report must make recommendations regarding the most appropriate use or development of the open area and may include preferable alternative use proposals consistent with the conservation of such areas. All such reports must be made available for public inspection.

In addition to preparing reports dealing with the open areas of the municipality, the board may also perform any other duties assigned to it by resolution of the local legislative body.

There are no provisions for state aid to local environmental conservation commissions or boards, in contrast to the provisions which are made for such aid to environmental management councils on the county level, which are discussed in the following chapter. Local commissions and boards generally must depend on local funding and gifts, though some money has been available to them from the Ford Foundation for a variety of different projects.

Although local environmental conservation commissions and boards are relatively new in New York State, they have for some time been established in the New England states and have spread to Midwestern and West Coast states as well. These commissions provide a means of focusing environmental concerns existing on the local level and of expressing these concerns within the framework of the local government. The strength of a particular commission or board depends on a number of factors, but perhaps the most important of these are the commitment, energy, and political awareness of its members. Different political structures and climates exist in different parts of the state, but citizen members of a local environmental conservation advisory commission should always evaluate circumstances realistically and seek to build strong public support for environmental values and a viable political base upon which protection of these values can be realized.

In summary, citizens should be aware that state enabling legislation exists for the establishment of local environmental conservation advisory commissions, and they should consider whether the establishment of such a commission within their own local government would be an effective way of expressing environmental concerns, of carrying out needed research, and of influencing decisions. If citizens feel that a local environmental conservation commission should be appointed, they should press for such action by the local legislative body. Finally, if such a commission is established, citizens should do all they can to see that it is a politically realistic and effective part of the local government.

NOTES

1. These laws are hereafter cited as TL, GCL, VL and GML, respectively. A publication of the New York State Office of Planning Services (OPS) entitled *A Guide to the Planning and Zoning Laws of N.Y. State* (rev. December 1973) is a compilation of the planning and zoning enabling acts drawn from these and other relevant laws. As part of a reorganization within the state government, the Office of Planning Services and the Office for Local Government ceased operation as such on March 31, 1975. Whereas some of their functions were terminated altogether and others were delegated to various state agencies, the major responsibilities of these two offices were transferred to the newly established Division of Community Affairs within the Department of State. In mid-April 1975 the question of whether an independent state planning agency might also be established, as recommended by the governor, had not yet been resolved by the legislature.

Reprinting of the Office of Planning Services (OPS) publications discussed in this book was postponed during the reorganization, but these publications should become available again from the Division of Community Affairs, New York State Department of State, 162 Washington Avenue, Albany, N. Y. 12225.

2. Robert M. Anderson, *New York Zoning Law and Practice* (Rochester, N.Y.: The Lawyers Co-operative Publishing Co., 1973), §3.03.

3. TL §261.

4. *See* Chapter 13 for a discussion of floodplain zoning and the federal Flood Disaster Protection Act of 1973.

5. The New York State Office of Planning Services (OPS) has published a useful booklet entitled *Adopting a Zoning Ordinance,* which outlines in detail the procedures that must be followed by towns, cities, and villages in the adoption of a zoning ordinance.

The Statute of Local Governments grants to cities, villages, and towns the general power "to adopt, amend and repeal zoning regulations." This statute also provides, however, that all the powers it grants "shall at all times be subject to such purposes, standards and procedures as the Legislature may have heretofore prescribed or may hereafter prescribe."

6. Anderson, *New York Zoning Law,* §17.02 *et seq.*

7. Some town planning boards have attempted to carry out site plan *approval,* but recent court decisions have held that this power cannot be exercised by a planning board. Mobil Oil Corp. v. Milton, 72 Misc.2d 505, 339 N.Y.S.2d 704 (Sup. Ct. 1972); Nemeroff Realty Corp. v. Kerr, 38 App. Div.2d 437, 330 N.Y.S.2d 632 (1972), *aff'd,* 32 N.Y.2d 873, 299 N.E.2d 897, 346 N.Y.S.2d 532 (1973).

Legislation which would enable local legislative bodies across the state to delegate site plan approval to planning boards is expected to be introduced in the state legislature in the spring of 1975, and bills authorizing such action in two specific areas (Westchester County municipalities and the town of Clarkstown in Rockland County) have already been passed.

8. TL §265–a. Uses of land which lawfully exist before a zoning ordinance is enacted and are allowed to continue after the ordinance becomes effective are commonly called "nonconforming uses." See Anderson, New York Zoning Law, Chapter 6, for a full discussion.

9. OPS, Interim—Stop-Gap Zoning (Legal Memorandum #2, 1969).

10. See Chapter 2 for a discussion of constitutional prohibitions against the "taking" of private property except for a public purpose and with just compensation.

11. TL §267.

12. Anderson, New York Zoning Law, §20.02 and §22.01 et seq.

13. TL §267(6); Chapmald Realty Corp. v. Board of Standards and Appeals, 76 N.Y.S. 2d 296 (Sup. Ct. 1948).

14. Galvin v. Murphy, 11 App. Div. 2d 900, 203 N.Y.S. 2nd 151 (1960).

15. See the discussion of official maps, pp. 49–51.

16. See Glossary.

17. Falvo v. Kerner, 222 App. Div. 289, 225 N.Y.S. 747 (1927); Eckels v. Murdock, 265 N.Y. 545, 193 N.E. 313 (1934); Anderson, New York Zoning Law, §22.16.

18. TL §268(2); Anderson, New York Zoning Law, §23.05.

19. TL §268(2); Anderson, New York Zoning Law, §23.06.

20. Anderson, New York Zoning Law, §23.07.

21. TL §268(1).

22. TL §272–a.

23. See Chapter 9.

24. 23 Op. State Compt. 226.

25. See pp. 45–46.

26. TL §277(1).

27. OPS, Control of Land Subdivision (rev. January 1974), p. 23.

28. TL §276(1). See also TL §272. Villages and cities must rely on less specific authority in VL §7–720 and GCL §28, respectively.

29. OPS, Control of Land Subdivision, pp. 39–54; Ulster County Planning Board, January 1971, revised April 1973. Model Subdivision Regulations (mimeographed).

30. OPS, Control of Land Subdivision, p. 21.

31. TL §277(1).

32. TL §277(3).

33. OPS, Control of Land Subdivision, p. 8.

34. See pp. 67–68.

35. GML §239–k.

36. See also OPS, Subdivision Regulation Enforcement (Legal Memorandum #3, July 1969) and Anderson, New York Zoning Law, §21–§24.

37. TL §270; GCL §26; VL §7–724. A helpful pamphlet entitled The Official Map (1974) has been published by the New York State Office of Planning Services.

38. TL §273.

39. TL §278(1).

40. *See* Chapter 2.
41. GML §99–g.
42. 30 N.Y. 2d 359, 334 N.Y.S. 2d 138, 285 N.E. 2d 291 (1972).
43. Most specifically: TL §130. A state building code exists, but it is not effective in a municipality unless expressly adopted by the local legislative body. When such enactments take place, the state code should be augmented by specifications reflecting local conditions.
44. TL §280, §280–a; GCL §36; VL §7–736.
45. TL §280, GCL §36, VL §7–736.
46. Putnam Valley Lumber & Supply Corp. v. Duell, 82 N.Y.S. 2d 407 (Sup. Ct. 1948); Petrie v. City of Rochester, 206 Misc. 96, 132 N.Y.S. 2d 501 (Sup. Ct. 1954).
47. GML §96–a.
48. *See* Chapter 2.
49. Anderson, *New York Zoning Law,* §8.46 *et seq.* The New York State comptroller has ruled that a town may regulate the construction or design of homes to promote the appearance of the town, provided that such regulation is not unreasonable, arbitrary, or discriminatory. 1963 Op. State Compt. 901.
50. GML §247.
51. *See* Chapter 15 for a discussion of development rights, conservation easements, etc.
52. GML, Article 12–F, §§ 239–x and 239–y. The New York State Office for Local Government has published a booklet entitled *Municipal Advisory Councils for Environmental Conservation* (September 1970) which provides a sample local law for such an enactment, as well as background information. As discussed in note 1 above, the Office for Local Government no longer exists as such. The publications of this agency are now available from the Division of Community Affairs, New York State Department of State, 162 Washington Avenue, Albany, N. Y. 12225. It is likely that these publications will be revised by the Division of Community Affairs.

CHAPTER 4

Land Use Controls at the County Level

THE DEGREE TO which counties in New York State are involved in land use control and planning varies greatly within the state and depends on a number of different factors, not the least of which are a particular county's financial resources, the sophistication and efficiency of its government, its political orientation, and the strength of its leadership. Some counties are acutely aware of the problems of uncontrolled land development and are actively working for county-wide cooperation in planning; others are not taking any initiative in this area at the present time.

New York State is divided into sixty-two counties, five of which lie wholly within New York City and form with the city a unique governmental unit. Considerable differences exist in the governmental structures of the other fifty-seven counties. Each has an elective legislative body, traditionally the board of supervisors, which must represent the people of the county in a manner consistent with the U. S. Supreme Court's "one-man, one-vote" ruling. Some counties, however, have adopted charters which permit considerable reorganization of county government, the separation of legislative and executive responsibility coupled with provision for a county executive or manager, and broadening of basic county powers. A charter may provide for the establishment of a new legislative body to replace the board of supervisors. State law clarifies that whenever the term "board of supervisors" appears in legislation, it means "the elective governing body of a county, by whatever name designated."[1] As of March 1975, seventeen of the state's fifty-seven counties lying outside New York City had adopted charters. Within this number are virtually all the counties in the state which have large populations.

As far as land use controls are concerned, some of the powers counties have are similar to those possessed by town, city, or village governments. For example, a county may establish a county planning board which may prepare a comprehensive master plan for the development of the county. In other cases, county powers differ considerably from those of the other forms of local governments in that they deal with review from a county perspective of particular matters which must be referred to the county by city, town, and village governments. An example of this type of power is the mandatory county review of certain local zoning actions. Noticeably lacking in the county's repertoire of powers is the authority to enact a zoning ordinance.

The basic topics covered in this chapter are the county planning board and its rights to prepare a comprehensive master plan and to review (1) certain local zoning actions, and (2) subdivision plats; the official county map; the county filing requirements for subdivisions; and county environmental management councils. Mention is made of control exercised by county health department officials, a subject which is discussed in Chapter 5. With respect to capital improvement programs, protection of historic places, and acquisition of open spaces (topics discussed in the preceding chapter) counties have exactly the same powers as do towns, cities, and villages. Consequently, these topics are not treated again in this chapter. In a final section, suggestions for citizen action are given.

COUNTY PLANNING BOARDS

Establishment of a County Planning Board

The board of supervisors of any county, alone or in collaboration with the governing bodies of cities, towns, or villages in the county may establish a County Planning Board (hereafter CPB) composed of representatives from the county and, if they participate, from local governments.[2] If the county has adopted a charter, this charter may provide that the members of the CPB be appointed by the county executive, subject to approval by the legislative body, rather than directly by the legislative body itself. The following officials, if existing in the county, must be *ex officio* members of the CPB: The county engineer, superintendent of highways, or district superintendent; and the comptroller or commissioner of finance. No compensation is permitted for the members of the CPB, but funds may be appropriated for expenses. All of the counties in the state, with the exception of Franklin County, have now established county planning boards.

The same statute which enables a county to establish a CPB also provides for the establishment of regional planning boards by the governing bodies of adjacent counties and of regional or metropolitan planning boards by the governing bodies of cities, towns, and villages in any county or counties. A majority of the state's counties are now involved in some type of regional planning board. These boards have basically the same planning and advisory powers that county planning boards have. Generally, regional planning boards have no implementation authority, but in some areas they have acquired some political muscle. For example, the Nassau-Suffolk Regional Planning Board on Long Island has been designated by the federal government as the official reviewing agent for all requests for federal assistance for public works programs in these two counties.

Preparation of a Comprehensive Master Plan

Once a CPB is established, it is empowered by statute to "perform planning work, including but not limited to surveys, land use studies, urban renewal plans, and technical services" and to "prepare and adopt . . . a comprehensive master plan for the development of the entire area of the county" which must include highways, parks, parkways, and sites for public buildings or works involving county or municipal participation, acquisition, financing, or construction.[3]

The county board of supervisors is empowered to adopt and to make changes in the comprehensive master plan prepared by the CPB. Before both the original adoption and any amendment, the board of supervisors must give two weeks' notice and hold a public hearing or hearings in which public officials as well as interested persons must be heard. Once the master plan is approved, in whole or in part, by the county board of supervisors, it becomes binding on this board and on county departments. Subsequently, all expenditures of public funds, except for state or federal projects, for acquisition of land or public improvements shown on the master plan must be made in accordance with this plan. Also, no expenditure of public funds can be made for acquisition of land or public improvements *not* shown on the plan, if these expenditures would cause a modification of the plan—until the plan itself is amended according to the required procedures.

One should note here the differences between comprehensive master plans prepared by town planning boards and those prepared by county planning boards. The former deal with all aspects of a town's future growth, public and private, and are advisory documents that are not formally adopted by the town's legislative body, the town board. The comprehensive master plan prepared by a CPB deals with public sites and facilities and is legally binding once it is adopted by the county's legislative body. Parts of a county master plan may cover other aspects of the county's growth, but these parts are not formally adopted by the county board of supervisors and, similar to town master plans, are advisory only.

Before holding a public hearing on a proposed change to the county master plan, the board of supervisors must submit these proposals to the CPB for a specified, reasonable period of time for consideration and advice. A majority vote of all members of the board of supervisors is necessary to take an action that is adverse to CPB advice on the proposed plan changes. Also, all plans involving construction of any state or county highway must be submitted to the CPB for examination and suggestions.

In addition to its preparation of the county comprehensive master plan, the CPB may also undertake a variety of activities involving the collection and distribution of planning information, research into business and industrial conditions, and recommendation of a comprehensive zoning plan to municipalities whose jurisdictions are served by the CPB.

Review of Local Zoning Actions

The law provides that where a CPB exists, cities, towns, and villages within the county must give that board at least thirty days to review proposed zoning ordinances or amendments and applications for special permits or variances when any of these measures would affect the zoning of land lying within 500 feet from any of the following:[4]

1. The boundary of any city, town, or village;

2. Any existing or proposed county or state park or other recreational area;

3. The right-of-way of any existing or proposed county or state highway or road;

4. The existing or proposed right-of-way of any stream or drainage channel owned by the county or for which the county has established channel lines; or

5. The existing or proposed boundary of any county or state owned land on which a public building or institution is situated.

A municipal body cannot take action contrary to CPB recommendations on such a measure except by a vote of a majority plus one of all of its members and after providing a full statement of reasons.

The sensible basis for this provision is that the public interest will be served by coordination of zoning actions and consideration of county-wide concerns.[5] The CPB is expressly directed to include the following important considerations, among others, in its review:

1. Traffic-generating characteristics of proposed land uses;

2. Protection of "community character as regards predominant land uses, population density, and relation between residential and non-residential areas";

3. Community appearance;

4. Matters pertaining "to the achievement and maintaining of a satisfactory community environment."

There is no provision for public participation in this county review. Needless to say, however, it offers opportunity for informal input and publicity—and given the range of qualifying circumstances, it should come into play whenever any large-scale land development project is proposed. The growing importance of, and interest in, county-wide or regional land use planning suggests that citizen effort should be exerted to make county review significant. This requires that there be a CPB, that it be well qualified, and that it have access to the services of qualified staff members or consultants.

Review of Subdivision Plats

The same type of CPB review procedure as that just described for local zoning actions is mandatory for all subdivision plats which are within 500 feet of the specified boundaries or facilities *if* there is a municipal planning agency and both this agency and the CPB have been authorized to approve subdivision plats.[6] The same objective of county-wide coordination is to be served by this review and the same considerations are to guide the CPB's recommendations.

Another, separate provision of the General Municipal Law gives counties an opportunity to exercise ultimate approval power over subdivisions, if they so choose.[7] A CPB authorized by a board of supervisors to approve subdivision plats may designate any area outside of a city or village as a subdivision control area and adopt subdivision regulations applying thereto. This county power would not apply to areas within the jurisdiction of a town with a planning board empowered to approve subdivision plats *unless* the town expressly consented through a resolution by its town board. The scope of a CPB's subdivision review power would be the same as that provided for town planning boards in the Town Law.[8] In the case of CPB review, public hearings must be held within the town in which a proposed subdivision is located. CPB subdivision regulations must apply to subdivision of two or more lots; and they become effective upon approval by the county board of supervisors.

The legislative bodies of cities, towns, or villages within a county that has a planning board can take the initiative of assigning to the CPB their own subdivision approval power. They can do this whether or not they have their own planning boards. The assignment becomes effective when accepted by the county, and can be terminated by either the county or the municipality.

County approval of subdivision plats could serve the need for county-wide planning very effectively if the CPB involved were a strong planning board and had a large enough staff to handle the review. As a fact of life, however, not many cities, towns, or villages are prepared to surrender their planning power and not many county boards of supervisors will agree to designate subdivision control areas, thereby reducing municipal autonomy.

THE OFFICIAL COUNTY MAP

The General Municipal Law provides for the establishment of an official county map "analogous in function and operation" to municipal official maps.[9] Such a county map may be established by a county board of supervisors for an entire county or parts thereof. It must show *existing* rights-of-way for county roads and drainage systems, and may show *proposed* rights-of-way. If the county has a CPB and a comprehensive master plan, additional features may be included on the official county map, such as rights-of-way for any proposed transportation network or sites for any proposed public building, whether these are to be constructed under county, state, or federal authority.

That part of an official county map that affects a particular municipality has the same status as an official municipal map when the municipality has no official map of its own. Note should be made, however, that an official county map does not show municipal roads or drainage systems.

A public hearing is not required before the original establishment of an official county map, but no change may be made on the map unless a public hearing is held. Ten days' notice of this hearing must be given in a newspaper of general circulation in the county and in a newspaper of general circulation in each municipality involved. Before making any changes, the county board of supervisors must also refer the matter to the CPB, if one exists, and to the county superintendent of highways or commissioner of transportation for a report within thirty days.

An official county map, where one exists, operates as a control on the issuance of building permits to developers. No permits may be issued for construction in rights-of-way or on the site of proposed improvements shown on an official county map unless an exception is allowed after a hearing on due notice. Decisions to grant or deny such exceptions are subject to judicial review under Article 78 of the Civil Practice Law and Rules.[10]

Also, no building permit may be issued by a city, town, or village for a building that has frontage on or access to or is otherwise directly related to an existing or proposed right-of-way or site shown on the official county map without prior notification to county authorities (the CPB and the superintendent of highways or commissioner of public works) who may report back approval, conditional approval, or disapproval. Action by a municipality on such a building permit application must be consistent with the county's recommendation, except in cases of unnecessary hardship or practical difficulties. Further, no subdivision plat which is directly related to a right-of-way or site shown on the map may be approved by a municipality without this same type of county review.

The county superintendent or commissioner, in cooperation with the CPB, if one exists, is required to promulgate rules and regulations governing county approval of building permits affecting features shown on the official county map.

THE COUNTY FILING REQUIREMENT FOR
SUBDIVISIONS

The New York Real Property Law requires that anyone who subdivides property into any number of lots for the purpose of offering these lots for sale to the public must file a map of the subdivision, certified by a licensed land surveyor, in the office of the county clerk or register of deeds before he offers these lots for sale.[11] A duplicate map must be filed in the county tax map department, if one exists, and in the office of the clerk of the city, town, or village in which the property is located. These maps are to be filed and numbered by the appropriate clerks according to the date of filing and indexed alphabetically by the name of the subdivision. It should be noted that the filing of deeds without the properly certified map does not fulfill the requirements of the law.

In itself, this requirement is probably less significant as a control than as an information resource, although the subdivider who sells and conveys a lot without satisfying the filing requirement is subject to a modest fine: $25 for each such violation.

The filing requirement has acquired greater significance as a control through other statutory provisions that bar the filing of a subdivision map or plat unless the project has received necessary approvals. As discussed in the previous chapter, when a city, town, or village (or county) planning board is authorized to review subdivision plats, a particular plat must be approved before it can be filed with the county clerk. As will be discussed in the following chapter, the adequacy of water supply and sewage disposal facilities must be approved, for subdivisions of five or more lots, under provisions of the state Public Health Law and Environmental Conservation Law, before this filing can be made.[12] Filings of subdivision plats which are made without the required approvals are in violation of the law. So also are filings in which a properly certified surveyor's map is not supplied. It appears that these statutory requirements are frequently violated.

COUNTY ENVIRONMENTAL MANAGEMENT COUNCILS

New York State law provides that the legislative body of any county may establish an environmental management council to "be responsible for reviewing and advising local and state government on present and proposed methods of using, protecting and conserving the environment for the benefit of all the people."[13] As of April 1975, thirty-two of New York's sixty-two counties have established such councils.[14]

In some respects county environmental management councils are similar to the local environmental conservation advisory commissions discussed in the previous chapter. Like the local commission, the county council has the authority to advise the governing body on matters relating to natural resources; to keep an index of all open areas and of all wetlands within its jurisdiction; to cooperate with other governmental and non-governmental boards or organizations; to conduct research on land areas; to publish materials about its work; and to submit an annual report to the governing body. In addition to these powers and duties, the county environmental management council *must* also prepare, in cooperation with the county planning agency and other appropriate agencies, a plan for the protection of the county's environment and the management of its natural resources. This plan must be submitted to the county's governing body as soon as practicable after the council's establishment. The council *must* also investigate and recommend to the governing body ecologically sound methods of planning the use of the county's resources.

Perhaps the most significant distinction between county environmental management councils and environmental conservation commissions at the city, town, and village level is the eligibility of county councils for state aid payments.[15] Up to one-half of the expenditures of a county council established pursuant to Article 47 of the Environmental Conservation Law is reimbursed out of funds appropriated to the New York State Department of Environmental Conservation (DEC). In connection with this program of state aid, the county environmental management councils maintain close ties with DEC, which has promulgated rules and regulations pertaining to aid payments.[16] Also, the law provides that the councils may make particular types of requests to DEC for assistance in their work.[17]

Each county environmental management council must include one member from each city, town, or village environmental conservation advisory commission within the county. Additional members may also be appointed. Members of the county legislative body and heads of those county departments whose work particularly affects or is affected by environmental considerations may be appointed as *ex officio* members of the council. The county may provide for compensation to be paid to members of the council and may make appropriations for expenses incurred, including the costs of maintaining staff employees to conduct council business.

The state enabling legislation authorizing the establishment of county environmental management councils was passed in 1970. Consequently, some of the county councils in the state have now been in operation for more than four years. Generally, these years of experience have brought to the councils a clearer understanding of political realities which must be faced, as well as greater recognition by local politicians. A growing trend toward the appointment of professional staffs by councils is also apparent across the state.

CONTROLS EXERCISED BY COUNTY HEALTH DEPARTMENTS

County health departments play an important role in land use matters when they promulgate their own water supply and/or sewage disposal regulations for subdivisions or are designated to perform review functions regarding water supply and/or sewage disposal for state officials. Such responsibilities of county health departments are best explained along with provisions of the New York State Public Health Law and Environmental Conservation Law, which are discussed in the following chapter.

CITIZEN ACTION

As has been mentioned in connection with CPB review of local zoning actions, citizen effort should be exerted to make county review of land development projects as effective as possible. The need for county-wide consideration of growth needs and development problems cannot be overemphasized.

County planning boards can sometimes be intimidated or dominated by developers or chambers of commerce, and can fail to use the powers which are available to them. Active citizen support, representing the interests of the public, can greatly increase the effectiveness of a CPB. Citizens should find out whether their CPB has a competent, professional staff and bring pressure to bear to obtain one if it does not. Where such qualified staffs exist, they can provide invaluable assistance to municipalities.

Citizen participation in public hearings on a county comprehensive master plan or official map should be encouraged. This is especially important in the case of the master plan, which when formally adopted by the county legislative body is a legally binding plan for the acquistion of land and for public improvements by the county. Citizens should also explore the possibility of establishing a county environmental management council or, if such a council already exists, find out about its activities and lend support. Whenever citizens think that a county planning board and/or an environmental management council should conduct certain kinds of studies which would benefit the county (such as a study of methods for preserving open space), they should express their feelings to the planning board, the environmental council and/or the county legislative body, and press for action.

NOTES

1. N.Y. General Construction Law §13–b.
2. N.Y. General Municipal Law (GML) § 239–b.
3. GML §239–d(1).
4. GML §239–m.
5. GML §239–l.
6. GML §239–l, §239–n.
7. GML §239–d (7).
8. In §§ 276, 277, and 278.
9. GML §239–g through §239–k. *See* Chapter 3 for a discussion of the official town map.
10. *See* Glossary.
11. N.Y. Real Property Law, Article 9, §334.
12. In a recent court case the authority of the Department of Health to approve all subdivisions of land of 5 or more parcels was challenged. *See* Chapter 5 for a discussion of this "Herrick case."
13. N.Y. Environmental Conservation Law (ECL) §47–0103. The New York State Office for Local Government's booklet *Municipal Advisory Councils for Environmental Conservation* (September 1970) provides a sample local law for the establishment of such a county council, as well as other background information. *See* note 52 of Chapter 3 for comments regarding the availability of Office for Local Government publications.
14. Five Adirondack counties are served by one environmental management council in accordance with a provision of the law authorizing this type of regional consolidation. *See* ECL §47–0113.
15. ECL §47–0115.
16. These rules and regulations can be found at 6 NYCRR Part 636.
17. ECL §47–0111.

CHAPTER 5

Major Land Use Controls at the State Level

New York State does not have a statewide program of land use controls. As will be discussed in later chapters, a regional program of planning and controls has been established for the Adirondack Park and special legislation has been passed to protect tidal wetlands.* In the state as a whole, however, state review of land development occurs primarily as a consequence of state government programs dealing with water supply, stream protection, and sewage disposal. In many cases, it has been possible under these programs for citizens to gain opportunities to bring development problems before the public that were not available at the local level, often because of local political pressures. It is very important, therefore, to know what controls exist at the state level and how they are implemented.

Before 1970, the authority to control water supply and sewage disposal systems resided in the state Department of Health, local health departments, and the state Water Resources Commission. In 1970, however, the Environmental Conservation Law was enacted, creating the New York State Department of Environmental Conservation (DEC) with a mandate to "conserve, improve and protect [the] natural resources and environment [of New York State] and

*Just as this book was going to press the state legislature passed two very important new environmental acts: a state "little NEPA" act and a fresh water wetlands act. See p. xiv of the Introduction.

control water, land, and air pollution, in order to enhance the health, safety, and welfare of the people of the state and their overall economic and social well being."[1] As part of a general consolidation of responsibilities for environmental programs under DEC, this department took over from the Water Resources Commission the power to control sources and distribution of public water supplies and, from the Department of Health, the authority to regulate the disposal of sewage. The Department of Health retained primary responsibility for approving the quality and quantity of particular water supply systems in terms of public health standards.

In practice, the roles actually played by DEC and the Department of Health (hereafter DH) in the implementation of laws dealing with water supply and sewage disposal are not always clear cut. Although DEC was given full statutory authority over sewage disposal systems, by agreement between the two departments DH continued to administer approval of all individual septic tank systems, while DEC assumed full responsibility for approval of communal sewerage systems. Even then, however, DEC did not at first have an engineering staff capable of reviewing the sewerage facilities for which it was responsible. On the other hand, DH had an experienced staff of forty-one field personnel in its ten district offices. Consequently, the two departments further agreed that DH could carry out review of community sewerage systems on behalf of DEC. Some of the nine DEC regional offices are still acquiring personnel, but most are now fully staffed and carry out review of communal systems independently of DH. As will be discussed below, DEC also plans to take over full administration of the approval of subdivisions which have septic tank sewage disposal systems if these subdivisions have five or more lots of less than ten acres each.

In addition, DH's broad responsibility to protect public health and DEC's broad responsibility to protect the environment are often intertwined. As a consequence, their specific administrative duties may often be very closely related. These circumstances have led to some disagreements between the departments and sometimes make it difficult to trace the path of a particular project that is being reviewed by both departments. In order to avoid being intimidated by real or apparent jurisdictional confusion, concerned citizens who want to monitor such review should develop a firm grasp of the basic responsibilities required by law of each department and an understanding of which procedures offer the most promise for full consideration of the environmental consequences of land development projects.

The role played by local health departments in the implementation of the Environmental Conservation Law, as well as the Public Health Law, is a further complicating factor. Some cities, counties, and part-counties in the state have established their own health departments which have legal authority to adopt subdivision regulations for their jurisdictions.[2] These regulations must conform to state law, but they may vary in other respects and no provision exists for state approval. Once a local health department has adopted subdivision regulations, then it carries out review and approval of subdivisions within its jurisdiction. In addition, it may also undertake responsibilities for DH and DEC in return for state aid payments. As a result, local health departments frequently handle all approvals required by proposed developments for their water supply and sewage disposal systems.

The basic responsibilities of DEC, DH, and local health departments in the review of land development projects are described in the discussion which follows. Access points for concerned citizens, important legal rights, and serious problems are indicated. A summary of the suggestions given for citizen action concludes the chapter.

THE NEW YORK STATE DEPARTMENT OF ENVIRONMENTAL CONSERVATION (DEC)

With respect to land use, DEC's review responsibilities in the following areas are most important:

1. Issuance of public water supply permits
2. Issuance of pollutant discharge permits
3. Stream protection
4. Environmental analysis

In general, it is safe to say that DEC will probably be involved in required review of almost any big, controversial land development project in the state. Even though developers may submit their sewage disposal and water supply plans to local health departments, applications from major projects almost always find their way to one of the nine DEC regional offices and the DEC central office in Albany. With respect to subdivisions of land, it is nearly impossible presently to plan a subdivision of fifty or more parcels without needing at least one DEC permit, and proposed regulations could reduce this threshold size to five or more parcels.

In the discussion which follows, it must be remembered, nevertheless, that DEC may delegate some of its responsibilities to the Department of Health or directly to local health departments.[3] As a result, the way basic procedures are carried out may vary from area to area.

It is important to note that whenever DEC must issue a permit for a particular aspect of a land development project, citizens have an opportunity both to contest the specific aspect of the project which is under review and also to urge DEC to broaden its evaluation of that permit application into a review of the proposed project's total environmental impact. Shortly after the creation of DEC in 1970, the commissioner of environmental conservation, Henry L. Diamond, made the following statement:

> We have taken a view now in any permit proceeding before the DEC that we will look at the full environmental impact of the permit.[4]

Citizens should do all that they can to see that this intent is carried out to the fullest extent possible. DEC's expansion of the water supply permit application submitted for the Ton-Da-Lay subdivision in the Adirondacks into a full review of the environmental impact of the proposed project is an example of how the policy has been implemented.[5]

1. Public Water Supply Permits

On July 1, 1970, DEC took over the powers and duties of the New York State Water Resources Commission, which had been authorized to adopt procedures for regulating the development of new or proposed water supply systems—that is, any new or increased taking of water from public water supply sources. At the present time, the state Department of Health is responsible for approving water supply quality and quantity in development projects that have individual wells and for approving the quality of water in public drinking water supply systems. DEC, in contrast, is responsible for approving the establishment of new public drinking water supply systems and the expansion of existing systems.

By law, maps and plans must be submitted to DEC for approval by any "person or public corporation who is authorized and engaged in or proposing to engage in, the acquisition, conservation, development, use, and distribution of water for potable purposes . . ." before any new or additional taking of water or any related construction can occur.[6]

Since an individual well on a private lot does not involve the *distribution* of water, it does not fall within the scope of this statute.[7] As will be discussed below, moreover, the Department of Health allows individual wells in subdivisions of up to fifty lots (or more, if a variance is granted). Consequently, many subdivisions in the state are not required to obtain a water supply permit from DEC.The many forty-nine-lot subdivisions in the state reflect the existence of this "escape hatch."

Also, no permit is required for the extension of the supply mains of a municipal water supply plant within the approved limits of its service area (even when this is done to supply water to territory not previously served), so long as the plant can supply the water needed without taking additional water.[8] Thus, land development projects which can obtain their water supply in this manner do not need to apply for a DEC water supply permit.

A development project is generally required to apply for a water supply permit only once, even though development may take place in stages, provided that the capacity of its water supply system is not increased. Thus developers usually only need approval for their original, comprehensive water supply concept. It is possible for DEC to ask for the application of a water supply permit in stages, but this is usually done only where the proposed development is very large and there is some uncertainty about the developer's ability to finance the entire proposed project.

Upon receipt of an application for a water supply permit, DEC publishes a public notice that a public hearing will be held on a specified day at a specified place to receive evidence and hear arguments from all those who "may be affected by the proposed project" and who have filed proper notices of appearance.[9] This notice must "be published in such newspaper or newspapers as the department shall deem appropriate, once in each week for not more than four weeks. At least one publication shall be in a newspaper of general circulation in the area affected."[10] This may mean that the notice may appear only once in a local newspaper, and even then it usually appears in fine print, embedded among a number of other legal notices.

If *anyone* who may be affected by the proposed project and wishes to speak in opposition to it files a proper notice of appearance with DEC, then a public hearing *must* be held. Only if no notices of appearance for opposition are received may DEC dispense with the hearing. Of all the procedures and permits discussed in this chapter, this is the only case in which a public hearing is mandatory.

In all other cases, hearings are held at the discretion of DEC. Concerned citizens should be aware of this opportunity to make certain that a public hearing is held on a development project. To avoid missing the notice of a hearing for a particular project, a written request may be sent to DEC, asking for personal notification whenever the permit application for this project is submitted. This request should be sent to the following address:

> Office of Hearing Officers
> New York State Department of
>   Environmental Conservation
> 50 Wolf Road
> Albany, New York 12233

Care should also be taken to file notices of appearance properly. The published notice of the hearing must specify the last day on which these notices of appearance can be filed with DEC. This date must be not more than ten days prior to the date of the hearing. Any person or public corporation who wishes to speak in opposition to the project under consideration must "recite in the notice of appearance their interests and specific grounds of objection."[11]

The prime considerations around which DEC water supply permit hearings revolve are whether the proposed plans:

1. Are justified by public necessity.
2. Take proper consideration of other sources of supply which are or may become available.
3. Provide for proper and safe construction of water supply facilities.
4. Protect the watershed from contamination.
5. Provide proper treatment of the water supply.
6. Provide for an adequate supply.
7. Are just and equitable to other affected areas of the state and their inhabitants, whose present and future water supply needs must be considered.

Citizens who plan to appear at such a hearing should do everything they can to be well organized and well prepared to give a strong presentation of their arguments. Individuals and groups should coordinate their efforts and try not to duplicate each others's testimony. Any research or studies that have been done in the area should be brought to bear. Any specialists, professional people, or prominent citizens who are willing to appear and speak at the hearing should be urged to do so. The more clearly and forcefully arguments are presented, the more weight they will carry with DEC.

Within ninety days after the closing of a hearing, which usually is held technically open until the official transcript is prepared and delivered to the hearing officer, DEC must issue a final decision on the water supply permit application. It can approve, approve with specified modifications, or reject the plans submitted.

2. State Pollutant Discharge Elimination System

Under the State Pollutant Discharge Elimination System (SPDES) program effective September 1, 1973,[12] no one may discharge pollutants into classified waters of New York State from a point source without a SPDES permit issued by DEC. Since both the ground and surface waters of the state are classified (that is, the state has developed and implemented a classification system for both), all discharges of pollutants from point sources are subject to this requirement—whether they are made above ground, underground, or directly into rivers and streams. Such discharges might be from municipal (including residential), industrial, agricultural, or commercial point sources.

The following is the definition of "point source" provided in the state law:

> "Point source" means any discernible, confined and discrete conveyance, including but not limited to any pipe, ditch, channel, tunnel, conduit, well, discrete fissure, container, rolling stock, concentrated animal feeding operation or vessel or other floating stock from which pollutants are or may be discharged.[13]

A pipe discharging pollutants from a factory or effluent from a sewage treatment plant is a clear example of a point source. General runoff from a virgin forest is a clear example of a non-point source. Certain other discharges, however, such as runoff via a man-made conveyance, fall within a gray area between point sources and non-point sources. Further clarifications in this area can be expected from regulations, administrative decisions, and court rulings on both state and federal levels.

The New York SPDES program was established in direct response to the Federal Water Pollution Control Act Amendments of 1972 which established a National Pollutant Discharge Elimination System (NPDES) and provided for delegation of authority to states with approved programs.[14] The New York State program has not yet received federal approval, but a formal proposal was submitted to the Environmental Protection Agency (EPA) on April 8, 1974. Approval is expected by July 1975.

Since the state program has not yet received federal approval, both federal NPDES and state SPDES permits are presently being granted in New York State. This has led to some confusion regarding jurisdiction. The following are important points which should be borne in mind:

1. Federal law requires that anyone discharging pollutants from a point source into navigable waters must obtain a NPDES permit.[15] (Note that this may be a discharge of any size.)

2. State law requires a SPDES permit for discharges of pollutants from a point source into either the groundwaters or the surface waters of the state. (Thus discharges into groundwaters require permits only under the state program.)

3. State law provided that until December 31, 1974, obtaining a NPDES permit would constitute compliance with the SPDES program—that is, a discharger who had obtained a NPDES permit for a discharge into navigable waters was not required to obtain a SPDES permit as well. DEC has continued this practice on a policy basis, and the regulations for the SPDES program, which are expected to be promulgated in the summer of 1975, also include such a provision. A NPDES permit will not be issued, however, unless state authorities have "certified," that is, approved, the discharge, or have waived certification.

4. It does not follow that obtaining a SPDES permit constitutes compliance with federal law. (Only if and when the state SPDES program is approved by the federal EPA will this be true.)

Thus citizens should be advised that prior to approval of the SPDES program by federal authorities, a land development project that obtains only a SPDES permit for a discharge into surface waters does not fulfill the requirements of federal law. Anyone who plans to discharge pollutants into navigable waters via a point source must obtain a NPDES permit. As pointed out above, the scope of the federal law is not confined to any particular size or volume of discharge; thus there is no cutoff point below which the federal law does not apply. Any advice to the contrary has no legal basis.

Important discharges of pollutants that are exempt from the SPDES program are:

1. Discharges from non-point sources.
2. Discharges conveyed directly into an existing sewage treatment plant (but discharges from the treatment plant itself are not excluded).
3. Discharges into the groundwaters of the state from a private dwelling designed to house less than three families and consisting of a flow of less than 1,000 gallons per day.[16]

Implementation procedures for the state SPDES legislation must be set out in official rules and regulations. DEC has prepared a draft version of these which was included in its proposal to the federal EPA and which will also, by agreement with EPA, be reviewed in a public hearing, probably during May or June of 1975. Final rules and regulations should be promulgated shortly thereafter.

One of the most important provisions of DEC's proposed rules and regulations for the SPDES program would require subdivisions of five or more lots of less than ten acres each to obtain a SPDES permit. Under this provision, private dwellings described in (3) above would not be exempt from permit requirements if they were part of such a subdivision. If this rule becomes official, it will greatly change the character and expand the scope of DEC's review of sewerage facilities.

At the present time, DEC requires only subdivisions of fifty or more lots to obtain permits for their sewage disposal facilities. According to the Environmental Conservation Law no subdivision of five or more lots can be offered for sale until DEC or local health departments have *approved* a plan or map showing "methods for obtaining and furnishing adequate and satisfactory sewerage facilities."[17] This approval need not, however, involve the issuance of a permit. DEC *permits* are required only for the construction or use of a new or modified sewage disposal system,[18] which effectively has meant a new or modified communal sewerage system as opposed to individual septic tanks (which have continued to be approved by health department officials). According to DEC's present regulations on sewerage facilities, a community sewerage system and thus a DEC permit (unless the sewage from the system can be discharged into an existing waste treatment plant) are required for subdivisions of fifty or more lots.[19] Under the new regulations, a SPDES permit from DEC would be required not only for subdivisions which are required to have community sewerage systems, but also from smaller subdivisions in which sewage is disposed via septic tanks into the groundwaters of the state.

Two considerations seem to be at the heart of DEC's effort to bring subdivisions of five or more lots under its permit-granting jurisdiction: (1) DEC recognizes the serious cumulative environmental problems caused by subdivisions within the 5–49 lot size range and wants to take effective action to control these problems; and (2) with federal funding available for state water pollution control programs, DEC can afford the manpower needed for this expansion of its review responsibilities.

To be sure, some developers have gone to considerable lengths to avoid DEC review and the expense of installing a community sewerage system. Thus, this is another reason why there are so many forty-nine-lot subdivisions in the state. For such subdivisions, developers must only get approval from health department officials of plans for individual septic tanks and then furnish lot purchasers with copies of these approved plans, which include specifications. The lot purchaser himself must bear the cost of installation.

To reap such benefits, some developers have even divided large tracts of land into several forty-nine-lot subdivisions. Others have sought a variance from the fifty-lot barrier which would allow individual septic tanks in larger subdivisions.[20] Such variances have been granted for surprisingly large developments, especially in the Adirondacks where engineers argue that sewage treatment plants are impractical for subdivisions of seasonal homes used only three months of the year. Yet much of the soil in the Adirondacks is not suitable for septic tanks, and runoffs of sewage which has collected on the surface of the ground have polluted streams and advanced the eutrophication of lakes.

It is important to note that under existing laws and regulations, only DEC, and arguably some local health department officials, have the right to grant variances for sewage disposal. Officials of the state Department of Health do not have the right to grant such variances, although in some areas they do so on a routine basis. Such actions are vulnerable to legal challenge.

Although the new state legislation instituting the SPDES program speaks primarily of prohibiting certain *discharges* of pollutants without a permit, the law clearly specifies that the *making or construction* of a point source or disposal system is also governed by the required SPDES permit.[21] Thus a developer is required to obtain a permit before beginning construction of a sewerage system, not simply before this system begins actual operation.

Within DEC, the Division of Pure Waters is responsible for the implementation of the SPDES permit program. Each SPDES permit issued must require compliance with standards established or approved by the U.S. Environmental Protection Agency (EPA) under federal law and with any stricter standards adopted pursuant to state law. Standards set by EPA include effluent limitations, standards of performance for new sources, and standards for toxic pollutants. DEC must also consider the impact of discharges on the quality of the receiving waters when it weighs the issuance of a SPDES permit. Both ground and surface waters of New York State have been classified and water quality standards have been adopted for each classification.[22] The classifications and standards for *surface* waters must be approved by the federal EPA before the state permit program can be authorized under the NPDES program. This federal approval of classifications and standards was granted in March 1975. DEC cannot issue any waste discharge permit that will lead to the contravention of standards for any classification. This means that conditions placed on a permit may be stricter than the federal effluent limitations or that a permit may be denied altogether. In case no classification has been made of the receiving waters involved in a permit application, DEC cannot grant a permit unless it finds that the proposed discharge will not injure public health and public enjoyment of the waters, the propagation and protection of fish and wildlife, and the industrial development of the state.

When the SPDES program was first established by the state legislature, the penalties set for violations were much weaker than those of the NPDES program. In April 1974, however, amendments were passed bringing state penalties more into line with federal penalties.[23] The only significant difference remaining is that federal law imposes heavy criminal penalties on all negligent violations, while state law distinguishes between simple and gross negligence and imposes heavy penalties only on the latter.

The following are the penalties for violations now established by state law for the SPDES program:

1. *Civil liability:* A person who violates the law, conditions of a permit, or a lawful DEC order is liable to a fine not to exceed $10,000 per day of violation. Such a person may also be enjoined from con-

tinuing the violation. Violation of a permit condition constitutes grounds for its revocation.[24]

2. *Criminal liability:* Any person who violates the law or a final DEC order made pursuant to the law *and* has "any of the culpable mental states defined in §15.05 of the penal law," is guilty of a misdemeanor and upon conviction must be punished by a fine of not less than $2,500 or more than $25,000 per day of violation or by imprisonment for one year or by both. If the conviction is for an offense committed after a first conviction under this law, then the punishment is a fine of up to $50,000 per day of violation or imprisonment for two years or both.[25]

Under the federal law establishing the NPDES program, special powers are granted to the administrator of the Environmental Protection Agency through which he can ensure enforcement of the federal law and of permit conditions by states which have federally approved permit programs.[26]

In keeping with the NPDES program, after which much of the SPDES program is modeled, broad provision is made in the state law for public participation and access to information.[27] These provisions are quoted below, almost in their entirety.

> Public notice of every complete application for a SPDES permit shall be circulated in a manner designed to inform interested and potentially interested persons . . . of such application.
>
> The department shall provide a period of not less than thirty days following the date of the public notice during which time interested persons may submit their written views with respect to the application. The period for comment may be extended at the discretion of the department.
>
> All written comments submitted during such thirty day or extended period shall be retained by the department and considered in the formulation of the final determination on the application.
>
> The department may, [at] its discretion, provide an opportunity for the applicant or any interested agency, person, or group of persons to request or petition for a public hearing with respect to such application.[28]
>
> The department shall promulgate rules and regulations with respect to notice, procedures and conduct of public hearings in accordance with due process of law for administrative proceedings and the

provisions of the [Federal Water Pollution Control Act, as amended]. (Such rules and regulations are included in the proposed SPDES rules and regulations on which a public hearing should be held in 1975. Concerned citizens should be sure to obtain copies of the final rules and regulations when they are promulgated.)

Except insofar as trade secrets would be disclosed, the following information shall be available to the public for inspection and copying;
(a) any SPDES permit, permit application, or form;
(b) any public comments, testimony, or other documentation concerning a permit application; and
(c) any information obtained pursuant to any monitoring, records, reporting or sampling requirements or as a result of sampling or other investigatory activities of the department.

The following features of the above provisions should be especially noted: A public hearing is not mandatory in the event of opposition to the application; written comments from the public must be considered by DEC in its decision regarding the permit; and public access to a wide range of information is required.

DEC's proposed rules and regulations for the SPDES program described above specify that any person or group may request to be on a mailing list to receive copies of notices for all SPDES applications within the state or within a certain geographical area. This means that citizens who are monitoring land development projects in a particular area would have a way of making certain that they know about every application for a pollutant discharge permit in that area and thus could avoid the risk of missing newspaper notices.

The proposed regulations indicate that requests to be placed on this mailing list for notices of SPDES applications should be sent to:

Division of Pure Waters
New York State Department of
Environmental Conservation
50 Wolf Road
Albany, New York 12233

Also according to these proposed rules and regulations a fact sheet will be prepared for every application that involves a discharge which has a total volume of more than 500,000 gallons on any day of the year. Upon request, DEC will add the name of any person or group to a mailing list for these fact sheets. All those who receive the notice or fact sheet for any SPDES application will also be sent a notice of a public hearing on the application, if one is held.

3. Stream Protection

Land development projects often include plans to disrupt or otherwise affect watercourses. Large subdivisions often involve plans to create an artificial lake or pond by damming a stream. Whenever such plans are proposed, it is likely that a permit from DEC may be required by law.

Such DEC permits are required to:

1. Change or disturb the course of, or remove sand, gravel, or other material from the bed or banks of any protected stream.[29]

2. Excavate from or place fill in navigable waters, or in marshes, estuaries, tidal marshes, and wetlands that are "adjacent to and contiguous at any point to navigable waters" and that are inundated at mean high water level or tide.[30]

3. Erect, reconstruct, or repair any dam or impoundment structure or any dock, pier, wharf, or landing structure, except for certain types of these structures which are precisely described in the law.[31]

The stream protection program through which the above permits are granted is administered by DEC's Office of Environmental Analysis in Albany and by the nine regional DEC offices. All applications involving dams receive engineering review in Albany. They are also reviewed for soil stability and structural safety by the state Department of Transportation.

In order to receive approval for a permit under this program, regulations require that a proposed project be in the public interest.[32] The project must be reasonable and necessary, and not dangerous to public health, safety, or welfare. It must not cause "unreasonable, uncontrolled, or unnecessary damage to the natural resources of the state," in terms of soil erosion, increased cost of water, pollution, siltation, and variation in the turbidity, velocity, temperature, and level of watercourses.

Applications for permits are submitted to the regional DEC offices. Each applicant must publish a "notice of application," provided by the permit agent, once a week for not more than two consecutive weeks in a newspaper of general circulation in the local area. This publication requirement may be waived at the discretion of the regional office for applications involving activities of a minor nature, small size, or limited impact. The published notice must specify the last date on which the public may file written objections to the project. In such written objections, grounds for the objections must be stated. Public hearings are not mandatory, but are held at the discretion of the DEC Office of Environmental Analysis. In practice, they are held less than 5 percent of the time, but public objections figure heavily in the office's decision on whether or not a hearing should be called.

The regional DEC offices may issue, but may not refuse permits. They refer all major or controversial projects, as well as projects for which they recommend denial of the permit application, to the Office of Environmental Analysis in Albany. They also refer to Albany any cases in which an applicant refuses to accept conditions imposed on a permit. After review of plans, the Office of Environmental Analysis may grant or refuse permits or issue permits subject to conditions, or it may decide that a hearing should be held before a decision is made.

Hearings are announced and conducted by DEC's Office of Hearing Officers, which is required to publish a public notice in a local newspaper "once in each week for not more than four weeks." Thus only one publication of the notice is strictly required, but DEC's general practice has been to publish the notice at least twice, usually in two consecutive weeks. Sometimes these two notices are published in different newspapers. Written objections may be filed prior to the hearing date. After the hearing, DEC makes its decision to approve, deny, or modify the application. It can also require that the applicant post a bond as security against environmental damage that might result from the project.

DEC can revoke or suspend a permit to construct a dam if it is revealed during construction that the dam is not being built in accordance with approved plans. DEC also has the authority to investigate dams and other impounding structures and, after public hearing on due notice, to serve an order requiring removal, repair, or reconstruction. If the owner does not comply with this order, DEC may enter upon the property and carry out the necessary removal, repair, or reconstruction itself. All expenses incurred may be added to the owner's property tax assessments.

A violation of these statutes involving stream protection is a misdemeanor, punishable by a fine of up to $500 for a first offense, up to $2,500 for a second offense, and up to $10,000 for a third or subsequent offense, or by imprisonment of up to one year or by both such fine and imprisonment.[33] Penalties apply to developers and prime contractors alike.

4. Environmental Analysis

Realty subdivisions in New York State traditionally were reviewed from an engineering standpoint by health department officials. So long as a developer's plans conformed to water supply and sewerage standards established for the protection of public health, approvals were virtually automatic. With the creation of DEC in 1970 serious attention was for the first time drawn to the full environmental consequences of developments. In keeping with the declaration of policy of the Environmental Conservation Law and the general functions, powers, and duties vested in DEC by this law, an Office of Environmental Analysis was set up within the department.[34] This office has primary responsibility for executing DEC's intent to consider the environmental impact of each project which is granted a DEC permit.

The regulations which govern the responsibilities of the Office of Environmental Analysis allow DEC to require a developer to submit an overall conceptual report and an environmental impact assessment whenever a proposed project will require a DEC permit of any kind (such as, but not limited to, the public water supply, SPDES, and stream protection permits discussed above).[35] DEC has issued general guidelines describing when such environmental information may be required, but these guidelines are not binding and the decision to request the information is discretionary.

The regulations further allow DEC to hold public hearings at the developer's expense to determine "whether and to what extent the proposed project or development will cause irreparable and irretrievable damage to the environment and the natural resources of the State of New York." The commissioner of environmental conservation determines when such an environmental impact hearing will be held. Again, the decision is discretionary and not subject to binding guidelines.

A decision of the Appellate Division of the Supreme Court of the State of New York made on May 16, 1974,[36] sharply criticized the DEC regulations dealing with environmental impact assessment. While upholding on other grounds DEC's denial of a water supply permit to the Ton-Da-Lay subdivision proposed in the Adirondacks, the court held that "[p]art 615 of 6 NYCRR does not reach the required definitive standards necessary to inform an applicant of exactly what is required for compliance."

After this holding, three courses of action were possible through which DEC could defend its environmental analysis program. The department could:

1. Rewrite Part 615 of its regulations, stating more clearly the standards by which applications will be reviewed. The need for this revision has long been recognized, and DEC has long been strongly urged to rewrite the regulations, which in their present form are vague with respect to both procedural and substantive matters.

2. Draft specific legislation to make unmistakably clear its right to review projects on the basis of their overall environmental impact.

3. Appeal the court's decision, which in several respects appears somewhat confusing.

As of mid-April 1975, the regulations of Part 615 have not been rewritten, but DEC has both (1) drafted new legislation, which it has submitted to the governor, and (2) taken action to appeal the Appellate Division decision. In the latter effort, the department has been denied "appeal as of right" by the Court of Appeals, but is now petitioning this court for "leave to appeal." It is hoped that these actions will lead to a stronger environmental analysis program, which can be used widely and effectively to assess the full environmental impact of proposed development projects.

The following discussion describes how the environmental analysis program actually operates at the present time.

When a developer files an application for a DEC permit, copies of the maps and plans which he submits or a notice of their availability is sent to both the central Office of Environmental Analysis in Albany and to the environmental analysis section of the DEC regional office for the area in which the proposed project is to be located. In most cases, evaluation of these maps and plans takes place in the regional offices.

Submitted maps and plans are also circulated for review and comment among the regional personnel of the fish and wildlife, forestry, and environmental quality units. Any of these regional units can recommend that the developer be requested to submit an overall conceptual report and an environmental impact assessment which provides a description of the proposed project or development and a detailed analysis of its environmental effects. Recommendations that these be required are reviewed by both the regional director and the director of the Office of Environmental Analysis. The endorsement of both these officials is necessary, but the final decision to require an overall conceptual report and an environmental impact assessment rests with the commissioner of DEC.

If a developer is required to submit either an overall conceptual report or an environmental impact assessment, the commissioner of DEC must "publish notice of the proposed project or development in at least one newspaper, designated by the commissioner as most likely to give notice to the members of the public concerned, at least once each week for not more than four weeks."[37]

After this notice, the public may submit to the DEC office in Albany written objections to the project, setting out specific grounds and reasons. The regulations do not specify that a deadline must be set for receipt of these objections by DEC, but in practice the published notices always specify a deadline. The failure of the regulations to establish an exact, proper procedure here should be noted.

The next provision of the regulations establishes that "within 30 days after the receipt of such application, assessment, and objections, if any, and after review of same" the commissioner must determine whether to limit the scope of DEC's review to the developer's application for a permit or to expand it to cover the total environmental impact of the proposed development, and to hold a public hearing.

It is clear that the regulations require that public opinion play a role in the commissioner's determination of whether a public environmental impact hearing should be held and that written objections from the public must be reviewed before this decision is made. It is important, therefore, that such objections be prepared and submitted to DEC. In practice, almost every time that DEC has requested an environmental assessment from a developer, a public hearing on the environmental impact of the proposed project has been held. This results in large part from the fact that DEC requires the assessment only in the case of very large-scale or controversial developments. As has been pointed out, the requirement of an environmental assessment must be approved by the appropriate regional director, by the director of the Office of Environmental Analysis, and by the commissioner of environmental conservation. It is far more an extraordinary action than the common rule.

DEC may, and often does, informally request that a developer submit additional information on the project for which he has filed a permit application. This information may relate to the environmental impact of the project and may be considered in the determination of whether a formal environmental assessment will be required. Since DEC does not, however, give public notice of the receipt of all permit applications, the public is not always given the opportunity to contribute to the environmental evaluation of a project that takes place before the internal decision is made to require a formal environmental assessment. DEC's issuance of public notice of the receipt of permit applications has fortunately become much more common since the establishment of the SPDES program, in which compliance with federal regulations is sought. DEC has always been required to give public notice of the receipt of applications for water supply permits, but now it is also required to give such notice with respect to applications for sewage disposal permits. When they feel that a full review of the environmental impact of a project is essential, citizens should take the initiative of setting out in written objections, filed with DEC pursuant to water supply or SPDES notices, why a full environmental assessment should be required. Further, they should state their environmental concerns and objections at DEC hearings held on water supply, SPDES, or stream protection permits.

The potential of the environmental analysis process and the opportunity to explore problems in the forum of an environmental impact hearing have to date been used very sparingly. As of April 1975 fewer than twenty such hearings have been held. Most of these hearings grew out of applications for a DEC water supply permit, and nearly all of them have resulted in decisions to allow some modified form of the proposed project to be built.

Although previously pointed out, it should be mentioned again that subdivisions of fewer than fifty lots, which often cause serious cumulative environmental damage, are at the present time rarely required to apply for a DEC permit. Therefore, these developments are not subject to any review by DEC's Office of Environmental Analysis.

THE NEW YORK STATE DEPARTMENT OF HEALTH (DH)

The Public Health Law (PHL) of New York State provides that no subdivision of five or more parcels may be sold, offered for sale, leased, or rented, and no permanent building may be erected on the land unless a plan or map of the subdivision has been filed with and approved by the state Department of Health or a city, county, or part-county department of health having jurisdiction over the area. After approval, the map or plan must also be filed with the local county clerk. This plan or map must "show methods for obtaining and furnishing adequate and satisfactory water supply" for the subdivision. In addition, the law requires that installation of facilities must be made in accordance with approved plans.[38]

If a city, county, or part-county department of health has been established in an area and if this department has adopted regulations for the control of realty subdivisions, as it is entitled to do by law,[39] then it will review and approve subdivisions within its jurisdiction. In all other cases, such approval is the responsibility of officials of the state Department of Health. Most of the review of subdivisions by state officials takes place through DH's regional offices and its ten district offices, where most of its field personnel are located.

As discussed earlier, DEC is responsible for controlling the geographical distribution of the water supply of the state through its water supply permits, while DH is responsible for seeing that public water supplies meet standards necessary for public health. These standards are compiled in the Sanitary Code.[40] Approval by health officials certifies that both the quality and quantity of a water supply system are adequate.

Rules and regulations for approval of realty subdivisions were issued by DH in 1966.[41] These regulations establish guidelines for water supply facilities and set forth conditions under which a developer is required to provide a community water supply system.[42] The most important of these conditions requires a community water supply system when a subdivision consists of fifty or more lots. In subdivisions of fewer than fifty lots, developers may submit plans which provide for private wells on individual lots. Private wells are less costly for a developer than a communal system. In fact he does not even have to install the wells himself. He must obtain approval of plans from health authorities; but the actual drilling can be left to future residents. A developer may apply to DH for a variance to allow private wells in subdivisions of over fifty lots—a practice which occurs frequently.

Two DH bulletins which are available from the Albany office set out standards for review and approval of water supply systems: (1) "Recommended Standards for Water Works" provides standards for communal systems; and (2) "Rural Water Supply" provides those for individual systems. DH review of applications for community water supply systems is centralized in its Bureau of Public Water Supply in Albany, while individual systems are reviewed in district and regional offices.

Although there are no provisions for public notice or public hearings associated with DH review and approval of subdivision plans, DH can urge DEC to conduct an environmental impact hearing on a subdivision under review by DH, if at least one DEC permit is also required by the development. Unfortunately, health authorities rarely take advantage of this opportunity. There are, however, lines of communication between the two departments. Both DH and local health department officials are notified of all applications for DEC *water supply* permits, and are given the opportunity to comment on plans and to testify at hearings.

It should be stressed that the Public Health Law requires that a *plan or map* which is approved by DH or a local health department be filed with the county clerk for subdivisions of five or more parcels before any parcel is offered for sale. The New York State Real Property Law requires further that anyone who subdivides property into any number of lots for sale to the public must file with the county clerk a map of the subdivision which has been certified by a licensed land surveyor, before offering the lots for sale.[43] Some developers attempt to bypass both of these laws by filing deeds rather than certified maps and plans with the county clerk. County clerks should be made aware that the acceptance of such deeds in lieu of certified and approved maps and plans is in violation of the law.

The Public Health Law exempts from its scope tracts of land which are divided into fewer than five lots or parcels. In many areas, landowners have developed several clusters of four lots or less on one piece of property to avoid the legal obligation of submitting to health officials maps or plans detailing methods of water supply. Other property owners have subdivided land into five or more lots and have simply not submitted plans to health authorities, often on the premise that offices were understaffed and would ignore violations.

One landowner in the Catskills, Everett W. Herrick, purchased thirteen farms in Delaware, Greene, and Ulster counties over a period of several years and sold 263 parcels of land subdivided from these farms without submitting any maps or plans to health authorities. Mr. Herrick contended that he sold recreational lands to sportsmen and vacationers and thus was not obliged to comply with Section 1116 of the Public Health Law which applies to subdivision parcels sold "as residential lots or residential building plots." When DH served Herrick with a "Notice of Hearing and Complaint," charging that he had violated the Public Health Law, Herrick sought and obtained a declaratory judgment that his land transactions fell outside the scope of the Public Health Law. In this judgment, given in September 1972, the judge went on to rule that Section 1116 and related sections of the Public Health Law, as DH attempts to apply them in cases such as this, are unconstitutional.

When DH appealed this case, the Appellate Division of the state Supreme Court upheld the judgment that Section 1116 of the Public Health Law did not apply to the Herrick sales, since the land was sold for recreational rather than explicitly residential purposes (although twenty-four year-round homes and many seasonal dwellings were constructed on the land after it was purchased from Herrick). The court did not rule on the constitutional issue.[44]

As a result of this decision, DEC and DH are working together to draft new legislation to clarify state review powers over subdivisions of land and to strengthen their ability to provide environmental protection.

Enforcement of the Public Health Law

The Public Health Law prescribes various penalties for violations of the law itself, as well as lawful orders and regulations issued by health authorities.

A person who violates any provision of the Public Health Law or of any lawful notice, order, or regulation pursuant to it for which a civil penalty is not otherwise prescribed by law, is liable for a fine of up to $1,000 for each violation.[45]

A person who willfully violates any provisions of the Public Health Law or any regulation established by a public officer under its authority, for which punishment is not otherwise prescribed by law, may be fined up to $2,000 or imprisoned for one year or both.[46]

Anyone who willfully violates a lawful order or regulation prescribed by any local health officer is guilty of a misdemeanor, except when such an order or regulation applies to a tenant's own dwelling unit or an owner-occupied one- or two-family dwelling. In the latter cases, a first violation carries a fine of up to $50 and a second or subsequent violation constitutes a misdemeanor which is punishable by a fine of up to $500 or by imprisonment for six months or by both.[47] An example of this type of violation would be the failure of a homeowner to install water supply facilities in accordance with conditions set forth in approved plans by local health officials.

The commissioner of health has the right to assess penalties of up to $1,000 for each violation, but this can be done only after a hearing or an opportunity to be heard has been granted the violator.[48] Among such hearings are those called when a person has subdivided land into five or more lots without submitting plans to health officials. Citizens who have knowledge of a clandestine subdivision, or of any other instance where statutes or regulations dealing with public health are being violated, should contact the nearest DH office in writing. In the case of a clandestine subdivision, it is best to inform DH as early as possible, ideally before lots are deeded and development of land begins.

The commissioner of health may also request the state attorney general to bring an action for an injunction against anyone who violates, disobeys, or disregards any provision of the Public Health Law or any lawful notice, order, or regulation pursuant to it.[49]

Special enforcement provisions apply to contamination of water supplies.[50] The enforcement procedure is always triggered by the discovery of a violation; there is no provision for preventive intervention before the act of contamination has occurred. When a source or act of contamination is discovered, the violator is notified of the rule or regulation violated and is ordered to comply immediately. If he does not comply, DH must immediately examine the violation. If it finds that a rule or regulation pertaining to contamination has been violated, it must order the local board of health in the affected area to convene and enforce compliance. If the local board does not do so within ten days, "any person interested in the protection of the purity of the water supply" may maintain a court action for the recovery of penalties incurred by such violation and for an injunction restraining continued violation.[51] A person violating a rule or regulation relating to a temporary source or act of contamination of public water supplies is liable to prosecution for misdemeanor for every violation and upon conviction can be fined up to $200 and/or imprisoned for up to one year. DH itself may impose a fine of up to $200 for each violation when rules or regulations relating to a permanent source of contamination are violated.[52]

CITY AND COUNTY HEALTH DEPARTMENTS

City, county, or part-county health departments, also known as local health departments, are responsible for much of the review and approval of land development projects that is carried out in New York State. When such a department has been established in a local area and has adopted subdivision regulations,[53] it reviews and approves maps and plans of subdivisions within its jurisdiction. In addition, both DH and DEC may delegate some of their responsibilities to such departments, under arrangements providing state aid payments for work performed. DEC does not at the present time delegate its authority to grant stream protection or water supply permits, but, aside from these exceptions, local health departments may carry out within their jurisdiction virtually all aspects of subdivision control required by the state, including reviews and approval of sewage disposal systems and water quality and quantity.

Despite the powerful roles local health departments may play in land development review, citizens' groups have to date known relatively little about them. The work done by these departments may be carried out without attracting public attention, since no notice need be given or public hearing held as long as a DEC permit is not involved. Moreover, since some local health departments do not review subdivisions and since the contractual arrangements made between DEC and other departments vary widely, it is frequently difficult to know what aspects of subdivision control are actually exercised by a particular local department. Citizens who are monitoring review of subdivisions should write to their local health departments and request a statement of its subdivision review and approval powers. They should also write to DEC's Office of Program Evaluation and Reporting in Albany to determine which, if any, of DEC's programs have been delegated to the local department.

When local health departments do have subdivision approval powers, the implementation of these powers should be carefully monitored by citizens. Local departments may, in fact, adopt strict water and sewerage regulations; they may be concerned about the environmental impact of development; and they may have experienced field personnel with great expertise regarding soil and groundwater characteristics in their area. On the other hand, it is quite likely that officials of a local health department may be subject to strong political pressure from local politicians who measure success in terms of growth and who are apt to be displeased with a health department that restricts growth. Also, established procedures do not exist at the local level for informing the public and involving them in decisions which are made. It is, therefore, important that concerned citizens find out what health department subdivision regulations are in effect in their area and press for conscientious enforcement.

Some provisions are made in state law for state supervision of local health departments and their personnel. Under the Public Health Law, DH has the authority to supervise the work and activities of local health officers, except in New York City, and to prescribe job qualifications.[54] Under the Environmental Conservation Law, DEC may delegate to "qualified personnel" of county and city health departments its duties to review and approve subdivision plans and to issue permits for sewage disposal systems.[55]

Most of the state supervision which is carried out, however, occurs in the administration and evaluation of state aid payments to local health departments for the work they do for DEC and DH.[56] The basic responsibility for administering and evaluating local environmental programs that are carried out in DEC's behalf rests with the DEC regional engineers for environmental quality. The DEC regional directors provide overall program direction and coordination at the regional level and DEC's Office of Program Evaluation and Reporting handles coordination and planning in Albany.

The city, county, or part-county health departments that wish to carry out environmental conservation responsibilities for which they would receive state aid must apply to DEC before November 1 of the year preceding the calendar year for which funds are requested. The departments which apply must state which programs they wish to adopt and provide a schedule of manhours available for each program and a statement of program objectives. Programs related to land development which local health departments may implement for DEC include the following:

1. Review and approval of realty subdivisions with community sewerage facilities. This may include conferences with developers, site inspection, approval of plans, and construction inspection.

2. Review and approval of sewage disposal facilities discharging more than 1,000 gallons per day (facilities smaller than this are not covered by the Environmental Conservation Law and their review for public health purposes is an existing responsibility of health officials).

3. Issuance of SPDES permits.

4. Inspection, sampling, and evaluation of waste treatment plants.

5. Comprehensive sewerage studies.

6. Promotion of the upgrading of existing waste treatment plants to required standards.

7. Training and approval of sewage treatment plant operators.

8. Identification of water polluters. This may include identification of discharge sources, formulation of abatement schedules, enforcement, and follow-up.

9. Participation in the assessment of the environmental impact of land development projects. This may include site inspection, review of plans, and presentation of testimony at hearings.

Citizens should find out what programs have been delegated to their local health departments by DEC, and should monitor implementation. This is particularly important when local health officers are participating in the environmental assessment of a project. It should be noted that since DEC does not delegate its authority to grant water supply and stream protection permits, local health departments may find themselves in the position of trying to assess the impact of a project over which they have limited environmental review power.

DEC conducts quarterly evaluations of work delegated to local health departments. In each of the nine regions, the regional engineer for environmental quality meets in April, July, October, and January with local health officials to review their performance of DEC programs.

DEC officials concede that their evaluation of the work done by local departments is primarily quantitative. According to DEC's *Policies and Procedures Manual,* "No formal reports are required from the counties, but they are expected to maintain sufficiently detailed records to enable the regional engineer for environmental quality to properly evaluate the degree and quality of services performed."[57] What this means in practice is that no efficient reporting system exists and that focus falls on the *amount* of work that has been done. It is not likely that DEC will learn of ground and surface water pollution, eutrophic lakes, soil erosion, and other environmental problems which are often associated with development projects unless an isolated misfortune receives sufficient publicity to reach the attention of DEC's regional engineer.

It is vital that DEC develop methods of qualitatively evaluating its local agents and that an adequate reporting system be developed. DEC must be made aware of failures that occur and must be prepared to withhold state aid from local health departments which are not capable of handling crucial environmental programs. The local personnel who carry out state programs must meet the qualifications established by the rules and regulations of the state Department of Health. If there are no established qualifications for a given position, DEC must approve personnel before delegating responsibilities.

Citizens can contribute to better evaluation by writing to the regional engineer for environmental quality in their DEC regional office whenever environmental problems are anticipated or result from mismanagement of local programs. A copy of any such correspondence should also be sent to the commissioner of environmental conservation. The more signatories, the better; and the best time to send such a letter is just before quarterly review meetings.

Subdivisions with septic tank sewage disposal systems approved by local health officials and also by DH personnel have been a major source of ground and surface water pollution in the state. There appear to be several reasons for these pollution problems:

1. Some health officials believe that septic tank systems offer the most effective and economical means of sewage disposal in subdivisions and approve such systems automatically as long as standards regulating lot size are satisfied by the developer. Such standards can be inadequate, allowing sewage effluent to contaminate wells on small lots. Furthermore, approvals for septic tanks are sometimes granted with little regard for soil conditions. Non-porous soil, for instance, does not adequately filter effluents, and as a result sewage can collect on the surface of the ground and be washed into waterways by rain.

2. Local departments have been known to rely solely upon site reports submitted by a developer's engineer in evaluating plans.

3. While local regulations might state that installation of water supply and sewage disposal facilities must be made in accordance with approved plans, and state law requires this, local departments sometimes fail to reinspect subsurface systems before they are covered over with soil. Thus while approved plans might require that a sewage leaching field be covered with sandy soil, it might actually be covered with three feet of clay—with no one the wiser until alerted by the rising odor of raw sewage.

4. In some cases, pollution has resulted from design errors in the equipment used.

5. Sometimes groundwater conditions may change after approvals have been granted or systems installed.

The frequency of failures in septic tank systems led the Office of the Counsel of DH in July 1972 to suggest procedures to local health officials for the revocation of approvals and the prevention of further development and sale of lots in subdivisions with such problems. Local officials were advised that when a subdivision approval was revoked, a copy of the revocation letter should be sent to the county clerk along with a request that this letter be filed with the subdivision's map or plan so that prospective purchasees would be alerted to the revocation.

Citizens should support the efforts of health department officials to correct sewage problems. They should inform these officials immediately whenever a malfunctioning sewage disposal system is discovered and they should press for effective action. If health authorities do not assume responsibility after concerted effort urging them to do so, citizens should contact the Environmental Protection Bureau of the state attorney general's office. As will be discussed in connection with land development problems in the Catskills, this bureau has taken a special interest in the problems caused by malfunctioning septic tank systems.[58]

CITIZEN ACTION

Because of the jurisdictional complications discussed in this chapter, suggestions for citizen action have been given in the course of the discussion. In summary, however, the following are important focuses for such action which have been recommended:

1. DEC Water Supply Hearings

When an application for a DEC water supply permit is made, DEC must issue public notice that a hearing will be held on a specified date if *anyone* objecting to the project files a notice of appearance for the hearing, stating specific objections and grounds. This is the only state review procedure in which public hearings are mandatory if objections are filed. Citizens should take care to make the most of these opportunities for public consideration of proposed developments. In all aspects of review for water supply permits, as well as the permits discussed in (2) and (3) below, citizens should press for evaluation of the total impact of a proposed project and, when needed, press for the environmental assessment and environmental impact hearing described under (4).

2. SPDES Permits

Under the new State Pollutant Discharge Elimination System (SPDES) program, citizens are by law guaranteed access to information about projects which have applied to DEC for SPDES permits. Public notice must be given for every application received by DEC; the public has thirty days in which to submit written comments; and these comments must be considered in the decision made on the permit application. Citizens may also place their names on a mailing list to receive individual notice of the receipt of applications, factsheets on very large discharges, and individual notice of hearings.

3. Stream Protection

Citizens are advised that disruptions and impoundments of streams require permits from DEC. Although public hearings are held on less than 5 percent of these permits, public objections figure heavily in DEC's decision on whether a hearing should be held.

4. Environmental Impact Assessments and Hearings

DEC may require an environmental impact assessment from any developer who is required to obtain at least one DEC permit. DEC is required by its regulations to give public notice of all proposed projects from whom it requests an environmental impact assessment and an overall conceptual report. The public is entitled to file written objections which the commissioner of DEC is required to review before determining whether a public hearing should be held on the environmental impact of the project. If a hearing is held, the public has the opportunity to give full consideration to the total environmental impact of the project.

5. Review of Projects by Health Authorities

a. Citizens should find out whether there is a city, county, or part-county health department in their area and, if so, whether it has adopted subdivision regulations or contracted to carry out environmental programs for DEC. If there is such a local department and it is carrying out either or both of these responsibilities, citizens should carefully monitor implementation, bearing in mind the possibility that there is local political pressure favoring as much growth as possible.

b. Citizens should report to DEC regional engineers for environmental quality any environmental problems anticipated or resulting from mismanagement of programs carried out for DEC by local health departments.

c. Citizens should report all violations of health laws and regulations to local and state health officials. In particular, they should report clandestine subdivisions, in which developers are subdividing land into five or more lots without submitting maps or plans to health authorities for approval.

d. Citizens should inform health authorities of malfunctioning septic tank systems which have been approved by health officials, and should press for corrective action. If health officials do not assume responsibility, then citizens should report the sewage problem to the Environmental Protection Bureau of the state attorney general's office.

In general, citizens should remember that DEC has stated the intent to consider the full environmental impact of every project which submits an application for a DEC permit. By keeping DEC informed of environmental problems and urging full assessment, citizens can play an important role in promoting the implementation of this policy. Citizens should appreciate their power to influence decisions which are made by DEC, DH, and local health departments. In particular, citizens should realize that their efforts (1) can lead to public hearings in which environmental problems can be openly discussed; and (2) can affect the outcome of development proposals and applications. Whenever citizens have the opportunity to appear at a hearing, they should take care to attract and organize as much support as possible for their arguments. They should work hard to identify the basic problems involved in a proposed development and to gather as much good information and evidence as possible to back up their position. They should seek to give well-organized, clear, and non-repetitive testimony at the hearing itself. The stronger the presentation they make, the more consideration they can expect from DEC.

The following episode is presented as just one example of the kind of citizen action that is currently being undertaken in New York State:

In late March 1974 a Catskills resident saw in a local paper a DEC notice that a hearing on both the water supply and SPDES permit applications of a proposed 34-building apartment complex would be held on a specified date if any notices of appearance for opposition were filed. This citizen organized a committee in opposition to the project, which would house 900 people and dump 97,000 gallons of treated sewage into the Plattekill Creek every day. The committee printed a simple leaflet advising the public that this complex would probably be approved by DEC. The leaflet raised the issue of what impact the development would have on "Roads & Bridges—Taxes—Fire Protection—School System—Hunting & Fishing—Future Land Development in the Towns of Mamakating, Shawangunk, Crawford." All those who objected to the proposed apartment complex were urged to come to a meeting at the Fire House in the village of Walker Valley. The overflow crowd of 250 people who attended this meeting decided to conduct a letter-writing campaign to DEC. These letters stated that a hearing should indeed be held, but requested a postponement of the date specified in the notice to allow more time for citizens to prepare testimony (another environmental hearing was in progress in the same town at that time, tying up legal and water quality experts). DEC agreed to this request. The citizens then hired an attorney to assist them. He advised a second letter-writing campaign urging DEC to expand the hearing into a full environmental impact hearing, provided for under DEC's environmental analysis program.

DEC denied this second request, but at the water supply and SPDES hearing held on the project in April 1975, the developer agreed to scale down the project to one-half the size originally proposed and to develop an underground system of sewage disposal which would remove the need for any discharge of sewage effluent into the Plattekill Creek.

NOTES

1. N.Y. Environmental Conservation Law (ECL) §1–0101.

2. ECL §17–1503 and N.Y. Public Health Law (PHL) §1118.

3. *See* pp. 97–98 for a discussion of the specific duties which DEC may delegate to local health departments.

4. From a speech given in Philadelphia on February 10, 1973, to the American Law Institute.

5. When DEC denied Ton-Da-Lay's application for a water supply permit, the developer sought judicial review of the decision. See pp. 88–89 of this chapter for a discussion of the Appellate Division decision.

6. ECL §15–1501.

7. There are special laws and regulations dealing with wells on Long Island, because of the serious groundwater problems there. *See* ECL §15–1525 and §15–1527.

8. 6 NYCRR §601.3.

9. ECL §15–1503(2).

10. ECL §15–0903(1)(b).

11. ECL §15–0903(2)(a).

12. ECL §17–0801 *et seq.*

13. ECL §17–0105. This definition, except for minor differences in wording, is identical to the definition of "point source" in the Federal Water Pollution Control Act Amendments of 1972, which are discussed later in this chapter and in Chapter 11. *See* 33 U.S.C. §1362(14).

14. 33 U.S.C. §1251 *et seq. See* Chapter 11 for a discussion of the Federal Water Pollution Control Act Amendments of 1972.

15. *See* Chapter 11 for a discussion of the meaning of "navigable waters" in federal legislation.

16. ECL §17-0701(5).

17. ECL §17–1505 and §17–1501.

18. ECL §17–0701.

19. 6 NYCRR §653.4. There are several other conditions and circumstances which require the provision of a community sewerage system. A community sewerage system is defined as a collection and disposal system serving more than one lot.

20. 6 NYCRR §653.6.

21. ECL §17–0701(1).

22. *See* ECL §17–0301 for the statute authorizing this and the regulations found at 6 NYCRR Parts 700–703 for the actual classifications and standards.

23. *See* ECL §71–1929 and §71–1933 and 33 U.S.C. §1319.

24. ECL §71–1929.

25. ECL §71–1933.

26. 33 U.S.C. §1319(a).

27. ECL §17–0805.

28. In closer agreement with federal regulations, the state's proposed SPDES regulations do not provide for any departmental discretion on this point. They state that any interested group of persons "may request or petition in writing for a public hearing with respect to any SPDES application." (§753.7.)

29. ECL §15–0501. Classifications of the streams protected are stated. These include trout streams and all higher classifications.

30. ECL §15–0505.

31. ECL §15–0503. An important exclusion states that no permit is required for a dam or impoundment structure where the area draining into the body of water formed is less than one square mile, if this structure is less than ten feet in height from all points of the stream bed and the quantity of water impounded is less than

one million gallons. Dams or impoundment structures include earth fills, roads, bridges, fords, or other structures which unduly impede the flow of water.

32. 6 NYCRR §608.6.
33. ECL §71–1107.
34. ECL §1–0101 and §3–0301.
35. These regulations can be found at 6 NYCRR Part 615.
36. Ton-Da-Lay v. Diamond, 44 App. Div.2d 430 (1974).
37. 6 NYCRR §615.3(b).
38. PHL §1116.
39. PHL §1118.
40. Found at 10 NYCRR Part 1.
41. These regulations can be found at 10 NYCRR Part 74.
42. A community water system is defined as a water supply source and distribution system serving more than one lot.
43. N.Y. Real Property Law, Article 9, §334.
44. Herrick v. Ingraham, 46 App. Div.2d 546 (1975).
45. PHL §12(1).
46. PHL §12–b(2).
47. PHL §12–b(1).
48. PHL §206(4)(c).
49. PHL §12(5).
50. PHL §1100 and §1102.
51. PHL §1102(2)(b).
52. PHL §1103.
53. Authority to adopt these regulations is granted in PHL §1118 and ECL §17–1503.
54. PHL §201(1)(a); §206(1)(b); and §225(b).
55. ECL §17–0701(6).
56. Statutory authority for state aid to cities and counties for health-related activities is found in Article 6 of the PHL; such authority for activities now under the administration of DEC is found at ECL §3–0117.
57. *See* §1551.41 (2) of the manual.
58. *See* Chapter 7.

CHAPTER 6

Regional Controls: The Adirondack Park Agency Act

THE ADIRONDACK PARK in New York State is the largest remaining wilderness area in the eastern United States. Comprising some six million acres, it is roughly the size of the state of Vermont. The Adirondack Mountains, in which there are more than 100 peaks over 3,500 feet high, dominate the landscape of the park. Lakes, streams, rivers, and wild forests abound. Both private and state lands, in random patterns of ownership, lie within the park's boundaries (commonly known as the "blue line," since the original boundary was marked by a blue line on the official map in 1892 when the park was created by the state legislature). The entire area is sparsely populated: Not a single town lying wholly within the park has a population of over 10,000.

The protection and preservation of the park as a wilderness area have been high priorities for the citizens of New York State since at least 1895. In that year, an article of the new state constitution declared that all the forest preserve lands owned by the state, most of which were in the Adirondacks,[1] would be kept "forever wild"— "They shall not be leased, sold, or exchanged, or be taken by any corporation, public or private, nor shall the timber thereon be sold, removed, or destroyed."[2] Established eighty years ago, this was the first constitutional protection ever provided by a state for a natural resource. Proposals to amend this unqualified preservation and to broaden recreational uses of the land have been consistently rejected by the people of the state.

Actions taken with regard to the Adirondack Park in the early 1970s have continued this tradition of protection. Regional programs of land use controls have been adopted for both private and state lands in the park, and are presently being implemented. Because of the immense size of the park, many New York residents are directly affected by these plans. For others, the story of what has happened and descriptions of the land use plans developed may offer valuable insights and possible models for other areas. The greater the number of citizens who understand what has been accomplished, moreover, the greater the likelihood that the plans adopted will be conscientiously and wisely carried out.

The roots of many present-day land uses and ownership patterns in the Adirondack Park lie many years in the past. Most of the region remained practically unsettled well into the nineteenth century. As late as 1843, the first official state surveyor wrote that this "Great Wilderness" was as little known and explored as central Africa. By the late 1800s, however, lumbermen and vacationers had penetrated the region. It was largely in response to rapacious stripping of the land carried out by some lumbering operations that the "forever wild" article of the constitution was adopted.[3] During this period, the Adirondacks also became popular as a resort for the wealthy who built castles and luxurious lodges in the area. The less affluent soon followed, generally arriving by train and finding accommodations in the big hotels which began to spring up. Wonderful opportunities for fishing, hunting, and hiking were discovered, and some of the local residents began to hire themselves out as guides to lead vacationers into the wilderness. During this period an important characteristic of the Adirondacks took form: Ownership of large tracts of land by wealthy families and timber companies.

The majority of the permanent residents of the park were then, as they are now, relatively poor. The timber operation offered employment for some and the paper industry it brought with it provided jobs for even more. Farming continued to be a way of life for many. Mining of such minerals as garnet, magnetite, and zinc also came to the region and has remained there.[4] On the whole, however, much of the area began to become economically dependent on the influx of vacationers.

With the advent of the automobile and the paved road, the steady growth of recreational use accelerated. Up until the end of World War II, however, the public lands in the park remained more or less inviolate and land use patterns in the private portions generally complemented the forest preserve holdings. The postwar tourist boom and the construction of the New York Thruway brought dramatic changes. Motels with TV and heated pools multiplied and more than a half a dozen synthetic tourist attractions such as a Santa's Workshop and a Frontier Town sprang up. As the years passed, more and more people came to vacation in the area. In the winter, thousands of people began to pour into the area to ski, and in the summer some areas began to overflow with campers and hikers. Discernible paths even began to appear on some of the "trail-less" peaks over 4,000 feet, as the summer traffic of climbers in search of a wilderness experience increased.

By the late 1960s signs began to appear that even more dramatic, large-scale, and rapid changes were likely. With the completion of Interstate 87, "the Northway," from Albany to the Canadian border, the Adirondacks suddenly became within a day's drive of some 55 million people. This ease of access for millions, combined with the great surge in demand for second homes, was almost certain to draw to the Adirondacks the kind of subdivision development and chaotic commercial growth that had already swept through other scenic parts of the country.

Many people who were concerned about the future of the region realized that something needed to be done. In 1967 a proposal was submitted to the governor suggesting that a portion of the Adirondacks be converted into a national park. Within New York State, opposition to this idea was almost universal, but the proposal brought the question of what was going to happen in the Adirondack Park to the forefront. What kinds of private development were going to occur? Were there ways of preventing destructive overuse of popular areas of state land?

CREATION OF THE ADIRONDACK PARK AGENCY

In 1968 Governor Rockefeller appointed a Temporary Study Commission on the Future of the Adirondacks to make a comprehensive study of the park. Two years later this commission published a report on its work, which carefully detailed 181 recommendations and stressed the vulnerability of the park. Largely in response to these recommendations and the strong support of the governor's office, the state legislature passed the Adirondack Park Agency Act in 1971.[5] This act created the Adirondack Park Agency with a mandate to do the following:

1. In consultation with the Department of Environmental Conservation (DEC), develop a master plan for all state lands in the park that (a) would classify these lands according to their characteristics and their capacity to withstand use and would provide guidelines for management; and (b) would reflect the actual and projected uses of private lands within the park.
2. In cooperation and consultation with local governments, prepare and submit to the governor and the legislature a land use and development plan for all private lands in the park which would classify different types of areas and establish the intensity and types of land use and development permissible in each.
3. While the above plans were being prepared, review any proposed development which might have an adverse effect on the park.

In creating the Adirondack Park Agency and instructing it to prepare plans for both private and public lands within the park boundaries, the legislature acknowledged the desirability and necessity of regional planning in the Adirondacks. The Study Commission had made it clear that what happened in the 3.7 million acres of private land in the park would directly affect the wilderness character of the 2.3 million acres of forest preserve land. Effective control over private development could not be expected to be initiated by local governments in the park area. Although empowered by state enabling legislation to enact land use controls, only a few of the park's municipalities up to that time had provided any kind of control (only about 10 percent of the private land in the park was zoned). In addition, small local governments might not be capable of making, and should not be obliged to make, decisions about developments that would have an impact on the entire park and thus affect the interests of the state as a whole.

The Study Commission also pointed out the unusual ownership patterns in the park. Only one percent of landowners together owned more than 50 percent of the private land. There were 626 owners whose individual holdings were more than 500 acres in size. Three timber companies owned more than 125,000 acres each. In addition, 60 percent of the private land in the park was owned by non-residents. These were not circumstances in which local governments in small, rural areas could be expected to carry out effective control.

Consequently, the Study Commission strongly recommended

that an independent agency be established to provide a centralized land use framework through which local, regional, and state concerns could be addressed. The state legislature followed this advice in establishing the Adirondack Park Agency and precisely stated in the Adirondack Park Agency Act that:

> The state of New York has an obligation to insure that contemporary and projected future pressures on the park resources are provided for within a land use control framework which recognizes not only matters of local concern but also those of regional and state concern.

In addition to appreciating the significance of the Adirondack Park Agency Act as a regional approach to land use control, it is also important to recognize that this act is pre-eminently an environmental law. This is made clear in its statement of purpose:

> The basic purpose of this [act] is to insure optimum overall conservation, protection, preservation, development and use of the unique scenic, aesthetic, wildlife, recreational, open space, historic, ecological and natural resources of the Adirondack Park.

PLANS FOR PUBLIC AND PRIVATE LANDS

On June 1, 1972, the Adirondack Park Agency submitted to the governor the State Land Master Plan which it had developed in cooperation with the Department of Environmental Conservation. One thousand copies of a draft of this plan had previously been distributed to a wide range of interested parties and a series of nine hearings had been held. Approximately 1,000 people attended these hearings and just under 200 testified. Following the hearings a complete review of the plan was carried out and a number of modifications were made.

The final plan classifies the state lands into the following seven categories: wilderness; primitive; canoe; wild forest; intensive use; wild, scenic, and recreational rivers; and travel corridors. The largest portions of land fall under the designations of wilderness (approximately 45 percent) and wild forest (approximately 51 percent). Specific types of activities, structures, and maintenance practices are permissible in each area. For example, only the most rustic and natural types of structures are allowed in wilderness areas, where all motorized access and equipment are prohibited, while a variety of recreational activities are permitted in wild forest areas. Primitive areas are managed in the same way as wilderness areas, but they may include some structures or uses which are prohibited in wilderness areas. (It is expected that some of these areas will be eligible for wilderness classification at some future date.) Intensive use areas contain such heavily used facilities as campgrounds, developed beaches, ski centers, and visitor information centers. Delineations and descriptions of the particular areas which fall into each of the seven classifications, as well as a map, are parts of the plan.

This State Land Master Plan was approved by the governor. The Department of Environmental Conservation, the legal administrator of the forest preserve, then began the development of individual management plans for the various units of classified land. DEC and the Adirondack Park Agency began work together on the formulation of rules and regulations for enforcement.

In December 1972 the Adirondack Park Agency released a Preliminary Land Use and Development Plan for the Private Lands of the Adirondack Park. As specified by law, this preliminary plan was reviewed in a series of public hearings, held in each of the twelve counties which have land within the park and in Buffalo, New York City, and Rochester. Some 6,000 people attended the hearings and over 430 offered testimony. Approximately 500 written statements were received in the course of the review. In addition, the agency held numerous informal meetings with local governments and with local and regional planning boards. The comments and views expressed during this review process led to revisions in the plan and a number of changes in the preliminary map.

The final Adirondack Park Land Use and Development Plan and Recommendations for Implementation was submitted to the governor and the state legislature in March 1973. A somewhat bitter debate ensued in which representatives from the Adirondacks tried to prevent approval of the plan. At the heart of this opposition was the belief that the plan would work economic hardship on the region, whose residents already suffered from low income levels and high unemployment rates. Both the assembly and the senate voted to postpone all action on the question for one year, but this measure was vetoed by the governor. Passage of a bill instituting the plan as law (as amendments to the Adirondack Park Agency Act) was possible only after a number of compromises were made.

In effect, these compromises allayed the fears of Adirondack legislators that the concerns of local governments would not receive adequate attention in agency decisions and that these governments would suffer financially, but the basic provisions of the plan remained unaltered. The strong support given the plan by the governor was decisive in working out these compromises. To strengthen the local voice in decisions, an Adirondack Park Local Government Review Board was set up to advise and assist the Adirondack Park Agency. This board has twelve members, each of whom represents one of the counties within the park. With respect to financial problems, agreements were made (1) to abandon a long-standing state proposal to cut state payments made to local governments in lieu of taxes on forest preserve lands; and (2) to increase considerably the amounts of money available for local planning under the plan.

Another fulltime resident of the Adirondacks was also added to the Adirondack Park Agency, bringing its membership to a total of eleven: The commissioner of environmental conservation, the secretary of state, the commissioner of commerce, and eight members appointed by the governor, of whom none may be state officials or employees, five must be fulltime residents of the park, and no more than five may be members of the same political party.

Now that plans for both state and private land within the Adirondack Park have been completed and approved, the Adirondack Park Agency is primarily concerned with putting these plans into action. The following section discusses the plan for private land use and development in detail and explains how it is to be implemented by the agency and by local governments.

PRIVATE LAND USE CONTROLS

The Land Use and Development Plan

The plan classifies all privately owned land within the Adirondack Park into six different types of land use areas: hamlets, moderate intensity use, low intensity use, rural use, resource management, and industrial use.[6] For each of these areas it specifies an "overall intensity guideline" which defines maximum development in terms of the number of principal buildings per square mile. Primary and secondary compatible uses are also specified for each land use area. Primary uses are those which are generally suitable anywhere in a given land use area, as long as they are in keeping with the overall intensity guideline. Secondary uses are those which are suitable only if they are appropriately located.

In keeping with the policy of the Adirondack Park Agency Act, the plan is committed to "the preservation of [the park's] open space character." Once such a commitment is made in planning, then the question must be answered: Where can growth take place? This plan basically accepts existing growth patterns and concentrates future growth primarily where development has already begun. In further classifying land use areas, it considers the following factors:

1. What is the carrying capacity of the land? How deep is the soil? How steep are the slopes? These are essential considerations for both construction and sewage disposal. They deal with the basic determination of the degree of human habitation and use which particular kinds of land can sustain.

2. Is the land located in or very near to an environmentally critical area, such as a wetland or floodplain; a river designated by the state as wild, scenic, or recreational; high elevations; forest preserve lands; or a travel corridor?

3. Is the land located in or very near to a critical wildlife habitat or the habitat of rare and endangered plant or animal species?

4. Is the land agriculturally or industrially productive?

All of these factors have a bearing on the way land lying outside existing developed areas is classified.

As far as population growth is concerned, the Adirondack Park Agency has estimated that the plan will ultimately allow a maximum population within the park of 2 million people.[7] At the present time, there are only about 125 thousand permanent residents in the park and some 90 thousand seasonal residents. Thus, a very large growth in population is allowed by the plan.

By far the largest proportion of private land in the park is classified in a way that is conducive to the preservation of open space. The most restrictive type of land use area with respect to the overall density guidelines, the resource management areas, accounts for 53 percent of the 3.7 million acres of private land. The next most restrictive areas, the rural use areas, cover 32 percent. Low intensity use areas account for 10 percent. The remaining 5 percent of the land falls either into moderate intensity use areas, or into hamlets or industrial use areas, neither of which is constrained by an overall intensity guideline. When considering this breakdown, one should bear in mind that under existing uses of land, about 80 percent of all private lands are devoted to open space uses.

In the following discussion, descriptions are given of the general character and purposes of each of the six types of land use areas. Table 1 (see p. 117), which should be used in conjunction with these descriptions, sets out the overall intensity guideline for each type of area and gives examples of primary and secondary compatible uses. In addition to stating intensity in terms of "principal buildings per square mile," as it is expressed in the plan, this table also shows, for purposes of comparison only, what an average lot size in acres would be if development were completely uniform in an area and if only one principal building were constructed on each lot. This is done only in an attempt to give some sense of the dimensions involved; and the following statement from the plan itself should be borne in mind:

> While a grid system of uniform lot sizes within a given land use area
> for a particular town may be appropriate at times, in many cases it will
> be damaging to both the resources of the Park and to the ability of local
> governments to provide services to merely translate the intensity guide-
> line to a uniform lot size.

As defined in the act, "principal buildings" include the following: a single family dwelling; a mobile home; a tourist cabin of 300 or more square feet of floor space; each dwelling unit of a multiple family dwelling; and commercial or industrial structures of specified dimensions. Special formulas are provided for hotel and motel units and agricultural structures and dwellings. The compatible uses given in the table are only a small sample from the lists of compatible uses set out in the plan. For example, under moderate intensity use areas in the plan, fourteen compatible primary uses and twenty-three compatible secondary uses are listed.

1. Hamlet areas

These areas are based on the existing developed communities of the park. They range from larger communities which have diverse residential, commercial, tourist and industrial developments, and public services to smaller, less varied communities. Basically, they are almost all small mountain villages, most of which still retain a certain amount of local charm and character. Under the park land use plan, they are intended to serve as the primary centers for growth and to provide services for the park's permanent, seasonal, and transient populations. By concentrating future development in such established areas, the plan seeks to further the preservation of open space and low density development in the rest of the park. No overall intensity guideline (that is, no building construction limit) is established for hamlet areas and all land uses are considered compatible. Local governments may, however, impose their own land use controls.

2. Moderate intensity use areas

These are areas in which relatively intense development, primarily residential in nature, is possible, desirable, and suitable. Generally located near hamlets, where community services can be most readily and economically provided, these areas are intended to provide for residential expansion and other related uses. They have topography and soil suitable for such construction. Some sections are located along highways or accessible shorelines where existing development has already established the character of the area. Other sections which are not yet developed have deep soils, moderate slopes, and easy access to hamlets. Given its overall intensity guideline, a moderate intensity use area should at maximum development be no more densely developed than a spacious residential suburb.

3. Low intensity use areas

These areas are also suited primarily for residential development, but of lesser intensity, with homes preferably clustered. They are normally reasonably close to a hamlet, and they have fairly tolerant physical and biological resources. It is anticipated that these areas will primarily be used to provide housing opportunities both for park residents and for the growing second home market.

4. Rural use areas

In these areas, natural resource limitations and public considerations require more stringent development constraints. The areas are characterized by substantial acreages of one or more of the following: Fairly shallow soils, relatively severe slopes, fragile ecological systems, critical wildlife habitats, proximity to scenic vistas or key public lands. In addition, these areas are frequently remote from hamlets or are not readily accessible. They are characterized by a low level of development and a variety of rural uses that are generally compatible with the protection of their relatively intolerant natural resources and the preservation of the open space atmosphere of the park. Residential development in these areas will be limited to large lots or to carefully planned small clusters. Strip development along travel corridors will not be allowed.

5. Resource management areas

In these areas the need to protect, manage, and enhance forest, agricultural, recreational, and open space resources is of paramount importance because of overriding natural resource and public considerations. Many of the areas are characterized by substantial acreages of one or more of the following: Shallow soils, severe slopes, elevations of over 2,500 feet, floodplains, proximity to designated or proposed wild or scenic rivers, wetlands, critical wildlife habitats, or habitats of rare and endangered plant and animal species. Other areas include extensive tracts under active forest management and agricultural areas of considerable economic importance. The basic objectives of resource management areas are to protect delicate natural resources; to encourage good management of forest, agricultural, and recreational resources; to protect open spaces; and to prevent strip development along travel corridors. Residential development will be allowed on large lots or in carefully planned small clusters.

6. Industrial use areas

Included here are areas that are substantial in size, are located outside of hamlet areas, and are either (1) presently predominated by industrial or mining uses, or (2) identified by local and state officials as having potential for new industrial development. Residential homes are not a compatible use. No overall intensity guideline is provided.

Before any significant new land development or subdivision of land can be undertaken in the park, consideration must be given to factors which might have an "adverse impact upon the park's natural, scenic, aesthetic, ecological, wildlife, historic, recreational, or open space resources." The plan specifically lists thirty-seven different "development considerations" which must be taken into account. The five basic categories of these are: Natural resource considerations; historic site considerations; site development considerations; governmental considerations; and governmental review considerations. Basic emphasis falls on environmental resources and characteristics upon which development would have an impact, such as existing air and water quality, erosion, and noise levels. Burdens imposed on the public for provision of services must also be weighed, as well as any commercial, industrial, recreational, or other benefit which might be derived.

Table 1
Overall Intensity Guidelines and Examples
of Compatible Uses by Land Use Type

Land Use Type	Overall Intensity Guideline*	Examples of Compatible Uses Primary	Secondary
Hamlet Area	None applicable	All uses compatible	
Moderate Intensity Use Area	500 prin. bldgs./sq. mi. (avg. lot size: 1.3 acres)	Single family dwellings	Multiple family dwellings Mobile home courts Public and semi-public buildings
Low Intensity Use Area	200 prin. bldgs./sq.mi. (avg. lot size: 3.2 acres)	"	"
Rural Use Area	75 prin. bldgs./sq. mi. (avg. lot size: 8.5 acres)	"	"
Resource Management Area	15 prin. bldgs./sq. mi. (avg. lot size: 42.6 acres)	Agricultural uses Open space recreational uses Forestry uses	Single family dwellings
Industrial Use Area	None applicable	Industrial uses Mineral extractions	Commercial uses

* See p. 114 of this chapter for an explanation of the use of average lot sizes in this table.

Special restrictions apply to land development along the shore-lines of all lakes and ponds; of any river designated as wild, scenic, or recreational; and of any river or stream navigable by boat, including canoe. Restrictions regarding removal of vegetation, including trees, on all shorefront lots are specified. Minimum lot widths or allowable numbers of buildings per linear mile of shoreline and minimum setbacks for buildings are established for the various types of land use areas. A minimum setback for sewage drainage fields and seepage pits of 100 feet from the mean high-water mark is required for shoreline development on *all* lakes, ponds, rivers, and streams.

Implementation of the Land Use and Development Plan

Implementation of the plan takes place principally through control of new projects by the Adirondack Park Agency and by local governments with land use programs approved by the agency. Development which was substantially underway when the act became effective is not affected, although the Agency did have interim review powers over private land development in the period between the agency's creation and the approval by the state legislature of its private land use plan.

Large-scale or potentially more critical proposed projects to be located in sensitive areas are called Class A regional projects and require agency approval. Less critical projects, called Class B regional projects, are controlled principally by local governments with approved land use programs. If a local government does not have an approved land use program, then a Class B project in its jurisdiction is reviewed by the agency. Criteria for classifying projects are different for each of the six land use areas. Definitions and particular types of projects falling into Class A or Class B are spelled out in the plan for each land use area, and will be discussed in more detail below.

Local land use programs are approved by the agency when they are deemed to support and further the park's Land Use and Development Plan in the light of local needs and conditions. These programs may allow greater and lesser intensities of development within different parts of a given land use area as long as the overall intensity does not exceed the plan guideline. They may, moreover, impose more restrictive intensity guidelines than the park plan requires. Local governments are allowed considerable flexibility in determining compatible uses for the different land use areas. Particular uses may be added, excluded, reclassified as either primary or secondary, or actually prohibited. It should be noted that when a local land use program is duly adopted by a local government, it is valid and enforceable whether or not it is approved by the agency. Thus a developer would always have to obtain approval for a proposed project under such a local program as well as any other local controls adopted in accordance with state enabling legislation, in addition to any required agency approval.

Subdivision control within the Adirondack Park is considered by many citizens to be one of the most important aspects of the agency's work, for here the greatest pressure has been anticipated. In particular, the purchase of huge tracts of land by out-of-state development corporations once presaged the entrance of large-scale second home subdivisions into the Adirondacks.[8] The development and approval of the Land Use and Development Plan has given the state and its citizens the means to control these, as well as smaller projects, in the public interest.

"Subdivision" is defined in the Adirondack Park Agency Act as "any division of land into two or more lots, parcels or sites, whether adjoining or not, for the purpose of sale, lease, license or any form of separate ownership or occupancy" (including any improvements or land development preparatory to such division)—except for the lease of land for hunting, fishing, and other open space recreational uses. Under the act, and apart from stricter requirements imposed by local land use programs, whether a subdivision developer must submit his plans for approval to the agency or to the local government or to neither one depends on the size and type of the project, the land use designation of the area where the project is located, and the characteristics of the particular location.

For example, if a proposed subdivision is in a rural use area, it is a Class A regional project, requiring agency approval, if (a) it involves twenty or more lots, parcels, or sites; or (b) no matter how many lots are involved, if it is located in any of several enumerated types of sensitive locations such as wetlands or elevations over 2,500 feet. It is a Class B regional project, subject to review and approval by a local government having an agency-approved land use program, if (a) it comprises from five to nineteen lots, parcels, or sites; or (b) it has less than five lots any of which is less than 320,000 square feet in size or 80,000 square feet when shoreline is involved; or (c) it involves mobile homes. If the project (a) has fewer than five lots, parcels, or sites and all lots are at least 320,000 square feet in size or 80,000 square feet when shoreline is involved; (b) involves no mobile homes; and (c) is not located in an environmentally critical area, then it requires no review or permit under the Adirondack Park Agency Act.

The following tables list by land use areas the kinds of subdivisions that are Class A regional projects (Table 2); Class B regional projects (Table 3); and those that require no approval under the act (Table 4).

These tables all deal with subdivisions. A full listing of all Class A and Class B projects by land use area can be found in the Adirondack Park Agency Act. The following are illustrative examples of

Table 2
Subdivisions That Are
Class A Regional Projects

Land Use Designation of the Site	Size and Character of the Project
Hamlet Area	a. Subdivisions involving wetlands b. Subdivisions involving 100 or more lots or residential units
Moderate Intensity Use Area	a. Subdivisions located in a critical environmental area b. Subdivisions involving 75 or more lots or residential units
Low Intensity Use Area	a. Subdivisions located in a critical environmental area b. Subdivisions involving 35 or more lots or residential units
Rural Use Area	a. Subdivisions located in a critical environmental area b. Subdivisions involving 20 or more lots or residential units
Resource Management Area	a. Subdivisions located in a critical environmental area b. Subdivisions involving 2 or more lots

NOTES: The act provides for more extensive agency review of subdivisions by special agreement between a local government and the agency.

Subdivisions are not a compatible use in industrial use areas.

Table 3
Subdivisions That Are
Class B Regional Projects

Land Use Designation of the Site	Size and Character of the Project
Hamlet Area	None
Moderate Intensity Use Area	a. Subdivisions of 15 to 74 lots (without any mobile homes) b. Subdivisions of less than 15 lots where any lot is less than 40,000 sq. ft. or when shoreline is involved, less than 25,000 sq. ft. c. Subdivisions involving mobile homes and 2 or more lots

Low Intensity Use Area	a. Subdivisions of 10 to 34 lots (without any mobile homes) b. Subdivisions of less than 10 lots where any lot is less than 120,000 sq. ft. or when shoreline is involved, less than 50,000 sq. ft. c. Mobile home subdivisions involving 2 or more lots
Rural Use Area	a. Subdivisions of 5 to 9 lots (without any mobile homes) b. Subdivisions of less than 5 lots where any lot is less than 320,000 sq. ft. or when shoreline is involved, less than 80,000 sq. ft. c. Mobile home subdivisions involving 2 or more lots
Resource Management Area	None

NOTE: Subdivisions are not a compatible use in industrial use areas.

Table 4
Subdivisions That Require No
Approval Under the Adirondack Park Agency Act

Land Use Designation of the Site	Size and Character of the Project
Hamlet Area	Subdivisions which have fewer than 100 lots or residential units and do not involve wetlands
Moderate Intensity Use Area	Subdivisions which have fewer than 15 lots and no lots of less than 40,000 sq. ft. or, when shoreline is involved, of less than 25,000 sq. ft.; are not located in a critical environmental area; and do not involve mobile homes
Low Intensity Use Area	Subdivisions which have fewer than 10 lots and no lots less than 120,000 sq. ft. or, when shoreline is involved, of less than 50,000 sq. ft.; are not located in a critical environmental area; and do not involve mobile homes
Rural Use Area	Subdivisions which have fewer than 5 lots and no lots of less than 320,000 sq. ft. or, when shoreline is involved, of less than 80,000 sq. ft.; are not located in a critical environmental area; and do not involve mobile homes

projects which are uniformly designated as Class A and Class B, respectively, in moderate intensity use areas, low intensity use areas, and rural use areas:

Class A: All structures in excess of 40 feet in height, except residential radio and television antennas; commercial or private airports; timber harvesting that includes a proposed clearcutting of any single unit of land of more than twenty-five acres; watershed management and flood control projects; major public utility uses.

Class B: Public and semi-public buildings; municipal roads; marinas, boatyards, and boat launching sites; golf courses; campgrounds; commercial sand and gravel extractions.

In reviewing a Class B project, a local government with an approved land use program is required to apply the "development considerations" spelled out in the Adirondack Park Agency Act and to assess potential adverse impact with respect to the thirty-seven enumerated factors. A Class B project cannot be disapproved by a local government without a public hearing, but it can be approved without such a hearing. The Adirondack Park Agency must be notified when a project application or an application for a variance from a local land use program is received. The agency can request any pertinent information, which must be supplied, and can participate in all stages of local review. It can nullify a variance from an approved land use program that is granted by a local government. It can also initiate judicial review of the issuance of a permit by a local government, as well as institute legal proceedings to enjoin or modify the project for which the permit is issued. Under certain circumstances, the agency can institute legal proceedings to revoke its approval of a local land use program.

The Adirondack Park Agency itself reviews all Class A projects and those Class B projects proposed in jurisdictions of local governments which do not have approved local land use programs. The agency follows basically the same procedures in reviewing both classes of projects.

All applications to the agency must conform to the requirements set forth in the agency rules and regulations.[9] Upon receipt of a complete project application, the agency notifies the Adirondack Park Local Government Review Board and appropriate local, county, and regional officials, who have the opportunity to submit advisory comments. In the case of a Class A project proposed for an area in which there is an approved local land use program, the agency must determine whether the project meets all pertinent requirements of the local program. Within ninety days after official receipt, the agency must decide either to approve the application outright, to approve it subject to conditions, to disapprove it, or, at its discretion, to hold a public hearing on the project before making its decision. If a public hearing is to be held, it must commence during this ninety-day period or as soon after the conclusion of the period as is practical. The agency's decision on the application must then be made within ninety days after the completion of the hearing. Unless a developer agrees to an extension, failure by the agency to make its decision within these time periods is tantamount to approval. The decision may take the form of approval, conditional approval, or disapproval. A permit is granted when a project is approved or when stipulated conditions have been fulfilled.

In cases of "practical difficulties or unnecessary hardships," the agency is empowered, after public hearing, to allow variances from the park plan's restrictions. On the other hand, a land use not included on the list of compatible uses for a land use area is presumed to be incompatible. The burden is on the developer to convince the agency that in a particular instance such a proposed use would be compatible.

Overall intensity guidelines are to be applied to the total area of a proposed project plus all adjacent land owned by the developer. The intensity of development on land under different ownership in the same land use area has no bearing on the number of principal buildings to be allowed in a proposed project. In general, a landowner cannot construct more principal buildings on his land than the overall intensity guideline for the given land use area in which the project is located. On parcels of land less than 2,500 acres, however, the agency can—after public hearing—allow greater intensity by reclassifying the land from one type of land use area to another. Such a reclassification can be initiated by the landowner, by the local legislative body, or by the agency. Two-thirds of the members of the agency must approve such a change. (Other reclassifications are possible in conjunction with agency approval of local land use programs.)

CITIZEN ACTION

Citizens can affect the course of events in the Adirondack Park on two different levels: (1) In the review of project applications by the Adirondack Park Agency or by local governments with agency-approved local land use programs; and (2) in the overall development of the agency. There are several organizations which take a vital interest in both of these concerns. The Sierra Club, the Adirondack Mountain Club, and the Association for the Protection of the Adirondacks are all deeply committed to protection of the Adirondack Park and have active programs monitoring activities and decisions of the Adirondack Park Agency. The Adirondack Mountain Club publishes a bimonthly magazine on the region called *The Adirondac*. The Environmental Planning Lobby, which lobbied for the creation of the agency and approval of its land use plan for private land, continues to give Adirondack bills high priority. Citizens who are concerned about the Adirondack Park would do well to contact any of these organizations:

> Sierra Club
> Atlantic Chapter
> 50 West 40th Street
> New York, N. Y. 10018
>
> The Adirondack Mountain Club
> 172 Ridge Street
> Glens Falls, N. Y. 12801
>
> The Association for the Protection of
> the Adirondacks
> 21 East 40th Street
> New York, N. Y. 10016
> *and*
> P. O. Box 951
> Schenectady, N. Y. 12301
>
> Environmental Planning Lobby (EPL)
> 211 East 43rd Street
> New York, N. Y. 10017

Naturally the strong support which was mobilized to establish the agency and to give it effective and workable land use control powers does not exist today in the same concentrated and focused way. The passage of strong legislation is not, however, an assurance that plans will be conscientiously and wisely enforced. Consequently, a great need exists for all those concerned about the Adirondack Park to keep abreast of developments there and to be ready to take action when they see that it is necessary.

The relationship between the agency and local governments within the park has always been somewhat sensitive. Citizens should consider how they might be able to ease any problems which might exist in this area. In particular, efforts should be made to see that wise selections are made of the county representatives to serve on the Adirondack Park Local Government Review Board. As a general rule, whenever any important position in the Adirondack Park needs to be filled—whether it is a staff or board position or a political office —energy should be exerted to see that competent people with a commitment to protection of the Adirondack region are chosen.

In the various local governments, residents should work for the institution of local planning and explore all possibilities of obtaining funds to do this well.

Review of Project Applications

Those who are concerned with project review should as a first step obtain and study the rules and regulations governing review procedures prepared by the agency.[10] These are available upon request from the agency at the following address:

> Adirondack Park Agency
> P.O. Box 99
> Ray Brook, N.Y. 12977

A major problem in monitoring project review is the fact that the agency is not required to give public notice of the receipt of applications, and may approve or disapprove a project without a public hearing. A local government with an approved local land use program must hold a hearing before disapproving a Class B project, but it may approve such a project without a hearing. Consequently, concerned citizens must find ways of keeping track of project applications. The agency is required by law to give official notice of receipt of a completed application to the following: The project sponsor; the Adirondack Park Local Government Review Board; the chairman of the county planning board, if one exists, of the county involved; the chairman of the appropriate regional planning board; and, if the application is for a Class A regional project, to the clerk of the local government in which the proposed project would be located.

There is no provision in the Adirondack Park Agency Act for agency consideration of written comments from the public in those cases in which public hearings are not held or in prehearing review in those cases in which they are. All those officially notified of the receipt of a project application are, however, encouraged to provide advisory comment, and informal local government involvement in agency review is mandatory. Citizens might want to approach local government officials about problems relating to particular projects in hopes that these concerns will be transmitted to the agency. If, however, local officials do not share their concerns, or there are other difficulties, citizens might submit comments directly to the agency or press for a hearing. Sometimes citizens may be able to offer the agency special expertise. Persuading the agency to hold a hearing which can serve to publicize genuine environmental threats is likely to be an important task for concerned citizens.

Whether or not a hearing is held, citizen effort regarding review of a project might be directed toward any of the following objectives: Agency disapproval of the application; agency approval subject to conditions; or the inclusion of requirements or conditions in permits granted. In issuing a permit, the agency is authorized to require the posting of performance bonds to ensure that the project will be adequately supported by the basic services and improvements which it requires. The agency may also insist that deeds to subdivision lots contain provisions limiting future construction.

When the agency decides to hold a hearing on a project application, the law requires that notice be given by publication at least once in a newspaper having general circulation in each local government in which the project is proposed to be located, by conspicuous posting of the land involved, and by individual notice to all involved landowners, to the Adirondack Park Local Government Review Board, and to various local, county, and regional officials.

The agency's rules and regulations provide that individual notice of a hearing must be sent to:

1. All immediately adjacent landowners.

2. All other public agencies that have previously filed with the agency a written request to be notified of particular hearings or of particular types of hearings.

3. "[A]ny person having a substantial and tangible economic

right or interest which might be directly affected by the decision of the agency concerning the project under review."[11]

Anyone claiming the right to receive individual notice of a hearing under (3) must file with the agency at its headquarters in Ray Brook, New York, a statement of his or her right and interest and a request to be notified of a particular hearing. The agency must inform such a person in writing by certified mail whether or not it decides to grant this request.

It is important to note that in the draft of proposed rules and regulations released by the agency on November 12, 1973, there were several important provisions with respect to citizen involvement that were dropped in the final, official version of the regulations. Notably, under the draft regulations, many more individuals and groups would have been allowed to request individual notice of hearings. While the final regulations restrict this opportunity to persons who have substantial and tangible economic interests which would be directly affected by a proposed project, the draft regulations extended this privilege to a wide range of individuals and groups who might have a direct or indirect interest in the impact of a proposed project or who might possess special expertise. The draft specifically stated that environmental organizations and various types of citizens' groups might well have such an interest.

In addition to restricting tremendously the range of those entitled to request individual notice of hearings, the final regulations also dropped the provision made in the draft for requesting individual notice not simply for a particular hearing but for particular types of hearings and for hearings in particular types of places. Under the draft regulations, individuals and groups could request on a yearly basis that they be sent individual notice of all hearings of a certain type. Under the final regulations, provision is made only for requesting individual notice for a single, particular hearing.

It is apparent that pressure was brought to bear on the agency to restrict the involvement of citizens' groups and environmental organizations in its review of projects, and to curtail the dissemination of information about its public hearings.

In an official hearing, it is important to know who qualifies as a "party" to the hearing and what the rights are of those who qualify. The rules and regulations of the Adirondack Park Agency specify that parties to its hearings on Class A and Class B regional projects include two different types of parties: "Parties as of right" and "parties by permission."[12] Parties as of right include the project sponsor, the agency staff, and those adjacent landowners, public agencies, and persons entitled to individual notice of the hearing. Parties by permission include all those persons who do not qualify as parties as of right, but who have:

> a right or interest in the hearing of such nature that their intervention is necessary to or would further the purpose of the hearing. Such a right or interest must include either (1) a demonstrable social, economic, or environmental interest in the proposed project or in the potential impact of such project relative to the development considerations specified [in both the act and the rules and regulations] or (2) expertise in some aspect of the project that is directly relevant to the ultimate decision of the agency.

Any person claiming such interest or expertise which would entitle him to be a party by permission must file in writing with the agency at least ten days prior to the hearing (except where good cause can be shown for a later filing) both a statement of right or interest and a request to be made a party by permission to the hearing. It is obviously important to convince the agency and its staff of one's interest and expertise by whatever means may be appropriate. The agency must send those seeking to become parties by permission written notification of its decision on such requests.

All parties (except the project sponsor and the agency staff) must file a written notice of the intention to intervene at least three days prior to the hearing.

In the proceedings of the hearing, all parties must be afforded the opportunity to present evidence and argument, but only parties as of right are granted the important right to cross-examine witnesses. Thus only the project sponsor, the agency staff, any public agency, and those persons entitled to individual notice of the hearing (that is, adjacent landowners and those who have substantial and tangible interests which would be directly affected by the proposed project) have the right to question witnesses on vital aspects of the project. Citizens' groups or environmental organizations which might be allowed by the agency to become parties by permission are not allowed to ask such questions. This procedure is in marked contrast to hearings held by the New York State Department of Environmental Conservation, in which citizens' groups and environmental organizations readily qualify as bona fide parties and are entitled to cross-examine witnesses.

Aside from the parties, any other person or public agency who wishes to appear at the hearing and make an oral or written statement may do so without having filed a written notice with the agency. Such statements may favor or oppose the project or simply express a position without specifically favoring or opposing. Statements become part of the record of the hearing, and written statements may be received up to and including the last day on which the hearing is held.

The presiding officer of a hearing is entitled to impose reasonable limitations regarding time and the number of persons heard. The agency must keep a verbatim record of the proceedings of each hearing and certified copies of such records may be obtained for a reasonable fee.

In addition to hearings on project applications held at the agency's discretion or prior to disapproval of a Class B project by a local government, public hearings are required for review of applications to the agency for variances from the strict letter of plan provisions or shoreline restrictions which claim "practical difficulties or unnecessary hardships."

The act encourages cooperation between the Adirondack Park Agency and other state agencies in the conduct of public hearings. Accordingly, the agency holds joint hearings with the New York Department of Environmental Conservation for projects which are being reviewed by both agencies.[13] In such cases, there is only one hearing officer, but each agency makes its own separate findings.

The Adirondack Park Agency Act contains a broad provision for judicial review by means of an Article 78 proceeding of any agency act, omission, or order.[14] Application for this review, should it seem essential to challenge an agency decision, must be made within sixty days of the effective date of the order or the date when the act or omission occurred. This can be done, however, only by an "aggrieved person." Under traditional court rulings, it is necessary to show an adversely affected property interest in order to qualify. The strongest claim for standing to obtain judicial review is a claim of threatened economic loss by a property owner or lessee adjacent to the proposed project. Aggrieved persons who have not utilized every opportunity offered by the administrative process (such as filing comments with the agency or participating in a public hearing) to make known their objections may discover, too late, that the court is not prepared to offer a forum for the grievances of a person who has failed to exhaust his "administrative remedies."

Overall Development of the Adirondack Park Agency

Citizens not only may become involved in the review of individual project applications; they also have played an important role in the overall development of the Adirondack Park Agency itself and have continuing legal rights with respect to future land reclassifications and amendments to agency rules and regulations.

Thousands of citizens took part in the public hearings that were held on the drafts of the Land Use and Development Plan and the State Land Master Plan. A number of environmental groups and citizens' organizations sent out informational materials on the drafts, and urged the public to attend hearings and to testify or submit written statements in areas of special interest or expertise. Efforts were made to make the plans as sound as possible with respect to the protection and use of natural resources, the rights and interests of park residents and landowners, and the continuous involvement of the public.

The development by the agency of rules and regulations to govern project review procedures and to provide further guidance to potential project sponsors offered another opportunity for concerned citizens to take part in public hearings. Any amendments to the final rules and regulations, moreover, can be made only after at least one public hearing. Fifteen days' notice must be given for the hearing at least once in a newspaper of general circulation in each county wholly or partially within the Adirondack Park and in at least three metropolitan areas of the state, and by individual notice to local, county, and regional officials. This notice must contain a statement describing the subject matter of the proposed rules and regulations, the time and place of the hearing, and where further information may be obtained.

In general, changes in land classifications on the map of the Land Use and Development Plan must be preceded by public hearings. Exceptions to this rule are (1) reclassifications of less than 2,500 acres of land allowed in the initial approval by the agency of a local land use program; and (2) amendments which clarify the boundaries of the land use areas, correct any errors on the map, or effect any other technical changes. In these two cases, the holding of a public hearing is at the discretion of the agency. Hearings concerning amendments to the plan map are to be held in each local government in which the land in question is located. Notice of not less than fifteen days must be given by publication at least once in a newspaper of general circulation in the area involved, by conspicuous posting of the land itself, and by individual notice to landowners, local, county, and regional officials, and the Adirondack Park Local Government Review Board.

NOTES

1. The remainder were in the Catskills.

2. New York State Constitution, Article XIV, Section 1.

3. Such lumbering practices not only destroyed the beauty of the land, they also endangered the stability of watershed systems upon which the canal transportation of the time depended.

4. Today the largest zinc-producing mine in the United States is located in the Adirondacks, as are the world's largest garnet mine, ilmenite mine, and open-pit magnetite mine.

5. N.Y. Executive Law, Article 27, §800 *et seq.* It should be noted that there is more than one Article 27 under this law and that under one of these there is even another §800. Those searching for the statute dealing with the Adirondack Park Agency should be forewarned of this confusion.

6. A map which delineates all of the classifications of private lands within the park by a color code was published with the final version of the Land Use and Development Plan. Copies of this map can be inspected at the State Capitol, at the headquarters of the Adirondack Park Agency in Ray Brook, N.Y. (which is near Saranac Lake), or in the office of the clerk of any county or local government within the park. The map was also widely distributed to interested organizations and individuals when it was first published.

7. Provisions of the agency's preliminary draft of the plan would have permitted a population of up to 1.2 million, but revisions of this draft led to the higher growth limit.

8. The Horizon Corporation, a land sales company based in Tucson, Arizona, bought 24,300 acres in the park from a lumber company. Luis Paparazzo, a Connecticut developer, purchased 18,500 acres, where he planned to build the Ton-Da-Lay development, which is discussed in Chapter 5.

9. These can be found at 9 NYCRR Parts 580–586.

10. *Ibid.*

11. 9 NYCRR §581.15 (a) (3).

12. 9 NYCRR §581.15 (d).

13. *See* Chapter 5 for a discussion of DEC hearings.

14. *See* Glossary.

CHAPTER 7

Land Development Problems in the Catskills

T HE CATSKILL REGION of New York State is known to the world as the setting of many of Washington Irving's tales and as the home of lavish resort hotels. It is also known to a more limited number of people as a beautiful rural area that is in imminent danger of being overtaken by an advancing urban surge emanating from the New York City metropolitan area. Productive dairy and truck farms, mountain slopes and peaks, clear trout streams of unmatched quality, and the historical and cultural traditions of rural villages stand face to face with the kind of modern land development practices that have destroyed rural lifestyles and caused severe environmental problems in other scenic areas of this country.

The Catskill region encompasses an area that is roughly fifty miles north to south and fifty miles east to west. It is situated between the Hudson and Delaware Rivers, and contains nearly all of the counties of Sullivan, Ulster, Greene, Delaware, Otsego, and Schoharie, as well as the southern tip of Albany County.[1]

Like the Adirondack region, the Catskill region contains a "blue line" park within whose boundaries lie both private land and forest preserve lands that are protected as "forever wild" by the New York State Constitution. While most of the Adirondack region lies within the huge Adirondack Park, the Catskill Park consists of a relatively small part of the Catskill region, basically the mountainous core in Greene, Delaware, and Ulster counties. The "forever wild" land in the Catskills consists of only about 650,000 acres, compared to over 2.3 million acres in the Adirondacks. State and private lands coexist in a random pattern in the Catskills just as they do in the Adirondacks. The degradation of forest preserve lands resulting from incompatible uses of adjacent lands is, however, probably a more serious problem in the Catskills because the area is more densely inhabited and proportionately less of the land is covered with trees.

Homes for both commuters and vacationers are involved in the subdivision development that is taking place in the Catskills. New York City's suburbs have advanced steadily northward toward the Shawangunk Mountains, the lower perimeter of the Catskill region. The opening of Route 17, known as "the Quickway," has placed lower Sullivan County within arduous commuting distance of Manhattan. A vigorous second home market exists for those who want to spend weekends and vacations in the Catskills. The fact that the lower Catskills are within the range of one tank of gasoline for motorists may become increasingly more important for this market, if fuel shortages continue.

The enormous expansion of Stewart Airport in Newburgh along with a high-speed connecting rail link to New York City, both of which are proposed by the New York Metropolitan Transportation Authority, would open up the Catskills to many more people. Stewart Airport is not actually in the Catskill region, but lies just to the south in Orange County. The future of this expansion is by no means certain, but developers in the Catskills generally favor it and some use it as a selling point. The developers of the proposed Shawanga Village subdivision, for example, stated in an environmental impact statement submitted to the New York State Department of Environmental Conservation that major sources of employment for potential residents of the development were expected to be Stewart Airport in the town of Newburgh, located approximately thirty miles away, the White Plains area, fifty-seven miles away, and the Middletown region, eight miles away.

The 1970 Census showed a population increase over the past decade of almost 19 percent in Ulster County and over 16 percent in Sullivan County, compared with a statewide average increase of 8.4 percent. Some small towns and villages, caught in the development wave, have doubled in population since 1960. These growth figures, moreover, do not reflect second home construction or seasonal use. In Sullivan County, nearly ten times as many subdivision lots were approved in 1972 as in 1969—a circumstance which is largely related to the growth of second home developments.

Tax assessment practices in New York State, in which land is usually assessed according to its potential for development rather than its existing use, encourage owners of large tracts of Catskill lands to sell or develop their properties. Many farmers and other landowners who hold highly taxed acreage that does not generate sufficient income come under increasing pressure to sell. Thus, the number of farms in the Catskills is dwindling rapidly, and land speculation companies are showing an increased interest in the area.

"Strip development" and subdivisions are two types of development around which many problems revolve. In the Catskills, strip development takes place along major access roads such as Routes 23 and 28. Ice cream stands, mobile home courts, gasoline stations, and shops have sprung up along these highways. Then people have sought homes within easy reach of the services offered by such establishments. This kind of development is a particular problem in the Catskills, since the major highways generally trace the paths made by tanners in the early nineteenth century through very narrow valleys. These valleys very quickly become crowded by competing land uses. Major developments begin to creep up the mountain slopes, where soil is thin and not suitable for absorption of sewage wastes, and the terrain often makes proper installation of septic tanks impossible. As a result, raw sewage which is not properly accommodated can rise to the surface of the ground and then either seep or be washed by rain into the streams below. In the valleys, development continues in piecemeal fashion, often in subdivisions of fifteen to thirty lots which are financed by local residents under pressure from rising taxes. The cumulative effect of several such developments upon stream quality can be severe.

While there are scattered examples of well-planned, environmentally sensitive subdivisions in the Catskills, many projects have caused real damage to natural resources. The non-porous nature of much of the soil in the area, along with failure by developers to abide by state regulations dealing with the proper location and installation of septic tanks, or to provide sewage treatment plants when the soil is not suitable for septic tanks, has led to many serious problems. In many cases, the question arises of whether the land used for subdivisions is actually capable of sustaining the concentrated human habitation placed upon it.

When septic tanks were improperly installed in non-porous soil in a Sullivan County subdivision, raw sewage bubbled up from the ground and was washed into nearby Sand Pond. This untreated waste constituted a threat of infection which forced a YMCA children's camp on the pond to curtail its water-related programs. The subdivision homeowners filed a complaint with the Environmental Protection Bureau of the state attorney general's office. After investigation, the attorney general's office sued the developer on behalf of the homeowners, asking that the court order the developer to stop the pollution and to install a sewage treatment plant. The court granted both orders and denied the developer's claim that his responsibility had ended when he sold the property.

A similar problem occurred in an Ulster County subdivision. Malfunctioning septic tanks, placed in non-porous soil in an improper manner, produced a direct flow of rancid sewage which ran next to a school and then found its way into Esopus Creek, which is famous for its purity and beloved by Catskill trout fishermen. The sewage entered the Esopus just one-half mile above the Ashokan Reservoir where water from the Esopus is impounded before it is conveyed by aqueduct to New York City for drinking purposes.

The residents of this subdivision formed a homeowners' association, notified the New York City Board of Water Supply and the Ulster County Health Department, hired an attorney, and informed the Ulster County press. When private negotiations between the homeowners' association and the developer stalled, the association contacted the state attorney general's office, whose Environmental Protection Bureau investigated the problem and ordered the developer to propose a solution which would abate the open sewage hazard. The developer offered the homeowners a cash settlement, which they rejected on the grounds that she should install an efficient sewage treatment system. The attorney general's office subsequently sued the developer, seeking either $125,000 in damages or the installation of a sewage treatment plant. As causes of action, the suit alleged that the developer had not complied with the regulations of the Ulster County Health Department, that the septic tanks were not installed according to the specifications detailed on partial plans submitted to that department, and that the sewage constituted a public nuisance. The homeowners also brought a separate legal action against the developer. Both of these suits are still pending.

Residents of another subdivision, located just below the Shawangunk Mountains, experienced both water shortages and malfunctioning septic systems, raw sewage from which killed fish in nearby Otterkill Creek. Schoharie Creek, a lovely but fragile trout stream, now carries the treated waste of four different subdivisions which have been built near the Hunter Mountain ski complex, and it is threatened by several additional proposed developments.

The Basherkill Wetlands, a 3,000-acre fresh water marsh in Sullivan County, boasts many important biological and geological resources and supports several endangered species of flora and fauna. Much of this marsh was purchased by New York State in 1972 with monies available through New York's Environmental Quality Bond Act of 1972. The area was purchased by the state in order to preserve its quality and character, but subsequently private developers have proposed to create six separate subdivisions with 2,400 housing units on 1,370 acres, the treated sewage from which would eventually find its way into the "protected" waters of the Basherkill. In the face of a virtual onslaught of subdivision applications in the town of Mamakating, in whose jurisdiction the Basherkill area falls, citizens of the town persuaded their planning board to declare a sixty-day moratorium on the processing of all subdivision applications before it, during which time a study of development patterns in Mamakating would be undertaken. When, at the end of sixty days this study was not completed, the moratorium was extended for thirty more days.

Despite the serious problems it faces, the Catskill region is generally ill-equipped to deal with land speculation and development. There is no regional planning framework at present and little regional consciousness among many of its residents. In general, the repercussions of concentrated development tend to conform to geographical rather than political boundaries. In a mountainous region like the Catskills, this problem is particularly acute. The saturation of a valley or watershed with second home communities has an impact that is not limited to the towns or villages which may have approved subdivision plans.

Local controls on land development are also usually very weak or virtually nonexistent in the Catskills. As of December 1974, only 71 of the 160 towns, villages, and cities in the Catskills had zoning ordinances or planning boards with subdivision regulations or both. Some of the existing zoning ordinances, moreover, are based on urban models that allow a twenty- or thirty-fold population increase and the eventual despoilment of natural features.

TEMPORARY STATE COMMISSION TO STUDY THE CATSKILLS

The absence of adequate land use controls and the need for a regional approach to the problems involved led to the establishment by the state legislature in 1971 of a Temporary State Commission to Study the Catskills (hereafter the Catskill Study Commission). The creation of this commission was encouraged by citizens in the Catskills who had taken note of the work done by the Adirondack Study Commission and felt that the Catskills were equally worthy of study and protection.

There are, however, significant differences between the Catskill Study Commission and the Adirondack Study Commission. The latter was a gubernatorial commission in which the governor appointed all of the commissioners and personally received all findings. The governor's office very strongly supported the commission and actively participated in the effort to enact legislation creating the Adirondack Park Agency, to focus this agency's mandate on the creation of binding land use plans for public and private lands, and to get the private land use plan through the state legislature.

The Catskill Study Commission is, by contrast, a legislative commission which was created by and is responsible to the New York State legislature. Six of its nine commissioners were appointed by the legislature, while the other three were appointed by the governor. The commission submitted an interim report of its activities and recommendations to the legislature on March 31, 1974, and submitted final findings and recommendations in the spring of 1975. In general, the Catskill Study Commission has not received the kind of politically powerful support that was forthcoming for the Adirondacks and has not been characterized by the same degree of commitment and leadership that was evident in the earlier commission.

The mandate of the Catskill Study Commission also differed significantly from that of the Adirondack Study Commission. Whereas Governor Rockefeller directed the commissioners he appointed to study the Adirondacks to scrutinize closely several narrow and specific questions aimed at defining management and development policies within the large Adirondack Park, the Catskill Study Commission's mandate was much broader and more vaguely worded. It encompassed examination of the natural resources, cultural resources, social organizations, economy, and general well-being of rural communities within an extremely diverse region including both the Catskill Park and the surrounding Catskill region. The commission was charged to study ways to protect the Catskills from unplanned population growth and "measures to be taken by local governments to assure that the development of private lands is consistent with long range plans." Based on this study, it was charged to make recommendations to the legislature.[2]

After considerable organizational delays, the Catskill Study Commission and its administrative staff began work in February of 1973. In their first six months of work, they reported that they met with 100 different organizations. They also made contracts with independent research groups for studies, including an updating of the Catskill portion of the New York State Land Use and Natural Resources Inventory, a survey of the attitudes of Catskill residents toward land use planning and regional planning, and exploration from a regional perspective of the following topics: The Catskill resort industry; transportation; unique natural areas; agriculture; forestry; industrial development; subdivisions; water resources; wildlife management; and land uses and their relative impacts on taxes.

In its interim report submitted to the state legislature on March 31, 1974, the Catskill Study Commission documented "the increasing menace of uncontrolled growth" in the Catskills and identified this menace as a regional problem. But while the interim report added to the fund of information on the region, it failed to provide any strong, promising recommendations regarding how this critical situation could be effectively met. The following are several of the explanations which the commission offered for its failure to take a more decisive stand:

1. Only in its final report, due March 1975, would the commission offer "comprehensive recommendations" on "more comprehensive and fundamental legislative questions."
2. Detailed studies, then underway, would suggest draft recommendations to which public response would be elicited before the final recommendations were prepared.
3. Enabling legislation already existed through which local governments could adopt strong land use controls.

The original legislation establishing the Catskill Study Commission provided that the commission would submit its final report on March 31, 1975, and would terminate its activities at that time. In

March 1975, however, the legislature extended the existing term of the commission through July 1, 1975, to give itself time to review proposed legislation dealing with the question of whether the commission's life should be extended for several more years. The commission actually submitted its recommendations to the legislature in April 1975. The report setting out these recommendations was based on the preliminary report released for discussion purposes by the commission in February 1975.

The central recommendations made by the commission were that a regional land use program and an economic development program be developed for the Catskill region. It was proposed (1) that the legislature extend the life of the Catskill Study Commission, authorizing it to develop these two programs by 1977, and (2) that a permanent regional body be established by the legislature to implement the programs developed.

The commission recommended that the regional land use program include both a state lands master plan and a private land use program. The former would be developed in conjunction with the New York State Department of Environmental Conservation and other state agencies to guide use and management of the state lands in the Catskills. The latter would (1) define critical areas and areas of greater than local concern, in which the permanent regional body should carry out review of development projects, and (2) establish *minimum* performance standards for local and county governments.

The proposed economic development program would identify both areas where economic growth and development are most desirable and types of development that should be encouraged. Examples of the latter suggested in the report were tourism, forest products, and agriculture.

In addition, the commission also recommended that a moratorium be established on the location of nuclear plants in the Catskill region until the safety question is better defined and understood. Further, the commission took a strong stand against any further exportation of water from the Catskill region.

In mid-April 1975 it is impossible to predict how the legislature will respond to the recommendations of the Catskill Study Commission. Citizens who are concerned about the region will need to find out what actions are taken and what plans are made for the future. It is to be hoped that the search for an effective regional approach to the land development problems of the Catskill region is neither abandoned nor ineptly carried out.

CITIZEN ACTION

It is very important that all citizens who have an interest in the Catskill region or who are concerned about the development problems existing there express their concerns to the Catskill Study Commission during its life span. Strong public support is needed to push for the development of environmentally protective measures and effective regional land use controls in the Catskills.

The following is the commission's address:

> Temporary State Commission to Study the Catskills
> Rexmere Park Hotel
> Stamford, N.Y. 12167, Telephone: (607) 652–7512

A good way to express concern for the Catskills is to join and work with the Catskill Center for Conservation and Development, a citizens' organization founded in 1969 to serve as a base for concerted citizen action in behalf of the Catskills. In 1970 it conceived the idea of working to get a state commission to study the Catskills, and it supported the bill which implemented this idea. Three of the nine commissioners of the Catskill Study Commission are on the board of directors of the Catskill center.

The center conducts a monthly "Catskill Forum" at various locations throughout the area to provide an opportunity for exchange of viewpoints on vital regional issues. In the summer, it sponsors an intern program for graduate students specializing in such fields as land use planning, resource management, forestry, recreational development, and agriculture. The studies produced by these interns contribute to the creation of a new land use ethic for the region. The following is the address of this important organization:

> The Catskill Center for Conservation
> and Development
> Hobart, N.Y. 13788

Several environmental organizations have formed Catskill committees and have passed resolutions supporting Catskill regional planning. The Adirondack Mountain Club, the Sierra Club (Atlantic Chapter), and the Environmental Planning Lobby are three organi-

zations which are actively involved with the problems of the Catskills. Their addresses follow:

> The Adirondack Mountain Club
> 172 Ridge Street
> Glens Falls, N.Y. 12801[3]

> Sierra Club
> (Atlantic Chapter)
> 50 West 40th Street
> New York, N.Y. 10018

> Environmental Planning Lobby
> 211 East 43rd Street
> New York, N.Y. 10017

Active work for any of these groups could be a strong way of supporting the Catskills as a region whose natural and cultural character
should be preserved.

In local areas of the Catskills, residents should press for wise
planning and the institution of careful control over land development, and work actively with local and county planning boards.

NEW YORK CITY WATERSHED LANDS IN THE CATSKILLS

There is a special set of rules and regulations affecting land use
in a large section of the Catskills of which citizens concerned about
the region should be aware: The rules and regulations which protect
the New York City water supply from contamination.

New York City receives almost 90 percent of its water supply
from streams and rivers in the Catskills. Rain and snow that fall in
Catskill watershed areas drain into waterways which are impounded
by dams to form artificial lakes or reservoirs. This impounded water
is then conveyed through pipes and aqueducts to serve the needs of
New York City.

There are three Catskill watershed systems, comprising five
reservoirs. They are:

1. The Catskill system, including the Schoharie and Ashokan
reservoirs.

2. The East Delaware system, including the Pepacton reservoir which flows into the Rondout reservoir.

3. The West Delaware system, including the Cannonsville reservoir which also flows into the Rondout reservoir.

New York City owns and maintains all of these reservoirs, as well as access roads and additional properties around reservoir perimeters.

Rules and Regulations

The Public Health Law of New York State establishes that the New York City Environmental Protection Administration (hereafter the city EPA) and Board of Water Supply (hereafter BWS) may make rules and regulations, subject to the approval of the state Department of Health, "for the protection from contamination of any or all public supplies of potable waters and their sources within the state where the same constitute a part of the source of the public water supply of said city."[4]

The current rules and regulations drawn up under this provision were approved by the state Department of Health in 1953.[5] Revision of these regulations is presently being considered. BWS has jurisdiction over rule making and enforcement involving New York City water supply sources during the construction of water supply facilities—such as dams, reservoirs, or roads. Upon completion of these facilities, jurisdiction is transferred to the city EPA, which maintains offices at all Catskill reservoirs and must approve almost all development in watersheds producing water for New York City. The regulations protecting this water supply from contamination provide (1) that city approval must be obtained prior to the alteration of any existing sewage disposal system or construction of any new system within the watershed jurisdiction; and (2) that systems must operate in accordance with approved plans.

The New York City regulations establish limiting distances within which activities that might contaminate water supply sources cannot take place. For example, current regulations do not permit the disposal of sewage within 250 feet of any spring, marsh, water course, or reservoir draining into the city's reservoirs, unless by means of an approved sewage disposal plant or a privy connected to an approved sewage disposal system by a watertight pipe. City officials can grant variances to such setback requirements only upon determination that the New York City water supply will not thereby be endangered. Sewage which can be washed into waterways by rain or snow cannot be deposited anywhere on the ground.

Enforcement

The New York City regulations provide for fines of $25 for first violations and $50 for subsequent violations of their provisions. In addition, the New York State Public Health Law provides that for temporary contamination of water supply sources a violator is liable to prosecution for a misdemeanor for every such violation and on conviction can be punished by a fine of up to $200 and/or up to one year's imprisonment. For violations leading to permanent contamination of public water supplies, the state Department of Health may impose penalties of $200 for each violation.

When the city EPA or BWS detects a violation of the New York City regulations, notice is served on the violator. If the violator fails to comply within five days, either agency "may summarily enforce compliance" and "may summarily abate or remove the cause" of the violation and "to that end may employ such force as may be necessary and proper . . ."[6] New York City can also go to court to recover penalties or for an injunction or both.

New York City's powers to protect its water supply can serve as an effective land use control if rules and regulations are forcefully administered. There is no provision in either the city regulations or the state Public Health Law for public hearings or comment upon subdivision plans submitted to the city EPA. At the present, this agency is not concerned that the rapid population growth in the Catskills will pose a major threat to the quality of New York City's drinking water in the near future. Nonetheless, sources such as the Ulster County subdivision discussed above have directly polluted Catskill streams feeding New York City reservoirs, and the city's enforcement of its regulations has to date been less than vigorous.

Citizen Action

Concerned citizens are encouraged to get to know New York City watershed personnel in the Catskills and to monitor the review and approval of subdivisions on land within the city's water supply jurisdiction. Violations of city regulations and of state and federal laws should be publicized. Citizens should press for strict enforcement and urge that subdivisions be approved only when soils can accept subsurface sewage or when wasteloads from sewage treatment plants will not degrade the quality of Catskill streams.

NOTES

1. This is the area that lies within the scope of the Temporary State Commission to Study the Catskills established by the New York State legislature and discussed later in this chapter.

2. Catskills—Temporary Study Commission, Ch. 688, McKinney's 1971 Session Laws of New York.

3. The Adirondack Mountain Club has five chapters in the New York Metropolitan area: the Knickerbocker, the New York, the Long Island, the Ramapo, and the North Jersey, but all correspondence should be addressed to the home chapter in Glens Falls, New York.

4. N.Y. Public Health Law (PHL) §1100.

5. These rules and regulations can be found in the state compilation of regulations at 10 NYCRR Part 128. They are also separately printed and distributed by the New York City Environmental Protection Administration.

6. PHL §1102 (3) (a).

CHAPTER 8

Protection of Wetlands

WHAT IS A WETLAND?

THERE ARE BASICALLY two kinds of wetlands: (1) tidal or salt water wetlands which include banks, bogs, salt marshes, swamps, and meadows that border on, lie beneath, or are subject to tidal waters; and (2) fresh water wetlands or marshes that can be found almost anywhere there is a lake, stream, river, pond, or spring.

Tidal wetlands can be classified into two types depending on the primary type of grass found on them. The low marsh is covered with *Spartina alterniflora,* or cordgrass, while the high marsh is covered by *Spartina patens,* or salt hay. The high marsh is infrequently washed by tidal flows, usually only during lunar tides or sizable storms. The primary salt water wetlands of New York State lie on Long Island, along the coastline south from Port Chester, and on Staten Island.

WHY ARE WETLANDS IMPORTANT?

Swamps and lowlands once had a very bad name—dating back to times when malaria was a major killer—and were long considered unhealthy or wasted areas that should be filled as soon as possible.

Only in the very recent past has the great importance of wetlands been widely recognized and have efforts been launched to save the ones that are still left. Among the most important reasons for preserving wetlands are the vital roles they play in nurturing marine life, providing flood and storm protection, converting pollution into useful nutrients, accommodating sedimentation, and harboring wildlife and waterfowl.

Tidal wetlands are crucially important to marine life. They serve as nurseries for the many species of game and commercial fish that are spawned in their protective reaches, where thick plant life affords shelter from predators. The unique characteristics of wetlands— their abundant plant life, their absorption of nutrients which are washed in from the sea and down from the land, their natural processes of decay and oxidation—lead to the production of a rich growth of microscopic plants and animals which serve as food for fish, mollusks (such as clams, mussels, and oysters), and crustaceans (such as crabs). The benefits of wetlands accrue, moreover, not only to the creatures who are born and live there; they are also vital to marine life in the open sea. Much of the organic matter produced in wetlands, as well as many larger animals, is washed out to sea where it supports marine life that does not itself inhabit the wetlands. Approximately two-thirds of Atlantic fish are dependent at some point in their life cycle on the existence of wetlands.[1] The significance of this fact for the fisheries of New York State in particular and of the East Coast in general is obvious. It has been estimated that a single acre of tidal wetlands yields 535 pounds of fish a year in catches in coastal waters or at sea.[2]

Abundant growth of plant and animal life also takes place in fresh water wetlands in a similar sort of natural chain. In New York State such fresh water fish as the pickerel, the bass, the crappie, the perch, and the sunfish all thrive in the waters of wetlands, while the crawfish and many types of minnows and insects live among the bulrushes and reeds.

The capacity of tidal wetlands to absorb and store water makes them a natural buffer which protects upland and developed areas from storm tides and floods and retards erosion. Coastal wetlands can store as much as 300,000 gallons of water per acre and are flexible enough to withstand wave surges which would tear apart artificial breakwaters.[3] The same ability to absorb and hold water makes the fresh water wetland invaluable in flood control.

Wetlands, both tidal and fresh water, serve as natural biological and chemical oxidation basins in which organic runoff and pollution are converted into useful nutrients. The vast quantities of oxygen necessary for this process come from the photosynthesis process which takes place in the wetland's thriving plant life. Wetlands also serve as settling and filtering basins for silt and other organic matter which would otherwise obstruct streams, channels, and harbors.

The tidal wetlands of Long Island have been described as "the most important coastal waterfowl area in the North Atlantic states."[4] During the spring and fall over twenty-five species of migratory birds rest and feed in these areas. Numerous other species breed and live there. Fresh water wetlands also provide homes and nesting areas for many birds of the state, such as the hooded merganser and the colorful wood duck.

In addition to these natural and economic values, wetlands also provide direct benefits, such as open space and recreational areas. In New York State, tidal wetlands comprise a large portion of the remaining open space and unspoiled natural areas along the crowded coastline. They, and fresh water wetlands as well, offer recreational space and settings for thousands of fishermen, hunters, bird watchers, campers, trappers, and hikers each year.

HOW ARE WETLANDS DESTROYED?

Destruction of wetlands occurs by direct and indirect means. Directly, wetlands are destroyed when they are filled with garbage, dirt, rocks, tree stumps, and other refuse. Indirectly, they are destroyed by the encroachment of oil, sewage, and industrial waste. Also, a roadway, dock, dike, dam, causeway, channel, or other man-made incursion can cause the gradual erosion or destruction of a wetland which no longer receives the proper nutrients or which no longer can withstand the onslaught of current or waves.

Runoff pesticides from agricultural spraying and mosquito control can also cause serious damage in wetlands. Such pesticides kill not only the target insects, but also have a pernicious effect on exposed birds and fish. The birds can no longer lay fertile eggs, while the fish build up the pesticides in their tissues. Such affected fish, when they leave the protection of marshes and inlets, are in turn eaten by larger fish who also store the poisons—in a chain that eventually leads to human consumption of contaminated fish.

Whether direct or indirect, destruction of wetlands in the United States as a whole and in New York State in particular has been extremely efficient. It has been estimated that in colonial times New York State had about one million acres of wetlands. By 1955, it had less than 500,000 and was continuing to lose them at the rate of about 3 percent per year.[5] In 1936 the South Shore of Long Island alone had 30,000 acres of tidal wetlands. In 1967, only 16,000 were left— in only 30 years 14,000 acres had been lost.[6]

THE TIDAL WETLANDS ACT OF NEW YORK STATE

As far as tidal or salt water wetlands in New York State are concerned, powerful protective measures are set out in the state's Tidal Wetlands Act, which went into effect on September 1, 1973.[7] Stating that "tidal wetlands constitute one of the most vital and productive areas of our natural world," this act establishes that it is "the public policy of this state to preserve and protect tidal wetlands, and to prevent their despoliation and destruction, giving due consideration to the reasonable economic and social development of the state." Although "economic and social development" are thus given due notice, the act's strong affirmation of the importance of tidal wetlands, its full descriptions of the different ways in which they are valuable, the absence of further emphasis on development, and the strength of its protective provisions make clear that the paramount concern of the Tidal Wetlands Act is the preservation of wetlands.

The act basically provides for:

1. A *moratorium* on all alterations of tidal wetlands, beginning September 1, 1973, and extending until the adoption of land use regulations called for by the act—unless a hardship permit for a specific alteration has been granted by the commissioner of environmental conservation.

2. An *inventory* of all tidal wetlands in New York State.

3. *Land use regulations* to govern uses of the inventoried wetlands through the establishment of a permit system.

4. The development by the New York State Department of Environmental Conservation (DEC) and local governments of a *program and cooperative agreements for the protection of wetlands.*

5. Measures for *enforcement,* including specific penalties for violations.

Public hearings are mandatory in many aspects of the implementation of the act by DEC.

The act does not apply at all to any wetlands appropriated by the state under the power of eminent domain. Wetlands acquired by the state through other means, such as purchases or donations, are regulated by the act.

1. Moratorium

After September 1, 1973, and up to the effective date of the land use regulations to be adopted for the protection of inventoried wetlands, the act states that no person may "alter the state of any tidal wetland" unless he or she has first received a permit from DEC. This prohibition also applies to any area immediately adjacent to a tidal wetland which DEC deems necessary to protect in order to carry out the act. The final moratorium regulations which DEC belatedly released in June 1974 state that unless the commissioner of environmental conservation determines otherwise in a particular case, an "adjacent area" includes lands that "extend for a distance of 300 feet in any direction landward from the landward boundary of the tidal wetland or to an elevation of 10 feet above mean sea level, whichever is closer to such boundary."[8] In a particular case, such an adjacent area may be determined by the commissioner to extend for a farther distance if he finds that "one or more activities on the lands in question may directly or indirectly cause an alteration to the existing state of such tidal wetland."

"Alter" is defined by the regulations to include the performance of any activity "which directly or indirectly may have a significant adverse effect on the existing condition of any tidal wetland. . ."[9] Such activities include but are not limited to draining, dredging, excavation and removal of natural products, dumping, filling, erection of structures or construction of roads, and driving of pilings or erecting other obstructions. Excluded from regulation are "[o]rdinary and necessary maintenance and repair of existing structures and areas, including but not limited to docks, piers, wharves, pilings, dolphins, and paved areas . . . where such activity does not directly or indirectly have a significant adverse effect on the existing condition of such wetland." Also excluded from regulation under the act are the depositing and removal of natural products in the process of "recreational or commercial fishing, shellfishing, aquaculture, hunting, or trapping."

To obtain a permit during the moratorium, a person must show that hardships have been imposed upon him and DEC must determine that the action in question is not contrary to the policy and provisions of the act. A public hearing must be held within thirty days of the receipt by DEC of the petition for a permit. Notice of this hearing must be published in at least two newspapers which have general circulation in the area in which the wetland involved is located. DEC regulations make broad provisions for public participation in such hearings during the moratorium period. Namely, anyone who files properly can become a party to a hearing with the right to cross-examine witnesses, and even those who have not filed notices of appearance may be (and usually are) allowed to intervene at the hearing.

Once a permit is granted, it may be revoked if any of its terms are violated. Any aggrieved person may seek judicial review of a DEC decision under Article 78 of the Civil Practice Law and Rules.[10]

2. Inventory

DEC is charged to prepare an inventory of all tidal wetlands in the state, using photographic and cartographic techniques which will provide clear and accurate maps of the boundaries of these wetlands. Upon completion of a tentative boundary map for a particular area, DEC must hold a public hearing "in order to afford an opportunity for any person to propose additions [to] or deletions from such map." Public notice of this hearing must be published at least once, not more than thirty days or fewer than ten days before the hearing date, in at least two newspapers of general circulation in the area where the wetland is located. After the hearing DEC must establish the final boundaries of the wetland, and then file a copy of the map delineating these in the office of the clerk of the county in which the wetland is located. These boundary maps must be available to the public for examination. Any person who is aggrieved by the final DEC decision may seek judicial review under Article 78 of the Civil Practice Law and Rules.

The statewide tidal wetlands inventory must be readjusted from time to time when it is necessary to reflect such natural changes as erosion and accretion and also such changes as have occurred as a result of permits granted under the Act.

DEC completed taking the aerial photographs needed for the inventory in October 1974. Actual maps based on these photographs are being processed. Release of tentative boundary maps by DEC is expected in the spring and summer of 1975.

3. Land Use Regulations

Once the inventory is completed, DEC must adopt regulations governing uses of land in the inventoried tidal wetlands. These regulations must take into consideration "the present and potential value of the particular wetland for marine food production, as a wildlife habitat, as an element of flood and storm control, and as a source of recreation, education and research." DEC must determine what uses are compatible with these values and prepare land use regulations that permit only such compatible uses. Once established, "no permits may be granted by any local body, nor shall construction or activity take place at variance with these regulations." When a tidal wetland is placed under a land use regulation restricting its use, this will be deemed a limitation on the use of the land for the purposes of property tax valuation.

It will probably be mid-1975 before these land use regulations are issued in final form by DEC. There is no specific provision in the law requiring a public hearing on the regulations before their adoption, but one will be held.

The list of activities that will, by statute, require a permit under the land use regulations is very comprehensive. Those activities subject to regulation include:

any form of draining, dredging, excavation, and removal either directly or indirectly, of soil, mud, sand, shells, gravel or other aggregate from any tidal wetland;

any form of dumping, filling, or depositing, either directly or indirectly, of any soil, stones, sand, gravel, mud, rubbish, or fill of any kind;

the erection of any structures or roads, the driving of any pilings or placing of any other obstructions, whether or not changing the ebb and flow of the tide; and

any other activity within or immediately adjacent to inventoried wetlands which may substantially impair or alter the natural condition of the tidal wetland area.

Whenever dredging or filling of navigable waters is proposed or the reconstruction or repair of certain dams and docks *and* such activity would substantially affect tidal wetlands, permission must be obtained under this act as well as under any other applicable law.[11]

The following activities are excluded from regulation:

The depositing or removal of the natural products of the tidal wetlands by recreational or commercial fishing, shellfishing, aquaculture, hunting, or trapping . . .

Activities, orders, and regulations of the department of health or of units of local governments with respect to matters of public health . . .

As has already been mentioned, lands appropriated by the state under the power of eminent domain are not subject to any of the provisions of the act.

Applicants for permits to carry out any of the activities regulated by the act must apply in writing and submit maps and plans to DEC. They must show that the activity proposed "will be in complete accord with the policies and provisions of the Act." A public hearing, at which anyone may be heard, must take place no sooner than thirty days and no later than sixty days after DEC receives the application. Public notice of this hearing must be published in at least two newspapers of general circulation in the area where the affected wetland is located. All applications, maps, and related documents must be available for public inspection at the regional DEC office serving the area.

DEC is empowered to grant, deny, or issue conditional permits. It may also suspend or revoke permits when activities do not conform to conditions set forth in the permit, go beyond the scope of the work proposed in the application, or do not comply with the terms and conditions set forth in the application.

Any person aggrieved by a DEC decision regarding a permit to carry out any of the activities regulated by the act may seek judicial review under Article 78 of the Civil Practice Law and Rules. If a court should find that a particular DEC decision effects a taking of property without due compensation, and thus violates both state and federal constitutions, the court may—at the election of the commissioner of environmental conservation— either set aside this DEC decision or require the commissioner to acquire the wetlands or whatever rights in them are deemed by the court to have been taken, proceeding under the power of eminent domain.[12] In simpler terms, if the court finds that a taking has occurred, the commissioner of environmental conservation has the option of (1) nullifying the DEC decision in question; or (2) actually purchasing the land or particular rights to it, proceeding under the power of eminent domain.

4. Program and Cooperative Agreements for the Protection of Wetlands

The act provides that when the inventory is completed, DEC must work with local government officials to establish a program for the protection of tidal wetlands and may enter into cooperative agreements with any of these governments for the purpose of preserving, maintaining, and enhancing tidal wetlands.

5. Enforcement

Any person who violates provisions of the act dealing with regulated activities is guilty of a misdemeanor and subject to fines of $500 to $1,000 for the first violation and $1,000 to $2,000 for each subsequent violation. Violators are also liable to the state for the full cost of restoring wetlands damaged by their activities. In the case of a continuing violation, each day's continuance is considered a separate and distinct offense, and is thus subject to a separate fine.

The state attorney general is responsible for prosecuting violators of the act, either on his own initiative or at the request of DEC. The attorney general may also seek an injunction of any violation or threatened violation.

DEC and the attorney general can also take action to abate the pollution of wetlands. DEC may restrict or forbid solid waste disposal, deep well disposal, or liquid waste disposal that pollutes a tidal wetland. When pesticides, chemical products, or fertilizer residues are the pollutants involved, the commissioner of environmental conservation "shall confer with other appropriate public officials to limit the use of such substances at their source. . . ."

In the tidal wetlands, DEC can also make recourse to other state laws prohibiting pollution, such as the law protecting shellfish or fish under which it is illegal for any substances injurious to these forms of marine life to "be placed or allowed to run into waters of the state in the marine district."[13]

OTHER STATE LAWS

While New York State has taken steps to provide protection for its *tidal* wetlands, it has not yet passed any special legislation to protect its *fresh water* wetlands.* It has been possible for the state

*A new fresh water wetlands act was passed just as this book was going to press. See p. xiv of the Introduction.

to purchase some fresh water wetlands with monies made available through the Environmental Quality Bond Act of 1972.

As far as defensive protective measures are concerned, however, only scattered provisions of state law are available. Those who are involved in an effort to save a threatened fresh water wetland should be ready to look in all directions for legal tools. They should explore controls existing at all levels of government—local, county, state, and federal. At the state level, provisions of the Environmental Conservation Law (ECL), which is enforced by DEC, may be relevant. In particular, all opportunities for public hearings held by DEC under this law (as discussed in full in Chapter 5) should be pursued. The effect of a proposed land development project on a wetland is a very important aspect of the project's environmental impact and should be fully explored in any DEC hearing concerning the issuance of any permit for such development.

There are a number of state statutes dealing with water pollution, stream disruption, and fish and wildlife protection which might be helpful in attempts to forestall destruction of fresh water wetlands. The following are examples of such laws, the enforcement of which is the responsibility of DEC under the enforcement provisions of the ECL:

Polluting Streams Prohibited (ECL §11–0503)

Under this law no deleterious or poisonous substance may be thrown or allowed to run into any waters, private or public, in quantities injurious to fish, to protected wildlife or waterfowl inhabiting such waters, or to the propagation of these species. The statute further prohibits dumping soil or refuse into any stream or its tributaries which are inhabited by trout.

Throwing Gas, Tar, or Refuse into Public Waters (ECL §71–3503)

This statute establishes that it is a misdemeanor for anyone to deposit any noxious, offensive, or poisonous substance into any public waters, or into any sewer or stream running into public waters.

State Pollutant Discharge Elimination System (SPDES) (ECL §17–0801 et seq.)

This legislation and DEC's implementation of it is described in detail in Chapter 5. Basically the SPDES program requires a permit for all discharges of pollutants via a point source into the classified waters of the state (which include both streams and groundwater). This state program was developed in response to the federal pollutant discharge system which was established under the Federal Water Pollution Control Act Amendments of 1972,[14] but DEC has not yet received approval to grant permits required under the federal law on behalf of the federal Environmental Protection Agency.

Protection of Water (ECL §15–0501; §15–0503; §15–0505)

These three statutes deal with disturbances of protected streams, dredging and filling of navigable waters, and construction of dams and docks. Their specific provisions, the permits they require, and their implementation by DEC are discussed in full in Chapter 5. With respect to wetlands, it should be especially noted that under the statute prohibiting disturbances of protected streams without a permit, small ponds or lakes with a surface area at mean low water level of ten acres or less which are located in the course of a stream are considered part of the stream and are subject to regulation. The dredging and filling statute also specifically applies not only to navigable waters of the state, but also to marshes, estuaries, tidal marshes, and wetlands that are adjacent to such waters.

Interference with Fish and Wildlife (ECL §11–0505)

This law prohibits the destruction of a beaver dam, house, or den or a muskrat house or den, or any structure constructed by a muskrat in which it can take shelter. These are structures that are common in wetland areas.

Private Rights in Waters (ECL §15–0701)

Under certain circumstances a riparian property owner or lessee with an interest in a natural watercourse or lake has the right to go to court when an alteration of that watercourse or lake causes or would cause him or his property unreasonable harm. Under this statute, "harm" means (1) interference with a present use of the water or with present enjoyment of riparian land, whether or not such interference has caused or will ever cause measurable financial loss; or (2) a decrease in the market value of riparian land. Interference with the present enjoyment of riparian land may be established by proof that the alteration in question is or would immediately render riparian land owned or occupied by the complainant less suitable or useful for the purpose or purposes to which he is presently devoting it. Admissible evidence includes that which indicates a diminution in "the desirability for recreational purposes, or the natural beauty of the body of water to which the land owned or occupied by the complainant is riparian."

Possible legal actions include suits for damages, actions for injunctive relief, and actions for a declaratory judgment defining the extent of one's rights and privileges, as well as those of others.

THE FEDERAL COASTAL ZONE MANAGEMENT ACT OF 1972

A number of federal laws exist which might have bearing on the protection of wetlands, but the law which focuses most directly on this problem is the Coastal Zone Management Act of 1972.[15] This act acknowledged that:

> [t]he increasing and competing demands upon the lands and waters of our coastal zone occasioned by population growth and economic development . . . have resulted in the loss of living marine resources, wildlife, nutrient-rich areas, permanent and adverse changes to ecological systems, decreasing open space for public use, and shoreline erosion . . .

In the light of these losses, Congress established that it would now be national policy "to preserve, protect, develop, and, where possible, to restore or enhance the resources of the Nation's coastal zone for this and succeeding generations."

Under this act, the "coastal zone" means the coastal waters and adjacent shorelands of the coastal states, and "includes transitional and intertidal areas, salt marshes, wetlands, and beaches." The coastal states include not only those states which border on the oceans or bodies of salt water, but also those bordering on the Great Lakes. Thus, in New York State the coastal zone includes not only Long Island and areas bordering on sea water or estuaries, but also areas bordering on the Great Lakes (Erie and Ontario), their connecting waters, and their "estuary-type areas." The exact inland limits of the coastal zone are left to the discretion of the states, but they should include shorelands, "the uses of which have a direct and significant impact on the coastal waters."

Basically the act provides for federal grants to coastal states to develop and implement management programs for the land and water resources of their coastal zones. Application for these grants is optional. The management program developed must include the following:

1. An identification of the boundaries of the coastal zone to be subject to the program;
2. A definition of what will constitute permissible land and water uses within the zone;
3. An inventory and designation of areas of particular concern within the zone;
4. An identification of the means by which the state proposes to exert control over land and water uses;
5. Broad guidelines on priority uses in particular areas, specifically including those uses of lowest priority; and
6. A description of the organizational structure proposed to implement the management program.

The grants are made by the secretary of commerce. Program development grants covering up to two-thirds of costs are available to states for three consecutive years, and implementation grants for up to two-thirds of the cost of administering the management program are available thereafter. According to the act, the authority to make program development grants will expire on June 30, 1977. Special grants are also authorized to aid coastal states in the acquisition, development, and operation of estuarine sanctuaries to serve as natural field laboratories. Up to 50 percent of costs may be granted, to a maximum of $2 million per sanctuary.

One of the basic policies of the act is "to encourage the participation of the public" as well as of federal, state, and local governments and regional agencies, in the development of the state coastal zone management programs. The secretary of commerce cannot approve a management program which is submitted by a state unless the state has provided opportunity for full participation in the development of the program by all interested parties, public and private, and public hearings have been held during the process of development. At least thirty days' notice must be given for such hearings, and all agency materials pertinent to the hearing must be made available to the public for review and study.

In New York State the governor authorized the Office of Planning Services (OPS) to submit an application to the secretary of commerce for an initial one-year program development grant and designated OPS as the agency to carry out program development under the act. An application requesting a grant of $550,000 and promising $275,000 in state matching funds was submitted by OPS in May 1974 and was approved in mid-November 1974.

New York State thus entered the Coastal Zone Management program late, and somewhat reluctantly as well. Futher difficulties ensued when OPS was terminated in March 1975, as part of a reorganization within the state government. In this process, the state legislature failed to make clear determination regarding the future of the state planning responsibilities which OPS had carried out. By mid-April 1975 it was still not clear whether these responsibilities would rest with the Division of Community Affairs of the Department of State or whether some other arrangements, such as the establishment of an independent state planning division, might be made. Thus the future administration of the Coastal Zone Management program, a state planning effort, was undetermined. These difficulties of reorganization have made execution of coastal zone planning and development of future grant proposals very difficult. It is to be hoped that once the legislative and administrative questions are resolved, work on the program can be effectively carried out.

The first-year planning program for New York State was designed to emphasize (1) determining the need, desirability, and feasibility of developing a coastal zone management program in New York State, and (2) compiling information on the state's coastal zone areas. A draft of the overall planning design was sent out for comment in January 1974 to 400 interested parties, including elected officials in coastal zone areas, regional planning boards, environmental organizations, and economic groups. As a result of responses to this distribution, special provisions were made for pilot demonstration projects in Rochester, Troy, and New York City.

In its development of Coastal Zone Management planning, OPS worked closely with DEC. Obviously, coordination of this planning effort with the work being done by DEC under the state's Tidal Wetlands Act is essential. It is noteworthy that most of the state's matching funds for the one-year program development grant sought under the Coastal Zone Management Act are provided by state funds appropriated for the inventory and mapping of tidal wetlands under the Tidal Wetlands Act.

The public participation in planning which must, by statute, take place under the Coastal Zone Management Act is very important. One significant factor of which citizens should be aware is that the state has only committed itself to applying for a one-year program development grant. Citizens thus need to give full support to the basic idea that planning and management of resources are necessary in the state's coastal zone areas, and they should press for full utilization by the state of federal funds which are available for this purpose.

A second vital area of citizen concern is the need to speak out for the protection of natural resources in coastal zone areas. As quoted above, the act emphasizes the loss of natural resources which has resulted from the competing demands on these areas occasioned by population growth and economic development, "including requirements for industry, commerce, residential development, recreation, extraction of mineral resources and fossil fuels, transportation and navigation, waste disposal, and harvesting of fish, shellfish, and other living marine resources." This emphasis is repeatedly restated in the act:

> Important ecological, cultural, historic, and esthetic values in the coastal zone which are essential to the well-being of all citizens are being irretrievably damaged or lost . . .

> Special natural and scenic characteristics are being damaged by ill-planned development that threatens these values . . .

> In light of competing demands and the urgent need to protect and to give high priority to natural systems in the coastal zone, present state and local institutional arrangements for planning and regulating land and water uses in such areas are inadequate . . .[16]

Despite this clear, basic orientation of the act toward the need to protect natural resources in coastal areas and to develop effective means of regulating development, efforts may well be made in the implementation of the act to treat special economic interests on an equal footing with environmental interests in coastal zone areas. If this happens, citizens should be quick to point out the overriding statutory emphasis on the protection of natural resources.

OTHER FEDERAL LAWS

There are other federal laws which are relevant to the protection of wetlands. The following examples deal with such varied areas as wildlife refuges, control of activities which are damaging to wetlands, flood insurance, environmental education, and environmental impact statements:

National Environmental Policy Act (NEPA) (42 U.S.C. §4321 *et seq.*)

Chapter 9 of this book is devoted to a discussion of the significance of NEPA for land use control. In brief, this act requires that federal agencies prepare environmental impact statements on all proposed activities which would significantly affect the human environment. Included among such activities are many actions which would have significant impact on wetlands. For example, a dam or dredging and filling operations proposed by the U.S. Army Corps of Engineers, any stream channelization proposed by the Soil Conservation Service of the U.S. Department of Agriculture, or any construction or expansion of highways involving federal funds would require the preparation of a NEPA environmental impact statement.

Rivers and Harbors Acts (33 U.S.C. §401 *et seq.*)

Among the provisions of this federal legislation are the requirements that permission must be obtained from the U.S. Army Corps of Engineers to carry out (1) any construction of a dam, dike, bridge, or causeway over or in any navigable water; or (2) any excavation, filling, or other modification of any lake or channel of any navigable water. These provisions, as well as the meaning of "navigable waters," are discussed in Chapter 11.

Federal Water Pollution Control Act Amendments of 1972 (33 U.S.C. §1251 *et seq.*)

This important water pollution legislation is discussed both in Chapter 5, in connection with the state SPDES permit program which has been developed in response to the federal enactment, and in Chapter 11. Under these amendments, the national goal is set forth that, wherever attainable, "water quality which provides for the protection and propagation of fish, shellfish, and wildlife, and provides for recreation in and on the water be achieved by July 1, 1983."[17] By 1985 it is the national goal that the discharge of pollutants into navigable waters be eliminated altogether.

One of the many aspects of this federal legislation is the establishment of a National Pollutant Discharge Elimination System in which permits are required for all discharges of pollutants from point sources into navigable waters. The discharge of certain hazardous substances is prohibited altogether, and the federal Environmental Protection Agency is authorized to establish effluent limitations for existing sources and standards of performance for new sources. Special effluent standards must be set for toxic substances.

A very significant provision of the 1972 amendments as far as the protection of wetlands is concerned is the requirement that a permit must be obtained from the Army Corps of Engineers for the discharge of any dredged or fill material into navigable waters. As is discussed in full in Chapter 11, these permits are required for all such discharges into navigable waters *as defined by the 1972 amendments.* Since this statute defines "navigable waters" very broadly, activities above mean high tide—the limit of Corps of Engineers' jurisdiction under traditional concepts of navigability—must be regulated. Initially, the Corps of Engineers was unwilling to accept this extension of its jurisdiction, even after two federal district courts and a federal court of appeals ruled that the requirements of the Federal Water Pollution Control Act Amendments of 1972 are not limited by traditional concepts of navigability. There are many important coastal and estuarine wetlands which are flooded periodically but lie above mean high tide, and it is essential that all protective measures set out by law for these areas be fully implemented. Consequently, the Natural Resources Defense Council brought suit to force the Army Corps of Engineers to fulfill its legal obligation to require permits for discharges of fill material in such wetland areas. This suit was upheld in March 1975.

The 1972 amendments also make broad provisions for control of water pollution through land use planning and regulation, but these provisions have not yet been effectively implemented.

National Flood Insurance Program (42 U.S.C. §4001 *et seq.*)

Federal flood insurance legislation, which has very important implications for development in wetland areas, is discussed in full in

Chapter 13. The two essential acts which comprise this legislation are the National Flood Insurance Act of 1968 and the Flood Disaster Protection Act of 1973. The former established the National Flood Insurance Program under which all flood-prone communities in the United States are to be identified and areas with special flood hazards are to be delineated. Flood insurance coverage is available in flood-prone communities only after they have qualified for the program, principally by adopting adequate land use controls regulating development in special flood hazard areas to minimize potential flood damage. The subsequent act put new teeth into this program by establishing that after July 1, 1975, no federal assistance and no loans from any financial institution supervised, regulated, or insured by the federal government will be available in any area identified as having special flood hazards unless the community in which it is located has qualified for participation in the National Flood Insurance Program.

The significance of this legislation for wetlands is considerable. It marks a dramatic reorientation in federal flood control policy. Formerly, emphasis was placed almost entirely on dam construction and dredging and filling operations which (1) involved the destruction of countless wetland areas, whose natural deterrence to flooding was then lost, and (2) encouraged development in flood plain areas. Today, a much greater appreciation of natural water patterns and the tremendous costs to the federal government of flood damage (which has not been forestalled by engineering "improvements") have led to the policy of taking effective action to bring about regulation of development in flood-prone areas.

National Wildlife Refuge System (16 U.S.C. §668dd and §715s)

The United States Fish and Wildlife Service of the Department of the Interior administers lands and waters acquired or reserved as federal wildlife refuges. Under the statute governing this system, provision is made for cash payments to counties in which such refuge areas are located. These payments are made from a fund comprised of revenues derived from the management of the areas by the Fish and Wildlife Service. Such revenues may come from the sale of animals or of agricultural or mineral products, or from fees (such as hunting fees, fishing fees, admission fees) which are charged for privileges consistent with the basic purposes of the refuge areas. After the secretary of the interior has paid from the fund all necessary expenses incurred in the revenue-producing measures, he must at the end of every fiscal year make the following payments to appropriate counties (such payments must be used by the counties only for public schools and roads):

1. In the case of reserved public lands in the National Wildlife Refuge System, each county in which such an area is located is entitled to 25 percent of the net receipts collected in that particular area.

2. In the case of areas in the system that have been acquired in fee by the United States, each county in which such an area is located is entitled to *either* (a) three-fourths of 1 percent of the cost of the area; *or* (b) 25 percent of the net receipts collected, *whichever is greater.*

If the net receipts in the fund are insufficient in a given fiscal year to pay the aggregate amount to all counties involved, the payment to each county is reduced proportionately.

This federal program offers means by which lands can be given to or acquired by the federal government and yet still provide revenue to local governments which lose their taxing power over the land once it comes under federal stewardship. Because of their abundant animal life, wetlands are prime locations for wildlife refuges. At the present time, the federal government is acquiring many small tracts of land along coastlines as part of a mini refuge program.

Endangered Species and Migratory Birds (16 U.S.C. §1531 *et seq.* and 16 U.S.C. §701 *et seq.*)

In addition to the above statutes, there are also a number of federal laws dealing with endangered species, migratory birds, and other types of wildlife, some of which inhabit wetlands and marshes. Special funds are set up to establish federal refuges, and there are protective provisions dealing with the habitats of endangered species. Whenever citizens are involved in an effort to preserve a threatened wetland, they should find out if endangered species or migratory birds live in or use the area and then explore the possibility that either federal or state law contains protective provisions for the species involved.

CITIZEN ACTION

Public awareness of the importance of wetlands and marshes is essential if remaining wetland areas are to be saved. Concerned citizens should do everything within their power to increase general appreciation of the vital natural functions which wetlands perform and to take action to avert their destruction.

With respect to the New York State Tidal Wetlands Act, there are certain specific areas in which citizen attention should be focused. First of all, there should be citizen monitoring of DEC's issuance of permits to make alterations in wetland areas, both during the moratorium period and after land use regulations are adopted. Conscientious enforcement of the act's provisions and policies should be strongly supported.

Care should be taken to keep abreast of all public hearings held pursuant to the Tidal Wetlands Act. In particular, hearings held to review the inventory and mapping of the boundaries of specific wetlands should not be missed. The act's definition of what constitutes a wetland is not precise; therefore, public vigilance is necessary to assure that all areas requiring protection are included in the wetland areas for which land use regulations are to be enacted.

Violations of the Tidal Wetlands Act should be reported to DEC and to the state attorney general's office, which is responsible for prosecuting violators (either on its own initiative or at the request of DEC). The Environmental Protection Bureau of the state attorney general's office has taken an active interest in the preservation of tidal wetlands and works closely with DEC in this regard.

The preservation of fresh water wetlands requires considerable citizen resourcefulness since there is no existing state law specifically protecting this kind of wetland. To defend these vital natural resources, citizens must be prepared to explore all possibilities for control at all levels of government. In particular, when a proposed development would threaten a fresh water wetland, citizens should take full advantage of all opportunities for DEC hearings provided for in the Environmental Conservation Law and should press DEC to hold a full environmental impact hearing on the project (under Part 615 of its regulations).[18]

To strengthen their position, citizens should marshal as much public support as possible and seek the advice and assistance of as many experts (e.g., sanitary engineers, hydrologists, fishermen, economists, lawyers) as they can find. Many citizens' groups have found local colleges to be an excellent place to look for experts. Professors, instructors, graduate students, and undergraduates have participated in various kinds of environmental studies for citizens' organizations. Even high school biology classes have made important contributions to needed research in some areas.

All possibilities of establishing wetlands as wildlife refuges and/ or educational field laboratories should be explored. Several state and federal statutes through which assistance might be sought for such uses have been discussed in this chapter. Citizens might also seek to have their own local government establish a wetlands preserve. For example, in 1970 the town of Hempstead on Long Island designated a fifty-two-acre salt water marsh as its Marine Nature Study Area. In this area, the town's Conservation and Waterways Department has developed ways of explaining and demonstrating the value of wetlands both to school groups and to the general public. In 1973 alone, over 14,000 people visited Hempstead's Marine Nature Study Area.

Citizen action is also needed to press for the development of a sound state program under the federal Coastal Zone Management Act. Citizens should press the state to apply for program development grants which are available to it, to provide ample opportunities for citizen participation in the developmental process, and to formulate an effective management program, for which further federal funding is available. Public support for the protection of natural resources in coastal zone areas—a goal repeatedly emphasized by the act—should be marshalled to combat claims made by development, industrial, and commercial concerns that their special interests deserve equal consideration under the act. Attention should be given to the importance of coordinating planning under the Coastal Zone Management Act with the implementation of the Tidal Wetlands Act. Above all, citizens should be alert to the fact that the federal Coastal Zone Management Act mandates full public participation in planning.

In summary, wetlands and marshes are indisputably one of the most vital of our natural resources, yet they have been subjected to relentless destruction. Citizens should, therefore, be ready to explore all avenues through which remaining wetlands can be protected and enhanced.

NOTES

1. Denis Binder, "Taking versus Reasonable Regulation: A Reappraisal in Light of Regional Planning and Wetlands," 25 *U. Fla. L. Rev.* 1, 21 (1972).

2. R.H. Stroud and P.A. Douglas, eds., *A Symposium on the Biological Significance of Estuaries* (Washington, D.C.: Sports Fishing Institute, 1971), Introduction.

3. Binder, p. 19.

4. Joel S. O'Connor and Orville W. Terry, *The Marine Wetlands of Nassau and Suffolk Counties* (Marine Sciences Research Center, State University of New York, 1972), p. 19, quoting U.S. Department of the Interior, "Progress Report on Waterfowl Resources of the Great South Bay Region" (1969), p. 2.

5. James E. Forbes, "Environmental Deterioration and Declining Species," *The Conservationist* (August–September 1970): 21.

6. Peter L. Johnson, *Wetlands Preservation* (New York: Open Space Institute, 1969), p. 3.

7. N.Y. Environmental Conservation Law (ECL) §25–0101 *et seq.*

8. 6 NYCRR §660.1(c).

9. 6 NYCRR §660.1(b).

10. *See* Glossary.

11. *See* Chapter 5 for a discussion of permits required under DEC's stream protection program and Chapter 11 for a discussion of permits which must be obtained from the U.S. Army Corps of Engineers.

12. *See* Chapter 2 for a discussion of the "takings" issue.

13. ECL §13–0345.

14. *See* Chapter 11 and p. 160–161 of this chapter.

15. 16 U.S.C. §1451 *et seq.*

16. 16 U.S.C. §1451 (e)–(g).

17. 33 U.S.C. §1251(a) (2).

18. *See* Chapter 5 for a discussion of DEC hearings and review procedures.

CHAPTER 9

The Significance of NEPA for Land Use Control

T HE NATIONAL Environmental Policy Act (NEPA),[1] which was signed into law on January 1, 1970, laid the foundation for environmental analysis and regulation by the federal government.* Every federal agency proposing an action that will significantly affect the quality of the human environment must prepare a statement assessing the environmental impact of the proposed action. Since this crucial requirement applies to all federal agencies and requires a broad analysis of proposed agency actions, it provides an effective means of evaluating the environmental impact of expenditures of federal funds and the granting of licenses, permits, and other federal privileges. What is more, it lays this information not only before federal agencies, Congress, and the President, but before the public as well. To be sure, the enforcement of the act has required vigilant monitoring by environmental organizations, but the judicial review which has resulted from extensive litigation has served to strengthen the act.

The act sets out generalized goals for environmental policy in the country but with the caveat that this policy is to be achieved by means "consistent with other essential considerations of national policy." Within these constraints it is federal policy to:

---

*Just as this book was going to press the New York State legislature passed a "little NEPA" act, establishing evironmental impact statement requirements for state and local agencies. See p. xiv of the Introduction.

(1) fulfill the responsibilities of each generation as trustee of the environment for succeeding generations;
(2) assure for all Americans safe, healthful, productive, and esthetically and culturally pleasing surroundings;
(3) attain the widest range of beneficial uses of the environment without degradation, risk to health or safety, or other undesirable and unintended consequences;
(4) preserve important historic, cultural, and natural aspects of our national heritage, and maintain, wherever possible, an environment which supports diversity and variety of individual choice;
(5) achieve a balance between population and resource use which will permit high standards of living and a wide sharing of life's amenities; and
(6) enhance the quality of renewable resources and approach the maximum attainable recycling of depletable resources.

These broad aims of policy do not dictate a particular result when a federal agency addresses an individual problem. Instead, the act requires a case-by-case analysis of federal agency actions which requires the weighing and balancing of environmental effects before an agency acts. It is the formal requirement of this particularized impact analysis that lies at the heart of the act.

The required NEPA environmental impact statements must include the following elements:

(i)   the environmental impact of the proposed action,
(ii) any adverse environmental effects which cannot be avoided should the proposal be implemented,
(iii) alternatives to the proposed action,
(iv) the relationship between local short-term uses of man's environment and the maintenance and enhancement of long-term productivity, and
(v)   any irreversible and irretrievable commitments of resources which would be involved in the proposed action should it be implemented.[2]

NEPA applies to federal agencies no matter how their actions significantly affect the environment. The act obviously applies to situations where a federal agency directly undertakes the alteration of the environment through the construction of a project. For example, a major Post Office development or the building of a flood control dam by the Army Corps of Engineers requires that a NEPA impact analysis be undertaken. NEPA also applies where federal funds are expended by state or local governments. The federal Department of Transportation which reviews plans for federal-aid highways and grants funds to the states for their construction must file NEPA impact statements as part of its approval of proposed highway programs.

An impact analysis under the act must also be done where a federal agency licenses the activities of private parties. Thus, before the Nuclear Regulatory Commission grants a license for a nuclear plant, it must evaluate not only radiological questions but also such matters as the effect of the cooling system of the plant on waterways and aquatic life. Federal agencies which are only indirectly involved in environmental questions have also been required to file NEPA statements as part of their process of consideration and review. For instance, the Interstate Commerce Commission has been required by the courts to prepare NEPA statements on proposed abandonment of railway lines.[3]

At the present time, the only major general exemption from the NEPA statement requirement is contained in the Federal Water Pollution Control Act Amendments of 1972[4] which excuse the federal Environmental Protection Agency (EPA) from filing NEPA statements on discharge permits (except those for new sources) authorized by that act.

The threshold of actions that will "significantly affect the quality of the human environment" and thus bring NEPA into play is impossible to define, but the courts have interpreted the phrase liberally. For instance, the construction of a sixteen-story apartment building has required a NEPA statement.[5]

The act requires more than a narrow analysis of the proposed action. The courts have ruled that one of the fundamental aims of the statute is to provide information on which rational decisions can be made, not only by the federal agency involved, but also by the President, the Congress, and the public.[6] Under this mandate, an agency must look beyond its own jurisdiction in examining alternatives to the proposed agency action. For example, an agency which is considering offshore oil drilling must consider alternatives (such as changes in the oil import quota system) over which it does not have control.[7] Agencies have not been allowed to obscure the total environmental impact of a project by dividing it into smaller undertakings. Thus the Department of Transportation was forbidden to break roads into segments, thus masking the total impact of a larger road project.[8] Similarly, the Army Corps of Engineers may be required to consider at one time its entire scheme of development for a river basin.[9]

Generally, federal agencies have also been required to prepare NEPA statements themselves to assure as far as possible that a public and impartial analysis of a proposal is made rather than the self-serving critique that might be prepared by an applicant for a license or for funds.[10] Federal agencies which grant funds to state or local governments or license the activities of private parties usually rely on the recipient of the grant or license to make the initial collection of data and the preliminary environmental analysis. The extent to which the federal agency must rework this material is not clearly defined, but certainly some independent judgment and not simply a blind rubber-stamping of the work of others is required. This issue has been most thoroughly tested out in the case of highway construction projects where the federal Department of Transportation has relied heavily on the work of state highway departments.[11] As far as New York State is concerned, a recent decision of the U.S. Court of Appeals for the Second Circuit has ruled that there must be genuine federal preparation of the impact statement.[12] It is generally believed that a true federal review and fully independent decisions by federal agencies will produce the most disinterested and most environmentally sound decisions.

NEPA Statement Procedures

The Council on Environmental Quality (CEQ), which was established by the National Environmental Policy Act, is responsible for establishing the guidelines under which environmental impact statements are drawn up.[13] The provisions of these guidelines have been supplemented both by executive order and by judicial interpretations of the act.[14] The present system requires that a given federal agency prepare a draft impact statement upon which it must then seek comments from other federal, state, and local agencies with expertise in the area under analysis, and from the public. This draft statement is usually available for comment for a period of ninety days.

The CEQ guidelines establish that each agency must establish formal procedures for providing "timely public information" on its plans and programs with environmental impact. These procedures should include provisions for facilitating comments by private organizations and individuals on draft impact statements.[15] The courts have held that public notice of the availability of an impact statement must be given,[16] and the CEQ guidelines provide that public hearings should be held where appropriate.[17] Public notice of the availability of a draft statement for comment is given in the *Federal Register*. Citizens who wish to comment on a particular draft statement should take special care to make sure that they know when it becomes available. In general, public hearings are held only when required under the provisions of other statutes or when they are already an existing aspect of agency procedures.

Not only must public comment on a draft environmental impact statement be sought, but also such comment must be seriously weighed in the preparation of the final statement. In a case dealing with an interstate highway, the court held that:

> The public may also raise environmental questions by way of comment to the draft impact statement. Since the final impact statement must respond to these comments, as well as to the comments of government agencies, environmental harm which might have been overlooked by highway officials may be brought to their attention. For this reason, highway officials must give more than cursory consideration to the suggestions and comments of the public in the preparation of the final impact statement. The proper response to comments which are both relevant and reasonable is to either conduct the research necessary to provide satisfactory answers, or to refer to those places in the impact statement which provide them. If the final impact statement fails substantially to do so, it will not meet the statutory requirements.[18]

The final environmental impact statement, which the agency drafts following the comment period, must accompany the proposal through the agency review process. This review process varies enormously from agency to agency. For example, when the Nuclear Regulatory Commission licenses nuclear power plants, the commission conducts a review, modeled on court procedures, that requires testimony under oath and examination and cross-examination of witnesses. On the other hand, hearings of the Army Corps of Engineers on permits to undertake construction in navigable waters are on a legislative hearing model. Numerous position statements are allowed, but the hearings do not follow rules of evidence or permit thorough cross-examination of the agency's experts.[19]

On the basis of the final environmental impact statement and the agency review, a decision on a particular proposal is made and whatever environmental protection the agency imposes becomes part of the course of action. The courts assure that the procedural requirements of NEPA are met, but, except in clear cases of abuse, they are unwilling to substitute their judgment on substantive matters for that of an agency which is deemed expert in the matters it considers. For this reason, working within the administrative process by which the statements are drawn up and reviewed is crucial to citizens who want to influence the environmental aspects of any proposal.

How NEPA Can Be Used in Land Use Control

Since NEPA is a statute which governs the actions of federal agencies, it comes into play in land use decisions only when there is a federal presence. In contrast to air and water uses, which are subject to federal regulation notably under the Clean Air Act of 1970[20] and the Federal Water Pollution Control Act Amendments of 1972,[21] there is no comprehensive federal statute dealing with land use. Nevertheless, NEPA can be an important statute in the land use area. For instance, highways are important determinants of future development and all federally aided highway projects must pass through a NEPA review. Any dredging or filling within the waters of the United States requires a permit from the Army Corps of Engineers,[22] and thus any development involving such dredge or fill operations may undergo a NEPA analysis. These examples could be multiplied and detailed in great number. The critical fact to remember is that an important federal presence in any development scheme will bring in its train the requirement of compliance with the terms of the National Environmental Policy Act.

A case in which a large subdivision in New York State required the preparation of a NEPA statement will be discussed here to demonstrate both the applicability of the act and how its effectiveness can be lost. Then the 701 planning program of the U.S. Department of Housing and Urban Development (HUD) and the way both NEPA requirements and citizen participation provisions have been integrated into this program will be reviewed.

The Sleepy Hollow Lake subdivision. In the fall of 1970 a corporation called U.S. Properties, which was established by former principals of Boise Cascade, sent a representative into an area bordering on Murderer's Creek in Greene County, New York.[23] This agent bought options on farmland for a land development company incorporated in New York State under the name of Sleepy Hollow Lake, Inc., whose stock was wholly owned by U.S. Properties.

Sleepy Hollow Lake, Inc., proposed to subdivide two thousand acres into a $10 million second-home community. A central part of the plan was the intended construction of a seventy-foot-high dam on Murderer's Creek, a winding tributary of the Hudson River, to form a four-hundred-acre artificial lake. The land surrounding the new "Sleepy Hollow Lake" was generally to be divided into lots of approximately one-third acre, although some lots were to be larger.

During the winter of 1970–1971, the Sleepy Hollow agent met with the planning boards of the two towns and the one village within whose jurisdictions the land to be subdivided was located. A local lawyer and real estate broker was retained as the corporation's attorney. Support for the project was solicited from local politicians, with emphasis being placed on the tax benefits the development would allegedly bring. One member of the village of Athens planning board has recalled that during this period "the local politicians were telling us all about the economic benefits we would reap."[24]

In June 1971 a public hearing was held by the New York State Department of Environmental Conservation on permit applications submitted by the project. Although a number of significant criticisms of the proposals submitted were made by witnesses, including health department and DEC officials as well as the engineer retained by the county, DEC approved the project and granted the necessary permits.

Neither one of the two towns nor the village had a zoning ordinance, and although the planning boards had been studying subdivision regulations, none were then in force. Consequently, once DEC approval was granted, development of the Sleepy Hollow Lake subdivision began. Work started on the dam, as well, which now was to be eighty feet high and to retain a three-hundred-seventy-five-acre lake containing some four billion gallons of water.

After construction on the dam had commenced, the requirement under federal law that a permit be obtained from the Army Corps of Engineers to build a dam in any navigable water[25] was enforced. This permit should have been obtained prior to any work on the dam, but the developers did not make the necessary application, the Army Corps did not enforce the law at that point, and public surveillance did not reveal these failings. Thus, when the Army Corps did perceive the necessity for a permit and required an application, considerable work had already been done on the dam.

When the Army Corps began the permitting procedures, the Corps was required under NEPA to prepare an environmental impact statement on the damming of Murderer's Creek. The draft impact statement was released on August 29, 1972. This statement acknowledged that the project was already underway, the land already denuded, and an investment already committed. If the construction were to be stopped at this point, the draft stated that "the effects of the construction would either have to remain or be removed. If they were to remain, the environmental value of the area would be degraded. . . ." Consequently, construction was allowed to continue and the dam was built.

Nonetheless, in their belated environmental impact statement, the Army Corps had determined that:

> The overall development would replace forestation, convert an open creek into an impoundment with high eutrophic potential, adversely affect local wildlife, and place added loads on existing public services and facilities. Construction operations would generate noise and air pollution . . . and accelerate erosion with resulting increases of turbidity and nutrient loads in the stream.[26]

But, after the fact, the opportunity to consider whether this damage should be allowed was effectively lost.

The U.S. Department of Housing and Urban Development (HUD)

HUD is deeply involved in aiding the states and localities both with land use planning and with land development and redevelopment. The major program under which planning is fostered is the so-called "701" program which takes its name from the original section of the act in which it was passed.[27]

Under the 701 program HUD may fund a local or regional planning body for up to two-thirds of the cost of undertaking various planning activities, of which the most important is the development of a comprehensive plan through an "ongoing comprehensive planning process" which is required of each 701 grant recipient.[28] The emphasis of the statute is on planning which ignores traditional jurisdictional boundaries in order to look at all of an area or region which has common or related development problems.[29] These are to be comprehensive plans and comprehensive planning is broadly defined in the act to include:

> (A) preparation, as a guide for governmental policies and action, of general plans with respect to (i) the pattern and intensity of land

use, (ii) the provision of public facilities (including transportation facilities) and other government services, and (iii) the effective development and utilization of human and natural resources;

(B) identification and evaluation of area needs (including housing, employment, education and health) and formulation of specific programs for meeting the needs so identified;

(C) surveys of structures and sites which are determined by the appropriate authorities to be of historic or architectural value;

(D) long-range physical and fiscal plans for such action;

(E) programing of capital improvements and other major expenditures, based on a determination of relative urgency, together with definite financing plans for such expenditures in the earlier years of the program;

(F) coordination of all related plans and activities of the State and local governments and agencies concerned; and

(G) preparation of regulatory and administrative measures in support of the foregoing.[30]

HUD has made a great many 701 planning grants to governmental entities throughout New York State, varying from large-scale studies by groups like the Tri-State Regional Planning Commission to small plans by individual towns for parts of their jurisdiction. The regulations by which HUD administers these grants are keys for citizen action in local planning which is funded under 701.

HUD's interim regulations now in effect emphasize the importance and necessity of citizen involvement in the planning process. The planning body which receives the HUD grant must include in each progress report to HUD a statement of citizen involvement, and stringent criteria have been established by HUD to assure that citizens are not only informed but actively involved in the planning activity:[31]

[Citizens] should have the opportunity to help initiate as well as react to proposals. . . .

The applicant should provide citizens with access to the decision making process. Citizens should be involved where major plans, policies, priorities or objectives, are being determined. . . .

Effective communication produces information that is readily available, timely, and easily understood by citizens. Information should be provided sufficiently in advance of public decisions to give citizens an adequate opportunity to review and to react to proposals. Applicants should seek to relate technical data and other professional material to the affected citizens so that they understand the impact of public programs, available options, and alternative decisions.[32]

These are fine goals, but their achievement depends very heavily on citizens asserting their rights and being willing to take an active part in the planning process. Often citizens' groups have found that town planning bodies are not sufficiently responsive to the HUD regulations and that only through citizen pressure can the lofty aims of the HUD regulations be realized.

In the planning carried out under 701 grants, the statute requires that each plan must include a housing element and a land use element. The land use element must include an analysis, standards, and implementing procedures for effectively guiding and controlling major decisions concerning where growth will take place. It must also include general plans for the pattern and intensity of land use for residential, commercial, industrial, and other activities which will be a guide for government policy and action.[33] HUD's interim regulations implementing this part of its program describe a wide-ranging land use analysis.[34] The intent of the regulations is to integrate all land use policies and planning. The plans developed under the program are to serve as a guide for communities on all matters related to the use of land, including "air and water quality concerns, waste disposal, transportation, protection of coastal areas, open space, environmental conservation, development and housing." If the plans live up to these requirements, they will indeed be comprehensive. HUD has made August 22, 1977, the effective date upon which such land use elements must be included in the plans funded.[35]

HUD has built the dictates of the National Environmental Policy Act into the 701 program.[36] Wherever it funds the development of land use plans or policies, HUD requires that the planning body prepare an environmental assessment of these plans or policies. The assessments follow the requirements of NEPA impact statements and are to be made available to the public on a timely basis, including availability before public hearings on the plan.

In its regulations HUD has gone further than simply requiring that the procedural requirements of NEPA be met. It has specified that the program must work to carry out the national policies established by NEPA and to "[i]mprove and conserve the quality of the air, water and earth resources for the benefit of present and future generations in the planning and shaping of man made environments."[37]

In all, the regulations provide for a thorough environmental review of all the federally funded planning activity carried out in the state. Unfortunately, the planning entities on the local and regional level in New York which have performed environmental assessments to meet these HUD regulations have generally not lived up to the standards established. The environmental assessments have frequently been cursory in dealing with environmental issues and self-serving in making conclusory statements that no adverse impact can be anticipated under a plan. Many planning agencies appear to start their environmental review with the conviction that their programs could never degrade the environment. HUD does not appear to have corrected this situation by any searching review of the environmental assessments which have been forwarded to it. In addition, funding for the 701 program is not presently at a level where effective planning over large areas of the country can be anticipated.

It is up to the citizens of the state to make use of the citizen participation provisions of the HUD regulations and through that mechanism to assure that meaningful environmental review under NEPA is in fact carried out under the 701 planning grant program. Only by taking this approach is it likely that fully effective land use planning and NEPA environmental reviews will become an important part of the continuing comprehensive planning program which HUD funds in New York.

Outside of the 701 program, HUD does an enormous volume of business in project development, passing on fifteen to twenty thousand applications for projects across the nation each year. The vast majority of these grants will now be administered under the terms of the Housing and Community Development Act of 1974.[38] This act allows the secretary to release funds to localities, which assume all the responsibilities of the federal official so far as the National Environmental Policy Act is concerned.[39] HUD has published regulations implementing this section of the act, so the process of environmental review is now effectively in the hands of the localities. The secretary does retain the statutory responsibility to see that an application for funds "takes into account appropriate environmental factors."[40] It remains to be seen how this clause of the act will be interpreted and implemented by HUD.

CITIZEN ACTION

Citizens who are faced with a land use problem in which a federal agency or federal funding is involved or a federal permit, license, or certificate is required should seek to answer the following questions:

1. Is an environmental impact statement under NEPA required before a decision can be made on any proposed action?

2. If an impact statement is required, is one being prepared?

3. If an impact statement is being prepared, what agency is preparing it and when will a draft statement be available for public comment?

4. Are all procedural requirements being properly met?

5. Will the draft statement be reviewed in a public hearing? If so, when and where?

It is important to become involved in the NEPA process as early as possible, since it is at this stage that administrators are most receptive to new information and approaches.

If an environmental impact statement is not being prepared in circumstances which appear to require one, citizens should investigate the reasons why no statement is being drawn up, discuss the problem with federal agency officials, and seek clarification of the issue.

If an impact statement is being required, citizens should do all they can to prepare perceptive, accurate, and hard-hitting comments on the draft statement. The adequacy of the statement should be assessed, both in terms of the information it is required by law to contain and in terms of its substantive content regarding the particular problems at hand. The advice and assistance of experts should be sought in the preparation of these comments. Local colleges and universities often prove to be good places to look for such expertise and assistance. Also, individuals who may themselves be faced with the same or a similar land use problem may be willing to contribute professional help to a concerted effort to deal effectively with a problem. If a draft impact statement is to be reviewed in a public hearing, determined efforts should be made to present strong and effective testimony. In all cases, a clearly stated and well-organized objective assessment of basic environmental problems that is supported by as much good evidence as possible will be far more convincing to government officials than emotional pleas.

Citizens who live in areas where planning projects are being carried out with funds from the HUD 701 program should work to see that the public is involved in the planning process as fully and effectively as is required by HUD regulations, and that environmental assessments and land use components of plans are being developed responsibly by the locality, with full citizen participation.

With respect to other grants made by HUD, citizens should find out what NEPA review system has been established by their locality and press for the most thorough review possible of projects which involve significant environmental problems.

NOTES

1. 42 U.S.C. §4321 *et seq.*

2. 42 U.S.C. §4332(2)(c).

3. City of New York v. United States, 337 F. Supp. 150, 3 ERC 1570 (E.D.N.Y. 1972).

4. 33 U.S.C. §1371(C)(1).

5. Goose Hollow Foothills League v. Romney, 334 F. Supp. 877, 3 ERC 1087 (D. Ore. 1971).

6. Committee for Nuclear Responsibility v. Seaborg, 463 F.2d 783, 3 ERC 1126 (D. C. Cir. 1971); Natural Resources Defense Council v. Morton, 458 F.2d 827, 3 ERC 1558 (D. C. Cir. 1972).

7. Natural Resources Defense Council v. Morton, *supra.*

8. Named Individual Members of the San Antonio Conservation Society v. Texas Highway Department, 446 F.2d 1013, 2 ERC 1871 (5th Cir. 1971).

9. Sierra Club v. Froehlke, 359 F. Supp. 1289, 5 ERC 1033 (S. D. Tex. 1973), *rev'd sub nom.* Sierra Club v. Callaway, 499 F.2d 982, 6 ERC 2080 (5th Cir. 1974).

10. Greene County Planning Board v. Federal Power Commission, 455 F.2d 412, 3 ERC 1595 (2d Cir.), *cert. denied,* 409 U.S. 849, 4 ERC 1752 (1972). The Housing and Community Development Act of 1974 discussed later in this chapter established a major exception to this general rule.

11. I–291 Why? Association v. Burns, 372 F. Supp. 223, 6 ERC 1275 (D. Conn. 1974); Committee to Stop Route 7 v. Volpe, 346 F. Supp. 731, 4 ERC 1329 (D. Conn. 1972); Citizens Environmental Council v. Volpe, 484 F.2d 870, 5 ERC 1989 (10th Cir. 1973), *cert. denied,* 416 U.S. 936, 6 ERC 1440 (1974); FAIR v. Brinegar, 484 F.2d 638 (5th Cir. 1973); Life of the Land v. Brinegar, 485 F.2d 460, 5 ERC 1780 (9th Cir. 1973), *cert. denied,* 416 U.S. 961, 6 ERC 1512 (1974); Iowa Citizens v. Volpe, 487 F.2d 849, 6 ERC 1088 (8th Cir. 1973).

12. Conservation Society of Southern Vermont v. Secretary of Transportation, 508 F.2d 927, 7 ERC 1236 (2d Cir. 1974).

13. *See* 40 CFR §1500 *et seq.*

14. *See* Protection and Enhancement of Environmental Quality, Exec. Order No. 11514, 35 *Federal Register* 4247 (March 5, 1970); Frederick B. Anderson, *NEPA in the Courts: A Legal Analysis of the National Environmental Policy Act* (Washington, D.C.: Resources for the Future, Inc., 1973; distributed by the Johns Hopkins Press, Baltimore and London), Chapter VI.

15. 40 CFR §§1500.3(a) and 1500.9(d).

16. Brooks v. Volpe, 319 F. Supp. 90, 2 ERC 1004 (W.D. Wash. 1970), 329 F. Supp. 118, 2 ERC 1571 (W.D. Wash. 1971), *rev'd.* 460 F.2d 1193, 3 ERC 1858 (9th

Cir.), 350 F. Supp. 269, 4 ERC 1492 (W.D. Wash.), 350 F. Supp. 287, 4 ERC 1532 (W.D. Wash. 1972); Daly v. Volpe, 326 F. Supp. 868, 2 ERC 1507 (W.D. Wash. 1971), 350 F. Supp. 252, 4 ERC 1481, *opinion on rehearing,* 350 F. Supp. 260, 4 ERC 1486 (W.D. Wash. 1972).

17. 40 CFR §1500.7(d).

18. Lathan v. Volpe, 350 F. Supp. 262, 265, 4 ERC 1487, 1489 (W.D. Wash. 1972).

19. *See* Citizens for Clean Air v. Corps of Engineers, 349 F. Supp. 696, 4 ERC 1456 (S.D.N.Y. 1972).

20. 42 U.S.C. §1857 *et seq. See* Chapter 10.

21. 33 U.S.C. §1251 *et seq. See* Chapter 11.

22. 33 U.S.C. §§401, 403, and 1344. *See* Chapter 11.

23. A full account of the developments related here appears in an article by Walter Reinsdorf entitled "Another Legend of Sleepy Hollow," *The Catkills* (Summer 1973).

24. Reinsdorf, "Another Legend," p. 16.

25. *See* the discussion on navigable waters in Chapter 11.

26. Reinsdorf, "Another Legend," pp. 18–19.

27. 40 U.S.C. §461.

28. *See* Chapter 3 and Chapter 4 for a discussion of planning bodies which may apply for HUD grants to carry out comprehensive planning.

29. 40 U.S.C. §461(a).

30. 40 U.S.C. §461(m)(4).

31. 39 *Federal Register* 43384 (December 12, 1974). These interim regulations were effective upon publication. Promulgaton of final regulations, which will no doubt contain some revisions, is expected in 1975.

32. *Ibid.*

33. 40 U.S.C. §461(c)(2), (as amended by the Housing and Community Development Act of 1974).

34. 39 *Federal Register* 43378 (December 12, 1974).

35. 40 U.S.C. §461(d).

36. 24 CFR §600.65.

37. 24 CFR §600.65(a)(1).

38. 42 U.S.C. §5301.

39. 42 U.S.C. §5304(h).

40. 42 U.S.C. §5304(a)(2)(C).

CHAPTER 10

Land Use Controls Under the Federal Clean Air Act

THE CLEAN AIR Act, passed in 1970,[1] required the administrator of the U.S. Environmental Protection Agency (EPA) to establish national ambient air quality standards for six major air pollutants: carbon monoxide, particulates, hydrocarbons, sulfur oxides, nitrogen dioxide, and photochemical oxidants.[2]

Congress required that two types of ambient standards be designated: (1) "primary standards" to establish the level of air quality necessary, with an adequate margin of safety, to protect human health; and (2) "secondary standards" to safeguard all values other than health, including visibility, plant and animal life, buildings, and materials. The primary standards are to be attained by mid-1975, or by 1977 where extensions have been granted. The secondary standards must be attained within a "reasonable time," the exact determination of which is left to the federal EPA administrator. The standards refer to the measurement of concentrations of specific pollutants in "ambient" air—that is, in the air we breathe.

The act requires each state to develop implementation plans to attain and maintain the standards. The plans must be submitted to the federal EPA for approval, and Congress set forth in the act specific requirements which each plan must meet in order to be approved. Where the EPA administrator determines that a state plan, or parts of the plan, are not approvable, he is required by the act to promulgate federal regulations to correct deficiencies.

To assist in the development and implementation of the state plan in New York, the federal EPA divided the state into eight air quality control regions. In each of these eight geographical regions, a unified approach to meeting and maintaining standards can be developed. Each region is classified as priority I, II, or III for each pollutant, based on the level of air quality in that region, with priority I indicating the most polluted air. Table 5 lists the eight air quality control regions and their priority classifications, thus providing a rough picture of air quality levels across the state. The classifications were originally made in 1972, based on 1970 air quality data. More recent monitoring data do not indicate any basis for reclassification.

It must be stressed, however, that the designation of different control regions does not affect in any way the uniform applicability of all federal and state standards and regulations. For example, national primary and secondary air quality standards, emission limitations, and prohibitions against degradation of clean air are binding in all areas of the state. Whether or not a proposed new source of air pollution would cause a violation of such standards or regulations must always be considered.[3]

Although the Clean Air Act does not define a national land use policy for protecting air quality, it does require state plans to include land use or transportation controls where they are necessary to achieve the air quality standards.[4] This chapter discusses the following four aspects of the New York plan which bear on land use decision-making:

Table 5
Classification of Air Quality Control Regions in New York State

Air quality control region	Particulate matter	Sulfur oxides (SO_x)	Nitrogen dioxide (NO_2)	Carbon monoxide (CO)	Photochemical oxidants (hydrocarbons)
Niagara Frontier Intrastate	I	I	I	III	I
Champlain Valley Interstate	II	II	III	III	III
Central New York Intrastate	I	II	III	I	I

Genesee–Finger Lakes Intrastate	II	II	I	III	I
Hudson Valley Intrastate	I	II	III	III	III
Southern Tier East Intrastate	II	II	III	III	III
Southern Tier West Intrastate	II	II	III	III	III
New Jersey–New York–Connecticut Interstate	I	I	I	I	I

SOURCE: 37 *Federal Register* 10882 (May 31, 1972); 40 CFR §52.1671.

Legend

Pollutant	Priority		
	I	II	III
	Greater than	From–to	Less than
Particulate matter			
annual geometric mean	95 μg/m³*	60–95 μg/m³	60 μg/m³
24-hr. maximum	325 μg/m³	150–325 μg/m³	150 μg/m³
SO$_x$			
annual arithmetic mean	.04 ppm**	.02–.04 ppm	.02 ppm
24-hr. maximum	.17 ppm	.10–.17 ppm	.10 ppm
3-hr. maximum		greater than .50 ppm	less than .50 ppm
	Equal or greater than		*Less than*
NO$_2$			
annual arithmetic mean	.06 ppm		.06 ppm
CO			
1-hr. maximum	48 ppm		48 ppm
8-hr. maximum	12 ppm		12 ppm
Photochemical oxidants			
1-hr. maximum	.10 ppm		.10 ppm

*μg/m³ = micrograms per cubic meter
**ppm = parts per million

SOURCE: 36 *Federal Register* 22399 (November 25, 1971); 40 CFR §51.3.

1. Pre-construction review of major new stationary sources of pollution;[5]

2. Pre-construction review of indirect sources;[6]

3. Development of a maintenance plan;

4. Prevention of significant deterioration of air quality in existing clean air areas.

1. Pre-Construction Review of Major New Stationary Sources

The Clean Air Act requires state plans to include a procedure for reviewing, prior to construction, the location of every new stationary source of air pollution (or modification of an existing source) for which a new source performance standard is established by EPA.[7] In order to insure maintenance of the national air quality standards, which the act requires, the federal EPA regulations require pre-construction review of all new sources which might jeopardize the standards.[8] To insure the viability of state review and permit systems, moreover, Congress required that each state obtain adequate authority to prevent the construction of a source if it would prevent the attainment or maintenance of the national ambient air quality standards.[9]

In 1973 the New York State permit system was challenged in federal court by the Natural Resources Defense Council (NRDC),[10] because the New York regulations allowed applicants to receive provisional permits to construct a new source. A provisional permit could be obtained when the applicant showed that application and review prior to construction would result in "undue hardship or delay." Upon completion of construction under a provisional permit, the owner could then apply for a certificate to operate without ever having requested an actual construction permit. To obtain a certificate to operate, the polluter did not have to demonstrate that he would comply with air quality standards.

The court upheld NRDC's challenge to this permit system. The federal EPA agreed that a revision of the regulations involved was called for and New York has amended its state plan to indicate that construction under a provisional permit is at the owner's own risk, subject to a finding that the source will not jeopardize attainment of air quality standards.

The requirement that proposed stationary sources be reviewed prior to construction obviously has very significant implications for land use. The New York State plan already contains emission limitations which individual stationary sources must meet. These emission limitations prescribe the maximum amount of particulate matter or gases, such as SO_2, NO_2, and HC, which can be emitted from the stack. However, these limitations cannot insure attainment and maintenance of ambient air quality. For instance, a new source, such as a power plant or incinerator, located in Manhattan or other urban areas of the state, would almost certainly jeopardize the attainment or maintenance of the ambient air quality standards in that region, even if the source met specified emission limitations. Likewise, the location of a large source in a valley would have a substantially greater adverse impact on ambient air quality than the location of the same source on a mountaintop, where pollutants are more widely dispersed.

In fact, since an elevated site allows a source to take advantage of the greater dispersion capability of the elevated location, the power and smelting industries have pushed hard for the use of tall stacks, as high as one thousand feet, to allow greater dispersion of pollutants, rather than the installation of available stack gas-cleaning equipment which actually removes pollutants from the gas stream. The use of dispersion techniques such as tall stacks was ruled illegal by the Fifth Circuit U.S. Court of Appeals on two grounds: (1) Congress intended that pollutant emissions should be reduced, not merely diluted; and (2) such dispersion violates the principle of non-degradation, which is discussed below.[11]

The relationship between a single source of emissions and the total quantities of pollutants measured in the air at ground level is difficult, if not impossible, to define accurately. The development of a dispersion model involves computing the rate of emissions, determining the prevailing wind direction and speed, preparing an inventory of total emissions in the region, and assessing the effect of local topography. The ultimate determination sought is whether emissions directly attributable to a proposed new source will push ground concentrations over the acceptable limits. It was precisely because of the difficulty of relating emissions from a single source to ground-level concentrations which result from many different sources that Congress required state plans to include emission limitations applicable to each source at the stack, to insure that ambient standards are not violated.

It may be virtually impossible for the layman to assess the validity of a dispersion model. Citizens concerned that the location of a particular source will jeopardize air quality should obtain the assistance of a professional air quality planner from a private consulting firm or enlist the aid of professionals within DEC or a local air pollution control agency to provide a critique of the state's assessment of the air quality impact of a proposed source.

If New York State grants a permit for construction of a source which, because of its location, would cause a violation of ambient air quality standards, the only recourse for citizens under the Clean Air Act would be the filing of a citizen's suit as described in Section 304 of the act.[12] In such an action, the citizen-plaintiff must be prepared to show either (1) that the state did not meet procedural requirements, such as review of the proposed source prior to construction; or (2) that the pre-construction review indicated that violations would occur, yet the permit was granted anyway; or (3) in the case of a state determination that violations would not occur, that the calculations or the model is incorrect.

2. Pre-construction Review of Indirect Sources

New York State is required by the Clean Air Act and subsequent court decisions interpreting the act to prepare a plan to insure the maintenance of the national primary and secondary standards across the state, and to develop a procedure for pre-construction review of indirect sources, similar to the procedure developed for review of stationary sources.

Indirect sources are defined as those sources which attract mobile sources of pollution. Examples are highways, shopping centers, sports stadiums, coliseums, and airports. During the last two decades in this country, we have experienced such tremendous growth in automobile ownership and usage that existing data indicate that even stringent control of exhaust emissions from automobiles is not sufficient to prevent the accumulation of hazardous concentrations of CO, NO_2, and photochemical oxidants at facilities where large numbers of vehicles converge. Therefore, in order to fulfill Congress' mandate to maintain healthful air quality levels, the state must consider, prior to construction, the impact of facilities which will attract large numbers of automobiles.

EPA required every state to submit plans for reviewing indirect sources by August 15, 1973. New York submitted its indirect source review plan in the fall of 1973, but EPA disapproved it as inadequate, and promulgated a federal regulation in its place in February 1974.[13] Under the federal plan, the New York State Department of Environmental Conservation—acting as the EPA administrator's designated agent—must conduct a review of any proposed highway, airport, or shopping or parking facility which is over the size specified in the federal promulgation. Table 6 and Table 7 define the categories of proposed indirect sources which must be reviewed in urban areas and in non-urban areas, respectively.

Originally, the EPA regulation required that a permit be obtained for such facilities if construction was to begin on or after January 1, 1975. On December 30, 1974, however, EPA amended this regulation, suspending implementation of federal indirect source review procedures until further notice.[14] Specifically, EPA stated that "[n]o facility which commences construction or modification prior to July 1, 1975, will be subject to the Federal indirect source regulation." This suspension has no effect on existing or future state laws or regulations on indirect source review.

EPA announced this suspension of the implementation of its controversial indirect source review regulation after passage by Congress of an appropriations bill that prohibited EPA from spending any money to regulate parking programs through June 30, 1975. It is to be expected that implementation of the federal regulation will commence at a later date, but that the sensitivity of the issue will not diminish.

Meanwhile, the New York State Department of Environmental Conservation (DEC) promulgated a new state indirect source review regulation, which went into effect on January 13, 1975.[15] DEC hopes that this new regulation, which is patterned on the federal regulation, will be approved by EPA, so that the state review will fulfill federal requirements; however, even before such approval is obtained or review under the federal regulation actually begins, indirect sources must comply with the state regulation, which is already in force.

Both the state and federal regulations require that after DEC receives an application for the construction of an indirect source subject to review, the agency must make a preliminary determination of whether to approve or disapprove the application. Public notice of the application must be made in the area's newspaper(s) and the opportunity for the public to submit written comments on the application for at least a thirty-day period must be publicized. The application itself, DEC's preliminary determination, and other related materials must be made available for public inspection and copying. The state regulation provides that the commissioner of environmental conservation may call a public hearing to obtain further information if "there is sufficient public interest in and reason for such a hearing or if the applicant so requests." The type of information which DEC must consider in making its determination of whether a proposed indirect source is to be approved or disapproved is specified in both the state and federal regulations.

Unfortunately, there is little available data upon which to base

Table 6
Indirect Sources to Be Reviewed in
Urban Areas
(Standard Metropolitan
Statistical Areas)

Roads and Highways

New | 20,000 vehicles per day (average)
Modified | 10,000 vehicles increase per day over existing traffic (average)

Airports

New | 50,000 operations (incoming and outgoing flights) or 1.6 million passengers per year
Modified | 50,000 operations per year increase over existing level, or 1.6 million passenger increase per year

Other Indirect Sources

New | Parking for 1,000 cars or more
Modified | Parking for 500 cars over existing number

Table 7
Indirect Sources to Be Reviewed in
Non-Urban Areas

Roads and Highways

No review

Airports

Same as in urban areas

Other Indirect Sources

New | Parking for 2,000 cars or more
Modified | Parking for 1,000 cars or more over existing number

predictions of the impact of particular facilities on total air quality. To date, most of the data published by the federal EPA deal with predicting emissions *at* the source itself (i.e., in the parking lot of a shopping center or on a particular segment of highway) and do not define procedures for predicting the additional emissions generated by automobiles traveling to the source or the additional emissions resulting from increased trip demand generated by new highway facilities. The EPA guidelines for indirect source review and the development of maintenance plans contain data on predicting emission concentrations.[16] It is necessary, however, to scrutinize these guidelines carefully to determine the underlying assumptions used in

EPA's analysis. For instance, in the EPA guidelines for predicting CO emissions from indirect sources, the graphs used to predict the air quality impact of highways and parking lots are based on the assumption that CO monitors would be located not at curbside but as far as twenty meters away. Concentrations recorded twenty meters away would not reflect the high concentrations to which a driver, cyclist, or pedestrian traveling or standing at the curbside would be exposed.

From the environmentalists' point of view, the EPA regulation on the review of indirect sources which was promulgated in February 1974 is wholly inadequate to protect air quality against mounting pollutant levels due to automobile exhaust gases. EPA's decision to confine review to sources of a gargantuan character is one of the greatest failures of the regulation. In order to provide adequate coverage, the regulation should apply to sources of a size small enough that no one source or any collection of sources would interfere with the attainment or maintenance of the standards or result in any significant deterioration of air quality. The preamble to the regulation does not even imply that the selected size parameters are adequate to prevent such effects. In fact, according to the preamble, the "cutoff levels" are justified only in terms of some unspecified "nationwide context."

Not only are the cutoff levels not justified, but on their face they are demonstrably inadequate to prevent interference with attainment and maintenance of the standards and also to prevent significant deterioration. First, the cutoff levels ignore the fact that many areas of the country have existing high levels of pollution, at or in excess of the standard. In such areas, construction of facilities exempt from review will violate or will increase violations of standards.

Second, the cutoff levels ignore the cumulative impact of a number of unreviewed sources on air quality. There is nothing in the regulation to prevent the accumulation of sources that have a total associated activity greater than the cutoff level but which are each below that level when considered separately: for example, four parking lots around a single intersection or on a single block, each with a parking capacity of 600 cars, would have a total capacity of 2,400 cars.

Existing conditions demonstrate that these cutoff levels will not provide protection against violations of standards. For example, most of the intersections in midtown Manhattan or downtown Washington, D.C., do not contain a single source large enough to be subject to review under the established cutoff. Yet at many of these same intersections the eight-hour carbon monoxide standard is being exceeded regularly by large margins. If the present federal EPA regulation had been in effect since the time the sites of these intersections were virgin countryside, the regulation would have done nothing to prevent the present violations from occurring. Similarly, the regulation does nothing to protect present virgin areas from such developments.

The choice of a two-stage cutoff level which distinguishes between urban areas and non-urban areas, moreover, directly violates the principle of no significant deterioration which EPA is under court order to implement.[17] By exempting from review in non-urban areas the construction of highways of any size and of other sources twice the size allowed in urban areas, EPA is adopting an approach which allows at least twice as much pollution impact to occur in clean air areas as in dirty air areas. The Supreme Court has affirmed lower court holdings that the Clean Air Act does not permit this, and EPA has a legal duty to obey these court rulings.

Another controversial aspect of the federal regulation is the definition of "construction," which determines which proposed sources must apply for a permit. A permit is required only for projects which *begin* construction after a certain date (originally January 1, 1975, but now unspecified as a result of the suspension discussed above). However, EPA has defined construction so broadly that even the clearing of land—which could have taken place years before the developer even determined what to build on the site[18]—might qualify as "commencing construction" and allow the owner or developer to escape review. Review procedures were supposed to begin in the summer of 1974 to accommodate developers who were planning facilities six months or more in advance, but this did not occur in any state. On October 1, 1974, Connecticut became the first state to begin review of indirect sources.

There are still two possible remedies through which realistic indirect source review regulations may be achieved:

a. Although a federal EPA regulation has been promulgated for New York, an approved state plan would replace the federal regulation. Since states are not precluded from developing regulations stricter than those promulgated by EPA, adequate regulations could be established through state action. In fact, in the preamble to the federal regulation the EPA administrator states that this regulation is not and could not be designed to "reflect special local conditions," and he "supports and encourages the enactment of more restrictive indirect source provisions and regulations by states where the needs, conditions and/or public desire so indicates."[19]

b. If a suit brought by the Natural Resources Defense Council at the federal level is successful, it may result in a court order for new federal regulations.[20]

3. Development of a Maintenance Plan

The Clean Air Act and the court decision in *Natural Resources Defense Council* v. *Environmental Protection Agency*[21] require EPA to review state implementation plans to assure that the national air quality standards will be not only attained, but also maintained. EPA regulations implementing this requirement[22] call for submission of specific maintenance plans by the states for those areas in which study indicates the national standards will be violated by 1985 as a result of growth and development. The purpose of these plans is to prevent such violations from occurring, and they must include whatever measures are necessary "to insure that projected growth and development will be compatible with maintenance of the national standards . . ."

The EPA regulations, which were promulgated in June 1973, required each state by March 10, 1974 (a deadline that was later extended to May 10, 1974) to submit preliminary designations of areas in which national standards could be violated during the next decade. EPA was then supposed to publish in the *Federal Register* by August 16, 1974, its determinations of which of these areas would be subject to further study. For such identified areas, each state was then to prepare a more detailed air quality analysis of the impact of growth and development. Where this analysis indicated that standards would in fact be exceeded by 1985, the states were required by June 18, 1975, to submit ten-year maintenance plans to prevent such violations.

According to a tentative timetable developed by EPA on the basis of this deadline,[23] the agency hoped by September 1974 to have published guidelines for analyzing the air quality impact of projected growth and for developing an approvable maintenance plan. The states were then to complete their draft plans by February 1975, announce public hearings in April, hold these hearing in May, and submit final plans to EPA by the June 1975 deadline.

Unfortunately, despite the ruling federal statute, court order, and

Table 8
Maintenance Areas in New York State

Area	Part.	SO$_2$	CO	O$_X$	NO$_2$
		Contaminant			
New York Metropolitan Area	x	x	x	x	x
Niagara Frontier	x	x			
Capital District	x	x			
Mid-Hudson	x				
Utica-Rome Area	x				
Binghamton Area	x				
Syracuse Area	x				
Elmira-Corning Area	x				
Rochester Area	x				
Jamestown Area	x				

Legend:
Part. = particulate matter
SO$_2$ = sulfur dioxide
CO = carbon monoxide
O$_X$ = photochemical oxidants
NO$_2$ = nitrogen dioxide

MAP 2: Areas Served by the Nine Regional Offices of the New York State Department of Environmental Conservation

regulations, this entire time frame has now been abandoned. First, the states were very late in submitting their preliminary designations. Then, EPA failed to identify by August 1974 which of these proposed designated areas would require further air quality analysis and planning by the states, and as of March 1975, has still failed to make these determinations. Further, EPA fell badly behind in the publication of its guidelines, which grew into a thirteen-volume set, the last volume of which, it is hoped, will be released in the summer of 1975.[24]

It is now anticipated that EPA will publish new proposed regulations on maintenance plans in the *Federal Register* in May 1975. In draft versions of these regulations, the deadline for submission of air quality analyses and maintenance plans is extended to December 1975, and provision is even made for a longer extension at the request of a state governor. Moreover, the maintenance plans due then would not be the full-fledged plans for the ten years from 1975 to 1985, as originally required, but three-year "work plans" to cover the period through 1978. A second phase plan would then have to be developed by the states to provide for maintenance of standards through 1985.

This account of broken deadlines and extensions reflects the great reluctance EPA has shown to move forcefully ahead with those aspects of the Clean Air Act that involve land use control. Perhaps fearful of opposing forces that have now proposed amendments to the Clean Air Act that would greatly weaken or delete the transportation and land use controls provision of the act, EPA has not been willing to assume strong leadership in this area. Support and pressure from citizens who are well informed about the Clean Air Act and the regulations promulgated under it are badly needed to see that EPA and the state carry out ther legal obligations to assure that national air quality standards are attained and maintained.

Table 8 and Map 1 indicate the general areas submitted by the New York State Department of Environmental Conservation (DEC) as preliminary designations of areas in which national standards may be violated by 1985. For the initial naming of these areas, New York established the following designation criteria which are consistent with federal guidelines:

a. Particulate matter: (1) areas where national secondary standards will not be achieved by 1985; (2) areas now in compliance with national standards, but where growth to 1985 may increase particulate emissions to the degree that standards will not be maintained; or (3) areas where the state plan may not be sufficient to achieve or maintain standards.

b. Sulfur dioxide (SO_2): areas where national primary standards will not be maintained until 1985 because of increases in the use of fossil fuels. For the preliminary analysis it has been assumed that, for the present, this potential has not been exacerbated by the current energy crisis. This will be further analyzed during the coming years.

c. Carbon monoxide (CO): areas where a recent maximum eight-hour average exceeds 25 parts per million (ppm).

d. Photochemical oxidants (O_X): areas where a transportation implementation plan for photochemical oxidants is needed.

e. Nitrogen dioxide (NO_2): New York City area.

Both the federal EPA guidelines on inclusion criteria and New York State's determination of which areas warrant preliminary designation should be carefully scrutinized. For instance, the criterion for carbon monoxide pollutants covers only those areas where the existing eight-hour average for CO exceeds 25 ppm, a level almost three times the primary eight-hour standard (9 ppm) established to protect human health. In presuming that maintenance plans are necessary only for those areas where present CO levels are above 25 ppm, the state and EPA are counting heavily on the capability of still unperfected automobile exhaust emission control devices to reduce CO emissions drastically. They presume that these devices will not only cut existing concentrations by two-thirds, but will also offset the increased emissions resulting from increased automobile usage expected in the next ten years.[25] Despite the trend toward increased automobile usage and the concomitant increases to dangerous concentrations of pollutants caused by automobiles (CO, O_X, and NO_2), New York State has designated only one area—New York City—as an area for which a maintenance plan may be required to meet and maintain automobile pollutant standards. Even the state's own sampling indicates that at least two areas outside New York City (Rochester and the Niagara frontier region) have over the last year suffered increases in CO concentrations to levels above the eight-hour standard. In the Syracuse area, one of the two CO monitors for the area recorded levels above 12 ppm for an eight-hour period.

Limited monitoring in New York State is the chief constraint to ascertaining which areas of the state may violate standards by 1985. For instance, in four of the ten designated areas DEC has examined, the state has only one monitor for measuring automobile pollutants. In two of the six remaining areas (Jamestown and Elmira–Corning) the state has no data at all on automobile pollutant concentrations, but has rejected each of these areas for CO, O_X, and NO_2 maintenance plans on the grounds that "areas of comparable size indicate that standards will be maintained in this area." Two of the remaining four areas have only two monitors, while a third (the Niagara frontier region) has three monitoring stations.

Unlike monitoring for automobile pollutants, monitoring for SO_2 and particulate matter, which are primarily caused by stationary sources, has been conducted for a longer period of time and at more sites. In determining whether the state is monitoring in enough locations and in the proper places in an area to define pollution problems with respect to these two contaminants, citizens will need to call upon their knowledge of the particular area and of the number of sources (especially large sources), as well as their firsthand experience with pollution problems, such as a decline of visibility on poor days. Monitors for SO_2 and particulate matter should be located so that they measure the worst conditions in the area; in addition, they should be stationed at proper heights, to reflect concentrations to which the public is exposed. The proper location of monitors for pollutants from stationary sources is also highly dependent on prevailing meteorological conditions which affect the dispersion of the pollutants. Further, many stationary sources contribute "fugitive emissions"—i.e., emissions of gases and particulates from the building through windows, vents, and doors—as well as emissions from the stack. Such fugitive emissions result in seriously high ground concentrations in the vicinity of a plant, but very frequently the state's monitors are located too far away to measure them.

In summary, like virtually every other state in the nation, New York suffers from an inadequate network for the monitoring of air pollution. Lack of data, however, cannot legally serve as a justification for failing to consider whether a maintenance plan will be necessary in an area.

A list of the ten areas identified for preliminary designation by New York State, along with maps of monitoring locations and data, can be obtained from DEC's Albany office:

Division of Air Resources
New York State Department of Environmental Conservation
50 Wolf Road
Albany, N.Y. 12233

If an area of particular interest is not included on this list, inquiries should be made concerning how monitoring is carried out in this area and what measurements have been recorded. It is quite possible that an area was not included on the list of designated areas simply because no data existed to indicate that standards were being violated or that violations were very likely in the future. For example, the inclusion criteria for particulate matter require a maintenance plan for areas where present violations of the secondary standard will continue through 1985, *and* for areas presently in compliance where projected growth will lead to increased emissions and violation of the standard by 1985. Yet the list drawn up by New York State contains no explanations or growth projections for particulate emissions. In fact, nine of the ten areas designated by New York State are already above the secondary standard for particulates. While these nine areas certainly need maintenance plans, it is difficult to believe that Binghamton, New York, is the only area in the state that is presently below this secondary standard but may exceed it in the next ten years if unplanned growth is allowed.

As has been pointed out above, there is a great need for citizens to work for the adoption of a strong maintenance plan which effectively comes to terms with the impact of growth and development on air quality. The considerable delay which has already taken place in EPA's actions regarding maintenance plans accentuates the need for this effort.

4. Prevention of Significant Deterioration

Another aspect of air quality maintenance which will have an impact on land use is the development by the federal EPA and the state of measures to prevent significant deterioration. Simply stated, the principle of non-deterioration is that areas where air quality is presently better than the national standards should be protected. Although this specific language was not used in the Clean Air Act, the legislative history of the act demonstrates Congress' intent to prevent further degradation of air quality. In fact, this policy had already been adopted by the National Air Pollution Control Agency (NAPCA), a branch of the Department of Health, Education, and Welfare (HEW), even before the passage of the 1970 Clean Air Act.

Simply on the face of the matter it is clear that while conducting a major state–federal effort to clean up the air in those areas of the country we have polluted to unhealthful levels, we should not at the same time allow existing pure air areas to be sacrificed. But even more conclusive reasons exist for protecting our clean air regions.

The national standards were established on the basis of existing scientific evidence to protect human health and to prevent damage to animal life and vegetation. As research continues, however, and as measuring instrumentation grows more sophisticated, it is presumed by leading scientists in the field that we will discover adverse effects at lower and lower levels of pollution. Congress acknowledged this likelihood when it provided that the national standards should be reevaluated and revised when necessary to reflect new evidence.[26] Strong evidence of adverse effects on human health from sulfur dioxide at levels below even the present primary standards has already been uncovered.[27] Thus the potential for finding adverse health effects and vegetation damage at levels lower than the existing standards is a very strong argument for protecting our existing clean air areas. An additional consideration is that if these areas are diminished and high levels of pollutants are allowed to hang in the air nationwide, it will become more and more difficult to conduct the kinds of scientific testing necessary to determine threshold levels of damage to health and vegetation.[28]

When federal EPA officials balked at applying the principle of non-degradation in the early 1970s, the Sierra Club initiated a suit to force the agency to protect existing air quality. In May 1973 the Supreme Court affirmed the lower court decisions requiring EPA to prevent significant deterioration.[29]

EPA proposed alternative plans for the prevention of significant deterioration in July 1973, but final regulations were not promulgated until December 5, 1974.[30] The regulations provide for a regulatory scheme in which areas that have air quality better than national standards are to be designated as class I, class II, or class III, depending on the amount of pollution that is to be allowed in each. The greatest degree of deterioration is permitted in class III areas, where air pollution can be increased up to the national secondary standards. In class II areas, the allowable increase in SO_2 and particulate emissions is compatible with what EPA terms "moderate well-controlled growth." For instance, in a class II area, a controlled 1,000-megawatt utility plant could be accommodated within the allowable increment. The best protected areas are those designated class I, where the permitted increment in SO_2 and particulate emissions is the smallest. In all classes, "increment" refers to the allowable increase in ground-level concentrations of pollutants, not to an increase in pounds of total emissions.

Unless or until a state decides to classify its regions, all of its areas which have air quality that is better than the national secondary standards will be considered class II areas. If the state does wish to redesignate clean air areas as class I or class III, it must conduct public hearings, and must make a discussion of the reasons for the redesignation available for public inspection at least thirty days before the hearing.

The major drawback to this three-class approach is that unless designations of class II and III areas are carefully limited, substantial deterioration of air quality will result in vast areas of the country. It is estimated that in over 80 percent of the nation air quality is presently cleaner than required by the secondary standards. Under the three-class plan it is likely that only a few areas, akin to wilderness areas, will enjoy full protection from gradually deteriorating air quality.

EPA's response to the significant deterioration issue thus has been less than wholehearted and eager. It is especially important to note that the regulations which EPA has promulgated limit the increase of pollutant concentrations in ambient air, but do not limit the total amount of emissions allowed from the stack. Depending on particular meteorological conditions, this could permit stack emissions to despoil clean air over large regions, contributing further to the problem of suspended sulfates and acid rain.[31]

Concerned citizens should try to determine the practical implications for New York State of the federal EPA's regulations on non-deterioration. EPA Region II officials or New York State DEC officials should be pressed to equate the allowable increases of pollutants to actual projects, numbers of steel plants, smelters, incinerators, and electric plants—and to establish the total amount of pollution that will be allowed in a given area, such as Saratoga, Kingston, or Corning. The following are the addresses of the EPA Region II office and DEC's central office:[32]

EPA Region II
26 Federal Plaza
Room 908
New York, N. Y. 10007

New York State Department of
Environmental Conservation
50 Wolf Road
Albany, N. Y. 12233

Since the state is not required to redesignate any area as class I or class III, it is not required to hold public hearings on which areas should be protected and to what extent. It is likely, however, that the state will conduct a hearing or hearings to consider redesignation. Any hearing held must be conducted "in or near" the area affected. Since, however, the preservation of clean air areas is a matter of statewide and national concern rather than a strictly local issue, individuals or organizations should not hesitate to participate in hearings held in other localities or even in other states, particularly in neighboring states whose decisions regarding allowable increases in pollution may mean more pollution in this state.

The Sierra Club, which won the original court decision mandating EPA to take action to prevent significant deterioration, is now challenging EPA's regulatory scheme in the courts on the grounds that it does not adequately protect clean air areas.[33] However, citizens should proceed as if the EPA regulations on non-deterioration are finally binding, and should consult DEC on its plans regarding public hearings.

CITIZEN ACTION

Of the four aspects of the New York state plan discussed above, only two have been implemented with regulations that establish definite procedures for reviewing sources of air pollution. Even though these regulations for the pre-construction review of the new stationary sources and indirect sources suffer from inadequacies, they may still be effective tools in preventing large, ill-planned developments. Moreover, it is not too late to improve the regulations. Whenever New York State submits a new state regulation and it is approved by the federal EPA, citizens may file a court challenge within thirty days of the EPA approval.[34] As has been pointed out, a court challenge led to a court-ordered revision of the New York new stationary source permit system.

It is most important to remember that regulations are merely intended to implement a state or federal statute. They are not inviolate. When a state or federal regulation is inadequate to meet the requirements of the 1970 Clean Air Act, then it can be challenged or changed. Furthermore, citizens who are concerned with a particular proposed project which developers or the state assert meets regulatory requirements should be quick to point out that the project must also meet statutory requirements, i.e., it must not lead to the violation of any national standard.

In order to be able to use the provisions of the Clean Air Act, citizens should familiarize themselves with the act itself, with the regulations published in the *Federal Register,* and with applicable state regulations. Procedural requirements for new stationary source review and indirect source review are found at 40 CFR §51.18 and were published in the *Federal Register* on June 18, 1973 (38 *Federal Register* 15836). These regulations contain the requirements for public notice, advertisement of DEC's preliminary approval or disapproval, and provision of a thirty-day public written comment period. Specific requirements which must be met by DEC and by applicants in the review of indirect sources are found at 40 CFR §52.22 (38 *Federal Register* 7276, February 25, 1974). Regulations which specify the categories of stationary sources subject to new source performance standards and these standards themselves are included in 40 CFR Part 60. These regulations, as promulgated and amended, were published in the *Federal Register* on several different dates. Copies of all the regulations published in the *Federal Register* and a copy of the 1970 Clean Air Act may be obtained from:

> U.S. Environmental Protection Agency
> Office of Public Affairs
> Waterside Mall
> 401 M Street, S.W.
> Washington, D.C. 20460

The New York State permit system, covering pre-construction review of both direct and indirect sources, is set forth in the New York Code of Rules and Regulations at 6 NYCRR Part 201. As pointed out earlier, these regulations have been found inadequate and are being revised according to the court decision in *Natural Resources Defense Council* v. *Environmental Protection Agency.*[35] The state regulations on indirect sources which became effective in January 1975 are found at 6 NYCRR Part 203. Copies of these regulations, as well as other informational materials can be obtained from the New York State DEC regional offices.

For information on the status of an application or the review of any particular proposed source, contact should be made with the chief air engineer in the appropriate DEC regional office. If the staff of a regional office cannot answer questions raised, they should refer one to appropriate officials in the DEC central office in Albany.

With respect to the review of indirect sources, it may still be possible to persuade DEC to make its plan for indirect source review in New York State more environmentally sound than the regulations of the federal EPA. But persuading the state to take a stronger stand on this problem will not be an easy task. While adequate review of indirect sources is extremely important to the quality of the air we breathe, it is a very controversial issue. Across the country a number of organizations and influential interest groups such as chambers of commerce, merchants' associations, and real estate developers have resisted, on both national and local levels, proposals for indirect source review. Most opponents of indirect source review insist that it is a no-growth policy that would have a devastating impact on local and regional economies. It is important that citizens who recognize the importance of indirect source review counter this gross exaggeration. Review and regulation of indirect sources should be developed to provide for planned growth that does not sacrifice healthful air quality; they are not intended to prevent growth altogether. There is no reason why large shopping centers or stadiums cannot be constructed, as long as adequate mass transportation service, either public or private, is made available so that the number of automobiles traveling to the facilities can be kept to a minimum. Private developers can use their influence to help strengthen mass transit systems: they can urge local governments to extend or improve transit service and to seek new federal money to do so; they may themselves apply to the Urban Mass Transit Administration for federal funding to sponsor particularly innovative transit proposals. Developers also have the option of considering construction in central business districts, where public transportation is usually already available.

An additional problem that citizens working for effective indirect source review should expect to run into is that firm data do not exist for predicting with great accuracy the air quality impact of particular types of indirect sources. The EPA guidelines for analyzing the air quality impact of projected growth[36] may offer more insight on this problem, but their methodology is not infallible. The very lack of firm data means the layman may be in as sound a position as the technician to evaluate the adequacy of a proposed plan, or to prepare a critique of the DEC assessment of the air quality impact of a particular proposed source. The most effective approach for the layman is to determine—either through his or her own reading of the EPA guidelines and the state's analysis or by questioning agency officials—what assumptions were used in calculating the projected air quality impact of a proposed source. The following are very important questions which should be asked:

1. *Where did the state assume the monitor would be located?* One hundred feet from the curb, sixty feet, or at the roadside? Twenty feet off the ground, twelve feet, or five to six feet? In short, would the monitor measure the concentrations to which the average person would be exposed?

2. *Did the state use emission factors which take into account the vehicle age mix which is representative for the area?* Old cars have considerably higher emission rates than new cars.

3. *Did the state assume that new cars would meet the federal vehicle emission standards?* Originally, stringent emission standards for automobiles were to take effect in 1975, but this deadline was extended by Congress and by EPA until 1978. Now Congress is considering legislation to extend the deadline until 1981, making 1982-model cars the first to achieve the maximum reductions of HC, CO, and NO_2 required by the act. Furthermore, there is considerable evidence available now that new cars are not meeting the interim emission standards they were designed to achieve. In actual on-the-road use, these cars are emitting much higher levels of pollutants than prototype models emitted in certification tests conducted at the factory.

4. *Do the traffic volumes used in the model reflect the worst situation?* For example, in a shopping center the peak volumes probably occur during the Christmas shopping season at the close of business. The model for a sports stadium should reflect the traffic volume leaving the stadium—when everyone cranks up and attempts to leave at the same time. In the case of a proposed highway, the model should not necessarily depend on the design capacity of the highway—our existing highways are daily clogged with traffic levels exceeding their design capacity.

5. *Does the model reflect the impact a proposed source may have on other "hot" spots in the area?* While a single source may not cause violations at the site, the traffic it generates may lead to increased congestion or violations at prominent intersections in the region. The state's review must consider the projected traffic volumes at intersections in the immediate vicinity of the source; but depending on the roadway network in a region, a single source such as a coliseum, stadium, or elaborate shopping mall may generate trips from great distances which cause bottlenecks at intersections which are not in the immediate vicinity of the source.

Faulty assumptions such as those revealed by questions like these should be identified and corrected as quickly as possible.

With regard to the last two aspects of the New York state plan which deal with land use, efforts should be made immediately to build citizen pressure for an adequate state maintenance plan and state action to prevent significant deterioration. Educating members of the public who are not already involved with environmental issues is of primary importance. In their past experience in working on the New York Transportation Control Plan for New York City, environmental groups found to their dismay that they were communicating primarily with other environmentalists at the citizen workshops and through their mailings. Moreover, even though the preponderance of testimony offered at the public hearings held supported a strong air quality plan, many officials apparently regarded environmental spokesmen as an elite guard whose views were not representative of the electorate.[37] While citizens may not be able to overcome the bias of public officials on this point, the broader the base of support, the more effective it will be.

Contacts should be made with officials in the DEC's Albany and regional offices, and with federal officials in the EPA Region II office. These contacts are important in keeping abreast of the state's compliance, the flow of EPA guidelines and technical documents, and any changes in regulations or deadlines. Moreover, agency officials can be invaluable in explaining technical reports, describing the data available, or suggesting other sources of information. Citizens should, however, be as specific as possible in their inquiries and should press for specific responses.

"Politics" and "social and economic impact" are phrases citizens may hear bandied about in response to inquiries or suggestions for strict review procedures or enforcement provisions in the state plan. In writing the 1970 Clean Air Act, however, Congress pointedly rejected language which would require consideration of social and economic costs in plans to abate air pollution. The Fifth Circuit U.S. Court of Appeals has reaffirmed this reading of the act in a forceful decision which struck economic considerations from enforcement provisions in the Georgia State Implementation Plan:

> Under 1970 amendments to [the] federal Clean Air Act, Congress intended that considerations of economic cost or technical feasibility be always subordinate to considerations of public health, and that cost and feasibility are not to be considered in meeting three-year deadlines for attaining national primary standards. . . . The approach of the Amendments, as one commentator has expressed it, was to shift from the

approach of earlier legislation of "establishing air pollution standards" commensurate with existing technological feasibility" to a bolder "policy which forces technology to catch up with the newly promulgated standards." Note, The Clean Air Amendments of 1970: Better Automotive Ideas from Congress, 12 B.C. Ind. & Comm. L. Rev. 571, 581 (1971). As Senator Muskie, the Senate sponsor of the Amendments, put it: ["]The first responsibility of Congress is not the making of technological or economic judgments—or even to be limited by what is or appears to be technological or economically feasible. Our responsibility is to establish what the public interest requires to protect the health of persons. This may mean that people and industries will be asked to do what seems to be impossible at the present time. But if health is to be protected, these challenges must be met.["] 116 Cong. Rec. 16091 (daily ed. Sept. 21, 1970), quoted at Note, *supra,* at 581. . . . The Senate Subcommittee on Air and Water Pollution, which had been responsible for drafting the Senate version of the Amendments, sent a briefing paper to the Administrator in early 1972. In that paper, the Subcommittee stated its understanding of the matter: ["]Inclusion of a test of social and economic feasibility or compliance with those control requirements necessary to achieve protection of public health as part of implementation plan guidelines compromises the intention of the Act. . . .["] Hearings Before the Subcomm. on Air and Water Pollution of the Senate Comm. on Public Works on the Implementation of the Clean Air Act Amendments of 1970, 92d Cong., 2d Sess. at 308 (1972).[38]

Citizens should not be timid about requesting information or assistance from air pollution control officials. The Clean Air Act of 1970 was exemplary in requiring assurances that the state planning process be opened to citizen participation. The debate on the bill at the time of passage reflects the strong congressional intent that citizens be represented in the planning process and be provided with tools to assist in enforcement of the act. Congress took an unprecedented stand in requiring that the confidentiality of "process" data from private companies must be waived when it pertains to pollutant emissions and thus conflicts with the need for the public to know.

Armed with a knowledge of the legal obligations of the state and a basic understanding of some of the assumptions used in estimating emissions from projected developments, citizens should press agency and elected officials to commit the state to adequate plans for reviewing indirect sources, for maintaining standards, and for preventing deterioration of existing air quality. Public opinion combined with the threat of citizen suits to overturn an inadequate plan offer considerable leverage for influencing state proposals.

Most importantly, the public hearings held on the state proposals —for the maintenance plan, the redesignation of clean air areas under the federal non-deterioration plan, and indirect source review —should represent the *culmination* of citizen efforts, not the beginning. By the time a public hearing is held, it is probably too late to effect major changes in the state's proposals. In the past, public hearings have been scheduled only a week to ten days before the deadline for the submission of plans to the federal EPA and only minor changes, if any, were made after the hearing. This does not mean that efforts should not be made to prepare strong testimony, to arrange for witnesses, and to encourage a large number of people to attend. The public hearing is the citizens' first opportunity to "build a record," i.e., to introduce formal evidence, present pertinent statistics, and express public opinion. Under the act the transcript of the hearing must be considered by EPA in its review of the plan, and this record is vital in pursuing a legal challenge to an inadequate plan.

After the plan(s) have been submitted to EPA, there is still an opportunity to influence EPA's review, and to press EPA to correct by federal regulation any deficiencies in the state proposals. Review of New York State plans is conducted primarily in the EPA Region II office. Citizens should find out who is heading up a particular review and should communicate criticisms of the plan directly to this person. He or she should be made aware of possible inadequacies in the plan such as the state's failure to consider important statistics or use of invalid assumptions in projecting future growth rates, emissions, or air quality.

The EPA review offers another opportunity to "go on record." The EPA administrator publishes in the *Federal Register* his proposed approval/disapproval of each state plan and allows a thirty-day written comment period before making the final determination.[39] Even if citizens' comments do not reverse EPA's position, detailed and specific examples of the inadequacy of a state plan can be an effective tool in preparing a legal case against EPA or the state to remedy a weak plan. Not only do the comments and the hearing transcripts formally introduce important facts which can then be taken before the court, but they also serve notice to the court that these facts or issues were brought to the attention of the state—or the EPA administrator—*prior to the submission or approval of the plan.* This strengthens the citizens' position that they turned to the courts for remedy only as a last resort.

Table 9
National Primary and Secondary Ambient Air Quality Standards

Pollutant	Primary Standard	Secondary Standard
Sulfur Oxides:	(a) 80 micrograms per cubic meter (0.03 ppm)—annual arithmetic mean.	1,300 micrograms per cubic meter (0.5 ppm)—maximum 3 hour concentration not to be exceeded more than once a year.
	(b) 365 micrograms per cubic meter (0.14 ppm)—maximum 24-hr. concentration not to be exceeded more than once a year.	
Particulate Matter:	(a) 75 micrograms per cubic meter—annual geometric mean.	(a) 60 micrograms per cubic meter—annual geometric mean, as a guide to be used in assessing implementation plans to achieve 24-hour standard.
	(b) 260 micrograms per cubic meter—maximum 24-hr. concentration not be exceeded more than once a year.	(b) 180 micrograms per cubic meter—maximum 24-hr. concentration not to be exceeded more than once a year.
Carbon Monoxide:	(a) 10 milligrams per cubic meter (9 ppm)—maximum 8-hr. concentration not to be exceeded once a year. (b) 40 milligrams per cubic meter (35 ppm)—maximum 1-hr. concentration not to be exceeded more than once a year.	Same as Primary Standard.
Photochemical Oxidants:	160 micrograms per cubic meter (0.08 ppm)—maximum 1-hr. concentration not to be exceeded more than once a year.	Same as Primary Standard.
Hydrocarbons:	160 micrograms per cubic meter (0.24 ppm)—maximum 3-hr. concentration (6 to 9 a.m.) not to be exceeded more than once a year.	Same as Primary Standard.
Nitrogen Dioxide:	100 micrograms per cubic meter (0.05 ppm)—annual arithmetic mean.	Same as Primary Standard.

NOTE: All measurements of air quality are corrected to a reference temperature of 25°C. and to a reference pressure of 760 millimeters of mercury (1,013.2 millibars).

As has been indicated, the Clean Air Act of 1970 includes a special provision for citizen suits.[40] Under this provision, any person has the right to sue in federal district court to enjoin violations of the act or state implementation plans. This broad right is limited in the following ways: (1) a citizen may not sue for damages, but only to enjoin an illegal act or to force the performance of a nondiscretionary duty; (2) if the administrator of EPA or the state is diligently prosecuting a suit in federal courts, a citizen may not institute a separate suit, but he may intervene and become a party to the suit. The act also provides for the payment of litigation costs, including attorney and expert witness fees, at the discretion of the court.

NOTES

1. 42 U.S.C. §1857 *et seq.*
2. The standards which have been established are given in Table 9 on p. 207.
3. The state must apply a margin of error in approving or disapproving the construction of new sources, because the 1970 Clean Air Act requires the state to *insure* the attainment and maintenance of national standards [§110(a)(2)(B); 42 U.S.C. §1857c–5(a) (2)(B)]. Any construction which might jeopardize attainment and maintenance should be prohibited.
4. §110(a)(2)(B); 42 U.S.C. §1857c–5(a)(2)(B).
5. Stationary sources are sources which emit pollutants from a stack while operating. Examples are smelters, paper mills, fossil-fueled power plants, and steel mills.
6. Indirect sources are sources which cause air pollution because they attract mobile sources, notably the automobile. Examples are shopping centers, sports stadiums, highways, and airports.
7. §110(a)(2)(D); 42 U.S.C. §1857c–5(a)(2)(D). The administrator of EPA has established new source performance standards for the following categories: fossil-fuel-fired steam generators, incinerators, Portland cement plants, nitric acid plants, sulfuric acid plants, asphalt concrete plants, petroleum refineries, storage vessels for petroleum liquids, secondary lead smelters, secondary brass and bronze ingot production plants, iron and steel plants, and sewage treatment plants.
8. 40 CFR §51.18.
9. §110(a)(4); 42 U.S.C. §1857c–5(a)(4).
10. Natural Resources Defense Council v. Environmental Protection Agency, 494 F.2d 519, 6 ERC 1475 (2d Cir. 1974).
11. Natural Resources Defense Council v. Environmental Protection Agency, 489 F.2d 390, 6 ERC 1248 (5th Cir. 1974).
12. 42 U.S.C. §1857h–2. *See* Richard E. Ayres and James F. Miller, "Citizen Suits Under the Clean Air Act Amendments of 1970," *Natural Resources Defense Council Newsletter,* Vol. 1, No. 4 (Winter 1971). Copies are available at $.50 per copy from the Natural Resources Defense Council, 15 West 44th Street, New York, N.Y. 10036.
13. *See* 39 *Federal Register* 7270–7285 (February 25, 1974); 40 CFR §52.22.
14. 39 *Federal Register* 45014 (December 30, 1974).
15. 6 NYCRR Part 203.
16. U.S. Environmental Protection Agency, *Guidelines for Air Quality Maintenance Planning and Analysis, Volume 9: Evaluating Indirect Sources* (Draft) (Research Triangle Park, N.C.: Office of Air Quality Planning and Standards, 1975).
17. *See* the discussion of significant deterioration on pp. 197–200.
18. The definition states that construction includes land preparation "specifically

designed for an indirect source." However, this vague requirement may not be difficult for a developer to skirt in the case of a site which was cleared before building plans were made. Nevertheless, if the developer has not been steadily at work on the site since clearing the land, it may be successfully argued that his construction has not been "continuous" and that he must therefore be reviewed.

19. 39 *Federal Register* 7271 (February 25, 1974). The Natural Resources Defense Council does not agree that specifying large cutoff levels for review was necessary to reflect "nationwide" characteristics. Indeed, in virtually every area of the country, suburban or urban, existing conditions indicate that healthful air quality will be in jeopardy unless facilities smaller than EPA has specified are reviewed and designed for optimal access by public transit or bicycle and pedestrian travel in order to reduce projected emissions from automobile traffic. However, it is useful to note the administrator's admission that the categories for review established by EPA are not definitive and that more stringent review provisions may be called for.

20. Natural Resources Defense Council v. Environmental Protection Agency, Civil No. 74–1235 (D.C. Cir. 1974).

21. 475 F.2d 968, 4 ERC 1945 (D.C. Cir. 1973).

22. 38 *Federal Register* 15836 (June 18, 1973) and 39 *Federal Register* 16344 (May 8, 1974); 40 CFR §51.12.

23. U.S. Environmental Protection Agency, *Guidelines for Air Quality Maintenance Planning and Analysis, Volume18: Designation of Air Quality Maintenance Areas* (Research Triangle Park, N.C.: Office of Air Quality Planning and Standards, January 1974): OAQPS No. 1.2-016: I-7.

24. U.S. Environmental Protection Agency, *Guidelines for Air Quality Maintenance Planning and Analysis* (Research Triangle Park, N.C.: Office of Air Quality Planning and Standards, January 1974-   ). The volumes of this series are available from the U.S. Environmental Protection Agency, Air Pollution Technical Information Center, Research Triangle Park, N.C. 27711.

25. The number of vehicle miles traveled (VMT) by automobiles across the nation increased by 5 percent, 6 percent, and 8 percent in 1970, 1971, and 1972, respectively. The gasoline shortage in the winter of 1973–1974 curbed this increase temporarily, but with increased supplies at hand, the VMT is on the rise again. For more information on trends in automobile travel and the inaccuracies in federal EPA predictions regarding mechanical exhaust control devices, see the Natural Resources Defense Council, *Transportation Controls for Clean Air,* available from the Natural Resources Defense Council, 917 15th Street, N.W., Washington, D.C. 20005; and Calspan Corporation, *Automobile Exhaust Emission Surveillance* (March 1973) (Summary), available from the federal EPA.

26. At hearings held on the 1970 Clean Air Act, Dr. John T. Middleton, commissioner of the National Air Pollution Control Administration, testified that: "We know from the criteria published for sulfur oxides, that at certain levels definite adverse effects occur in the lung. We also know that at a little lower level there are more subtle effects on the action of the lung, and that below that some enzyme system begins to fail or to function improperly.

"The no-effect level would have to be somewhere below that, but as science progresses, it is very likely we are going to find still other body chemical systems that are being affected, so the no-effect level always corresponds, you might say, to the limitations of scientific knowledge in this area.

"It is because our knowledge is, hopefully, improving with time that . . . there is a need to revise the air quality criteria periodically . . . which . . . in turn may require different air quality standards." U.S. Congress Senate Subcommittee on Air and Water Pollution of the Committee on Public Works, *Hearings on S. 3229, S. 3466, S. 3546,* 91st Cong., 2d Sess., 1970, p. 1490.

27. The EPA CHESS study, released in 1973, reported: "Our data indicate that adverse effects on elderly subjects with heart and lung disease, and on panels of asthmatics, are being experienced even on days below the national primary standard for 24 hour levels of SO_2 and total suspended particulates." U.S. Environmental Protection Agency, *Health Consequences of Sulfur Oxides: Summary and Conclusions Based upon CHESS studies of 1970–1971* (August 15, 1973) (Draft), p. 22.

28. Unlike sulfur dioxide, sulfates (SO_4, which forms when SO_2 that is released into the atmosphere oxidizes) are distributed in dangerous concentrations over wide areas, not just at the points where plumes from specific sources touch down. A recent EPA memorandum indicated that high sulfate levels are being recorded even in rural areas of the country, hundreds of miles from large sulfur dioxide sources. The memorandum urged that unless study and control are initiated at once, the uniform levels of sulfate concentrations will make it impossible to conduct valid studies of the potential adverse effects of various concentrations and exposures.

29. Sierra Club v. Ruckelshaus, 344 F. Supp. 253, 4 ERC 1205 (D.D.C. 1972), *aff'd per curiam,* 4 ERC 1815 (D.C. Cir. 1972), *aff'd by an equally divided Court sub nom.* Fri v. Sierra Club, 412 U.S. 541, 5 ERC 1417 (1973). As previously pointed out, the Fifth Circuit U.S. Court of Appeals has subsequently held that the use of tall smokestacks and other means of dispersing pollutants violated the principle of non-degradation. Natural Resources Defense Council v. Environmental Protection Agency, 489 F.2d 390, 6 ERC 1248 (5th Cir. 1974).

30. *See* 38 *Federal Register* 18986 (July 16, 1973) and 39 *Federal Register* 42509 (December 5, 1974).

31. When sulfur dioxide (SO_2) is released in the atmosphere, it can oxidize to form sulfates (SO_4) which then combine with water molecules to form sulfuric acid (H_2SO_4), resulting in what is known as sulfuric acid mist or acid rainfall.

32. The addresses of DEC's nine regional offices are listed in the Appendix.

33. Sierra Club v. Environmental Protection Agency, Civil Nos. 74–2063 and 74–2079 (D.C. Cir. 1974).

34. §307; 42 U.S.C. §1857h–5.

35. 494 F.2d 519, 6 ERC 1475 (2d Cir. 1974).

36. *See* note 16 above.

37. Interestingly enough, a recent study of neighborhood governments in New York City conducted by Columbia University's Bureau of Applied Social Research found that local leaders perceived air pollution to be less of a problem than did their constituents. *See* Allen Barton *et al., Progress Report for Members of New York City Neighborhood Study* (November 1972).

38. Natural Resources Defense Council v. Environmental Protection Agency, 489 F.2d 390, 6 ERC 1248 (5th Cir. 1974).

39. The administrator is not required by the act to provide a thirty-day written comment period; however, this has become an established practice of EPA in recognition of its responsibilities to provide for citizen participation.

40. §304; 42 U.S.C. §1857h–2. *See* note 12 above.

CHAPTER 11

Land Use Controls Under Federal Water Pollution Legislation

T HE PASSAGE OF the Federal Water Pollution Control Act Amendments of 1972[1] marked a turning point in the approach taken toward the problem of water pollution control in this country. Whereas past legislation had endorsed the practice of allowing certain waters to remain severely degraded to permit industrial and other uses, the 1972 amendments rejected this concept and adopted the view that "no one has the right to pollute—that pollution continues because of technological limits, not because of any inherent right to use the nation's waterways for the purpose of disposing wastes."[2] The new law rejected the traditional reliance on the "assimilative capacity" of our waterways and made it clear, as Senator Muskie stated on the floor of the Senate, that our "streams and rivers are no longer to be considered part of the waste treatment process."[3]

In implementing these new principles, the 1972 amendments recognized and came to grips with economic and technological constraints in such a way as to produce a regulatory program that is both strong and workable. They also recognized that if water quality is to be protected, there must not only be effective regulation of existing sources of water pollution, but also land use planning and controls to regulate the location of new sources. Before discussing in more detail the portions of the amendments which deal most directly with land use, a brief overview of this new act's most important provisions will be presented to outline the overall attack on water pollution, of which land use planning and control are an essential component part.

The New Act: An Overview

The objective of the 1972 amendments is "to restore and maintain the chemical, physical, and biological integrity of the Nation's waters."[4] Six national goals and policies are set out as means by which this objective can be achieved. The goals and policies established are that:

(1) . . . the discharge of pollutants into the navigable waters be eliminated by 1985;

(2) . . . wherever attainable, an interim goal of water quality which provides for the protection and propagation of fish, shellfish, and wildlife and provides for recreation in and on the water be achieved by July 1, 1983;

(3) . . . the discharge of toxic pollutants in toxic amounts be prohibited;

(4) . . . Federal financial assistance be provided to construct publicly owned waste treatment works;

(5) . . . areawide waste treatment management planning processes be developed and implemented to assure adequate control of sources of pollutants in each State; and

(6) . . . a major research and demonstration effort be made to develop technology necessary to eliminate the discharge of pollutants into the navigable waters, waters of the contiguous zone, and the oceans.

The regulatory program established by the 1972 amendments to implement these new national policies is innovative and far-reaching. Primary responsibility for implementation resides with the U.S. Environmental Protection Agency (EPA), but state–federal cooperation is an essential aspect of the total effort.

A basic distinction is made by the act between point sources and non-point sources of pollution. A point source is any confined, discrete conveyance such as a pipe, ditch, or even a floating craft.[5] Typical point sources include discharges via a pipe of effluent from industrial works or municipal sewage treatment plants. Uncollected runoff from an agricultural area or a mining operation is a typical non-point source of water pollution.[6] For point sources, the act provides the following regulatory scheme:

1. By July 1977 all dischargers other than municipal sewage treatment plants must have achieved effluent limitations based upon the "best practicable" pollution control technology currently available, and municipal sewage treatment plants must have achieved limitations based upon secondary treatment. [§301(b)(1)]

2. By July 1983 non-municipal point sources must have the "best available technology economically achievable" in operation, and municipal sewage treatment plants must have installed the "best practicable waste treatment technology." [§301(b)(2)]

3. Special effluent standards for toxic water pollutants must be based solely on environmental and safety considerations and must be met substantially before the 1977 deadline. [§307(a)]

4. New source performance standards based upon the "best available demonstrated control technology" must be met by all new facilities or installations. [§306]

5. Special effluent restrictions for particular dischargers based upon existing water quality standards must be employed whenever it is apparent that application of the toxic and technologically based standards above will not achieve water quality standards in a given basin by 1977.[7] [§301(b)(1) and §303(d)]. For 1983, a similar upgrading of the technologically based standards must be applied to dischargers in those basins where the technological standards will not achieve the 1983 "swimmable and fishable" water quality standard. [§302]

6. These effluent restrictions must be applied to point sources through a permit program—the National Pollutant Discharge Elimination System (NPDES)—administered either by EPA or the states.[8] [Section 402]. The 1972 amendments contain strong monitoring and enforcement provisions, including provisions for citizen suits, for ensuring that permit conditions are actually met. [§308, §309, §505]

The act's regulatory program for controlling non-point source pollution is set out primarily in Section 208 of the act. Under this section, the land use implications of which will be discussed in more detail below, comprehensive plans for the abatement of point and non-point source pollution must be prepared either by designated local agencies or by the state. The plans must be submitted to the administrator of EPA for his approval and, once approved, must be implemented by appropriate regulatory agencies. The overall purpose of Section 208 planning is to ensure that the act's goal of "water quality which provides for the protection and propagation of fish, shellfish, and wildlife and provides for recreation in and on the water" is achieved by 1983. Thus, Section 208 plans should be submitted to EPA in time for their full impact to be felt by the 1983 deadline.

Among other provisions of the act are those which establish a grant-in-aid and planning program for the construction of municipal sewage treatment plants [§201] and which require that each state develop a continuing planning process [§303(e)]. Both of these aspects of the act are discussed more fully below.

EPA's implementation of the 1972 amendments has been disappointing in many respects. The following actions of the agency have all been met by lawsuits brought by the Natural Resources Defense Council and other environmental organizations:

Nixon

1. Failure, because of stern directives from the Office of Management and Budget, to allot half of the money authorized for the construction of municipal sewage treatment plants (because of this impoundment, a substantial number of municipalities will not meet the 1977 requirements of the act applicable to sewage treatment works);[9]

2. Failure to meet more than a score of deadlines set by the act, thus prompting litigation which resulted in the establishment of substitute or replacement dates for the statutory deadlines missed;[10]

3. Failure to include in its list of toxic pollutants many metals and other substances which are toxic to humans or aquatic organisms (in fact, not including on this list most of the substances regulated because of their toxicity in the 1962 Public Health Service drinking water standards);[11] and

4. Exclusion of a wide range of non-industrial point sources from the National Pollutant Discharge Elimination System permit program which is intended by statute to regulate all point sources.[12]

In large part these shortcomings can be attributed to a lack of adequate resources. Sent out by Congress to do battle with almost the entirety of American industry and agriculture, as well as with other federal agencies which speak for powerful commercial interests, EPA has been armed with woefully inadequate resources. This weakness has often led to overcautious, hesitant, and intimidated behavior by EPA in implementing the act.

It is important that citizens who are concerned with the problems of water pollution and with the land use considerations which cannot be separated from these problems recognize both (1) that Congress has passed strong legislation that mandates the cleaning up of the country's waters; and (2) that implementation of this legislation often falls short of the legal requirements established. In whatever ways possible, citizens should support the provision of adequate resources for the federal EPA and press for conscientious and legally responsible implementation of environmental legislation by this agency.

Land Use Planning Provisions of the 1972 Amendments

1. Section 208. At least six sections of the 1972 amendments are concerned with planning.[13] Of these, Section 208 is by far the most important, in large measure because it provides a basis for regulating non-point sources of pollution. As discussed above, typical examples of non-point sources are runoff from agricultural land and runoff from mining operations. The water pollution caused by such non-point sources is extremely serious. In fact, it has been estimated that runoff accounts for perhaps half of our total water pollution problem.[14] Consequently, to achieve the goals established by the amendments, non-point source controls must be instituted. This will require that land uses which may result in this type of pollution be carefully planned, designed, and regulated. Section 208 requires such land use planning throughout the entire nation.

In addition to its vital role with respect to non-point sources, Section 208 also greatly strengthens the act's control of point sources and their impacts on land use. Section 208 plans must establish a regulatory program to control the location, modification, and construction of *all* facilities which may discharge pollutants, and they must also contain long-term specifications for the construction and use of public sewage treatment plants.

The requirements of Section 208 apply throughout all portions of each state. The governor may designate particular areas with severe water quality control problems for "area-wide" planning by local agencies.[15] The state, on the other hand, is responsible for Section 208 planning in all areas of the state which are not so designated. Special federal funds are available for planning under Section 208.[16]

If a governor chooses not to designate particular areas, he has two alternative courses of action: He may either remain silent, thus allowing local areas to designate themselves under special provisions of the act; or he may make a determination not to designate certain areas or even the entire state, thereby precluding both local self-designation and special federal funding for intensive area-wide planning under Section 208, as well as obligating the state to carry out 208 planning.

In 1974 the governor of New York State originally made a determination not to designate the entire state; however, after the Environmental Defense Fund filed a legal suit seeking, among other things, a coordinated water resources planning and management program for Nassau and Suffolk Counties on Long Island,[17] the governor designated these two counties as a 208 planning area in December 1974. An application for planning funds for this area was made, and in the spring of 1975 a grant of $5.2 million was approved. A number of local agencies will participate in the development of the area-wide 208 plan, which will be coordinated by the Nassau-Suffolk Regional Planning Board.

The required contents of Section 208 plans are carefully laid out in the act. The following are some of the most important requirements:

1. The plan must identify waste treatment needs, both municipal and industrial, for the next twenty years (an analysis of alternative waste treatment systems must be included).

2. It must provide for the establishment of a program to regulate the location, modification, and construction of all polluting facilities, whether involving a point or non-point source.

3. It must establish a program to identify and control non-point sources of pollution, including sources related to agricultural, silvicultural, mining, and construction activities. Land use requirements must be imposed to control this non-point source pollution.

4. It must develop a process to identify and control salt water intrusion into rivers, lakes, and estuaries resulting from any reduction of fresh water flow.

5. It must establish a process to control the disposal of pollutants on land or in subsurface excavations to protect ground and surface water quality.

6. It must identify the agencies that will implement the Section 208 plan.

Plans meeting these requirements must be prepared and approved before the middle of 1977 under the time frame provided by the act. It is imperative that Section 208 plans be ready by then so that they can be implemented in the Phase II period of the act, from 1977 to 1983. The full impact of these plans should be felt by the 1983 deadline for achieving the "fishable and swimmable" water quality standard.

Once a Section 208 plan has been approved by EPA and the implementing agency has been designated by the governor, all grants for the construction of publicly owned sewage treatment plants[18] must be made to the designated agency and must be in conformity with the approved plan. Also, no permit may be issued under the National Pollutant Discharge Elimination System[19] if it conflicts with such an approved plan. Thus, the Section 208 plan must be implemented. Once approved, it cannot be left on the shelf to gather dust.

EPA has elaborated on the statutory requirements of Section 208 in two documents, both released in May 1974. (1) It has promulgated regulations governing federal grants to designated area-wide agencies which prescribe the contents of the plans these agencies are to produce.[20] (2) It has published proposed guidelines to aid area-wide agencies in carrying out the actual planning required by Section 208.[21]

There are, however, serious shortcomings in EPA's implementation of Section 208. Perhaps the most glaring has been the agency's failure to give direction to the states regarding planning in non-designated areas, thus giving the misleading impression that Section 208 planning is unique to designated areas. Since fewer than thirty areas (almost all of them urban-industrial areas) have been designated, it is clear that most of the non-point source pollution in the nation will remain unabated unless EPA requires implementation of Section 208 in non-designated areas. Accordingly, the Natural Resources Defense Council filed suit in October 1974 to compel EPA to carry out its mandatory responsibility to implement Section 208 planning on a statewide basis, and to do so in a timely manner.

EPA's unsatisfactory leadership with respect to Section 208 is also apparent in the pace at which the agency is implementing this section in designated areas. The timetable set forth by Congress called for area-wide designations or non-designations by July 1973. However, EPA produced regulations for this process nine months late and designations were not made until after March 1974.[22] Thus, the development of Section 208 plans is already running badly behind schedule and EPA is showing few signs of more aggressive implementation. The timing of Section 208 planning is especially important because the provision for full federal funding for area-wide planning ends on June 30, 1975. Under the timetable established by Congress in Section 208, full funding would have carried the planning agencies in designated areas through two years of the three-year planning process. Because of EPA's sluggishness, the funding for the handful of areas already designated will decrease after only one year, just as the agencies are getting underway. Funding after June 30, 1975, will be less than the 75 percent maximum. Just how much less remains to be seen, but past Administration policy on pollution control expenditures is far from reassuring.

One approach under discussion within EPA is that of implementing statewide Section 208 requirements through the basin plans it is requiring the states to prepare under Section 303(e) of the act. These basin plans are essentially management documents, spelling out what needs to be done regarding the water pollution problems of the basins. They do not, however, create any major new regulatory or source control programs such as those required by Section 208. The EPA guidelines on basin planning do require analysis and description of non-point source problems and possible remedies,[23] but no provision is made for the development of the regulatory programs mandated by Section 208. Thus the basin planning program as developed to date has not established a base for adequate statewide 208 planning.

As will be discussed below under Citizen Action, the 1972 amendments include strong provisions for public participation. If these provisions are to be meaningful as far as Section 208 is concerned, it is essential that a 208 plan be drawn up as a discrete document (or at least as a separate, discrete part of a larger plan) which is made available in draft form for public review and participation at an early stage of the planning process. If, for example, in the case of statewide 208 planning, different aspects of required programs were scattered through a basin plan, it would be very difficult for citizens to assess whether the state was adequately meeting the statutory requirements of Section 208 and was responsibly addressing the state's problems.

2. Non-degradation. The non-degradation principle in water quality planning is analogous to the principle of non-deterioration of air quality discussed in Chapter 10. It holds that all bodies of water whose actual water quality is better than that required by water quality standards should be protected from degradation. Without a non-degradation principle, such waters could be legally degraded down to the standards. Protection in these instances is very closely tied to land use regulation, since degradation can result from the location of new sources or changes in existing streamside land use patterns. If clean water is to be preserved, adjacent land uses must be regulated.

As discussed in the preceding chapter, it has been established through the courts that the Clean Air Act of 1970 mandates the establishment by EPA of a non-degradation standard to protect clean air areas.[24] The 1972 amendments to the Federal Water Pollution Control Act also mandate a non-degradation standard for the country's waters. In view of the similarities both in language and in legislative history between these amendments and the Clean Air Act, it might be expected that EPA would have come forward with a major program to prohibit the deterioration of higher quality waters. Unfortunately, this has not been the case. As of March 1975, all that EPA has done is to state that all basin plans must incorporate any existing state anti-degradation clauses—which are notoriously weak. The necessity of establishing a program to prevent significant deterioration has been under discussion within EPA, but no action has been taken nor have any proposals been officially published. Under such circumstances, the door is left open for high quality streams to deteriorate.

This prospect certainly exists in New York State, where no strong non-degradation policy is embodied in state law. An "antidegradation statement," which has the status of a policy rather than a law, was adopted in May 1970 by the New York State Water Resources Commission (a former state agency whose functions and powers were assumed by the New York State Department of Environment Conservation) at the behest of the U.S. Department of the Interior (the federal EPA also had not yet been established at this time). Like most state non-degradation provisions, this policy statement is very weak in that no mechanism was established for its implementation, and it is vaguely worded, allowing degradation when "it has been demonstrated to the satisfaction of the commissioner of environmental conservation that other uses and different standards are justifiable as a result of necessary economic or social development." Although similarly worded statements have been adopted by most of the states in the nation, there is little evidence to indicate that they have provided any actual protection of waters from degradation. In New York State, the effort to determine what action had been taken by the state with respect to non-degradation clearly indicated that most DEC officials are not aware of the existence of the state's antidegradation statement. This, of course, does not preclude the possibility that in particular circumstances DEC may act to prevent the degradation of waters.

The problem of non-degradation should not be confused with other aspects of water quality protection. For example, the establishment and enforcement of standards, as well as the protection of particular high quality streams, are separate issues from the question of what happens to *all* waters that have water quality that is *better* than standards.[25]

In 1973, in an effort to spur the adoption of a strong non-degradation policy by EPA, the Project on Clean Water of the Natural Resources Defense Council (NRDC) developed a policy on non-degradation of water quality which it recommended to EPA. The following is a statement of that policy:

Policy on Non-Degradation of Water Quality

The new Federal Water Pollution Control Act of 1972 requires the Environmental Protection Agency to develop a program to protect high-quality waters and prevent deterioration in existing water quality. To assist EPA in carrying out this responsibility, NRDC suggests the following policies be followed regarding non-degradation of water quality.

An effective program for preventing significant degradation of water quality should include (1) specific substantive standards defining significant degradation and (2) effective procedural mechanisms for enforcing these standards.

Substantive Standards. After public hearings, all water segments in the state should be divided into two categories. Category I would be segments which should be kept in their present condition because they constitute an outstanding natural resource, *e.g.*, rivers in parks and refuges and other waters of great recreational or ecological significance. No degradation in these segments would be allowed.

Category II would be all other segments. Water quality here would be allowed to degrade by a small predetermined percentage. The percentage would vary depending on the water quality parameter but in no case would the percentage be large enough to allow the waters to degrade significantly. Moreover, if existing water quality meets the 1983 interim standard expressed in Sections 101(a)(2) and 302 of the Federal Water Pollution Control Act, the quality should in no case fall below that standard. The water quality required by 1983 is that "which provides for the protection and propagation of fish, shellfish and wildlife and which provides for recreation in and on the water." Section 101(a)(2).

The baseline water quality against which to measure degradation should be that existing near the end of 1972 when the Act was passed. If data [are] sparse, the 1972 water quality should be estimated.

Procedural Requirements. Non-degradation programs should be implemented immediately in order to play a part in the issuance of the first round of permits under the Act. Permits for new sources should be issued only upon a showing by the discharger that significant degradation will not result.

The non-degradation program would be primarily a state program, but it would be EPA's responsibility to review the classification of waters into Categories I and II, to establish national standards defining significant degradation, and to establish general procedures to ensure that these standards are enforced.

3. Construction of municipal sewage treatment plants. Section 201 authorizes the administrator of EPA to make grants for the planning and construction of publicly owned sewage treatment plants. While the purpose of Section 201 is to improve water quality, construction grants awarded under this section can have enormous implications for land development, since in large measure the size and location of sewage treatment facilities, along with the size and placement of connecting interceptor sewer lines, determine the extent and shape of community growth. Past evidence has indicated that where facilities are built for a population considerably larger than that existing in an area, growth to the capacity of the system is generated. Thus, great care should be taken before new sewerage facilities are constructed to assess their land use impacts, to consider alternative dimensions, and to provide for needed land use planning and regulation.

Unfortunately, it appears that very little attention has been paid to the land use implications of Section 201 grants. In 1974 a study of the impact of sewerage construction grants on residential land use was published by the Council on Environmental Quality (CEQ).[26] This study, which analyzed fifty-two EPA grants for sewerage construction, showed that the grants had provided for substantial excess sewerage capacity,[27] and that either the land use impacts of the grants had not been assessed or negative secondary effects of residential development had not been considered. In eight detailed case studies which were prepared on areas as diverse as Tulsa, Oklahoma, and Ocean County, New Jersey, urban planners and local officials expressed the belief that nothing could halt development in their respective areas and that sewage treatment systems had to be provided.

In fact, according to the CEQ study, procedures used in the physical design of interceptors, local planning and review procedures for project plans, and methods of project financing may encourage the "inevitability" of development. The summary of the report states that "[s]tudy findings indicate that current financing procedures—on both the local and federal level—may encourage the construction of sewerage systems tailored to the needs of future developers rather than the control of pollution problems." For example, in communities which intend to finance the local share of project costs by assessing connection fees on new development, pressure is created to encourage rapid growth to ensure financial viability for the project. Further, since the federal program is viewed as a one-time-only opportunity, communities are encouraged to seek as much excess capacity as possible.

One of the most disturbing findings of the CEQ study is that over half of the land to be served by the projects studied is presently vacant. Thus it appears that many localities are seeking not only to improve water quality, but also to obtain a federal subsidy for suburban growth on vacant land. This appears to run counter to the intent of the act which requires the EPA administrator to encourage sewerage schemes which combine open space and recreational considerations with waste management.[28]

The 1972 amendments to the Federal Water Pollution Control Act provide some safeguards for the construction grant program to assure that it is focused on improving water quality, and that the land use effects of the program are assessed adequately. Unfortunately, these safeguards are either not working properly, or their implementation is too new to be evaluated.

First, before a treatment plant or sewerage system is constructed, federal funding is available for the development of a facilities plan that assesses the effects of the proposed construction.[29] However, many projects which EPA has considered to be beyond the stage of facilities planning have been funded without such a plan. Even where the facility planning process is carried out, moreover, there is no assurance that environmental effects, including land use impacts, are assessed adequately, since EPA does not appear to be implementing aggressively the regulations governing this planning.

In addition, the act requires integration of Section 201 grants with the planning provisions of Sections 208 and 303. As has been pointed out above, once a Section 208 plan has been approved by EPA, all grants for the construction of sewage treatment works must be in conformity with this plan. This provision reflects Congress' intent that the construction of waste treatment facilities be coordinated with the land use planning and regulation required under Section 208. However, this requirement does not affect construction grants that are made before an approved Section 208 plan is in existence, and, as has been discussed, EPA's implementation of Section 208 has proceeded at a very slow pace.

Grants for sewerage construction must also be in conformity with state planning under Section 303, through which statewide construction priorities must be established. Unfortunately, the continuing planning process program under Section 303 has just gotten underway and as yet has had little effect.

Another safeguard is the National Environmental Policy Act (NEPA).[30] Although EPA is excused by the act from preparing environmental impact statements under NEPA for permits (except those for new sources) granted under the National Pollutant Discharge Elimination System (NPDES) established by Section 402, EPA is not excused from preparing such impact statements in the construction grant area. Initially, EPA was not preparing NEPA statements for construction grants, but under pressure from Congress and from citizens in particular areas where construction of sewerage facilities was proposed, the agency has altered its position somewhat. As of December 1974, EPA had prepared environmental impact statements for about 65 out of a total of approximately 4,000 project grants. The prospects for fuller EPA review in the coming year are no more promising. For fiscal 1976, EPA has set as a *goal* preparation of environmental impact statements for 5 percent of the construction grants awarded.

In general, the movement toward the preparation of NEPA statements, which must consider alternative possibilities, land use implications, and other environmental consequences, exists in tension with EPA's desire to expedite the granting of funds available for waste treatment facilities. The latter motivation has in a number of cases led EPA to overlook important land use considerations, while environmental impact statements have often been prepared on a "squeaky wheel" basis. The present administrative trend in EPA suggests that environmental impact statements are more likely to be filed for large projects. EPA officials believe that while the percentage of impact statements prepared is small compared to the large number of grants, the statements cover a larger percentage of the total number of grant dollars.

In essence, then, the sewerage construction grant program established under Section 201 is extremely important in terms of land use.

Concerned citizens should be aware of its potential impact on their communities and ready to monitor its implementation.

Another important provision of the 1972 amendments with which citizens who are concerned about land use problems should be familiar is Section 402(h),[31] which authorizes EPA to stop any new sewer hookups where treatment plants are in violation of an NPDES permit condition. EPA actually has the right to seek a court order prohibiting such connections, and should be pressed to do so, if necessary.

Further, on January 15, 1974, EPA released a policy memorandum authorizing the inclusion of special growth-related planning conditions in NPDES permits issued for municipal sewerage facilities that are threatened by rapid growth.[32] Such municipalities can be required, as an enforceable condition of an NPDES permit, to anticipate and regulate new sewer hookups which would overload the treatment plant. Although EPA permit writers are not required to impose such conditions, they are required to consider doing so when sewerage systems are already utilized to 85 percent of capacity and are experiencing or anticipate growth at 3 percent or more per year. Unfortunately, EPA permit writers have largely ignored this policy memorandum. A municipal permit that contains a growth-related condition is a rarity.

Army Corps of Engineers Permits and the Federal Water Pollution Control Act Amendments of 1972

Prior to the passage of the 1972 amendments to the Federal Water Pollution Control Act, it was unlawful to put any refuse matter (except liquid municipal sewage effluent and runoff from streets) into any navigable water or tributary thereof without a permit from the U.S. Army Corps of Engineers. This permit program, which was authorized under the so-called "Refuse Act,"[33] was replaced by the permit programs established under Sections 402 and 404 of the 1972 amendments. Although the Refuse Act itself is still on the books, it has been almost completely superseded by the Federal Water Pollution Control Act, as amended in 1972.

The Army Corps of Engineers is still responsible under legislation enacted prior to the 1972 amendments for issuing permits for dredging and filling operations and construction activities in navigable waters. The following activities, variations of which are often involved in land development projects, are unlawful without a permit from the Corps of Engineers:

1. Construction of a dam, dike, bridge, or causeway over or in any navigable water.[34]
2. Excavation, filling, or in any manner modifying any lake or channel of any navigable water.[35]

Note should be made that the Army Corps of Engineers is subject to the requirement of the National Environmental Policy Act (NEPA) that every federal agency must prepare an environmental impact statement before taking any action that significantly affects the environment.[36] Thus, for example, before issuing a permit for the construction of a dam, the Corps of Engineers must prepare an environmental impact statement which must be available for public comment. Chapter 9 discusses the Corps of Engineers' permit and environmental impact statement which were involved in the damming of Murderer's Creek by a large subdivision in New York State.

The 1972 amendments gave new responsibilities to the Army Corps of Engineers in the regulation of dredging and filling operations. Section 404[37] of the amendments establishes that no dredged or fill material can be discharged into the waters of the United States unless a Section 404 permit has been obtained from the Corps of Engineers. While earlier statutory provisions requiring that a permit be obtained from the Corps of Engineers for any dredging or filling in navigable waters focused on the possible interference of such operations with navigation, the focus of Section 404 is on the discharge of materials into receiving waters or surrounding wetlands and on the biological effects of such discharges. In some respects the new Section 404 permits overlap dredge and fill permits required by earlier legislation, but they differ in their prime concern with water quality and their applicability to wetlands. Thus the Section 404 program does not supplant the older permit program, but is in addition to it.

A very significant difference between the older Corps of Engineers permit programs and the provisions of Section 404 is that the former are subject to traditional concepts of navigability, whereas the latter are not. Some explanation is needed to clarify this distinction.

In a number of respects the concept of navigability that has been developed over the years by the Corps of Engineers is quite broad.[38] For example, the fact that in the past hunters and trappers who were engaged in interstate or foreign commerce used canoes on a waterway would be sufficient to establish it as navigable water. Also, once a determination of navigability is made, it is not extinguished by later actions or events which impede or destroy navigable capacity. Further, a waterway may be deemed navigable water even if it possesses falls, rapids, sand bars, or similar obstructions.

Nevertheless, the principle of navigability has always been central to the Corps of Engineers' work. One very important limitation that has resulted from this is the restriction of Corps jurisdiction in tidal areas to below mean high tide. In other cases, feeder streams and waters have been excluded from Corps jurisdiction because they were not classified as navigable.

The 1972 amendments go beyond traditional concepts of navigability by very broadly defining "navigable waters" as "the waters of the United States, including the territorial seas."[39] In commenting on the far-reaching significance of this new definition, an EPA legal memorandum points out that it "eliminates the requirement of navigability,"[40] leaving only the requirement that the pollution of waters covered by the act be capable of affecting interstate commerce. With respect to the latter the memorandum states that EPA will proceed on the assumption that federal jurisdiction extends to point source discharges not only into interstate waters and their tributaries, but also into intrastate waters from which fish or shellfish are taken for sale in interstate commerce, intrastate waters used by industries engaged in interstate commerce, and intrastate waters utilized by interstate travelers for recreational or other purposes.

Those aspects of EPA's approach which have been reviewed by the courts have been sustained. Two United States district courts and a United States circuit court of appeals have now held that federal jurisdiction under the Federal Water Pollution Control Act Amendments of 1972 is not limited by traditional concepts of navigability.[41] In so ruling, the courts have pointed out the overall dangers posed by water pollution to interstate commerce, as well as to the general health and welfare. They have documented Congress' resolve to control this problem, holding in one case that "Congress' clear intention as revealed in the Act itself was to effect marked improvement in the quality of the total water resources of the United States, regardless of whether that water was at the point of pollution a part of a navigable stream."[42]

Thus, the courts have held that "the waters of the United States" include not only navigable waters and their tributaries, but also waters which feed into them, including small streams, man-made canals, and the waters of wetland areas. In a case dealing with the filling of wetlands in Florida, the court held that "[t]he defendants' filling activities on land periodically inundated by tidal waters constituted discharges entering 'waters of the United States' . . ." and thus were subject to the permit requirements of the 1972 amendments.[43]

Unfortunately, the Corps of Engineers initially refused to incorporate the broader federal jurisdiction of the 1972 amendments into its administration of the Section 404 permit program. Relying on historical concepts of navigability, the Corps stated in regulations for Section 404 promulgated in April 1974 that it did not have authority to regulate activities above mean high tide.[44] The environmental implications of this position were very serious, since it excluded from regulation important coastal and estuarine wetlands which are flooded periodically but lie above mean high tide.[45]

Further, the Army Corps of Engineers refused to honor the court opinions which had ruled that federal jurisdiction under the 1972 amendments is not limited by traditional concepts of navigability (which include the traditional mean high tide demarcation). The Corps took this stand in spite of the fact that in two of these opinions, the court specifically quoted the following statement which was made in Congress just before the amendments were passed: "No longer are the old, narrow definitions of navigability, as determined by the Corps of Engineers, going to govern matters covered by this bill."[46]

In March 1975 the Natural Resources Defense Council, along with the National Wildlife Federation, obtained a court ruling which held that the Corps of Engineers' regulations which cover the Section 404 permit program are unlawfully restrictive and required the Corps to exercise its jurisdiction over dredging and filling operations in the waters of the United States, which include all wetland areas.[47]

CITIZEN ACTION

Citizens of New York State who want to work to realize the considerable potential which the Federal Water Pollution Control Act Amendments of 1972 have with respect to land use planning and regulation could profitably focus their attention in the following areas:

1. It is essential that New York State develop adequate plans under Section 208 of the 1972 amendments by the 1977 deadline. These plans must include means of identifying and controlling non-

point sources of pollution and must provide for regulation of the location, modification, and construction of all sources of pollution. Citizens should press for prompt and conscientious development of planning under this vital section of the act. EPA must also be strenuously pressed to provide needed guidelines to the states.

Making use of the general provisions for public participation under the act, which are discussed below, citizens should see that public involvement and contributions to the 208 planning process are maximized.

The task facing the agency responsible for 208 planning will be a politically difficult one. The land use implications of an effective 208 plan may be distasteful to land developers and local governments. Constant public scrutiny will be required to minimize the political pressures that will be brought to bear during the development of the plan.

As important as the development of an effective 208 plan is the establishment of the necessary means for effective implementation of the plan. This may well mean that new legislation must be passed to give the agency designated to carry out the plan the legal authority to do so. Public support for the passage of such measures will be needed.

2. A strong policy of non-degradation must be established by EPA to assure protection of high quality waters. Such a policy is mandated by the act and must be instituted and implemented if high quality waters are to be preserved from environmentally disastrous deterioration down to existing water quality standards. Although leadership by EPA in this problem is both required and necessary to establish protection on a nationwide basis, the state should also be urged to take action to avert degradation of water quality in New York.

3. Careful planning needs to be carried out in connection with the construction or expansion of sewage treatment facilities. Citizens should be aware of the profound effect additional sewerage capacity has on growth, should make certain that the dimensions of proposed facilities are carefully scrutinized, and should take action to see that necessary land use planning provisions and regulations are established when new plants are built.

Citizens should demand that an environmental impact statement be prepared by EPA before funds are granted to build a new waste treatment plant. This impact statement must consider the land use implications of the new construction, as well as other environmental consequences. Citizens should study the draft impact statement and prepare effective comments.

Citizens should be aware that EPA is authorized by Section 402(h) of the 1972 amendments to stop additional hookups to a sewage treatment plant that is violating a condition of its NPDES permit to discharge pollutants into navigable waters. Such proposed hookups should be reported to EPA and pressure should be brought to bear to assure that EPA takes action to prevent any further overloading of the plant in question.

It is important that citizens fully appreciate that public participation in water pollution control is required by the 1972 amendments: "Public participation in the development, revision, and enforcement of any regulation, standard, effluent limitation, plan, or program established by the Administrator [of EPA] or any State under this Act shall be provided for, encouraged, and assisted by the Administrator and the States."[48]

Regulations spelling out particular requirements for public participation have been promulgated by EPA and should be carefully read by concerned citizens.[49] These regulations establish that although primary responsibility for decision-making regarding water quality is vested by law in public agencies, "active public involvement in and scrutiny of" governmental decision-making is desirable. It is required that each agency carrying out activities under the act conduct a continuing program for public involvement. Among other things, such a program must include:

1. Provision of technical information to interested persons and organizations.

2. Public access to agency records.

3. Procedures for receiving information and evidence submitted by citizens.

4. Invitation, reception, and consideration of written comments from interested persons or organizations regarding proposed rule making.

In addition, whenever applications are made for certain kinds of grants (including construction grants under Section 201 and planning grants under Section 208 or 106), a summary of public participation must be a part of every application. This summary must "describe the measures taken by the agency to provide for, encourage, and assist public participation in relation to the matter; the public response to such measures; and the disposition of significant points raised."

Citizens should seek to take full advantage of the rights granted to them under the Federal Water Pollution Control Act Amendments of 1972 in their attempts to find solutions for both water pollution and land use problems.

NOTES

1. 33 U.S.C. §1251 *et seq.* These amendments were passed by Congress on October 18, 1972, as Public Law 92–500. The citations to particular sections of the act (i.e., the Federal Water Pollution Control Act Amendments of 1972) in this chapter refer to the section numbers of Public Law 92–500, a copy of which can be obtained from the Office of Public Affairs, U.S. Environmental Protection Agency, Waterside Mall, 401 M Street, S.W., Washington, D.C. 20460.

2. U.S. Senate, Committee on Public Works, *A Legislative History of the Federal Water Pollution Control Act Amendments of 1972,* 93rd Cong., 1st Sess., 1973, p. 1460 (hereafter *Legislative History*).

3. *Legislative History,* p. 165. For an informative discussion of these concepts, see Walter E. Westman, "Some Basic Issues in Water Pollution Control Legislation," *American Scientist* 60 (1972): 767.

4. §101(a); 33 U.S.C. §1251(a).

5. §502(14); 33 U.S.C. §1362(14).

6. There is a gray area between clear examples of point sources and non-point sources. Determinations of whether particular types of "conveyances" are to be considered point sources or non-point sources can be expected to come both from administrative clarifications by the U.S. Environmental Protection Agency and from litigation.

7. The act continues the federally approved interstate water quality standards adopted by the states pursuant to 1965 water quality legislation and requires the states to adopt standards for intrastate waters which also must be federally approved. All standards must be reviewed and upgraded at least once every three years. The first major revision of water quality standards, which should take place primarily in 1976, must implement the act's objective of maintaining the natural integrity of high quality waters and thus must require adoption by the states of strong non-degration provisions.

8. *See* Chapter 5 for a discussion of the State Pollutant Discharge Elimination System (SPDES) program which has been established in New York with the goal of receiving approval from EPA to issue permits under NPDES.

9. Several suits have been brought to require EPA to allot the authorized funds among the states. In February 1975 the U.S. Supreme Court ruled that the EPA administrator was required by the Federal Water Pollution Control Act to allot these funds. Train v. City of New York, 420 U.S. 35, 7 ERC 1497 (1975).

10. The Natural Resources Defense Council has brought two suits to enforce the deadlines established by the act: Natural Resources Defense Council v. Fri, Civil

No. 849–73 (D.D.C. June 19, 1973) (consent decree) and Natural Resources Defense Council v. Train, 6 ERC 1033 (D.D.C.1973), *aff'd,* _____F. 2d_____, 7 ERC 1209, (D.C.Cir. 1974).

11. The Natural Resources Defense Council's suit to require that additional substances be added to the toxic pollutants list was dismissed by the District Court, _____F. Supp._____, 6 ERC 1702 (D.D.C. 1974), but is now pending on appeal. Natural Resources Defense Council v. Train, Civil No. 74–1538 (D.C. Cir. 1974).

12. In March 1975 the Natural Resources Defense Council won its suit to require the NPDES permit program to cover all point sources. Natural Resources Defense Council v. Train, _____F. Supp._____, 7 ERC 1881 (D.D.C. 1975).

13. §§ 102, 106, 201, 208, 209, and 303; 33 U.S.C. §§ 1252, 1256, 1281, 1288, 1289, and 1313.

14. The contribution of pollutants from non-point agricultural sources (such as fertilizer and pesticide runoff) has been recognized for years. *See,* for example, Council on Environmental Quality, *Environmental Quality: The Third Annual Report of the Council on Environmental Quality* (1972), pp. 11–16.

Only recently, however, has attention been focused on runoff from city streets. A recent report prepared for the Council on Environmental Quality concluded that only about 20 to 60 percent of the total annual oxygen-demanding materials entering receiving waters from a city come from the sewage treatment plant and that the remainder comes from runoff and discharges into storm sewers which do not feed into sewage treatment plants. During a single storm event, 94 to 99 percent of the oxygen-demanding materials entering receiving waters is from runoff and sewer overflows. The street runoff from a typical moderate size city, moreover, will contain up to 250,000 pounds of lead and 30,000 pounds of mercury per year. *See* Enviro Control, Inc., *Total Urban Water Pollution Loads: The Impact of Storm Water,* 1974. Available from National Technical Information Service (NTIS #PB 231 730), 5285 Port Royal Road, Springfield, Va. 22151.

15. Regulations for identification of areas with water quality control problems and designation of responsible planning agencies have been promulgated by EPA. *See* 38 *Federal Register* 25681 (September 14, 1973); 40 CFR Part 126.

16. *See* §208(f) (2); 33 U.S.C. §1288(f)(2). Under this provision, grants covering 100 percent of the costs of developing and carrying out 208 planning were available through June 30, 1975, and grants for up to 75 percent of costs are available thereafter.

17. Environmental Defense Fund v. Train, Civil No. 74–C1698 (E.D.N.Y. 1974).

18. Under §201(g)(1) of the act; 33 U.S.C. §1281(g)(1).

19. Established under §402 of the act; 33 U.S.C. §1342.

20. *See* 39 *Federal Register* 17201 (May 13, 1974); 40 CFR §35.1050 *et seq.*

21. This document, which is entitled *Draft Guidelines for Areawide Waste Treatment Management,* is available from EPA's Office of Public Affairs.

22. 38 *Federal Register* 25681 (September 14, 1973); 40 CFR Part 126.

23. *See* 40 CFR §§130.23 and 131.306; 39 *Federal Register* 19634 (June 3, 1974).

24. Sierra Club v. Ruckelshaus, 344 F. Supp. 253; 4 ERC 1205 (D.D.C. 1972), *aff'd per curiam,* 4 ERC 1815 (D.C. Cir. 1972), *aff'd by an equally divided Court sub nom.* Fri v. Sierra Club, 412 U.S. 541, 5 ERC 1417 (1973).

25. Thus DEC's establishment of the new Class N classification and standards

for high quality waters may provide special protection for certain streams, namely those which are able to make it through a reclassification process, but this does not deal with the overall problem of degradation.

26. Council on Environmental Quality, *Interceptor Sewers and Suburban Sprawl*, September 10, 1974. This two-volume study was prepared by Urban Systems Research and Engineering, Inc., and is available in paperback and microfiche from: Ordering Department, National Technical Information Service (NTIS), 5285 Port Royal Road, Springfield, Virginia 22151. Volume I (Analysis; NTIS # PB236477) costs $7.00 in paperback and $2.25 in microfiche; volume II (Case Studies; NTIS # PB236871) is $8.70 in paperback and $2.25 in microfiche. The first section of volume I is a summary of the entire study.

27. The fifty-two grants studied were chosen from a list of 160 projects (in three EPA regions) that had reached the stage of construction. The grants selected were those which appeared most likely to have been used to finance excess sewer capacity. As a result of errors in original estimates of excess capacity, however, the fifty-two projects studied now appear to be more representative of all EPA sewerage construction grants than they were at first thought to be.

28. §201(f); 33 U.S.C. §1281(f).

29. 39 *Federal Register* 5252 (February 11, 1974); 40 CFR §35.900 *et seq.*

30. 42 U.S.C. §4321 *et seq. See* Chapter 9 for a discussion of NEPA.

31. 33 U.S.C. §1342(h).

32. U.S. Environmental Protection Agency, "Guidance for Conditioning of Municipal Permits in High-Growth Areas," January 15, 1974. This memorandum is public information and may be obtained from EPA.

33. 33 U.S.C. §407.

34. 33 U.S.C. §401.

35. 33 U.S.C. §403.

36. 42 U.S.C. §4321 *et seq. See* Chapter 9.

37. 33 U.S.C. §1344.

38. 33 CFR §209.260.

39. §502(7); 33 U.S.C. §1362(7).

40. As quoted in *Environment Reporter: Current Developments* 3:41 (February 9, 1973): 1240. Published by the Bureau of National Affairs, Washington, D.C. 20037.

41. United States v. American Beef Packers, Inc., _____F. Supp._____, Crim. No. 74-0-30 (D. Neb. 1974); United States v. Holland, 373 F. Supp. 665, 6 ERC 1388 (M.D. Fla. 1974); United States v. Ashland Oil & Transportation Co., 504 F. 2d 1317, 7 ERC 1114 (6th Cir. 1974).

42. United States v. Ashland Oil & Transportation Co., 7 ERC at 1118.

43. United States v. Holland, 6 ERC at 1395.

44. *See* 39 *Federal Register* 12118 (April 3, 1974); 33 CFR §209.120.

45. *See* Chapter 8 for a discussion of the vital importance of protecting wetlands.

46. 118 *Congressional Record* 33756-57 (1972), as quoted in United States v. Holland, 6 ERC at 1392, and United States v. Ashland Oil & Transportation Co., 7 ERC at 1119.

47. Natural Resources Defense Council v. Callaway, _____F. Supp._____, 7 ERC 1784 (D.D.C. 1975).

48. §101(e); 33 U.S.C. §1251(e).

49. 38 *Federal Register* 22757 (August 23, 1973); 40 CFR Part 105.

CHAPTER 12

Consumer and Investor Protection

LAWS AND PROGRAMS basically designed to protect purchasers of real estate, or which serve to protect such purchasers, have been established at federal, state, and city levels of government. The following such protective measures are discussed in this chapter:

1. The Federal Interstate Land Sales Full Disclosure Act
2. New York State Land Subdivision Disclosure Requirement
3. SEC Registration of Condominiums and Co-ops Sold Primarily as Managed Investment Opportunities
4. New York State Registration Requirement for Condominiums, Co-ops, and Homeowners' Associations
5. Federal Laws Against Mail Fraud
6. Licensing of Real Estate Brokers and Salesmen in New York State
7. New York City Consumer Protection Law

Vital provisions of the above require full disclosure of information about real estate offerings both to government agencies and to prospective purchasers; prohibit fraudulent practices, such as false or misleading advertising; forbid the omission of material facts in required documents; and establish penalties for violations.

These provisions are important to those concerned about land use for several reasons:

1. Certain types of real estate projects and practices are required to comply with them. If this compliance does not take place, then development which is carried out is unlawful and action can be brought to stop the development and/or to penalize the developer.

2. The preparation and filing of registration or "offering" statements involve both time and money. These expenses, as well as the legal obligation to disclose information, may deter irresponsible or highly speculative developers from attempting shaky projects.

3. The more that is publicly known about real estate projects, the better. The necessity of full disclosure can prevent secret deals which lead to windfall profits for developers and unexpected costs for both purchasers and communities. The requirement that developers reveal information—such as facts about their financial stability, the terms of sales or leases, the physical layout of the project and its relationship to other facilities and services—not only offers the prospective purchaser the opportunity to detect flaws in the offering, it also serves a similar disclosure purpose as far as the community is concerned. If misrepresentations of truth, omissions of material facts, or fraudulent schemes occur, there are existing mechanisms through which complaints can be made and pressure for corrective action brought to bear. In addition, access to detailed information about particular projects is provided by disclosure statements for citizens who are monitoring land development projects in their area. This information can be helpful in assessing whether a project is in compliance with all state and local laws and regulations.

4. In some cases, such as filings with the federal Office of Interstate Land Sales Registration (OILSR),[1] disclosure information on environmental factors, such as water supply and sewage disposal, is specifically required. The intent of these requirements is to protect purchasers, not the environment, but environmental protection may nonetheless be a by-product. For example, a land sales corporation in the Pocono Mountains of Pennsylvania has been convicted of falsely representing to purchasers that sewage could be disposed via individual septic tanks which would be approved by local officials, while actually soil conditions were not suitable for this method of sewage disposal.

In short, as time passes, the distinction between what is a fair deal for an individual land purchaser and what is a fair deal for a community and its natural resources is disappearing. Even though he may not be a committed environmentalist, the individual who buys land for a second home does not want to find himself faced with an inadequate water supply, sewage problems, bad air quality, noise, and traffic congestion. The soundness of an investment is, moreover, directly affected by these factors. Thus, as land becomes more and more scarce and as scientific evidence on the interrelationships of land uses accumulates, the needs of consumer and investor protection and the needs of environmental protection can be expected to come closer and closer together.

THE FEDERAL INTERSTATE LAND SALES FULL DISCLOSURE ACT

In 1969 the U.S. Congress, recognizing the tremendous growth of the land sales industry and the corresponding need for consumer protection, passed the Interstate Land Sales Full Disclosure Act.[2] Under this act it is unlawful for any developer or agent, directly or indirectly, to make use of any means of interstate commerce or of the mails to sell or lease subdivision lots unless:

1. A "statement of record" has been filed with the Office of Interstate Land Sales Registration (OILSR) of the U.S. Department of Housing and Urban Development (HUD);[3] and
2. A printed "property report" which meets all OILSR requirements is furnished to every purchaser before he or she signs any contract or agreement for sale or lease.

It is also unlawful for such a developer or agent, in selling or leasing, or offering to sell or lease, subdivision lots:

(A) to employ any device, scheme, or artifice to defraud, or
(B) to obtain money or property by means of a material misrepresentation with respect to any information included in the statement of record or the property report or with respect to any other information pertinent to the lot or the subdivision and upon which the purchaser relies, or
(C) to engage in any transaction, practice, or course of business which operates or would operate as a fraud or deceit upon a purchaser.

Full and detailed disclosure of information about the subdivision must be made in the statement of record. The property report is a shorter document, intended to be read in full by all purchasers, which includes some of the same material as the statement of record, as well as other information required by OILSR regulations.[4] A copy of the property report must be registered with OILSR along with the statement of record. The OILSR regulations explain the requirements for the preparation and filing of both documents, setting out a specified format and detailed instructions.

Exemptions

The act exempts certain types of sales and leases from its provisions, unless the method of disposition is adopted for the purpose of evading the act. In any administrative proceeding or litigation, the burden of proof rests with the developer to show that he is not attempting to evade the act.

Subject to this condition, the provisions of the act do not apply to the following:

1. The sale or lease of land in subdivisions which have fewer than 50 lots (there is no requirement that lots be contiguous, but only that they be offered or sold as part of a "common promotional plan").

2. The sale or lease of lots in subdivisions where *every* lot is 5 acres or larger in size.

3. The sale or lease of any improved land on which there is a residential, commercial, or industrial building, or to the sale or lease of land under a contract that obliges the seller to construct such a building on the land within two years.

4. The sale or lease of real estate under or pursuant to court order.

5. The sale of evidences of indebtedness secured by a mortgage or deed of trust on real estate.

6. The sale of securities issued by a real estate investment trust.

7. The sale or lease of real estate by any government or government agency.

8. The sale or lease of cemetery lots.

9. The sale or lease of lots to any person who acquires the lots for the purpose of engaging in the business of constructing residential, commercial, or industrial buildings or for the purpose of resale or lease of such lots to persons engaged in such business.

10. The sale or lease of real estate which is zoned by the appropriate government authority for industrial or commercial development, as long as certain other stringent requirements are met.[5]

While none of the above require a written determination of eligibility from OILSR, there is one special statutory exemption regarding which such a decision is necessary. Under this exemption, a subdivider does not have to register with OILSR if this office determines that *all* of the following criteria are met:

1. At the time of the sale or lease, the real estate is free and clear of all liens, encumbrances, and adverse claims.
2. Each and every purchaser or his or her spouse had made a personal on-site inspection of the land before signing a contract, and the developer submits a written affirmation of this to OILSR.
3. The developer has filed a proper claim of exemption with OILSR.
4. The developer has obtained OILSR approval of a statement detailing all reservations, restrictions, taxes, and assessments applicable to the land (such as property taxes).
5. This statement has been furnished to every purchaser prior to the signing of a contract and the developer has obtained in writing the purchaser's acknowledgement of the receipt of the statement.

All of these statements, filings, and agreements in effect waive the prospective buyer's right to examine a property report containing detailed information about land for which he or she might pay thousands of dollars. The inclusion of this complicated exemption in the act stemmed from pressure to provide "on-site" exemptions, on the grounds that Congress' original intent was to regulate sight-unseen sales. As has been reported in the *Federal Register,* however, "it has been OILSR's experience from the outset of the Act that a purchaser's presence on-site does not in itself afford him adequate information and protection in making a decision to purchase or not to purchase a lot."[6] In keeping with this finding, Congress has recently abolished another provision, discussed below, which allowed on-site purchasers to waive their revocation rights.

In all cases, prospective purchasers of lots should seek to learn as much as possible about the land. When a developer has gone to considerable trouble to avoid filing disclosure information with OILSR and furnishing property reports, prospective buyers should seek to determine why he has done this.

In addition to statutory exemptions, there are also several other exemptions which have been established by OILSR regulations, as is authorized by the act. Under these, the provisions of the act do not apply to the following:

1. The sale or lease of lots when every lot will be sold for less than $100, including closing costs, provided that the purchaser is not required to buy more than one lot.

2. The lease of lots for less than five years, provided that the lessee is not obligated to renew the lease.

3. The sale or lease of subdivision lots, numbering less than 50 and constituting 5 percent or less of the total number of lots in the subdivision, when the other lot sales or leases are exempt under other provisions (such as those exempting sales or leases of lots on which there is a residential, commercial, or industrial building).

It is also possible for a developer to file a request for an exemption order with OILSR for a subdivision of fewer than 300 lots which are offered "entirely or almost entirely" to residents of the state in which the land is located. All advertising over which the developer has control must also be confined to that state. (An example of interstate advertising which is beyond a developer's control is the reception by television sets in New Jersey of advertising transmitted by New York City stations.) Finally, no more than 5 percent of all annual lot sales may be made to nonresidents of the state in which the subdivision is located.

State Filings

Prior to January 1, 1975, OILSR accepted materials initially filed under state subdivision disclosure laws in New York, California, Florida, and Hawaii, as meeting federal requirements. This practice was terminated in 1975 on the grounds that the extent of disclosure and consumer protection now provided through the OILSR statement of record and property report is much greater than that required by the states. Only if the states strengthen their provisions to correspond with the more demanding federal regulations established in 1973 and 1974 will state filings again be acceptable as OILSR filings. Barring this, developers to whom both federal and state laws apply must prepare separate materials to meet state and federal requirements. (The states of Florida and California have obtained a temporary injunction against this federal action and are seeking a permanent injunction. New York is neither involved in nor affected by this suit.)

In New York State confusion has existed in the past regarding the relationship between state and federal filings. As will be discussed in the following section, the New York State law governing disclosure by subdivisions within the state applies only to those subdivisions which are sold on the installment plan. Since this is not generally the case, most subdivisions in New York are not subject to the registration requirements of the state law. Apparently, many developers have believed that if they did not have to file with the state, they also did not have to file with OILSR, or they have used the existing confusion on this point as a cover for not filing with OILSR. The distinct separation between state and federal requirements that has now been made should clarify this situation.

The Statement of Record

The statement of record required by the act is a long, detailed report of various physical and financial aspects of the land offerings. While statements of record are available for public inspection at the OILSR office in Washington, D.C., developers are not obligated to furnish copies to prospective buyers.

After receipt of a statement of record from a developer, the OILSR reviews its contents for completeness and accuracy. No lots in the subdivision may be sold or leased until the statement of record becomes effective, which usually happens on the thirtieth day after the statement is filed with OILSR.

The statement of record includes comprehensive disclosure information about the subdivision. Information on all of the following must be included: the dimensions of the subdivision; its ownership; the financial and legal background and relationships of its owners; topography and climate; nuisances; permits, filings and licenses required by other authorities; the condition of the title and the conditions of the offer, including terms and selling prices; roads and access to neighboring communities; utilities; drainage and flood control; recreational and common facilities; taxes and assessments; occupancy status; shopping facilities; and the availability of all municipal services.

The Property Report

Developers must also register with OILSR a copy of the printed property report. The law requires that a copy of this property report be furnished to every purchaser before a sale or lease agreement is signed. If a property report is not so furnished, the purchaser may void the agreement. The statute of limitations requires that such action to void an agreement be taken within two years of the date on which it was signed. The act further provides that if a purchaser was given a copy of the property report less than forty-eight hours before he signed a purchase or lease agreement, he has until midnight of the third business day following the transaction to revoke the agreement if he so chooses. In the original act, this "cooling-off period" extended only for forty-eight hours following signing, but it was extended by Congress to three business days in 1974.[7] Also, it was previously possible for a purchaser who had personally inspected the property to waive his revocation rights, but this provision was stricken from the law by the same Congressional action.

The requirements which the property report must meet are set out in detail in the OILSR regulations. These disclosure requirements were significantly broadened and strengthened by new regulations promulgated in 1973 and 1974.[8] Developers must now reveal any past or pending disciplinary proceedings pertaining to land sales or related activities, bankruptcies, or litigation involving the development company or any of the parties involved in the subdivision and "which may materially affect lot purchasers in [the] subdivision." Statements must be made regarding the availability and cost to the purchaser of roads, utilities (including water supply and sewage disposal), and municipal services. It must be stated whether or not the developer has a program in effect to control soil erosion, sedimentation, and flooding throughout the entire subdivision. If there is such a program, it must be described. "Unusual conditions" affecting the subdivision must also be listed and fully explained. These include factors which affect the environment and safety of the subdivision, such as flooding and other natural hazards, as well as air pollution, traffic hazards, and unusual noises. The developer's obligations regarding proposed recreational facilities must be clearly stated and estimated completion dates must be given.

An audited and certified financial statement must now be furnished to buyers as an exhibit to the property report if the subdivision has 300 or more lots or if the aggregate price of all lots is more than $500,000. This statement must also be registered with OILSR. After the first filing, however, the developer is required to submit annual audited statements "only if they disclose a material adverse effect on the developer's financial position." The financial strength of the developer is of concern to the lot purchaser since the price paid for a subdivision lot typically includes costs of proposed improvements to be made by the developer. In view of this, audited and certified financial statements should be required of all subdivisions, regardless of their size.

What must not be forgotten, however, is that all the disclosures in the world are worthless unless they are read and understood. Developers routinely reveal to OILSR that the land they wish to sell is remote, or submerged, or covered with stumps which the buyer must clear at his own expense. Such negative information is reported in compliance with the law by developers who are confident that not many buyers will be able to pick out flaws which are embedded in a long, intimidating document.

OILSR believes that people should recognize that the purchase of land is usually an expensive and complex undertaking, and that those who are prepared to invest thousands of dollars in a parcel of land should also be prepared to seek assistance in interpreting a property report, even if such consultation costs money. It is, to be sure, much less expensive to refuse an offer on the basis of a clear understanding of detailed information than to seek legal remedies after a contract has been signed.

Advertising Standards

In 1973 OILSR promulgated regulations governing advertising in subdivisions covered by the act.[9] These regulations are described by OILSR as an effort to define for developers the kind of advertising which it considers unlawful under the act and capable of triggering its authority to seek injunctions or restraining orders. The detail of the 35 advertising guidelines provided reflect the ingenuity with which some developers have misled consumers in the past.

The OILSR regulations forbid advertisements containing false or misleading statements, pictures, or sketches, as well as misleading omissions. It is also illegal for advertisements to contradict statements made in the statement of record, the property report, or any required financial statements. The front page of all printed advertisements must bear a statement (1) advising potential buyers to obtain a property report from the developer and to read it before signing anything; and (2) stating that HUD has not approved the offer in any way.

Specific examples are given of the kind of misleading or vague advertising that is prohibited. Maps must be drawn to scale, and terms like "minutes away" cannot be used unless actual road distances are also indicated. Advertising which refers to roads and streets, lot sizes, improvements, pre-development price bargains, public facilities, property exchange privileges, water supply, sewage disposal, and resale schemes must be accompanied by detailed clarifying information.

An inference which can be reasonably drawn from advertising material is considered by OILSR to be a positive assertion of fact, unless the inference is negated in clear and unmistakable terms in the same material. If, for example, lots are advertised, OILSR considers that it can be inferred that these lots can be used immediately, that all major subsurface improvements necessary for the construction of dwellings have been made, and that roads, potable water, and sewage disposal facilities are available.

Condominiums

In recent years, condominiums have become an increasingly common type of property ownership. In this type of development, individual dwelling units are purchased outright and common property and facilities (such as hallways, swimming pools, and grounds) are owned collectively by all residents. As is discussed later in this chapter, condominiums which are sold primarily as managed investments must be registered with the U.S. Securities and Exchange Commission.

In the *Federal Register* of September 4, 1973, OILSR clarified its policy regarding the application of the Interstate Land Sales Full Disclosure Act to condominiums.[10] As explained there, OILSR views a condominium as "equivalent to a subdivision, each unit being a lot." Thus, for the sale of a condominium unit to be exempted from the act, "either it must be completed before it is sold, or it must be sold under a contract obligating the seller to erect the unit within two years from the date the purchaser signs the contract of sale." In February 1974 OILSR published additional guidelines specifying that in the case of "primary residence condominiums in metropolitan areas," a unit must be ready for occupancy within two years to qualify for exemption; in the case of "condominiums in which the promotion of the common facilities is the primary inducement to purchase" (such as those in recreational developments), such facilities as well as the individual unit sold must be completed within two years.[11] Any delays in construction must be legally supportable as beyond the control of the developer.

Penalties and Enforcement

The Interstate Land Sales Full Disclosures Act has a three-pronged enforcement scheme:

1. *Civil liability.* Under the act, a buyer can void a sales or lease agreement if he was not given a property report before signing the agreement. If he received the property report within forty-eight hours before signing, he may revoke the agreement at any time up until midnight of the third business day following the transaction. A purchaser may also sue the developer for damages if the latter makes an untrue statement or fails to state a material fact in the statement of record or the property report.

2. *Administrative remedies.* The administrator of OILSR may suspend a subdivider's statement of record, if any untrue statement or omission of a material fact occurs in this document. If the developer corrects the statement of record, it can be reinstated, but no sales or leases can be made while the suspension is in effect. OILSR is authorized to make investigations concerning possible violations of the act or OILSR regulations and to publish findings.

3. *Injunctions and prosecution of offenses.* The administrator of OILSR may bring an action in a federal district court for a temporary or permanent injunction or restraining order whenever it appears that a subdivider is engaged in or is about to engage in acts or practices in violation of the act or OILSR regulations. OILSR is empowered to transmit evidence of alleged violations to the U.S. attorney's office for criminal prosecution under the act. The penalty for willfully violating any provision of the act or OILSR regulations is a fine of up to $5,000, imprisonment for up to five years, or both.

Enforcement action by OILSR under the act has been sporadic in the past, but examples of effective enforcement which demonstrate the potential of the act can be cited. In June 1973 the U.S. attorney for the southern district of New York brought a 42-count indictment against the Pocono International Corporation and its principal stockholder that was based in large part on violations of the act. This indictment alleged that Pocono International used several means of interstate commerce and the mails to offer and sell subdivided lands in the Pocono Mountains of Pennsylvania for which no statement of record had been filed with OILSR, as required by the act. It also alleged that the developers had falsely represented to prospective lot purchasers that sewage could be disposed of by means of individual septic tanks which would be approved by local officials, while in fact soil conditions were not suitable for this method of sewage disposal. Both defendants were convicted on 20 counts of the indictment.

In June 1974 OILSR added field representatives to its staff for the first time. These thirty new employees of the Land Sales Enforcement Division are stationed in offices throughout the country and are responsible both for seeking out unregistered subdivisions and for uncovering fraudulent practices by registered subdivisions. Presently, OILSR receives filings from approximately 6,000 subdivisions and relies heavily on citizen complaints for the initiation of investigative and enforcement actions.

Citizen Action

The Interstate Land Sales Full Disclosure Act was drafted primarily to protect the interests of purchasers of land. Still, it has indirect value as a tool for environmental protection. The act cannot generate land use planning, but it can, as the Pocono International indictment has shown, produce enforcement actions which bring environmental abuses to light. Specific disclosure information about environmental factors is also required in statements of record and property reports. Misrepresentations or omissions can lead to the suspension of statements of record or to injunctions or restraining orders, as well as to criminal prosecutions.

Concerned citizens should be aware of the act's requirements and of procedures for enforcement so that they can detect violations, report them to the proper authorities, and press for enforcement action. Although OILSR has greatly increased its enforcement staff, citizen complaints will continue to play a vital role in triggering investigations. Anyone who has reason to believe that a subdivider who is selling 50 lots or more, any one of which is less than 5 acres, has not registered with OILSR, and is not providing a property report to purchasers should notify the nearest office of the U.S. attorney[12] and OILSR at the following address:

Land Sales Enforcement Division
Office of Interstate Land Sales Registration
Department of Housing and Urban Development (HUD)
451 Seventh Street, S.W.
Washington, D.C. 20410

Material misrepresentations and/or omissions in a property report or in advertising, as well as any fraudulent practices, should also be reported. For a fee of $2.50, OILSR will send a copy of the property report for a specific subdivision to anyone who requests it. Statements of record are available for public examination only at the OILSR office in Washington.

Violations or suspected violations can be reported to OILSR or an office of the U.S. attorney by means of a personal letter or telephone call, but it is more effective to write or call on behalf of a citizens' group, a committee, or a homeowners' association.

Finally, all prospective property buyers should make sure that they receive a property report when one is required and that they follow the advice which must now be overprinted in large capital letters on the front page of every property report: "PURCHASER SHOULD READ THIS DOCUMENT BEFORE SIGNING ANYTHING." Professional help in interpreting this document should be sought if necessary. OILSR further advises against purchasing land under pressure from real estate salesmen or without actually having seen the land.

NEW YORK STATE LAND SUBDIVISION DISCLOSURE REQUIREMENT

New York State has a law requiring comprehensive disclosure of information by subdividers of vacant land, but, with regard to subdivisions within the state, this law applies only to those which are sold or leased on the installment plan.[13] The basic intent of the statute is to prevent fraudulent practices in transactions in which the purchaser of land makes periodic payments on the purchase price and does not receive title to the land until all payments are made. Since the vast majority of subdivisions in New York State are not sold in this fashion, but are rather financed by bank mortgages or purchase money mortgages from developers in which purchasers receive title to the land immediately, most subdivisions in the state do not fall within the scope of this law.[14] Whatever fraudulent or damaging practices may occur in subdivisions of land which are not offered for sale or lease on the installment plan are not subject to state scrutiny or penalties under this law.

The statute in question is Article 9–A of the New York State

Real Property Law, which is implemented by the New York Department of State. Under this statute no subdivider is allowed to sell, lease, or offer for sale or lease to the public within New York State any subdivided vacant land unless he has filed with the New York Department of State:

1. An "offering statement" containing detailed financial information and physical descriptions of the land being offered;
2. Any other information the Department of State might require; and
3. A statement signed by the subdivider affirming that all information submitted is true and providing other specific information such as a title search and a description of the proposed terms of sale.

As discussed above, this filing of information is actually required of only a limited number of subdivisions within the state, though it is required of all subdivisions located outside the state which are offered to New York State residents. This results because the term "subdivision" is defined in the statute as:

> vacant land or lands sold or leased on the installment plan or offered for sale or lease on such plan and also vacant land or lands situated outside the state of New York and sold or leased or offered for sale or lease on the installment plan or upon any and all other plans, terms and conditions of sale or lease.[15]

Thus, the law applies to all subdivisions outside the state from which land is offered for sale or lease to state residents, no matter what method of financing is used; but with respect to subdivisions within the state, it applies only to those sold on the installment plan.

Note should be made that the requirements of Article 9–A are not limited in any way by the number of lots in any given subdivision or by the size of those lots.

Before the New York Department of State accepts statements filed by subdividers pursuant to the requirements of Article 9–A, the department may actually inspect the land itself. In the case of subdivisions which are located outside New York State, the travel expenses of department personnel must be paid by the subdividers.

It should be pointed out that a subdivision within New York State which is not required to file a disclosure statement with the Department of State under Article 9–A will be required to file a disclosure statement with the Department of Law if the subdivision requires purchasers of land to buy memberships in a homeowners' association.[16]

The Offering Statement

Article 9–A provides that any offer to sell or lease subdivided vacant land which falls within its scope must be accompanied by a copy of a current "offering statement," the original of which must have been filed with and accepted by the New York Department of State. This offering statement provides descriptions and disclosures of many important facts about the subdivider and the land being offered. The subdivider must keep the statement up-to-date by filing at least every thirteen months a current, amended statement that reflects all changes that have taken place in the required information. Anyone planning to buy subdivided land in New York State on an installment plan should demand a copy of the necessary offering statement if it is not supplied, and should read it carefully.

The information which must be included in the offering statement is specified in Article 9–A and the regulations adopted pursuant to this statute.[17] All of the following must be included:

1. Information about the business background and finances of the subdivider and, if the subdivider is a partnership or corporation, its principals.

2. A statement of the title to the subdivision.

3. A statement of the terms and conditions on which the land is being offered and a price list of all lots offered.

4. A summary of all encumbrances or restrictions on the subdivision as a whole and on individual units.

5. A statement setting forth whether the subdivision has been approved or disapproved for mortgage loans (the names and addresses of all mortgage lending institutions involved must be listed).

6. All pertinent data and information with respect to: permissible land uses; distances to surrounding communities, services, schools, and public transportation facilities; terrain and climatic conditions; improvements and roads, completed and promised; availability and cost of water supply, public utilities, and sewage disposal facilities; all existing and proposed recreational facilities within the project, including any maintenance costs to the purchaser; and a certified financial statement of the assets and liabilities of the developer.

The first page of every offering statement as well as of all advertising or literature used to offer the property involved must have an easily readable statement pointing out that the Department of State has not made any judgment on the merits of the offering or approved it in any way. Anyone convicted of representing otherwise is guilty of a misdemeanor and subject to a fine of $1,000 or one year's imprisonment or both. The offering statement must be signed and affirmed to be true by the developer under penalties of perjury.

Roads, Streets, and Improvements

No filing can be accepted from a developer by the Department of State unless he can establish to the satisfaction of the department that every lot, plot, or site in the subdivision has at least one side contiguous to a street or avenue affording ingress and egress to and from streets and avenues in the subdivision. If the developer fails to establish this, the Department of State cannot accept his filing and he may not offer property for sale or lease.

All roads must be adequate in terms of width, construction, and materials. They must also conform to any local government requirements regarding road construction and maintenance. If all roads within the subdivision are not completed when the developer files the required statements with the Department of State, he must submit to the department a performance bond of twice the contemplated cost of the roads, to assure that the roads will be completed within one year's time. If other improvements, such as the development of recreational areas, are promised by the subdivider, but are not completed at the time he files with the Department of State, the subdivider must provide a completion bond, an escrow account, or other acceptable means to assure that sufficient funds are available for the completion of the improvements.

Sales Methods and Advertising

The subdivider must also submit to the Department of State a description of sales methods to be used, including copies of sales portfolios or materials. Copies of all advertisements must be accepted by the department before they can be published, distributed, or broadcast. No statement in any advertisement can be "inconsistent with or not covered in" statements filed with the department.

The Department of State has adopted standards governing the

content of advertising materials for subdivisions under its jurisdiction. These standards forbid:

1. The use of terms like "minutes away," "short distance," or "only miles" to indicate distance. Distances must be exactly computed and stated.

2. Advertisement of incompleted improvements unless it is stated in the advertising copy that such improvements are "merely proposed" or "under construction" or otherwise, as the case may be.

3. The use of artist's sketches.

4. The use of photographs portraying scenes not actually on the advertised property unless it is clearly indicated in the copy that the scene is not on the property and the actual distance in miles from the advertised land is given.

5. Reference to recreational facilities not in existence on the lands advertised unless it is clearly indicated in the copy that such facilities are merely proposed or the distance to the facilities from the land is stated.

6. Representations that the land advertised offers quick, immediate, or specific profits.

7. The use of maps showing proximity to other communities unless the maps are drawn to scale or actual mileages appear in easily readable print.

Enforcement

Any person who *knowingly* offers to sell or lease, or sells or leases, any subdivided lands which are subject to the provisions of Article 9–A without filing an offering statement and the verified statement required by the Department of State is guilty of a felony. Anyone who *knowingly* advertises to obtain money or property by means of false pretenses, representations, or promises concerning such subdivided lands, or who makes fictitious or pretended purchases or sales of such lands, is guilty of a misdemeanor. Anyone who *willfully* violates or fails to comply with any of the provisions of Article 9–A or who *knowingly* omits or neglects to comply with any order, permit, decision, demand, or requirement of the department under this statute is also guilty of a misdemeanor. If such violations are carried out by a real estate broker or salesman licensed by the state of New York, the Department of State may suspend or revoke his license.

The New York State attorney general or a local district attorney, at the attorney general's request, is responsible for prosecuting violators of Article 9–A. Such prosecutions may be instituted upon the written request or demand of the Department of State.

The Department of State also has the power to conduct special, independent investigations. It has the right to subpoena witnesses, to compel their attendance, to examine witnesses under oath, and to require the production of relevant books or records. Failure to cooperate with such an investigation can constitute a misdemeanor.

When the Department of State has reason to believe that a subdivider under its jurisdiction has engaged in, or is engaging in, or is about to engage in transactions constituting fraudulent practices, the Department of State or the attorney general may bring an action to enjoin him and any other persons involved from continuing such practices and/or from selling or offering any subdivided lands to the public within New York State. If it can be shown that the subdivider has or is engaged in fraud, a permanent injunction can be obtained. The court may appoint a receiver to hold any and all property derived fraudulently.

Generally, the Department of State relies upon citizen complaints to stimulate investigations. The investigation team within the department is, however, very small and claims to be inundated with work. As a matter of policy, the Department of State usually investigates only *registered* subdivisions, while the attorney general's office investigates *unregistered* subdivisions. Moreover, the department rarely sends cases involving registered subdivisions to the attorney general for prosecution, preferring rather to seek offers of restitution to purchasers making complaints. In actual fact, the Department of State and the attorney general's office very seldom deal with each other on matters related to Article 9–A.

Department of State personnel also attend various high-pressure dinner and film solicitations characteristically given by land sales companies with big advertising budgets. When, however, the staff of "Help," a public television presentation (broadcast early in 1974) which focused on fraud in land sales, interviewed members of the Land Sales Division of the Department of State, it was revealed that department personnel actually attend very few of these dinners and that, when they do, they identify themselves to land salesmen as representatives of the Department of State.

Citizen Action

Article 9–A is characterized by significant statutory limitations, and the investigation team of the Land Sales Division of the Department of State exhibits apparent weaknesses. Nevertheless, some subdivisions in the state are sold on the installment plan (the very large Sleepy Hollow Lake subdivision in the Catskills is one example).[18] Therefore, there are occasions when developers are legally required to comply with the provisions of Article 9–A and, thus, when concerned citizens can use this necessary compliance as a legal tool. In such situations, concerned citizens should first find out whether the subdivider has filed the proper statements with the Department of State. If this has been done, then citizens should obtain copies of the prepared offering statement and read it very carefully. Any violation of Article 9–A and any misrepresentation of truth or fraudulent practice should be clearly and forcefully reported to the Land Sales Division of the New York Department of State and to the state attorney general, whose addresses are as follows:

> New York Department of State
> Subdivision Unit
> 270 Broadway
> New York, N.Y. 10007

> Bureau of Securities and
> Public Financing
> Department of Law
> State of New York
> 2 World Trade Center
> New York, N.Y. 10047

The following are three more general areas where concerted citizen action is needed:

1. The Department of State should be urged to draft legislation amending Article 9–A to include all subdivisions in New York State within its purview, not just those which are sold on the installment plan.
2. The Department of State should be urged by citizens' groups

to modernize and expand its investigative work so that effective enforcement of the law can be provided.

3. The Department of State should be pressed to open its records to citizens who are interested in specific subdivisions. This effort should be greatly facilitated by the New York State Freedom of Information Law[19] which became effective on September 1, 1974. The force of this law, which states that "government is the public's business," should be very helpful to citizens who need to obtain information from the New York Department of State, which has often been reluctant to open its subdivision files to the general public.

SEC REGISTRATION OF CONDOMINIUMS AND CO-OPS SOLD PRIMARILY AS MANAGED INVESTMENT OPPORTUNITIES

Each year an increasing number of condominiums are being offered for sale throughout New York State. While at one time condominiums were built almost exclusively in urban and resort areas, they are now becoming more and more common in suburban and rural areas. Some of these condominiums, as well as certain cooperative apartment projects, fall within the scope of federal securities legislation[20] and are thus subject to disclosure requirements which are administered by the U.S. Securities and Exchange Commission (SEC).[21]

In the condominium form of ownership the owner of each condominium unit usually has an undivided interest in or title to his individual unit and also a part interest or share in common facilities and areas such as lounges, pools, or grounds. Some condominium developers simply wish to sell each unit in a project to purchasers who will be owner-occupiers. Other developments, especially those in vacation areas, offer special rental arrangements such as a "rental pool" agreement in which unit-owners place their units in an "inventory" of condominiums which are rented out on a revolving basis by a managing agent.[22] Typically, under such agreements the rents received on all units and the expenses incurred are pooled, and individual owners receive ratable shares of the proceeds whether or not their own units were actually rented. Arrangements of this type are obviously designed for unit-owners who only want to use their units part time. The condominium's managing agent takes on the day-to-day chores of attracting, servicing, and supervising transient, short-term rentals. The pooling of available units assures each participant of a fair share of the project's overall renting potential, avoids competition among unit-owners, and spreads the risk of vacancies. The SEC holds that the offer of a condominium unit together with the offer of an opportunity to participate in such a rental pool, designed to be used by unit owners for investment purposes and dependent on the services of a specified agent, involves the offer of an investment contract which must be registered with the SEC, unless exempted on other grounds.

The SEC described the kinds of condominiums which are subject to registration requirements in a publication entitled *Guidelines as to the Applicability of the Federal Securities Laws to Offers and Sales of Condominiums or Units in a Real Estate Development.* [23] As stated in this publication, if any one of the following elements is involved in a condominium offering, it will be viewed as the offering of an investment contract which must be registered with the SEC:

1. Offering participation in a rental pool arrangement to the unit-owner.

2. Offering a condominium which has any rental arrangement or similar service, with emphasis on the economic benefits to the purchaser to be derived through the managerial efforts of the promoter or a third party chosen by the promoter.

3. Offering a rental arrangement in which the purchaser must hold his unit available for rental for any part of the year, must use an exclusive rental agent, or is otherwise materially restricted in the occupancy or rental of his unit.

4. Offering participation in a condominium project in which there are commercial facilities in the common holdings which (a) provide income which is not used simply to offset common area expenses, and (b) are more than incidental to the project as a whole and are established as a primary income source for unit-owners.

The SEC does not consider that a continuing affiliation between the developers and promoters of a condominium project and the unit-owners in the form of maintenance arrangements for the upkeep of buildings and grounds brings the project under its jurisdiction.

The SEC guidelines point out that it is very difficult to anticipate the wide variety of arrangements that may be involved in a condominium offering. There may, in fact, be other situations not covered by the guidelines where a condominium offer would constitute an offering of securities. The guidelines conclude with the following statements: "Whether an offering of securities is involved necessarily depends on the facts and circumstances of each particular case. The staff of the [Securities and Exchange] Commission will be available to respond to written inquiries on such matters."

Some cooperative apartment projects are also subject to SEC registration. In the cooperative housing form of ownership, a corporation owns an apartment building or buildings and sells shares, coupled with proprietary leases for individual units, to residents or prospective residents. Such offerings are exempt from the requirements of federal securities legislation, if they meet the exacting standards set forth in SEC regulations.[24] Basically the units exempted under these regulations are those sold for owner-occupancy. More complex co-op offerings which have "investment contract" features, involving rental pool arrangements, exclusive rental agent provisions, or other investment management services, are subject to SEC registration requirements.

Under the Securities Act of 1933[25] it is unlawful for any person "directly or indirectly" to sell or to offer to sell any security "by means of instruments of transportation or communication in interstate commerce or of the mails," unless a registration statement is filed with the SEC and a prospectus which meets the disclosure requirements of the act is given to each offeree or purchaser before or during an offer or sale. In other words, before a condominium involving an investment contract can be offered for sale, a comprehensive disclosure statement must be filed with the SEC and a prospectus which discloses material information for prospective purchasers must be provided before or during the offer or sale of each condominium unit. The penalties for failure to comply with these provisions include civil sanctions (suits by purchasers for restitution of damages), criminal penalties ($5,000 fine and/or five years imprisonment for willful violations of the act), and administrative remedies (suspension of the registration statement by the SEC).

Prohibitions applicable to advertising and sales practices used in the sale of condominiums which must be registered with the SEC are discussed in the SEC publication *Advertising and Sales Practices in Connection with Offers and Sales of Securities Involving Condominium Units and Other Units in Real Estate Developments.*[26] The following restrictions are of prime importance:

1. Disseminating sales literature or advertising prior to the required registration of a condominium constitutes an illegal offer.

2. No deposits, payments, or purchase commitments may be accepted prior to the filing of the registration statement.

3. Once the registration statement is filed but before it is effective: (a) *offers* may be made, but *no written offer* may be made that does not include a proper prospectus; and (b) no purchase commitments, payments, or deposits may be accepted, even if they are placed in escrow or are fully refundable.

4. After the effective date of the registration statement, *sales* may be made only if a proper prospectus is provided to every offeree before or during every written offer.

The Securities Act of 1933 exempts certain types of offerings from registration. The SEC and the courts generally view these exemptions narrowly, however, and most condominiums which are offered for sale as managed investments will not be exempt. The following are two notable exemptions:

1. The Intra-State Exemption

The act exempts from registration those securities which are offered for sale and sold entirely within one state. To qualify for this exemption, the offeror, all purchasers, and all offerees must be residents of the same state. If an offer is made to only one person who is not a resident of that state, the exemption is lost.

2. The Private Offering Exemption

The act exempts "transactions by an issuer not involving any public offering." In other words, offers are exempt which are so limited as to be private in character. This exemption is of little consequence with respect to condominium sales, since it is virtually impossible under the usual marketing and advertising techniques of developers to sell condominium units in this way.

It should be noted, however, that since 1933 there have been many suits and much debate on the issue of exactly what constitutes a private offering. The courts have consistently held that the private offering exemption cannot be mechanically based on the fact that only a given number of offerees are involved in a particular project. The ultimate test of the exemption has been held to be whether the offerees' association with, or knowledge of, the offeror is such that they have available to them the information which would otherwise be provided by the registration requirements and thus do not need the protection necessary in public offerings.[27] More exact guidelines have recently been established by a new SEC regulation, "rule 146," which became effective June 10, 1974.[28] This rule establishes that a *sale* of securities to thirty-five people or less will be considered a private offering if certain investor tests are met, notably if all purchasers are adequately informed or have access to adequate information about the issuer.

Citizen Action

Citizens who are concerned about particular condominium developments should seek answers to the following questions:

1. Does the condominium have any of the managed investment features (rental pool, mandatory rental arrangements, extensive commercial facilities) described above?

2. If so, has the condominium been registered with the SEC and is a formal prospectus being supplied before or with every written offer?

3. Are there any misleading statements or serious omissions in the prospectus?

If a condominium appears to be subject to SEC jurisdiction and (1) it has not been registered, or (2) a proper prospectus is not being provided before or with every written offer, or (3) misleading statements or omissions exist in the prospectus, a full written report should be filed with the SEC and the advice of SEC officials should be sought. The following is the address of the SEC division which handles the registration of investment contract condominiums:

U.S. Securities and Exchange Commission
Division of Corporation Finance
500 North Capitol Street
Washington, D.C. 20549
(202) 755-1200

Because of the many complexities involved, citizens may wish to consult a securities attorney. If it turns out that a violation of federal securities laws or regulations has occurred, the SEC should be pressed to take appropriate enforcement action.

NEW YORK STATE REGISTRATION REQUIREMENT FOR CONDOMINIUMS, CO-OPS, AND HOMEOWNERS' ASSOCIATIONS

The General Business Law of New York State requires that an offering statement be filed with the Department of Law before any public offering or sale, in or from the state, of real estate syndication interests, including cooperative interests in real estate.[29] "Cooperative interests in real estate" generally include shares in a cooperative housing corporation together with proprietary leases permitting occupancy of specific apartments; condominium units; and memberships in homeowners' (property owners') associations, which own, lease, or maintain common areas in a real estate development, when such memberships are obligatory for purchasers of property in a development. (Note that subdivisions in New York State which are excluded from registering with the Department of State under Article 9–A of the Real Property Law, discussed earlier in this chapter, must register obligatory homeowners' associations when they exist.)

The state attorney general may grant certain discretionary exemptions from the law, which also applies to other types of securities offerings involving real estate syndication, but these exemptions are not normally granted for condominiums, cooperative apartments, or homeowners' associations.

The required offering statement must include disclosure of the following types of information:

1. Detailed terms of the transaction.
2. A good physical description of the property.
3. The rights and liabilities of purchasers.
4. Specifics pertaining to leases, mortgages, and any other encumbrances on the property.
5. Background information on project sponsors and promoters, as well as a statement of their expected profits in the project if they have owned the property for less than three years.
6. Detailed descriptions of expenditures necessary for operation and management of the project, as well as any contracts binding the project.
7. Details concerning the hiring and firing of management.
8. Tax consequences.

All project sponsors, as well as any brokers or dealers selling condominiums, co-ops, or homeowners' association memberships, must file a "broker-dealer statement" and all salesmen employed by the sponsor or such broker-dealers must file a "salesman statement." These documents must disclose:

1. Previous business activities of brokers or dealers and the employment history of every salesman.
2. Any criminal or administrative sanctions which have been levied against the broker, dealer, salesman, or any principal of the project.

In general, the law provides that the state attorney general may require the disclosure of such information "as will afford potential investors, purchasers, and participants an adequate basis upon which to found their judgment and shall not omit any material fact or contain any untrue statement of a material fact."

The offering or sale of all cooperative interests in realty must be made only on the basis of the information filed in the offering statement, a true copy of which must be furnished to every purchaser. The law also prescribes that all advertising of such offerings must be consistent with this information and must state that offers are made only by an offering statement which has been filed with the Department of Law. A statement must also be prominently included in all advertising that the filing of an offering statement with the Department of Law does not constitute approval of the offering by this department or the state attorney general.

Pursuant to a policy statement of the Department of Law on "testing the market" (Cooperative Policy Statement No. 1), it is permissible for the sponsor of a cooperative apartment, condominium, or homeowners' association venture to accept a nominal sum, not to exceed $50, as an indication of interest in purchasing a cooperative apartment or condominium *prior* to the filing of the required offering statement, provided that the following conditions are met:

1. The money must be fully returnable at the will of the prospective purchaser, who must not be considered to be legally bound to make an actual purchase.
2. All monies so received must be kept in a special trust account pending return to the prospective purchaser or consummation of a purchase agreement.

3. Any advertising material must make these conditions clear and must state that the advertisement is not an offering and that an offering can only be made by an offering statement filed with the Department of Law.

4. The sponsors or their sales agent must provide a receipt setting forth the above terms to all those from whom they receive such funds.

5. All advertising proposed to be used in testing the market must be submitted for examination to the state attorney general's office at least forty-eight hours prior to its use and may not be used until it is cleared by that office.

In addition, before the above procedures may be utilized, an application to test the market must be filed with and approved in writing by the attorney general's office. These procedures may not be used, moreover, for condominiums or cooperative apartments which have rental pool arrangements or other "investment contract" features. Disclosure statements for this type of offering must be filed both with the state and with the federal Securities and Exchange Commission before any funds may be accepted from prospective buyers.[30]

It appears that some out-of-state developers use the "testing the market" procedure to sell a limited number of units to New York residents. Developers of small projects who expect to sell only a few units in New York State and do not want to incur the costs of filing with the Department of Law seem to be illegally using testing-the-market advertising to make these sales, without objections being raised by the state attorney general. No reporting requirement is imposed by the attorney general on developers who file applications to test the market.

The law provides that all offering statements filed with the Department of Law, as well as any accompanying exhibits or documents, must be available for inspection by any person who has purchased a cooperative interest in real estate covered by this statute or who has participated in the offering of such an interest.

The state attorney general is authorized to initiate an investigation of any alleged fraudulent practice, misrepresentation, or other violation of statutory provisions or regulations pertaining to the offering or sale of securities within the state of New York.[31] The attorney general may initiate an action to enjoin any such violation and he may bring criminal prosecutions against any person charged with committing fraudulent practices.[32] The courts have held, moreover, that:

The words "fraud" and "fraudulent practice" should be given a wide meaning so as to include all acts, although not originating in any actual evil design or contrivance to perpetrate fraud or injury upon others, which do by their tendency to deceive or mislead the purchasing public come within the purpose of this article.[33]

Finally, the courts have also ruled that the statutory prohibitions against the use of intentionally deceptive statements or advertising in the sale or offering of securities give rise to private cause of action for damages.[34]

Citizen Action

Citizens should be aware of the legal requirements pertaining to real estate transactions which are established by the General Business Law and be ready to determine if particular projects are in compliance with the law. Any failure by a condominium or cooperative apartment project (or by a project involving an obligatory homeowners' association) to file an offering statement with the Department of Law, any failure to provide a true copy of such an offering statement to every offeree, or any misrepresentation, deception, or other fraudulent practice should be reported in as clear, precise, and complete detail as possible to:

> Bureau of Securities and
> Public Financing
> Department of Law
> State of New York
> 2 World Trade Center
> New York, N.Y. 10047

FEDERAL LAWS AGAINST MAIL FRAUD

Under federal law it is a crime to use the mails, radio, television, telephone, or telegraph for the purpose of carrying out fraud—a prime example of which would be the intentional misrepresentation of truth to induce sales of land, homes, or condominiums.[35]

Sending promotional materials through the mail which use "false or fraudulent pretenses, representations, or promises" to sell land or dwellings constitutes mail fraud. It is, in addition, a crime for a developer or promoter to use "a fictitious, false, or assumed title, name or address, or name other than his own proper name" in connection with a fraudulent sales scheme conducted through the mails.

Anyone who for the purposes of fraud "transmits or causes to be transmitted by means of wire [telephone or telegraph], radio, or television communication in interstate or foreign commerce any writings, signs, signals, pictures, or sounds" also commits a federal crime.

The penalty for each of these crimes is a fine of not more than $1,000, or imprisonment for not more than five years, or both.

Citizen Action

A concerned citizen who has good reason to believe that a developer or promotor may be violating any of the above provisions of federal law in the promotion of land, homes, or condominiums should notify the nearest office of the U.S. attorney. The following are the four district offices of the U.S. attorney in New York State:

Northern District
Federal P.O. Building
Clinton Square
Syracuse, New York 13201

Eastern District
225 Cadman Plaza E.
Brooklyn, New York 11201

Southern District
40 Centre Street
New York, New York 10007

Western District
502 U.S. Court House
Niagara Square
Buffalo, New York 14204

LICENSING OF REAL ESTATE BROKERS AND SALESMEN IN NEW YORK STATE

All real estate brokers and salesmen engaged in business in New York State must be licensed by the New York Department of State in accordance with the provisions of Article 12–A of the New York Real Property Law (hereafter Article 12–A).[36] "Real estate broker" is broadly defined to include anyone who, for another person, firm, or corporation and in return for a fee or commission, lists, sells, exchanges, buys, or rents an interest in real estate; offers or attempts to negotiate such transactions; collects rent for the use of real estate; or negotiates a loan to be secured by a mortgage or other encumbrance. A "real estate salesman" is defined as a person employed by a licensed real estate broker to carry out such functions in the broker's behalf.

Licenses for both brokers and salesmen are issued by the Albany office of the New York Department of State. An applicant for a broker's license must be over the age of twenty-one and must either be an American citizen or have declared the intention of becoming one.[37] An applicant for a salesman's license must be over the age of eighteen and may not have been convicted of a felony (unless granted an executive pardon or a certificate of good conduct from a parole board). Those seeking a broker's license must pass a written examination and answer questions posed by the Department of State to determine the trustworthiness and competence of applicants. Those seeking a salesman's license must pass a written examination designed to satisfy the department with respect to applicants' "character and general intelligence." Since 1971 all new applicants for a broker's license must have successfully completed at least forty-five hours of study in real estate courses approved by the Department of State. Unless they qualify as non-resident licensees, all licensed brokers must maintain a definite place of business within New York State. All brokers must also conspicuously display their license in their place of business. An attorney who is licensed to practice law in New York State is not required to obtain a license from the Department of State in order to act as a real estate broker.[38]

Licenses are valid for a maximum of two years and may be renewed. A temporary license for not more than sixty days may be issued to an applicant for a salesman's license if the broker who wishes to employ him files a written request stating his willingness to be responsible for the actions of the salesman. Every license must have imprinted or impressed upon it the seal of the Department of State.

The Department of State also issues to every licensed broker and salesman a pocket card which identifies the holder as a licensee. These cards, which also bear the imprint or impress of the seal of the Department of State, must be shown upon request.

The Department of State can revoke or suspend, for as long a period as it deems proper, the license of any broker or salesman, impose fines up to $500, or reprimand any licensee who:

1. Is convicted of a violation of Article 12–A;
2. Misstates a material fact in an application for a license;
3. Is found guilty of fraud or fraudulent practices;
4. Conducts dishonest or misleading advertising; or
5. Demonstrates his untrustworthiness or incompetence to act as a real estate broker or salesman.

If a license is revoked or suspended, both the license and the pocket card must be returned within five days to the Department of State. The display of a real estate broker's license after it has been revoked or suspended is prohibited. Whenever the license of a broker or salesman is revoked, such a broker or salesman is ineligible for relicensing for a period of one year. Revocation of a broker's license, moreover, also serves to suspend the licenses granted to all salesmen employed by the broker. Any broker or salesman who is notified that disciplinary action is pending against him has an opportunity to be heard by officials of the Department of State before action is taken.

Any person who violates any provision of Article 12–A is guilty of a misdemeanor, as is any broker who employs an unlicensed salesman. If a violator received money as commission, compensation, or profit from the violation, he is also liable to penalties at least equal to the amount received, but not more than four times that amount. Such penalties may be sued for and recovered by any person aggrieved.

The Department of State is responsible for the enforcement of Article 12–A, and can investigate the business, practices, or methods of any licensee. Such investigations can be triggered by citizen complaints. Criminal actions for violations of Article 12–A are prosecuted by the New York State attorney general.

Citizen Action

Citizens should be aware of licensing requirements for real estate brokers and salesmen and of the legal obligation of both to show their pocket cards upon request. Failure by brokers or salesmen to produce pocket cards, any other violation of Article 12–A, or evidence of untrustworthiness or incompetence on the part of a real estate broker or salesman should be promptly reported to the Department of State. The following is the Albany address of the Licensing Services Office of the Department of State:

Licensing Services
New York Department of State
162 Washington Avenue
Albany, New York 12225

Complaints regarding any irregularities should be filed in writing with this office, though investigation may be carried out through a field office of the Department of State. As much information as possible should be supplied—for example, the complete name of the salesman, broker, and/or company involved, the address of the business, and a full explanation of the complaint.

NEW YORK CITY'S CONSUMER PROTECTION LAW

New York City has a broad consumer protection law which may apply to certain sales of land, homes, or condominiums intended for family, household, or personal use.[39] This law prohibits "any deceptive or unconscionable trade practice in the sale, lease, rental, or loan or in the offering for sale, lease, rental, or loan of any consumer goods or services, or in the collection of consumer debts." It applies to any such action which is made in the city to a city resident. The phrase "deceptive or unconscionable trade practice" is defined very broadly to include any false or misleading oral or written statement, visual description, or other representation; the use in any oral or written representation of exaggeration, innuendo, or ambiguity as to a material fact or failure to state a material fact, if such use deceives or tends to deceive; and the use of any act or practice which unfairly takes advantage of the lack of knowledge, ability, experience, or capacity of a consumer or which results in a gross disparity between the value received by a consumer and the price paid.

The law, in effect, applies to use of all advertising media in the city—including newspaper, radio, and television—even if the land or dwelling offered for sale is located outside the city. It need not be shown that consumers are being, or actually were, injured for the Department of Consumer Affairs to act. The use of deceptive or unconscionable trade practices simply in the advertising or offering for sale or lease of land, homes, or condominiums is in itself a violation of the law and thus is sufficient for the department to have jurisdiction.

The Department of Consumer Affairs has already charged a New Jersey developer selling land and second homes in the Pocono Mountains of Pennsylvania with violating New York City's Consumer Protection Law by employing deceptive advertising in television commercials carried by New York stations. The developer challenged the department's characterization of subdivision lots and second homes as "consumer goods and services," but the court upheld the department.

The enforcement powers of the Department of Consumer Affairs are extensive. It may impose civil penalties of $50 to $350 for violations of the Consumer Protection Law and up to $500 for "knowing violations." On a finding of repeated, multiple, or persistent violations of the law, the department may bring an action compelling the defendant to pay into the court all monies received as a result of the violations, and direct that this money be used to compensate consumers' losses due to such practices, including costs incurred by these consumers in making and pursuing their complaints. The defendant may also be directed to pay to the city the costs of bringing the action and making the investigation leading to the judgment. The city may at any time seek a court order for a temporary or permanent injunction or restraining order to stop deceptive or unconscionable practices.

Citizen Action

A citizen who knows of offers to sell, lease, or rent land or dwellings for family, household, or personal use, which involve "deceptive or unconscionable acts or practices" and which are made in New York City or use advertising media in the city, should notify the New York City Department of Consumer Affairs at the following address:

Consumer Advocate
Department of Consumer Affairs
80 Lafayette Street
New York, N.Y. 10013

NOTES

1. *See* the discussion on pp. 235–245 of this chapter.

2. 15 U.S.C §1701 *et seq.*

3. The secretary of HUD was authorized by the act to establish the OILSR to administer the act's provisions.

4. These regulations can be found at 24 CFR §1700 *et seq.*

5. This exemption was added by the Housing and Community Development Act of 1974, which contained amendments to the Interstate Land Sales Full Disclosure Act. Regulations implementing these new amendments were published at 39 *Federal Register* 38098–38101 (October 29, 1974).

6. 38 *Federal Register* 23873 (September 4, 1973).

7. Housing and Community Development Act of 1974, §812(c); 15 U.S.C. §1703(b).

8. *See* 38 *Federal Register* 23866–23909 (September 4, 1973); 39 *Federal Register* 7824–7825 (February 28, 1974); 39 *Federal Register* 9431–9433 (March 11, 1974); and 39 *Federal Register* 38098–38101 (October 29, 1974).

9. 24 CFR Part 1715; 38 *Federal Register* 23897 (September 4, 1973).

10. 38 *Federal Register* 23866 (September 4, 1973).

11. 39 *Federal Register* 7825 (February 28, 1974).

12. *See* Appendix for the addresses of the four district offices of the U.S. attorney in New York State.

13. N.Y. Real Property Law, Article 9–A.

14. In a purchase money mortgage the seller of property, rather than a bank, issues a mortgage to the purchaser. Since title to the property is conveyed upon receipt of a down payment (rather than after *all* payments are made, as is the case under an "installment plan"), subdivisions sold in this manner do not fall within the scope of Article 9–A, even though buyers in such circumstances make their mortgage payments to the developer.

15. N.Y. Real Property Law, Article 9–A, §337(1).

16. *See* pp. 257–260 of this chapter.

17. These regulations can be found at 19 NYCRR Part 135. Provisions dealing with offering statements are at §135.14.

18. It should be pointed out that many out-of-state subdivisions register with the Department of State under Article 9–A.

19. N.Y. Public Officers Law, Article 6, §85 *et seq. See* Chapter 1 for a full discussion of this new state law.

20. 15 U.S.C. §77a *et seq.*

21. On July 4, 1974, the Federal Trade Commission announced that it would undertake a nation-wide investigation of the development and management of residential condominiums. The intent of this investigation was to determine whether companies that build, sell, or operate condominiums "have been or are engaging in unfair or deceptive practices in connection with these activities." This investigation, which might have led to broad new federal rules governing activities of the industry and legal actions on specific issues, was abruptly terminated by the commission without explanation in March 1975.

22. A number of hotels are now being converted to "rental pool" condominiums.

23. SEC Securities Act Release No. 33-5347, issued January 4, 1973; 38 *Federal Register* 1735 (January 18, 1973).

24. 17 CFR §230.235.

25. 15 U.S.C. §77a *et seq.*

26. SEC Securities Act Release No. 33-5382, issued April 9, 1973; 38 *Federal Register* 9587 (April 18, 1973).

27. Securities and Exchange Commission v. Ralston Purina Co., 346 U.S. 119 (1953).

28. 17 CFR §230.146; 39 *Federal Register* 15266 (May 2, 1974).

29. §352–e.

30. See pp. 252–256 of this chapter for a discussion of SEC requirements.

31. General Business Law §352; Charles H. Greenthal & Co., Inc. v. Lefkowitz, 32 N.Y.2d 457, 299 N.E.2d 657, 346 N.Y.S. 2d 234 (1973).

32. General Business Law §§352–i and 353, §§352–c and 358. The attorney general may also bring actions under Article 22–A of the General Business Law, which deals with false advertising, and under §63(12) of the Executive Law, which deals with repeated fraudulent or illegal acts.

33. People v. Federated Radio Corp., 244 N.Y. 33, 154 N.E. 655 (1926). *See also* People v. Tellier, 7 Misc. 2d 43, 155 N.Y.S. 2d 245 (Sup. Ct. 1956); People v. Abbott, 4 Misc. 2d 565, 147 N.Y.S. 2d 256 (Sup. Ct. 1955).

34. Barnes v. Peat, Marwick, Mitchell & Co., 69 Misc. 2d 1068, 332 N.Y.S. 2d 281 (Sup. Ct. 1972).

35. 18 U.S.C. §§1341–1343.

36. §440 *et seq.*

37. A person who has declared the intention of becoming an American citizen must do so within seven years if he wishes to retain his eligibility for a real estate broker's license.

38. Weinblatt v. Parkway–St. Johns Place Corp., 136 Misc. 743, 241 N.Y.S. 721, *aff'd,* 229 App. Div. 865, 243 N.Y.S. 810 (1930).

39. Administrative Code of New York, Chapter 64, Title A, "The Consumer Protection Law of 1969."

CHAPTER 13

Other Special Controls

IN ADDITION TO the legislation providing for land use planning and regulation that has already been discussed, both the state and federal governments have enacted other laws which involve land use controls in particular types of circumstances. Three important instances of such action are discussed in this chapter:

1. The National Flood Insurance Program
2. Federal and State Wild, Scenic, and Recreational Rivers Systems
3. Siting of Power Plants and Utility Transmission Facilities in New York State

In a brief concluding section, reference is made to some of the special commissions and public authorities not treated in this book which have impact on land use patterns and decisions in various parts of New York State.

THE NATIONAL FLOOD INSURANCE PROGRAM

The National Flood Insurance Program is designed to play a very important role in land use control in floodplain areas. The program was established by the National Flood Insurance Act of 1968, under which flood insurance, previously unavailable from the private sector, was made available to residents of communities which participate in the program.[1] The prime requirement for such participation is the establishment of satisfactory land use controls to regulate development within floodplain areas identified as having special flood hazards. The act provided that the federal government would identify flood-prone communities and would provide data to guide local governments in the adoption of adequate controls.

This legislation marked an important reorientation in federal policy regarding floods, which previously had concentrated almost entirely on the construction of public works such as dams and levees for flood prevention. By 1968 it had become apparent that while such works cannot prevent all floods, the illusion of full protection that they project was resulting in rapidly increasing development in flood-risk areas. When floods occurred, the federal government then had to come in with millions of dollars of disaster relief funds to aid those whose settlement in floodplains had been encouraged by very expensive federal public works programs. In addition to these direct economic costs, awareness had also developed of the great environmental costs associated with such projects as dams and channelization. Consequently, Congress now sought to encourage flood protection through regulation of land uses as a counterpoint to federal public works programs, using flood insurance as an alternative to disaster relief payments.

When, in 1973, Congress saw that only a small percentage of eligible flood-prone communities were participating in the National Flood Insurance Program, it passed new and stronger legislation, increasing both the benefits and sanctions of the program. The Flood Disaster Protection Act of 1973[2] established that:

1. On and after March 2, 1974, no *federal assistance* can be granted for the acquisition or construction of property within any area identified by the federal government as having special flood hazards and in which flood insurance is available, *unless the property is covered by flood insurance.*[3]

2. The federal agencies "responsible for the supervision, approval, regulation, or insuring of banks, savings and loan associations, or similar institutions" must by regulation direct that on and after March 2, 1974, such institutions may not make, increase, extend, or renew any *loans* secured by property in an area identified

as having special flood hazards and in which flood insurance is available, *unless the property is covered by flood insurance.*[4]

3. On and after July 1, 1975, no *federal assistance* can be granted for the acquisition or construction of property within any area identified by the federal government as having special flood hazards, *unless the community in which such area is located is then participating in the National Flood Insurance Program.*[5]

4. The federal agencies which supervise, approve, regulate, or insure banks, savings and loan associations, or similar institutions must issue regulations prohibiting such institutions on or after July 1, 1975, from making, increasing, extending, or renewing any *loans* secured by property in an area identified as having special flood hazards, *unless the community in which the area is located is then participating in the National Flood Insurance Program.*[6]

These are powerful sanctions, requiring action by individuals in (1) and (2) and action by communities in (3) and (4) to avoid the loss in flood hazard areas of federal aid and of loans from financial institutions that are subject to any kind of federal supervision, regulation, or insurance (which includes virtually all banks and savings and loans associations). This means that an individual in a community which is participating in the program will not be able to get a mortgage for construction or repairs in special flood hazard areas unless he has purchased flood insurance. If a flood-prone community fails to adopt adequate land use controls to qualify for participation in the program before July 1, 1975 (or one year after the community is identified as flood prone, whichever is later), no one will be able to obtain federal aid or loans for use within special flood hazard areas.

In New York State, testament to the "teeth" of the federal Flood Disaster Protection Act of 1973 can be found in recent state legislation[7] which expresses the desire "to prevent the termination of critically needed financial assistance." The new state law not only provides for technical assistance by state agencies to local governments to help them qualify for the National Flood Insurance Program, but also stipulates that if a local government fails to qualify or if its qualification is revoked by the federal government, the commissioner of environmental conservation has the authority to promulgate and administer flood hazard regulations for that locality that meet minimum federal requirements. This authority extends until such time as the local government qualifies under the federal program. Such assertion by the state of its right to exert the police power on the local level is not traditional, and demonstrates the power of the federal flood insurance legislation to bring about needed land regulation in flood hazard areas.

As mentioned above, the 1973 federal Flood Disaster Protection Act also increased the benefits of the National Flood Insurance Program. The limits of available coverage for both structures and contents were greatly increased while rates were substantially reduced. In addition, the act increased from $250 million to $500 million the amount that the secretary of housing and urban development (HUD) can borrow from the U.S. Treasury to finance the program. Moreover, whereas the 1968 act had established a monetary limit on the total amount of claims that could be outstanding at any one time, the 1973 act replaced this dollar restraint with a time limit on the writing of flood insurance contracts. No such contracts may be written after June 30, 1977, at which time a federal review of the program will be conducted.

Administration of the Program

The National Flood Insurance Program is administered by the Federal Insurance Administration of the U.S. Department of Housing and Urban Development (HUD). The private insurance industry, which is represented by the National Flood Insurers' Association, cooperates with the federal government in this subsidized program and writes all flood insurance policies. The National Flood Insurers' Association appoints servicing companies, generally on a statewide basis, to disseminate information both to the public and to insurance agents, to process all flood insurance policies, and to handle the adjustment of claims for loss payments. Policies may be purchased by property owners in eligible communities from any licensed property and casualty insurance agent or broker.

Information and assistance regarding qualification for the program is available to communities directly from the Federal Insurance Administration. In addition, the governor of each state has appointed a state coordinating agency to assist communities in qualifying for the program, especially in developing acceptable land use and control measures. The coordinating agency appointed in New York State is the Department of Environmental Conservation (DEC).

The secretary of HUD is charged by statute to identify all floodplain areas within which there are flood hazards, and to delineate the boundaries of flood hazard areas. He is authorized to consult and contract with other federal departments and agencies (such as the Army Corps of Engineers, the U.S. Geological Survey, and the Soil Conservation Service), as well as with state and local agencies, in making these determinations. A provision of the 1973 act established that the identification of special flood hazard areas and determination of the degree of hazard in each area must be completed at the earliest date possible.

By June 30, 1974, the secretary of HUD was required to have notified all known flood-prone communities which were not participating in the program of their tentative identification as a community containing one or more areas having special flood hazards. After this notification, each community was required either (1) to apply promptly for participation in the program; or (2) within six months to submit technical data to HUD establishing that the community either is not seriously flood prone or has corrected flood hazards by floodworks or other flood control measures. The secretary of HUD may grant a public hearing to any community when there is conflicting data on the nature and extent of a flood hazard; or, alternatively, the community may be given the opportunity to submit written evidence. In either case, the secretary's determination is conclusive, if supported by substantial evidence.

As further information on flood hazards becomes available, the secretary of HUD may identify additional flood-prone communities.

The standard which has been adopted by HUD for the identification of special flood hazard areas and as the base flood elevation for the adoption of local land use controls is the so-called "100-year flood." This standard represents the flood level that on the average will have a 1 percent chance of being equaled or exceeded in any given year. Thus special flood hazard areas are those areas in which there is a 1 percent chance of flooding in any given year. Determination of this probability is not based on historical data alone, but takes into consideration factors such as topography, wind velocity, tidal surge, and man-made devices such as levees and dams.

Once a community has been identified as flood prone (that is, as a community which contains one or more areas which have special flood hazards), it must qualify for the National Flood Insurance Program within one year after notification or by July 1, 1975, whichever is later, to avoid the sanctions discussed above.

As was also pointed out above, in order to qualify for the program, a flood-prone community must adopt adequate land use and control measures consistent with federal criteria. HUD promulgated regulations setting forth such criteria in December 1971.[8] These regulations provide that "the minimum requirements governing the adequacy of the land use and control measures for flood-prone areas adopted by a particular community depend on the amount of technical data formally provided to the community by the [federal insurance] Administrator." Optimally, the federal insurance administrator will provide data which will:

1. Define the special flood hazard areas within the community;
2. Identify water surface elevations, setting forth the heights which would be reached by the "100-year flood" at points within the floodplain; and
3. Identify the "floodway," which includes the stream channel and immediately adjacent areas which during the "100-year flood" would carry the major portion of flood waters moving at great velocity; or
4. Where applicable, identify the "coastal high hazard area," which is that part of the coastal floodplain that is subject to high-velocity waters.

The following minimum standards for flood-prone communities apply according to the amount of data provided to a given community by the federal insurance administrator. A community must meet the respective minimum requirements of (2) through (5) below within six months after it receives the specified data from the administrator. A participating community which does not adopt land use and control measures in accordance with these minimum standards within six months will lose its eligibility. A community can also have its eligibility suspended if it allows development which violates the measures it has enacted, thereby violating its agreement with the Federal Insurance Administration. Although some participating communities have been suspended for such actions, monitoring efforts need to be strengthened. When a community's eligibility is suspended, no flood insurance policies may be sold or renewed until it is formally reinstated by the Federal Insurance Administration; and as a non-participant in the program, the community incurs the federal sanctions.

1. When the administrator has not defined the special flood hazard areas within a community, has not provided water surface eleva-

tion data, and/or has not provided sufficient data to identify the floodway or coastal high hazard area, the community must:

a. Require building permits for all proposed construction or other improvements in the community;
b. Review all building permit applications for new construction or substantial improvements to determine whether proposed building sites will be reasonably safe from flooding;
c. Review subdivision and development proposals to assure that they are consistent with the need to minimize flood damage; that all public utilities and facilities are located, elevated, and constructed to minimize or eliminate flood damage; and that adequate drainage is provided; and
d. Require new or replacement water supply systems and/or sanitary sewerage systems to be designed to minimize or eliminate infiltration of flood waters into the systems and discharges from the systems into flood waters, and require on-site waste disposal systems to be located in a manner that will avoid impairment and contamination during flooding.

2. When the administrator has identified the floodplain area having special flood hazards, but has not provided data on water surface elevation, the floodway, or the coastal high hazard area, the minimum land use and control measures adopted by a community for the floodplain must:

a. Take into account floodplain management programs, if any, already in effect in neighboring areas;
b. Apply at a minimum to all areas identified by the administrator as having special flood hazards;
c. Provide that within the floodplain areas having special flood hazards, the laws and ordinances concerning land use and control and other measures designed to reduce flood losses will take precedence over any conflicting laws, ordinances, or codes;
d. Require building permits for all proposed construction or other improvements in the floodplain area having special flood hazards;
e. Review building permit applications for major repairs in the special flood hazard area to determine that the proposed

repair uses construction materials that are resistant to flood damage and methods that will minimize such damage;

f. Review building permit applications for new construction or substantial improvements within the special flood hazard area to assure that the proposed construction (including prefabricated and mobile homes) is protected against flood damage; is designed and anchored to prevent flotation, collapse, or lateral movement; and uses construction materials that are resistant to flood damage and methods that will minimize such damage; and

g. Meet all the requirements of (c) and (d) listed above under (1).

3. When the administrator has identified the floodplain area having special flood hazards, and has provided water surface elevations for the 100-year flood, but has not provided data sufficient to identify the floodway or coastal high hazard area, the minimum land use and control measures adopted by a community for the floodplain must:

a. Meet all the requirements listed above under (2);

b. Require new construction or substantial improvements of residential structures within the special flood hazard area to have the lowest floor (including the basement) elevated to or above the level of the 100-year flood;

c. Require new construction or substantial improvements of non-residential structures within special flood hazard areas to have the lowest floor (including the basement) elevated to or above the level of the 100-year flood or, along with utility and sanitary facilities, to be floodproofed up to this level; and

d. In riverine situations, provide that until a floodway has been designated, no use, including landfill, may be permitted within a special flood hazard area unless the applicant for the use has demonstrated that the proposed use, when combined with all other existing and anticipated uses, will not increase the water surface elevation of the 100-year flood more than one foot at any point.

4. When the administrator has identified a riverine floodplain area having special flood hazards, has provided water surface elevation data for the 100-year flood, and has provided floodway data, the

land use and control measures adopted by the community for the floodplain must:

a. Meet all the requirements listed above under (2);
b. Meet the requirements of (b) and (c) listed above under (3);
c. Designate a floodway for passage of the water of the 100-year flood. Selection must be based on the principle that the area chosen must be designed to carry the waters of the 100-year flood, without increasing the water surface elevation of the flood more than one foot at any point;
d. Provide that existing nonconforming uses in the floodway shall not be expanded but may be modified, altered, or repaired to incorporate floodproofing measures, provided that such measures do not raise the level of the 100-year flood; and
e. Prohibit fill or encroachments within the designated floodway that would impair its ability to carry and discharge the waters resulting from the 100-year flood, except where the effect on flood heights is fully offset by stream improvements.

5. When the administrator has identified a coastal floodplain area having special flood hazards, has provided water surface elevation data for the 100-year flood, and has identified the coastal high hazard area, the land use and control measures adopted by the local government for the floodplain must:

a. Meet all the requirements listed above under (2);
b. Meet the requirements of (b) and (c) listed above under (3);
c. Provide that existing uses located on land below the elevation of the 100-year flood in the coastal high hazard area shall not be expanded; and
d. Provide that no land below the level of the 100-year flood in a coastal high hazard area may be developed unless the new construction or substantial improvement (i) is located landward of the reach of the mean high tide; (ii) is elevated on adequately anchored piles or columns to a lowest floor level at or above the 100-year flood level and securely anchored to such piles or columns; and (iii) has no basement and has the space below the lowest floor free of obstructions.

In addition to setting out these minimum standards, the HUD regulations make recommendations for the development of overall comprehensive management plans for flood-prone areas. Central to these considerations is the need to divert unwise development from flood-prone areas and to encourage land uses there which are consistent with the flood damage potential of such areas.

On March 26, 1975, the Federal Insurance Administration of HUD published in the *Federal Register* proposed amendments to the existing regulations for the National Flood Insurance Program.[9] The public comment period for these proposals extended through May 26, 1975, and public hearings were scheduled to be held across the country after that date. Promulgation of the final regulations is expected in the second half of 1975.

The proposed amendments contain a number of very important provisions. For example, after the administrator has identified the floodplain area having special flood hazards, the flood-prone community:

> Must in riverine situations, submit to the Administrator evidence of coordination with upstream, downstream or adjacent communities adversely affected by any development, fill, encroachment, or alteration or relocation of a watercourse.

Further, once special flood hazard areas have been identified, communities may not simply sit back and wait for the Federal Insurance Administration to supply further flood data, but must take "reasonable measures to consider and use" any available 100-year flood data as criteria for administering the required floodplain regulations adopted by the community.

Where the adminstrator has supplied 100-year flood elevation data, the proposed regulations require that floodproofing of all new construction and substantial improvements of non-residential structures be carried out in accordance with the standards for completely flood-proofed structures contained in the U. S. Army Corps of Engineers publication "Flood-Proofing Regulations." A registered professional engineer or architect must also certify that all floodproofing measures used for a structure are reasonably adequate to enable it to withstand the various impacts and effects of the 100-year flood.

Special new provisions are also proposed for mobile homes. These distinguish between new and existing mobile home parks within special flood hazard areas. Elevation to the 100-year flood level is required for mobile homes in new parks, while mobile homes moving into existing parks where facilities are already in place do not have to be elevated. In the latter case, however, full disclosure must be made to every new mobile home purchaser that the mobile home is being located in a special flood hazard area. In addition, within a designated floodway or coastal high hazard area, no new mobile home park, expansion of an existing park, or location of new mobile homes is permitted.

Once a floodway is designated, the proposed regulations would prohibit all new construction and substantial improvements which would result in an increase in flood heights during the 100-year flood. The existing regulations permit fill and encroachments where the effect on flood heights is fully offset by stream improvements, but the proposed amendments do not include this exception.

In the case of designated coastal high hazard areas, it is proposed that the use of fill for structural support be prohibited.

Prior to the comment and review period for this proposed revision of the HUD regulations for the National Flood Insurance Program, it is not possible to predict exactly what form the final regulations will take. Citizens who are aware of the significance of this important program should take special care to obtain copies of the final regulations when they are published in the *Federal Register*.

In New York State a very large majority of the 1,600 communities which have zoning and building code jurisdiction are affected by federal flood legislation and regulations. As of April 1, 1975, some 1,425 of these communities had been identified as flood-prone communities and had received maps delineating special flood hazard areas. Another 78 communities had been tentatively identified as flood prone and were under further study. Four hundred and thirty-three communities had already qualified for participation in the National Flood Insurance Program and thus were eligible for the sale of flood insurance.

Data on water surface elevations and coastal high hazard areas have been provided to only a very few communities, and it is likely to be a number of years before such data are supplied to all flood-prone communities. While the land use and control measures required for initial qualification in the program can be a rather vague building permit system, the provision of additional data will require that more sophisticated land use and control measures be adopted in line with the HUD criteria spelled out above.

As discussed above, new legislation has been enacted by the New York State legislature to facilitate technical assistance by state agencies to local flood-prone communities seeking qualification for the

National Flood Insurance Program, and to provide for state promulgation of adequate land use regulations in cases where local governments fail to qualify.[10] When a local government is notified by the secretary of HUD of its formal identification as a flood-prone community, it must notify the commissioner of environmental conservation within ten working days. Upon receipt of such notification, DEC is responsible for providing technical assistance to the local government, including assistance in the development of joint programs by two or more local governments and the provision of model flood hazard regulations.

If within three months of the date by which a local government must qualify for participation in the program or be subject to sanctions, the commissioner of environmental conservation judges that this local government may fail to qualify, DEC must develop flood hazard regulations for the jurisdiction which meet minimum federal requirements. As discussed earlier, DEC also has the authority to promulgate and to administer such regulations in communities which fail to qualify for the program or which have their qualification revoked.

The state law also requires that state agencies take affirmative action to minimize flood hazards and losses in connection with state-owned and state-financed buildings, roads, and other facilities; the disposition of state lands and properties; the administration of state and state-assisted planning programs; and the preparation and administration of state building, sanitary, and other pertinent codes. The commissioner of environmental conservation is granted the authority to establish standards and procedures to govern the review of potential flood hazards at the proposed construction sites of state and state-financed facilities.

Citizen Action

Citizens should be aware that the strong provisions of the Flood Disaster Protection Act of 1973 may not be strictly and smoothly implemented. In many quarters the required land use and control measures may be politically unwelcome. While a vague resolution supporting the principle of land use regulation in flood hazard areas may not meet much opposition, more specific and stringent requirements pertaining to elevation precautions, floodproofing, or prohibition of new residential uses in a floodway are likely to be resisted by those planning or supporting construction in flood hazard areas.

Although the federal statutes and regulations are actually more concerned with the regulation of development in flood hazard areas than with stopping development, compliance with the standards established will increase the costs of construction. Thus various political and administrative maneuvers to avoid full compliance with laws and regulations can be expected.

In some areas, there may be extended delays in the provision of needed data by the federal government. When this occurs, flood-prone communities can retain their eligibility in the National Flood Insurance Program with loose and unsophisticated land use and control measures, since they are not required to comply with stricter standards until data are received on water surface elevations, the floodway, and coastal high hazard areas.

Consequently, there is a great need for citizen monitoring of the implementation of the National Flood Insurance Program. Citizens should familiarize themselves with the provisions of federal and state laws and regulations, and make sure that officials in their community are conscientiously carrying out the requirements of the program. Any efforts that are made to thwart such implementation should be subjected to full public scrutiny and reported to the Federal Insurance Administration. The following is this agency's address:

Federal Insurance Administration
U.S. Department of Housing and Urban Development
Washington, D.C. 20410

Once a flood-prone community has qualified for participation in the program, citizens should make sure that developments approved for special flood hazard areas by such local bodies as the planning board or the zoning board of appeals comply with the land use requirements of the flood insurance program. The likelihood that a community will lose its eligibility under the program if it approves developments in violation of its agreement with the Federal Insurance Administration should be stressed. Any such violations should be reported to the Federal Insurance Administration and investigation requested. Citizens who report the violations of their own local government, of course, run the risk that if the community is suspended, their own individual flood insurance policies cannot be renewed. This problem has been somewhat ameliorated in New York State by the passage of state legislation providing that the state will take action to rectify the loss of eligibility in suspended communities.

FEDERAL AND STATE WILD, SCENIC, AND RECREATIONAL RIVERS SYSTEMS

Both the federal government and New York State have passed legislation to protect certain rivers and adjacent land areas. The following discussion describes both of the new systems which have been established.

The Federal Wild and Scenic Rivers Act

In 1968 Congress passed a Wild and Scenic Rivers Act[11] establishing the national policy

> that certain selected rivers of the Nation which, with their immediate environments, possess outstandingly remarkable scenic, recreational, geologic, fish and wildlife, historic, cultural, or other similar values, shall be preserved in free-flowing condition, and that they and their immediate environments shall be protected for the benefit and enjoyment of present and future generations.

The act implemented this policy by instituting a National Wild and Scenic Rivers System (hereafter the system), by designating all or portions of eight rivers and adjacent lands as the original components of this system, and by setting out methods and standards for future additions to the system. The system is administered by the secretary of the interior, and, where national forest lands are involved, by the secretary of agriculture.

Several different kinds of protection are afforded the river areas in the system. First of all, the act now authorizes the appropriation of $37.6 million for the acquisition of land in designated river areas. Secondly, restrictions are placed on water resources projects directly affecting river areas of the system. The Federal Power Commission is prohibited from licensing "the construction of any dam, water conduit, reservoir, powerhouse, transmission line, or other project works" on or directly affecting a river in the system. Also, no department or agency of the United States may "assist by loan, grant, license, or otherwise in the construction of any water resources project that would have a direct and adverse effect on the values for which such river was established . . ." This does not preclude licensing of or assistance to developments below or above a designated river area or on a tributary stream which "will not invade the area or unreasonably diminish the scenic, recreational, and fish and wild-life values" present in the area on October 2, 1968, the date the act was passed. No federal department or agency may recommend authorization of *any* water resources project that "would have a direct and adverse effect on the values for which such river was established" or request appropriations to begin construction of any such project, no matter when it was authorized, without (1) advising either the secretary of the interior or the secretary of agriculture (whichever is responsible for the administration of the river area in question) in writing sixty days in advance of its intention to do so; and (2) specifically reporting to Congress at the time of the recommendation or request how construction of this project might affect the river area and its protected values.

In general, each component of the National Wild and Scenic Rivers System must be administered in a manner that protects and enhances the values which led to its inclusion in the system. Primary emphasis in this administration must be given to protecting esthetic, scenic, historic, archeological, and scientific features.

The land acquisition provisions established by the act authorize the secretaries of the interior and of agriculture to acquire lands and interests in land, such as scenic easements, within the authorized boundaries of any component of the system.[12] Neither secretary may, however, acquire fee title to an average of more than 100 acres per mile on both sides of the river. State-owned lands may be acquired only by donation. If 50 percent or more of the entire acreage within a river area is owned by the federal, state, or local government, the secretaries are prohibited from acquiring fee title to any lands by condemnation under the authority of the act. However, they are permitted in such circumstances to use condemnation to clear a title or to acquire scenic easements or other easements which are "reasonably necessary" to give the public access to the river. Land cannot be acquired by condemnation if it is located within any incorporated city, village, or borough which has a "duly adopted, valid zoning ordinance" that conforms to the purposes of the act. In order to carry out this provision, the appropriate secretary must issue guidelines specifying standards for local zoning ordinances. These standards must have the object of (1) prohibiting new commercial or industrial uses that are not consistent with the purposes of the act; and (2) protecting bank lands by means of acreage, frontage, and setback requirements on development.

Authorization is also given for exchanges of property in which a grantor may trade land within a river area for federally owned land elsewhere in the same state that is under the jurisdiction of the appropriate secretary. Other federal agencies and departments which have administrative jurisdiction over lands within a river area may transfer this jurisdiction to the appropriate secretary. The secretaries are also empowered to accept donations of lands and interests in land, as well as funds and other property which can be used in the administration of the system.

Owners of detached, one-family dwellings acquired under the act may retain rights of use and occupancy for non-commercial residential purposes for a term of up to twenty-five years. These rights may be terminated if the appropriate secretary is given reasonable cause to find that use and occupancy are being exercised in a manner that conflicts with the purposes of the act. In such a case, a fair market price for the unexpired portion of the rights must be paid to the holder.

As pointed out earlier, the act not only designates the original nine component river areas of the system, it also provides for future additions to the system. A river area can become part of the system in two ways:

1. If, like the original nine components, it is authorized for inclusion by an act of Congress; or
2. If it is (a) designated as a wild, scenic, or recreational river by an act of the legislature of the state or states through which it flows; (b) permanently administered as such a river by an agency or political subdivision of the state without expense to the federal government; and (c) approved by the secretary of the interior for inclusion in the system.

To be eligible for inclusion in the system, a river area must include a free-flowing stream and adjacent land areas that possess one or more of the values set out by Congress—that is, scenic, recreational, geologic, fish and wildlife, historic, cultural, and other similar values. A river that is not presently free-flowing can, if restored to this condition, become eligible for inclusion. "Free-flowing" as defined by the act means "existing or flowing in natural condition without impoundment, diversion, straightening, rip-rapping, or other modification of the waterway." The act further states that the existence of "low dams, diversion works, and other minor structures at the time any river is proposed for inclusion . . . shall not automatically bar its consideration for such inclusion: *Provided,* that this shall not be construed to authorize, intend, or encourage future construction of such structures within components of the national wild and scenic river system." Under the act, a river is "a flowing body of water or estuary or a section, portion, or tributary thereof, including rivers, streams, creeks, runs, kills, rills, and small lakes."

Each river area included in the system must be classified and administered as one of the following:

> (1) Wild river areas—Those rivers or sections of rivers that are free of impoundments and generally inaccessible except by trail, with watersheds or shorelines essentially primitive and waters unpolluted. These represent the vestiges of primitive America.
> (2) Scenic river areas—Those rivers or sections of rivers that are free of impoundments, with shorelines or watersheds still largely primitive and shorelines largely undeveloped, but accessible in places by roads.
> (3) Recreational river areas—Those rivers or sections of rivers that are readily accessible by road or railroad, that may have undergone some development along their shorelines, and that may have undergone some impoundment or diversion in the past.

Different stretches of the same river can be classified into different categories. For example, a section of a river which is otherwise designated as "scenic" may be too developed to warrant this classification, but may qualify for a "recreational" designation.

In addition to the eight rivers designated as original components of the system, the act also specifically named twenty-seven other rivers as potential additions to the system. One of these specified rivers was the Delaware River from Hancock, New York, to Matamoras, Pennsylvania. The events that have followed this particular designation are discussed in more detail below. Each of the twenty-seven rivers proposed as potential additions must be studied by the secretary of the interior or of agriculture to determine whether it should be included in the system. All of these studies must be completed by 1978, and the cooperation of appropriate state and local government agencies must be sought in their preparation. Rivers which are most likely to be developed in a way that would render them unsuitable for inclusion must be studied first. The secretary of the interior is responsible for eighteen of these studies and the secretary of agriculture for the other nine.

In January 1975 Congress added twenty-nine new rivers to the list of rivers to be studied for possible inclusion in the system.[13] River studies and reports for these rivers must be completed by October 1979. No New York rivers were included in this designation.

Through October 2, 1978, and, under specified conditions, one to three years longer, the Federal Power Commission and other federal agencies are prohibited from licensing and assisting water resources projects which would have a direct effect on any of the rivers designated as potential additions (unless during this period the appropriate secretary determines, upon study, that a particular river should not be included in the system). In addition, federal agencies must promptly advise either the secretary of the interior or the secretary of agriculture of other activities which might affect these rivers.

The act also states that in all planning for the use and development of water and related land resources, consideration must be given by federal agencies involved to potential national wild, scenic, and recreational river areas, and all river basin and project plan reports submitted to Congress must consider any such potential.

Each proposal submitted to Congress for the inclusion of a new river area within the system must be accompanied by a report, including maps and illustrations, that treats the following matters:

1. The characteristics which make the river area worthy of inclusion.
2. The current status of land ownership and use in the area.
3. The effects inclusion of the area in the system would have on potential uses of land and water.
4. The federal agency proposed to administer the area.
5. The extent to which it is proposed that administration, including costs involved, be shared by state and local agencies.
6. The estimated federal costs of acquiring necessary lands and interests in land, as well as of administration.

Each such report of a river area is printed as a Senate or House document.

Before the report is submitted to the President and Congress, copies are circulated among the secretaries of the interior, agriculture, and the army, the chairman of the Federal Power Commission, the heads of other affected federal agencies, and the governor of the state or states in which the river area is located, unless adjacent land areas are already owned by the federal government or have been authorized for acquisition by Congress. After a ninety-day comment period, the entire proposal, including the report and comments, is submitted to the President and to Congress.

State applications for the inclusion of rivers in the federal system must be approved by the secretary of the interior after comment from the secretaries of agriculture and the army, the chairman of the Federal Power Commission, and the heads of other affected federal agencies.

As pointed out earlier, one of the twenty-seven river areas designated by the act as a potential addition to the system was a section of the Delaware River extending from Hancock, New York, to Matamoras, Pennsylvania. The secretary of interior assigned the mandated study of the Delaware to the Bureau of Outdoor Recreation. This study, which was begun in 1969 and completed in the summer of 1973, found all of the designated portion of the Delaware to be of outstanding quality, but recommended that only two sections, totalling twenty-five miles, be classified as "scenic," with the remaining fifty miles to be classified as "recreational." Bureau of Recreation officials believed that nearby railroad tracks disqualified some stretches of the river from a "scenic" designation.

Shortly after the study was completed, the Bureau of Outdoor Recreation presented its findings at two informal public meetings. At these meetings, the bureau proposed five alternative model management plans for the designated portions of the Delaware. Key to each of these management plans was a determination of what proportion of the 14,700 acre management area along the river was to be owned and managed by the federal government and what proportion was to be owned and controlled by present residents and local governments.

The five alternatives presented by the Bureau of Outdoor Recreation ranged from a "total federal management plan" in which 6,000 of the 14,700 acres would be purchased outright by the federal government, with the remaining 8,700 acres to be controlled through "scenic easements, zoning, and local land use agreements," to a plan in which the federal government would purchase outright only 35 acres. A prolonged and spirited public debate ensued, involving citizens and government agencies in both Pennsylvania and New York. The controversy essentially pitted those who felt that local zoning initiatives in both New York and Pennsylvania had repeatedly failed to protect land areas, and thus that total federal management was necessary, against those who believed that total federal management would intrude upon the right of communities to control their own affairs and would unnecessarily take private property from local citizens.

A second issue involved the extent to which the Delaware should be made accessible to the public if and when it becomes part of the system. Each of the five proposed plans called for a number of visitor and recreation centers along the river's banks, to be used for boat launching, camping, picnicking, and nature trails. The issues were how many such sites were appropriate for a protected river and whether any sites should be constructed within the two sections of the river to be designated as "scenic."

The Bureau of Outdoor Recreation decided that it would recommend to the secretary of the interior a management program in which 450 shoreline acres would be purchased by the federal government and five new visitor sites would be constructed, two of which would serve as visitor information centers. Before submitting its recommendations to the secretary of the interior, the Bureau of Outdoor Recreation sent them to federal, state, and local agencies and to the governor for review and comment. In these recommendations, the bureau maintained that a combination of federal and local management would be much cheaper than a major federal purchase program and expressed confidence that a coordinated effort by communities on both sides of the river to enact zoning ordinances consistent with the purposes of the act, along with the assistance of the Delaware River Basin Commission, would successfully protect the river.

The federal, state, and local comments on the proposed recommendations were returned to the Bureau of Outdoor Recreation at the end of April 1974. After reviewing these comments and revising its draft recommendations, the bureau prepared a final proposal and report which it expected to submit to the secretary of the interior late in the spring of 1975. One important revision that has been made is the decision to propose that only two rather than five new visitor sites be constructed.

The New York State Wild, Scenic, and Recreational Rivers System

In 1972 New York State passed its own legislation to protect rivers which possess "outstanding natural, scenic, historic, ecological and recreational values" for present and future generations.[14] This legislation, which was modeled after the federal Wild and Scenic Rivers Act, established a state system of wild, scenic, and recreational rivers; designated initial components of the system; and prescribed methods and standards for additions to the system. All sixteen of the rivers or sections thereof which were designated as the original components of the system lie within the Adirondack Park, but a five-mile section of the Connetquot River and approximately nine miles of the Carmans River in Suffolk County on Long Island were added to these designations by later legislative amendments.

The system is administered by the Adirondack Park Agency and by the New York State Department of Environmental Conservation (DEC). The Adirondack Park Agency is responsible for all privately owned parts of river areas which lie within the boundaries of the Adirondack Park. DEC is responsible for all river areas located in other parts of the state and for all parts of river areas owned by the state within the Adirondack Park. The two state agencies must cooperate in all management activities affecting river areas within the Adirondack Park.

Rivers or sections thereof which are included in the system are classified as "wild," "scenic," or "recreational," under the following definitions and with the following management objectives:

1. *Wild rivers.* "Those rivers or sections of rivers that are free of diversions and impoundments, inaccessible to the general public except by water, foot or horse trails and with river areas primitive in nature and free of man-made development except foot bridges." To be designated as "wild," a river section must be at least five miles long and, in general, a distance of at least one-half mile must separate the river shore from a public highway or private road open to the public for motor vehicle use, unless a physical barrier exists which effectively screens the sight and sound of motor vehicles. Management must be directed toward perpetuating the wild condition of the river area.

2. *Scenic rivers.* "Those rivers, or sections of rivers, that are free of diversions or impoundments except for log dams, with limited road access and with river areas largely primitive and largely undeveloped or which are partially or predominantly used for agriculture, forest management and other dispersed human activities which do not substantially interfere with public use and enjoyment of the rivers and their shores." There is no minimum required length for this classification. Management of scenic river areas must be directed

toward preserving *and restoring* the natural scenic qualities of such rivers.

3. *Recreational rivers.* "Those rivers, or sections of rivers, that are readily accessible by road or railroad, that may have development in their river area and that may have undergone some impoundment or diversion in the past." Again, there is no minimum required length, and management must be directed toward preserving *and restoring* the natural qualities of the river areas.

The law provides that limited existing exceptions to the criteria for the three classifications will not automatically disqualify rivers from designation. A river area is to be examined as a whole, with its overall worthiness for inclusion being the deciding factor. All rivers in the system must be "relatively free of pollution." All state agencies are directed to pursue policies appropriate to their functions, powers, and duties that will enhance the conditions of designated rivers in accordance with the classification criteria set forth.

Within one year after the inclusion of a river in the system, DEC and/or the Adirondack Park Agency must establish detailed boundaries for the river area. These boundaries cannot be wider than one-half mile from each river bank. The river areas must then be managed according to the policies of the law and the criteria established for "wild," "scenic," and "recreational" classifications.

DEC and the Adirondack Park Agency must make and enforce regulations for the management, protection, enhancement, and control of land use and development in the wild, scenic, and recreational river areas of the system. During the first half of 1975 the Adirondack Park Agency released draft regulations for private lands in river areas of the system which lie within the Adirondack Park. After this draft was reviewed in three public hearings, the agency decided to prepare another draft, which will also be reviewed in public hearings. Essentially, the regulations developed by the agency relate management of the river areas to the private land use and development plan of the Adirondack Park, which is discussed in detail in Chapter 6. In keeping with the need to provide special protection for the state's wild, scenic, and recreational rivers, however, the regulations are more restrictive than the provisions of the land use plan.

For areas outside of the Adirondack Park, DEC intends to develop a separate set of regulations for each river area that is added to the system. Presently, the department is working with town, county, and federal officials on the development of regulations for the Carmans River. (Federal officials are involved because the river corridor includes part of a federal wildlife refuge.) In mid-April 1975 development of regulations for the Connetquot River had not yet begun.

In its work on regulations for river areas outside the Adirondack Park, DEC does not have an existing state regulatory framework for land use, such as that provided by the Adirondack Park land use plan, within which to work. Consequently, the department is focusing on the formulation of minimum state standards and on cooperative efforts with local officials to develop suitable management programs. Emphasis is being placed on the use of local zoning and planning powers, in conjunction with minimum state standards, and on the effective coordination of legal requirements of other state and federal programs, such as the National Flood Insurance Program, which is discussed in Chapter 13.

From a legal standpoint, however, DEC interprets the state law as authorizing state zoning in river areas of the system and holds that final state regulations will prevail over less strict local regulations.

The administration of each river area must emphasize the protection of its "ecological, recreational, aesthetic, botanical, scenic, geological, fish and wildlife, historical, cultural, archeological and scientific features." After the inclusion of a river area in the system, no dam or "other structure impeding the natural flow" of the river may be constructed on the river. Land uses in existence before the inclusion of a river area may continue, but may not be altered or expanded except as permitted by the respective classifications. However, DEC or the Adirondack Park Agency may order that an existing land use be discontinued, but only if landowners are compensated for their loss either by agreement or through condemnation.

In wild river areas no new structures or improvements, no new development of any kind, and no access by motor vehicles is permitted. In scenic areas continuation of existing agricultural practices, selective timber harvesting, and the propagation of crops are permitted, but mining, excavation, and the construction of roads, except when involving existing private roads necessary for residential, agricultural, or forest management purposes, are prohibited. A further exception in case of roads allows construction of new public access roads if there is no other access within two land miles in either direction. In recreational river areas, lands may be developed for all agricultural and selective timber harvesting uses and small communities as well as dispersed or cluster residential developments and public recreational areas are allowed. Roads or railroads may provide public access on one or both river banks, and there may be several bridge crossings and numerous river access points.

The law directs DEC and the Adirondack Park Agency to encourage any federal studies for inclusion of New York river areas in the National Wild and Scenic Rivers System, and states that a river included in the New York State system may also be included in the federal system.

A river area which is part of the state forest preserve or of a state park, wildlife refuge, or similar area is subject both to the provisions of the state law establishing the wild, scenic, and recreational river system and to other applicable statutory and constitutional provisions. Stricter provisions apply in cases of conflict.

Any violator of the law establishing the state system or of any regulation or order issued pursuant to this law may be compelled to obey by means of injunction, mandamus, or other appropriate remedy. Violators are also subject to civil fines of from $100 to $1,000 per day of violation.

The law requires that DEC or the Adirondack Park Agency study and, from time to time, propose additions to the system to the governor and the state legislature. Each proposal must specify the class or classes of the proposed addition and provide a detailed report containing the following information:

1. A map of the area;
2. The characteristics which would make the area a worthy addition to the system;
3. The current status of land ownership and use in the area;
4. The anticipated acquisitions of land and scenic or other easements in the area;
5. The potential uses of the land and the water; and
6. The cost of acquiring land and scenic or other easements and improvements proposed.

The report must be sent to legislative authorities in each county, town, and municipal corporation any part of which lies within the river area in question and to the commissioners of transportation, agriculture and markets, health, and commerce before submission of a proposal to the governor and legislature.

In an important provision, the law opens the door for "studies and proposals by other agencies or by citizen groups working independently or with [DEC or the Adirondack Park Agency]." This amounts to an invitation to citizen groups to prepare their own river studies. In effect, the provision allows the substitution of the energy and efforts of citizens who are trying to defend a particular stream for state expenses involved in enabling DEC or the Adirondack Park Agency to hire or free personnel to do river studies. No funds at all were appropriated for the system when the law establishing it was enacted.

The law directed the Adirondack Park Agency and DEC to study and evaluate certain specified rivers as potential additions to the system. Most of these rivers are within the Adirondack Park. Proposals for additions must be made to the state legislature no later than 1975.

At public hearings held in March 1975, the Adirondack Park Agency presented for discussion the findings of its two-year study of Adirondack rivers which might be added to the system. On the basis of this mandated study, the agency recommended that 1,113 miles of rivers be added to the 171 miles of Adirondack rivers already in the system. In mid-April 1975 this recommendation was still under discussion and no formal proposal had been submitted to the legislature.

On April 22, 1974, DEC announced plans to study stretches of forty-six rivers that had been recommended by citizens' groups and DEC personnel for inclusion in the system.[15] A number of these studies have now been completed, many with the assistance of citizens' groups and organizations such as The Catskill Center for Conservation and Development. Requests for study of additional rivers have also been received.

DEC's river studies are coordinated by its Division of Lands and Forests in Albany, but the regional directors are responsible for seeing that the studies are actually carried out. DEC encourages citizen groups which are interested in conducting river studies under DEC supervision to contact the commissioner of environmental conservation or the director of the regional office with jurisdiction over the area in which the river to be studied is located. DEC recommends that participating groups have the technical expertise needed to carry out a river study. The department estimates that about four days are required to inventory ten miles of a river, and has prepared a "field data collection form" to guide citizens in preparing river studies. The form inventories and categorizes the study data required, so that groups need only fill in numbers and descriptions and then turn the form over to DEC. These forms are available in the regional offices.

A river study is only part of the overall report which forms the basis of a proposal by DEC or the Adirondack Park Agency for the inclusion of a river in the system. As pointed out, the law requires that these two agencies circulate reports which they prepare among county, town, and municipal legislative authorities and state agencies before submitting a proposal to the governor and the legislature. However, the studies and proposals prepared by citizen groups or other agencies working independently of DEC and the Adirondack Park Agency, do not have to be circulated among local and state authorities prior to submission to the legislature.

Citizen Action

Opportunities for citizen participation in the state's wild, scenic, and recreational river program have been explained in the previous section. These include both (1) the preparation of river studies in cooperation with DEC or the Adirondack Park Agency; and (2) the independent preparation of studies and proposals by citizen groups for the inclusion of rivers in the system. Many citizens across the state have already taken part in such work. For example, both of the Long Island rivers that have been added to the system by legislative amendment have been studied and strongly supported by local citizens. In both cases, high school biology classes played a vital role in the preparation of the required river study.

Also, citizens should support the adoption of effective management programs for river areas included in the system. A public hearing must always be held in each area before rules and regulations are promulgated for that area, and citizens should take care to attend. In addition, citizens should express their endorsement of river protection to their local government officials.

The federal Wild and Scenic Rivers Act does not have a clause comparable to that in the state law allowing and encouraging citizen studies and proposals. It is possible, however, for citizens to influence their elected representatives in Congress, federal officials who are charged with studying and/or proposing potential additions to the system, and state and local officials who may participate in the study process. Efforts can be made to urge the governor and the state legislature to propose river areas for inclusion in the federal system, whereby access can be gained to federal protective measures and funds for the acquisition of lands and easements. When public meetings are held to discuss the proposed recommendations of a federal agency regarding a particular river, citizens have the opportunity to work for the best possible means of protecting the river.

SITING OF POWER PLANTS AND UTILITY TRANSMISSION FACILITIES IN NEW YORK STATE

In recent years the tension between the demand for power in the United States and the environmental damage caused by power-generating facilities has been increasing. A phenomenal growth in energy demand has led to a proliferation of power plants, and, as the undesirable environmental effects of power plants have become better known to the public, there has been increasing controversy over where future plants are to be located.

A number of different kinds of environmental problems are associated with power plants. Those plants which consume fossil fuels such as coal and oil to produce electricity can cause serious air pollution problems. They can destroy a river's aquatic environment (1) by sucking in and destroying fish and fish eggs found in water used to cool condensors; and/or (2) by discharging heated or polluted wastewater, which reduces the oxygen content of the river (thus suffocating aquatic life), changes the metabolism and spawning patterns of fish, and disrupts the food chain. Severe damage to the aquatic life of rivers and streams can also be caused by hydroelectric plants, in which water itself directly turns turbines to produce electricity; by pumped storage plants, in which water is pumped to higher elevations during periods of low demand for electricity and then runs down to power generators during peak periods; and by nuclear plants, which may use stream water for cooling purposes. Hydroelectric plants and pumped storage plants can also disrupt the water-flow patterns in entire watersheds. Nuclear plants, in which nuclear energy is used to produce electrical power, are particularly controversial, with many scientists warning that, among other serious problems, adequate safeguards do not presently exist to prevent theft or leakage in the transportation, storage, and use of radioactive materials or to prevent accidents within plants which would produce serious emissions of radioactive material. In addition, power plants can occupy large areas of land, cast out long webs of power lines, and produce serious levels of noise.

There is at the present time no coordinated federal or state plan governing the siting of all power plants, but different types of plants are subject to different kinds of federal and state regulation. Nuclear power plants must be licensed by the U.S. Nuclear Regulatory Commission and both hydroelectric and pumped storage plants must be licensed by the Federal Power Commission. Both of these federal agencies must comply with the National Environmental Policy Act (NEPA) requirements which are discussed in Chapter 9. This means that each agency must prepare an environmental impact statement whenever it considers issuing a license for a power plant. In each case, a draft impact statement must be made available for public comment and the final statement must follow the application for a license through the entire review process, which in the case of both the Nuclear Regulatory Commission and the Federal Power Commission always includes a public hearing.

Fossil-fueled power plants do not require a federal license. In 1972, however, the New York State legislature set up a state regulatory program for the siting of all major steam generating facilities, which include both fossil-fueled plants and nuclear power plants. This program will be discussed in detail in the next section. Following that will be a discussion of state regulation of major utility transmission facilities.

In addition to the above requirements, all types of power plants must also obtain permits required by the Federal Water Pollution Control Act Amendments of 1972[16] for any discharge, whether of pollutants or of heated water, into navigable waters. As of March 1975 these permits, except those for the discharge of dredged or fill material, must be obtained from the U.S. Environmental Protection Agency (EPA); but as has been discussed in Chapter 5,[17] New York State has passed legislation establishing a State Pollutant Discharge Elimination System (SPDES) with the goal of receiving authorization from EPA to issue permits on its behalf.[18] An application by the state requesting such authorization is presently pending.

Permits for the discharge of dredged or fill material into navigable waters, as well as permits for any construction in navigable waters, must be obtained from the U.S. Army Corps of Engineers.[19]

Special provisions are made in the 1972 amendments for thermal discharges. Under Section 316,[20] EPA can allow a particular power plant to discharge heated water in excess of established standards if the owner or operator of the plant can show that the increased discharge of heat will still assure protection of a balanced, indigenous population of fish, shellfish, and wildlife in the water body. This relaxation of standards must be preceded by a public hearing. The section further requires that in reviewing thermal dischargers, EPA must require that "the location, design, construction, and capacity of cooling water intake structures reflect the best technology available for minimizing environmental impact."[21]

One very serious environmental problem frequently associated with power plants is the entrainment of small aquatic organisms such as fish eggs and larvae with the river water used for cooling purposes. As the organisms pass through the plant's cooling system, they are damaged or killed. This problem is not openly and explicitly addressed in Section 316. Consequently, it is presently unclear exactly what legal authority, if any, EPA will exercise to control the destruction of plant and animal life that is drawn into the cooling systems of power plants.

Siting of Major Steam Electric Generating Facilities

After July 1, 1972, no one may begin the preparation of a site for, or begin the construction of, a major steam electric generating facility in New York State without having first obtained a certificate of environmental compatibility and public need (hereafter, certificate) from the New York State Board on Electric Generation Siting and the Environment (hereafter, the siting board).[22] Any such facility for which a certificate is issued must be built, operated, and maintained in conformity with the terms of the certificate and with applicable state and municipal laws.

"Major steam electric generating facility" is defined by law as a facility with a generating capacity of 50,000 kilowatts or more. Steam electric generating facilities include power plants which use nuclear fuels such as uranium and plutonium or fossil fuels such as natural gas, coal, or oil to produce steam which turns turbines to create electricity. Not included are hydroelectric plants, which use water directly to turn turbines, or pumped storage plants (as pointed out above, these two types of plants are regulated by the Federal Power Commission).

Certain major steam electric generating facilities are also specifically exempted from the provisions of this law. Namely, no application for a certificate is required:

1. For a facility that was under construction on or before July 1, 1972, or for which, by that date, an application had been made for a license, permit, or approval from any federal, state, or local com-

mission, agency, board, or regulatory body, so long as the location of the plant was designated by the applicant in that application.

2. For the construction of a facility that was approved by a municipality or public benefit corporation which sold bonds or bond anticipation notes for its financing on or before July 1, 1972.

3. For a facility "over which any agency or department of the federal government has exclusive jurisdiction, or has jurisdiction concurrent with that of the state and has exercised such jurisdiction, to the exclusion of regulation of the facility by the state." (The question of whether this provision exempts nuclear plants from the state law is presently under litigation.)

4. For normal repairs, replacements, modifications, and improvements to a facility that do not violate any certificate issued or increase the capacity of the facility by more than 50,000 kilowatts.

5. For a facility (a) constructed on lands dedicated to industrial uses; (b) the output for which is to be used on the premises for industrial purposes; and (c) the generating capacity of which does not exceed 200,000 kilowatts.

The siting board, which was established as part of the Department of Public Service and is the body from which certificates must be obtained, is composed of five members: the chairman of the Public Service Commission, who serves as chairman of the siting board; the commissioner of environmental conservation; the commissioner of health; the commissioner of commerce; and one ad hoc member, appointed by the governor for the duration of a particular certification proceeding, who must be a resident of the judicial district in which the facility in question is to be located, as primarily proposed. The presence of three of the five members constitutes a quorum for the transaction of business. Each member except the ad hoc member can delegate an alternate to serve in his stead for any particular proceeding.[23]

A certificate cannot be granted unless the siting board finds and determines:

1. The public need for the facility and the basis thereof;

2. The probable environmental impact of the proposed facility;

3. That the facility (a) represents the minimum adverse environmental impact, considering the state of available technology, the nature and economics of the various alternatives, state interests with respect to esthetics, historical sites, forests and parks, fish and wild-

life, and other pertinent considerations; (b) is compatible with public health and safety; and (c) will not discharge any effluent that will be in contravention of water quality standards set by DEC;[24]

4. That the facility is designed to operate in compliance with applicable state and local laws and regulations (The board may refuse to apply any local ordinance, law, resolution or other action, or any regulation or standard "if it finds that as applied to the proposed facility, such is unreasonably restrictive in view of the existing technology or the needs of or costs to consumers whether located inside or outside of such municipality." Such a municipality must be given an opportunity to present evidence supporting its enactment.);

5. That the facility is consistent with long-range planning objectives for electric power supply in the state and for the protection of the environment;

6. "[T]hat the facility will serve the public interest, convenience, and necessity, provided, however, that a determination of necessity for a facility made by the power authority of the State of New York pursuant to . . . the public authorities law[25] shall be conclusive on the board"; and

7. "[T]hat the facility is in the public interest, considering the environmental impact of the facility, the total cost to society as a whole, the possible alternative available methods of power generation, or alternative available sources of energy as the case may be, both within the state and elsewhere, and the immediacy and totality of the needs of the people of the state for the facility within the context of the need for public utility services and for protection of the environment."[26]

Every applicant for a certificate must file with the siting board an application containing extensive and detailed information, including:

1. A full description of the proposed site and facility;
2. Maps;
3. Detailed information about the source and volume of water required for plant operation and cooling;
4. Studies which have been made of the expected environmental impact and safety of the project, during both construction and operation, including descriptions of (a) the wastes and noise to be produced; (b) what measures will be taken for abatement; (c) plans

indicating the compatibility of the facility with the environment; and (d) how the construction and operation of the facility would comply with all environmental, health, and safety provisions of state and municipal laws;

5. Estimated cost information;

6. A statement explaining the need for the plant;

7. A description of any reasonable alternate location or locations for the facility and alternate practical sources of power; and

8. Any other information which the siting board or Public Service Commission may require.

Copies of the application, including all required information, must be filed with the Public Service Commission and made available for public inspection.

The applicant must also submit to the siting board a detailed environmental impact report which contains statements regarding the projected impact, during both the construction and operation of the plant, on:

1. Air quality, including information on all projected air contaminants such as the sulfur and nitrogen oxides;

2. Aquatic ecology, including information on the composition and abundance of marine biota in affected wetlands and water bodies;

3. Water quality and quantity;

4. Noise levels;

5. Terrestrial ecology, focusing on surrounding vegetative cover, flora, and fauna; and

6. Land use and esthetics, including aerial photographs which identify visually sensitive land use areas and an assessment of social and economic impacts.

The environmental report must consider the state of available technology, the nature and economics of various alternatives, and the preservation of historic sites, forest preserve lands, and fish and wildlife. Data submitted must be based on environmental monitoring of at least one year, except in the case of applications filed before January 1, 1974, where six months of monitoring was sufficient so long as data for the remaining six months were submitted at a later date.

A fee of $25,000 must accompany each application. This fee is used to defray expenses incurred by municipal parties to the certification proceeding for expert witnesses and consultants. Any funds remaining after a decision is made and the time for applying for a rehearing and judicial review has expired are refunded to the applicant.

The applicant must see that a copy of the application is served on each municipality in which any portion of the facility may be located, either as primarily or alternatively proposed; on the state attorney general; on each member of the state legislature in whose district any portion of the facility may be located; and, where applicable, on the Hudson River Valley Commission, the St. Lawrence–Eastern Ontario Commission, and the Adirondack Park Agency.

The applicant must publish a public notice of his application once a week for not more than four consecutive weeks in a newspaper or newspapers of general circulation in each area in which the facility would be located as primarily or alternatively proposed. This notice must include a brief description of the site and the facility, a map, a statement of the alternative proposed sites, and the approximate date on which the application is to be filed. The applicant must also notify all persons who have filed a statement with the Public Service Commission within the last twelve months requesting that they be sent notices concerning all facilities proposed for location (whether as a primary or alternative site) in a specified area.

Upon receipt of a complete application, the chairman of the siting board fixes a date for a public hearing to begin within 180–210 days of this receipt. The hearing is conducted by a presiding examiner appointed by the Department of Public Service, who is aided by an associate examiner appointed by the Department of Environmental Conservation. Formal rules of evidence applicable to court proceedings do not apply in the hearing. Oral or written testimony may be presented, either by the parties themselves or through an attorney.

Parties to a certification proceeding include the applicant, the New York State Department of Environmental Conservation, the Department of Health, the Department of Commerce, and—where the facility is proposed to be located within their respective jurisdictions—the Hudson River Valley Commission, the St. Lawrence–Eastern Ontario Commission, and the Adirondack Park Agency. The Department of Environmental Conservation is vested with the responsibility of presenting expert testimony and information concerning the potential impact of the proposed facility and any alternative facility or energy source on the environment and concerning whether and how such facilities would comply with applicable state and municipal environmental protection laws, standards, policies, rules, and regulations.

The following may also become parties to a certification proceeding, provided that they file with the Public Service Commission a notice of their intent to do so within ninety days after the date of application given in the published notice:

1. Any municipality, or individual resident thereof, in which any portion of a proposed primary or alternative site is located.

2. "[A]ny non-profit corporation or association, formed in whole or in part to promote conservation or natural beauty, to protect the environment, personal health or other biological values, to preserve historical sites, to promote consumer interests, to represent commercial and industrial groups or to promote the orderly development of any area in which the facility may be located . . ."[27]

3. Any municipality, or resident thereof, within a five-mile radius of the proposed facility.

4. Any other municipality, or resident thereof, which the Public Service Commission or the siting board finds might be affected by the potential environmental impact of the facility.

All those filing a notice of the intent to be a party must state in their petition how the proposed facility might environmentally or economically affect them. Other persons besides those indicated above who wish to become parties to a certification proceeding may petition the Public Service Commission in writing, stating their interest in the proceeding and explaining why their participation would be in the public interest. Denial of such petitions can be appealed to the siting board.

The Public Service Commission, the siting board, or the hearing examiner may order the applicant to publish a notice that pre-hearing meetings may be conducted. Also, the applicant or any other party may confer informally with the commission staff before or during the hearing, but statements made in such conferences are not binding unless by written agreement. The presiding examiner may hold pre-hearing conferences at his discretion.

During the hearing the applicant must show that the location, design, construction, operation, and maintenance of the proposed facility are planned to comply with all applicable federal and state laws, rules, regulations, standards, and requirements, interstate compacts, and municipal laws or ordinances. The applicant must submit to the siting board copies of all applicable laws and controls. If the provisions of a particular law or control are not met by the specifications set forth in the application, the applicant must state how he proposes to insure compliance if the facility is certified.

In the proceedings the applicant must provide a number of exhibits, including all the environmental information required for the filing. In addition, the applicant must provide an analysis of the need for the proposed facility, considering the statewide power system, and must elaborate on the safety and reliability of the proposed facility.

The presiding examiner of the hearing must set a date thirty to sixty days after the beginning of the hearing as the time by which he must receive notification from any party who wishes to offer testimony recommending a site that is not proposed by the applicant as either the primary or an alternative site. Any testimony favoring a new site must be accompanied by a topographic map of the new site. The applicant himself must prepare a complete case for at least two sites or show why there is only one reasonable site; if he does not do so, the examiner may dismiss the application. If another party convinces the examiner that there is a "reasonable probability" that an unconsidered site may be environmentally, economically, or in some other way superior to the proposed sites, the applicant may be required to study in detail and prepare plans for this site.

Based on the record of the proceeding and the recommendations of the presiding and associate hearing examiners, the siting board renders a final decision on the application. It may also hear oral arguments before making its decision. The decision may be to grant or deny the application as filed or to certify the facility at any site considered at the hearing upon such terms, conditions, limitations, or modifications of the construction or operation of the facility as the siting board may deem to be appropriate. The statutory tests and standards listed on pages 279–298 above must be applied. The siting board must issue an opinion stating in full the reasons for its decision.

Any party aggrieved by any decision on an application for a certificate may apply to the siting board for a rehearing within thirty days after the issuance of the decision. If this application for a rehearing is denied, a petition may be filed with the Appellate Division of the Supreme Court of the state for judicial review. The grounds for and scope of review by this court are specified in the statute.

Except as provided by this part of the Public Service Law or by the siting board, no state agency, municipality, or municipal agency may require any type of permit, approval, or condition for the construction or operation of a facility for which an application for a certificate has been filed, except under provisions of state law pertaining to protection of employees. In the case of a municipality or an agency thereof, the municipality must have received notice of the filing of the application. The law also specifies that neither the Hudson River Valley Commission, the St. Lawrence–Eastern Ontario Commission, nor the Adirondack Park Agency may hold a public hearing for a major steam electric generating facility for which an application for a certificate has been filed.

Siting of Major Utility Transmission Facilities

A certificate of environmental compatibility and public need (hereafter certificate) is also required for the preparation of a site for the construction of a major utility transmission facility in New York State.[28] In this case, the certificate must be obtained from the Public Service Commission, but the procedures followed are similar to those established for the issuance of certificates for power plant sitings by the New York State Board on Electric Generation Siting and the Environment, discussed in the previous section.

According to the Public Service Law, "major utility transmission facility" means:

1. An electric transmission line of a design capacity of 125 kilovolts or more extending a distance of one mile or more, or of 100 kilovolts or more and less than 125 kilovolts, extending a distance of more than ten miles, including associated equipment, but not including any such transmission line located wholly underground in a city with a population over 125,000 or a primary transmission line approved by the Federal Power Commission in connection with a hydroelectric facility; and

2. A fuel gas transmission facility extending a distance of 1,000 feet or more to be used to transport fuel gas at pressures in excess of 125 pounds per square inch, not including any such transmission facility located wholly underground in a city.

Exempted from certification requirements are those facilities for which an application for a license, permit, or approval was made to a federal, state, or local regulatory body before July 1, 1970, provided that the location of the facility was specified in the application; the construction of which was approved by a municipality or public benefit corporation which sold bonds or bond anticipation notes for its financing prior to July 1, 1970; and over which any agency or department of the federal government has exclusive jurisdiction, or has jurisdiction concurrent with that of the state and has exercised such jurisdiction, to the exclusion of regulation of the facility by the state.

The Public Service Commission cannot grant a certificate for the construction or operation of a major utility transmission facility unless it finds and determines:

(a) the basis of the need for the facility;
(b) the nature of the probable environmental impact;
(c) that the facility represents the minimum adverse environmental impact, considering the state of available technology and the nature and economics of the various alternatives, and other pertinent considerations;
(d) in the case of an electric transmission line, (1) what part, if any, of the line shall be located underground; (2) that such facility conforms to a long-range plan for expansion of the electric power grid of the electric systems serving this state and interconnected utility systems, which will serve the interests of electric system economy and reliability;
(e) in the case of a gas transmission line, that the location of the line will not pose an undue hazard to persons or property along the area traversed by the line;
(f) that the location of the facility as proposed conforms to applicable state and local laws and regulations issued thereunder, all of which shall be binding upon the commission, except that the commission may refuse to apply any local ordinance, law, resolution or other action or any regulation issued thereunder or any local standard or requirement which would be otherwise applicable if it finds that as applied to the proposed facility such is unreasonably restrictive in view of the existing technology, or of factors of cost or economics, or of the needs of consumers whether located inside or outside of such municipality;
(g) that the facility will serve the public interest, convenience, and necessity, provided, however, that a determination of necessity for a facility made by the power authority of the state of New York pursuant to . . . the public authorities law[29] shall be conclusive on the commission.[30]

An applicant for a certificate must file with the Public Service Commission an application containing the following information: (1)

The location of the proposed site or right-of-way; (2) a description of the proposed facility; (3) a summary and description of any studies which have been made on the environmental impact of the project (copies of such studies must be filed with the commission and made available for public inspection); (4) a statement explaining the need for the facility; (5) a description of any reasonable alternate location or locations, a description of the comparative merits and detriments of each location submitted, and a statement of the reasons why the primary proposed location is best suited for the facility; and (6) any other information which the applicant may consider relevant or which the Public Service Commission may require.

Applicants must also file a number of exhibits containing general, environmental, economic, engineering, legal, and market considerations, as well as maps. The environmental impact information required includes statements of how the construction and operation of the facility might affect plant and animal life and what plans and provisions have been made to keep right-of-way clearing to a minimum, to protect natural vegetation and adjacent resources, to protect fish and other aquatic life from harm caused by the use of explosives or pollutants in or near streams or other bodies of water, to minimize the environmental impact (including visual and noise disturbance) of all structures, and to clean up and restore the project area after construction. Statements must also be made regarding what efforts, if any, have been made to assure:

1. That any right-of-way avoids scenic, recreational, and historic areas;
2. That any right-of-way will be routed to minimize its visibility from areas of public view;
3. That any right-of-way has been planned to avoid heavily timbered areas, high points, ridge lines, and steep slopes; and
4. That the selection of any proposed right-of-way preserves the natural landscape and minimizes conflict with any present or future planned land use.[31]

In addition, every filing with the Public Service Commission must also include the testimony, in written form, and exhibits which will comprise the applicant's direct case in support of his application at the certification hearing.

The applicant must serve a copy of the complete filing on each municipality in which any portion of the facility is to be located, both as primarily and alternatively proposed; on the commissioners of environmental conservation, commerce, and transportation; on each member of the state legislature through whose district any portion of the facility might pass; and, where applicable, to the Hudson River Valley Commission, the St. Lawrence–Eastern Ontario Commission, and the Adirondack Park Agency.

The applicant must also publish a public notice once a week for two consecutive weeks prior to the filing in a newspaper or newspapers of general circulation in all the areas through which the facility, as primarily or alternatively proposed, might pass. This notice must provide a brief description of the proposed facility, the location of the proposed right-of-way, and the date on or about which the filing is to be made with the Public Service Commission.

Upon the receipt of a complete filing, the Public Service Commission must set a date for the beginning of a public hearing sixty to ninety days after such receipt. A hearing of identical format must be held on an application for an amendment to a certificate already held, if the amendment would result in any material increase in environmental impact or a substantial change in the location of any portion of the facility involving sites other than those proposed as alternates in the original application.

Parties to a certification proceeding on major transmission facilities, in addition to the applicant, may include the Department of Environmental Conservation; the Department of Commerce; and, where applicable, the Hudson River Valley Commission, the St. Lawrence–Eastern Ontario Commission, and Adirondack Park Agency. The following may also become parties if they file a notice of the intent to do so within thirty days after the date given in the published notice as the date of filing: any municipality, or resident thereof, through which any portion of the facility might pass, any non-profit corporation or association representing the values and interests described in (2) on page 301 of the previous section, and any other person or entity the commission may deem appropriate. A notice of the intent to be a party should state the basis on which the claim to be a party is made.

Any person or organization may petition to become a party to a certification proceeding within the thirty days allowed for the notices of intent and may be allowed by the hearing examiner to intervene if such participation would contribute to the appropriate resolution of the proceeding. Petitions may also be filed for late intervention, and if denied, can be appealed within ten days to the commission. Any person may make a limited appearance in a proceeding, with the right to file a written statement which becomes part of the record but not to present oral testimony or cross-examine witnesses and parties, if he files the statement within sixty days after the date given in the newspaper notice as the date of the filing.

A record must be made of all testimony and cross-examinations at the hearing. On the basis of this record and upon application of the statutory tests and standards listed on page 304 above, the Public Service Commission renders a decision either granting or denying the application as filed or granting it upon such terms, conditions, limitations, or modifications as deemed appropriate. The commission must file an opinion describing its reasons for any denial, and may file such an opinion for any decision.

As in the case of power plant sitings, any party aggrieved by the decision made in a certification proceeding may apply to the Public Service Commission for a rehearing within thirty days after the decision is issued. If this is denied, a petition for judicial review can be filed with the Appellate Division of the Supreme Court of the state.

Again, no state agency, municipality, or municipal agency may require any approval, consent, permit, certificate, or other condition for the construction or operation of a major transmission facility for which an application for a certificate has been filed. Also, neither the Hudson River Valley Commission, the St. Lawrence–Eastern Ontario Commission, nor the Adirondack Park Agency may hold a hearing of its own for a major transmission facility for which such an application has been filed.

Citizen Action

Most of the advice given in Chapter 1 on the politics of citizen action is directly relevant to citizen action with respect to certification proceedings for major steam electric generating facilities and major electric transmission facilities. Organization is essential; care should be taken to give effective testimony at hearings; contacts should be made with agency officials who can explain procedures and complications involved in the proceedings. Although the assistance of specialists will probably be needed, citizens' groups should make full use of local talent. For example, in the assessment of the primary proposed site and the exploration of alternative sites, long-time residents can often provide helpful information, as well as make effective presentations at hearings regarding local historic, environmental, and esthetic values.

The regulations of the Public Service Commission encourage

informal consultations with its staff: "Applicants, other parties, and all interested groups and persons are invited and encouraged to confer on an informal basis with the staff of the commission with respect to any matter related to a filing or proposed filing."[32]

Citizens should take advantage of this opportunity. They should contact commission staff members to clarify any uncertainties and perhaps may want to request that a representative be sent to an organized public meeting to explain the certification proceeding, to point out what forms must be filled out and what deadlines must be met, and to answer questions. Contact with officials of the Department of Environmental Conservation may be desirable on matters related to the environmental impact of a proposed facility. It is likely that a citizens' group will need an attorney to assist them in a certification proceeding, if this is at all possible.

Note should be made that the public notice of the application for a certificate for a major steam electric generating facility must include a map of the primary proposed site. This distinctive feature makes this notice more prominent and easier to spot than is often the case with public notices.

In dealing with different power companies, citizens will find that some companies are more sensitive to citizen concerns than others. The former are more likely to follow citizen suggestions if they make sense; the latter may be much more unmovable. In either case, citizens should always avoid strident exhortations and emotional pleas. Arguments presented on the merits are much more effective.

Note on the Undergrounding of Electric Distribution and Telephone Lines in Subdivisions

The Public Service Commission also regulates the installation of electric and telephone wires in new subdivisions in which five or more buildings are planned.[33] The commission oversees the rates established by utilities for installation of lines as well as the method of installation.

Last year the commission promulgated new regulations for the installation of electric distribution and telephone lines for new residential buildings within subdivisions and for new multiple-occupancy buildings with four or more proposed dwelling units.[34] These new regulations, which became effective on February 10, 1974, modify previous regulations which generally mandated underground installation of electric distribution and telephone lines in subdivisions. The undergrounding mandate was intended to help preserve the natural appearance of the landscape of proposed subdivisions and reflected a concern for esthetic values. Since undergrounding is generally more expensive than overhead wiring, within a year after the regulations requiring undergrounding were promulgated the Public Service Commission found itself deluged with applications for variances from developers wishing to reduce costs. As a result, new regulations more generous to subdividers were drafted. The following are important provisions of these new regulations:

1. Subdivisions which do not require approval from "governmental authorities having jurisdiction over land use" do not have to have lines installed underground. Among land use authorities, the Public Service Commission includes the New York Department of State, the Department of Environmental Conservation (DEC), any health department, counties, cities, villages, and towns. In effect, all tracts of land which are subdivided into less than five parcels are exempted by this provision.[35]

2. A developer may direct a utility to install overhead lines if an approved subdivision will require more than 200 trench feet of distribution line per dwelling unit planned, unless undergrounding is required by a municipal ordinance. In effect, this provision eliminates required undergrounding in subdivisions which are divided into large lots.

3. Overhead lines are allowed when the developer of the subdivision is not primarily engaged in the construction of dwelling units within the subdivision (i.e., is primarily a land developer), when there is no municipal ordinance or other governmental regulation requiring underground service, *and* when development proceeds very slowly, according to standards established in the regulations.[36]

4. A utility or a developer may petition the Public Service Commission to allow overhead service in cases involving high costs for undergrounding, when undergrounding would be "impractical, unjust or discriminatory" to customers, or when undergrounding, in the developer's opinion, would cause environmental damage.

Citizen Action

Mandatory undergrounding of electric distribution and telephone lines in subdivisions is a significant control. Its esthetic importance is evident. From a tactical standpoint, the costs involved may prevent subdivision by developers who are working on a very narrow margin. A Public Service Commission paper entitled "Proposed Modifications of Rules Applicable to Underground Electric Facilities," dated March 26, 1973, stated that some developers have alleged that the costs of underground installation were instrumental in decisions not to subdivide land.[37]

Since the Public Service Commission regulations have now been considerably weakened, communities wishing to establish stronger control over the installation of electric distribution and telephone lines should enact a municipal ordinance requiring undergrounding in all subdivisions.

SPECIAL COMMISSIONS AND PUBLIC AUTHORITIES

It is not possible in a single volume to discuss all programs and agencies that affect land use planning and regulation in New York State. The following is a list of some of the bodies that are not treated in this book:

1. *Appalachian Regional Commission,* 1666 Connecticut Avenue, N.W., Washington, D.C. 20235. A federal commission with jurisdiction over specified counties in the Appalachian region that sponsors projects to foster economic development and the development of human resources. Fourteen counties in New York State participate in its programs. State coordination is provided by the Division of Community Affairs of the New York State Department of State.

2. *Delaware River Basin Commission,* P.O. Box #360, Trenton, New Jersey 08603. An interstate–federal commission created by a compact between Delaware, New Jersey, New York, Pennsylvania, and the United States to manage and protect the water resources of the Delaware River Basin.

3. *Hudson River Valley Commission,* South Swan Street Building, South Mall, Albany, New York 12223. A state commission empowered to review development along the Hudson River.

4. *Lake George Park Commission,* John Hancock Building, Ticonderoga, New York 12883. A state commission with planning, zoning, sign control, and limited development permit powers in the Lake George Park.

5. *Metropolitan Transportation Authority,* 1700 Broadway, New York, New York 10019. A public authority established to develop, improve, and operate transportation systems within the New York City metropolitan region.

6. *New England River Basins Commission,* 55 Court Street, Boston, Massachusetts 02108. A federal–interstate commission established to prepare plans for the management of water and related land resources in the river basins of New England, including Long Island Sound.

7. *Port Authority of New York and New Jersey,* 1 World Trade Center, New York, New York 10048. A public authority established by a compact between the states of New York and New Jersey to purchase, construct, and/or operate terminals and transportation facilities in the New York port area. For example, the Port Authority operates the New York–New Jersey bridge and tunnel connections and Kennedy, La Guardia, and Newark airports.

8. *St. Lawrence–Eastern Ontario Commission,* State Office Building, 317 Washington Street, Watertown, New York 13601. A state commission empowered to prepare a comprehensive plan for and to review development in towns and cities adjacent to the St. Lawrence River or eastern Lake Ontario in the counties of St. Lawrence, Jefferson, Oswego, and Cayuga.

9. *Temporary State Commission on Tug Hill,* State Office Building, Watertown, New York 13601. A commission, similar to the Temporary State Commission to Study the Catskills (discussed in Chapter 7), which was charged to study the problems and resources of the Tug Hill region near the Adirondack Park and to make recommendations to the state legislature on the basis of this study. Its legislative mandate expired on March 31, 1975.

Unfortunately, all too often commissions possess considerable statutory powers, but implementation falls far short of the intent of the law. For example, the Hudson River Valley Commission has broad project review powers over development along the Hudson River. If it reviews a project, sponsors are not permitted to "undertake or continue" the project during a thirty-day review period.[38] If within these thirty days the commission determines that "the project might have an unreasonably adverse effect upon the scenic, historic, recreational or natural resources of the Hudson River valley,"[39] it may order a further sixty-day suspension of the project so that a more complete review, including a public hearing, can be carried out. In practice, the Hudson River Valley Commission, with its eight to ten member staff, conducted only five hearings in 1974 in its entire 700-square-mile jurisdiction. Established as an independent agency in 1966, with a staff of almost sixty people, it is today a part of the New York State Office of Parks and Recreation (though an attempt to obtain the commission's telephone number from the New York City office of the state Office of Parks and Recreation was met with the response that the Hudson River Valley Commission was no longer in existence). The commission's statutory review powers have remained essentially unchanged, but the means granted it for implementation have been severely truncated.[40]

The Delaware River Basin Commission, which in 1974 had a budget of about $1.6 million, has statutory approval powers over any project "having a substantial effect on the water resources of the [Delaware River] basin."[41] This commission, however, has greatly limited the scope of its review powers by exempting in its regulations a large number of projects which it "deemed not to have a substantial effect on the water resources of the basin."[42] The following are among the fifteen types of projects *exempted* from review:

1. The construction of new impoundments or the enlargement or removal of existing impoundments, for whatever purpose, when the storage capacity is less than 100 million gallons.

2. Bridges and highways, unless they would pass in or across an existing or proposed reservoir or recreation project area as shown in the comprehensive plan.

3. Draining, filling, or otherwise altering marshes or wetlands when the area affected is less than twenty-five acres.

A detailed analysis of the operation of the Delaware River Basin Commission and its actual and possible methods of formulating policy is presented in a recent book entitled *The Uncertain Search for Environmental Quality.*[43]

In general, commissions often defer to state and local government decisions in politically sensitive areas such as land use regulation rather than aggressively carry out their statutory powers.[44]

A striking contrast exists in the case of public authorities, which are entities traditionally created to undertake major public works projects, typically issuing bonds to cover construction costs and paying off these bonds out of user charges. An active public authority, particularly when it has a protected source of income outside annual legislative appropriations, can be extremely powerful, often surpassing the range of activity which was originally conceived of by the legislators establishing it. An excellent example of this phenomenon is the power wielded by Robert Moses through the Triborough Bridge and Tunnel Authority and the related public authorities which he controlled from the 1930s to the 1960s.[45] Moses succeeded in obtaining seemingly innocuous but broadly phrased powers for his authorities, which were then insulated from direct interference from the executive and legislative arms of state government by two mechanisms: (1) the authorities were internally financed by the collection of user charges from their public works, particularly bridge tolls; and (2) the terms of the agreements with the authorities' bond holders were employed to repel efforts to alter the direction and policies adopted by the authorities. With such powers, the Triborough group of authorities were effectively used by Moses to alter profoundly the transportation and land use patterns of New York City and the surrounding metropolitan area. These authorities are pointedly analyzed and described in *The Power Broker* by Robert Caro, which provides many classic examples of the distinction between real and apparent power.[46]

NOTES

1. 42 U.S.C. §4001 *et seq.*

2. 42 U.S.C. §4001 *et seq.*

3. Section 102(a); 42 U.S.C. §4012a(a).

4. Section 102(b); 42 U.S.C. §4012a(b).

5. Section 202(a); 42 U.S.C. §4106(a).

6. Section 202(b); 42 U.S.C. §4106(b).

7. N.Y. Environmental Conservation Law (ECL) §36–0101 *et seq.*

8. 24 CFR Part 1910.

9. *Federal Register* 13420 (March 26,1975).

10. ECL §36–0101 *et seq.*

11. 16 U.S.C. §1271 *et seq.*

12. The act specified that the boundaries of each of the original rivers in the system could include an average of not more than 320 acres per mile on both sides of the river. 16 U.S.C. §1274(b).

13. 16 U.S.C. §1276 (February 1975).

14. ECL §15–2701 through §15–2723.

15. The names of these rivers, as well as the counties in which they are located and the sections to be studied, were stated in a DEC press release issued on that date.

16. 33 U.S.C. §1342 and §1344. *See* Chapter 11 for a discussion of this important federal water pollution legislation.

17. *See* pp. 79–86.

18. The state law provided that through December 31, 1974, a permit issued by the federal EPA under the National Pollutant Discharge Elimination System (NPDES) established by the Federal Water Pollution Control Act Amendments of

1972 would serve as compliance with state requirements. After that time, DEC continued this practice on a policy basis.

19. *See* pp. 224–227 of Chapter 11.

20. 33 U.S.C. §1326.

21. Section 316(b); 33 U.S.C. §1326(b).

22. N.Y. Public Service Law, Article 8, §140 *et seq.* Regulations adopted pursuant to this statute can be found at 16 NYCRR Parts 70–80.

23. Some apprehension has been expressed by officials of the Public Service Commission that this provision may lead to a lack of continuity, since it is likely that different alternates will serve on the siting board for different certification proceedings.

24. *See* p. 83 of Chapter 5.

25. §1005.

26. N.Y. Public Service Law §146 (2).

27. N.Y. Public Service Law §144 (1) (k).

28. N.Y. Public Service Law, Article 7, §120 *et seq.* Regulations adopted pursuant to this statute can be found at 16 NYCRR Parts 85–88.

29. §1005.

30. N.Y. Public Service Law §126 (1).

31. 16 NYCRR §86.5.

32. 16 NYCRR §85.6.

33. N.Y. Public Service Law §§66 and 94.

34. 16 NYCRR Part 100.

35. *See* Chapter 5 for a discussion of the approvals required from health officials and DEC for all subdivisions of five or more lots. *See* Chapter 3 for a discussion of the land use powers of towns, villages, and cities, Chapter 4 for those of counties, and pp. 245–252 of Chapter 12 for the disclosure requirements of the Department of State.

36. *See* 16 NYCRR §100.4 (7).

37. *See* p. 4 of the paper.

38. N.Y. Executive Law §721(4) (e) (2).

39. 21 NYCRR §750.31(e).

40. In its original mandate, the Hudson River Valley Commission was also charged to prepare a comprehensive plan for its jurisdiction, but this authorization has been rescinded.

41. Delaware River Basin Compact §3.8.

42. Delaware River Basin Commission, *Rules of Practice and Procedure* §2–3.5.

43. Bruce A. Ackerman *et al.* (New York: Free Press, 1974).

44. As discussed in Chapter 6, a notable exception to this rule was the Temporary Study Commission on the Future of the Adirondacks, which proposed that regional land use controls be established, since adequate initiatives could not be expected to come from local governments.

45. In 1968 the Triborough Bridge and Tunnel Authority was merged with the Metropolitan Transportation Authority when members of the board governing the MTA were made *ex officio* members of the board governing the Triborough Bridge and Tunnel Authority. (N.Y. Public Authorities Law §552.)

46. Robert A. Caro, *The Power Broker: Robert Moses and the Fall of New York* (New York: Alfred A. Knopf, Inc., 1974).

CHAPTER 14

Property Tax Myths and Realities[1]

TRADITIONALLY IT HAS been assumed that certain land uses have a favorable impact on local real estate taxes and are to be sought after. The reasoning has been as follows: Commercial or industrial development, resorts, and vacation homes all increase the assessed value of real estate in a jurisdiction and increase tax revenues without placing corresponding demands on local services, particularly on schools. Thus, revenues are enhanced without equivalent expenditure demands and taxes are lowered. Advocacy has also been expressed for intensive development in general on the grounds that it brings economic well-being to an area. On the other hand, it has often been assumed that if a jurisdiction has large areas devoted to agricultural or other open space uses, taxes will necessarily be high.

In fact, this kind of reasoning—which is frequently put forward as an unassailable argument for new development—is far too simplistic to account for the many complexities of the real world. Two basic realities should be recognized:

1. In any given locality, any number of complicating factors influence local revenue and expenditure patterns and thus play a role in determining whether property taxes are high or low. Land uses, of course, number among these factors, but there are many others.

In order to identify and assess the different factors at work in a particular jurisdiction, an in-depth study taking into consideration local circumstances and distinctive characteristics is required. Consequently, it is both specious and dangerous for communities simply to assume that certain types of land uses will necessarily result in reduced real property taxes.

2. It is becoming increasingly clearer that the costs to the public of new development projects frequently outweigh the additional tax revenues gained. Hidden or subtle costs that are not taken into consideration at the proposal stage often appear later to become necessary expenditures for the jurisdiction. Costs that were foreseen often turn out to be greater and to involve more complications than planned. In addition to direct new municipal expenditures, new developments also impose more indirect economic, social, environmental, and esthetic costs on communities. These costs have traditionally been overlooked when new developments are proposed, but their impact is becoming much more apparent as more and more communities experience serious growth and development problems.

Thus, in order to assess the probable effect of a proposed new development on the property taxes of a locality, it is necessary both:

1. To identify and evaluate the impact of the different factors affecting expenditures and revenues in that particular locality; and

2. To determine how the proposed development will interact with the existing local situation, by very carefully considering all possible costs to the community—including short-term and long-term, direct and indirect, obvious and subtle costs—that the project may involve.

The importance of recognizing the complications involved in property tax questions lies primarily in the need to place in perspective the unsubstantiated claims so often put forward by real estate developers and local politicians that particular new developments will bring substantial tax benefits to a locality. Traditionally, proponents of this claim have advanced it as a conclusive reason for approving a development project, without granting legitimacy to other important considerations. This situation needs to be righted— citizens need to become aware of the weaknesses of the "tax benefits" argument, and the simplistic rhetoric of its proponents needs to be scrutinized.

After a brief discussion of the basic facets of the real property tax, examples of factors which may affect local revenues and expenditures will be pointed out and checklists of the kinds of costs new developments may bring will be provided.

THE REAL PROPERTY TAX

In New York State the real property tax accounts for over 60 percent of all locally raised revenues, although in the decade from 1959 to 1969 real property tax revenues declined from 49 percent to 35 percent as a percentage of total local revenues from all sources —federal, state, and local. This decline occurred because of a substantial increase in state aid, an increase in federal aid, increased utilization of the county sales tax, and the imposition by New York City in 1966 of a city income tax. On the town and village level, however, this revenue shift has had less impact. The real property tax is the only levy imposed by these jurisdictions and is the major revenue base for local services. No federal or state program helps defray any substantial part of the cost of such local services as police, fire, and sanitation. The state does bear part of the road maintenance burden, but this aid amounted to less than one-third of total local road maintenance expenditures in 1970 ($126 million out of a state-wide total of $386 million) and the aid formula was revised in 1971, reducing the amount received by many localities. Road maintenance expenditures are of primary importance in town and village budgets. They represent the largest area of town expenditures in New York State (33 percent of current expenditures in 1969) and the second largest item for villages (21 percent, second only to public safety, which received 27 percent of the total).

Real property taxes are imposed by several different taxing entities, depending on where the property is located. Thus a village resident pays a county, town, school, and village tax, while the resident of a town outside a village only pays the first three. Residents of cities (except those larger than 125,000) pay separate city, county, and school taxes. Only New York City property owners pay one tax. In addition, a local tax bill may carry charges for services provided through special districts, which are special areas within a town or sometimes a county in which specific services such as sewerage, water supply, fire protection, or street lights are provided.[2] These districts are administered by the town or the county, respectively, and taxes levied for the services provided may be assessed on an *ad valorem* basis (that is, based on the assessed value of the property served) or on a benefits basis. These varying patterns are sometimes confusing, and make it difficult to compare the total real property tax burdens of different jurisdictions. In addition, as is discussed below, school taxes are paid to school districts whose boundaries are usually not coterminous with those of municipalities.

Comparability is made even more difficult by the fact that different jurisdictions assess the value of property at different percentages of full market value. Thus, one town may assess at 40 percent of full value and another at 80 percent. A tax rate of twenty dollars per thousand in the first jurisdiction would be equivalent to a rate of ten dollars per thousand in the second. Owners of property with the same market value would pay the same dollar amount in taxes in both towns. The state Board of Equalization and Assessment establishes equalization rates for each jurisdiction so that assessed values can be converted to full values. Table 10 demonstrates such conversions.

The largest single real property tax does not go to local government, but rather to school districts to pay for the local share of this single most expensive public function. In 1969 primary and secondary education absorbed approximately 53 percent of all local expenditures in the state outside of New York City (including New York City, school expenditures were almost 40 percent of the total). Approximately half of this cost was paid for by state aid to education. In 1970 this amounted to about 54 percent of all state aid to local government, or over $2 billion.

Since road maintenance and education tend to be the two largest local expenditures, they exercise a large influence in determining the need for local taxes. Welfare costs, an increasingly large area of expenditure, are borne jointly by federal, state, and county governments.[3] It is the largest single expenditure by counties, and has a

Table 10
Conversion of Tax Rates and Values

	Market Value of Sample Parcel	Assessed Value	Equalization Ratio	Tax Rate	Tax Paid
Town A	$30,000	$12,000	40	$5.00 per thousand	$60
Town B	$30,000	$24,000	80	$2.50 per thousand	$60

major impact on the county property tax. It should be noted, however, that counties have been making increasing use of the sales tax as a revenue source. Due to this factor, and the shared aspect of welfare costs, county property tax rates do not reflect the full burden of welfare expenditures.

Factors Which May Affect Local Revenues and Expenditures

As discussed above, in any given locality property taxes are determined by the interaction of many different factors, some of which are related to land use, others of which are not. The following examples indicate the breadth of factors which may be involved:

1. Topography and climate often directly affect municipal expenditures. For example, other things being equal, a mountainous area with much snow and rainfall can be expected to have higher road maintenance expenses than a community at a lower altitude with relatively flat terrain. No state or federal aid program, moreover, is tailored to compensate for such variations.

2. State and federal aid programs, in general, have different effects on different localities. Such programs are often based on permanent population figures and thus may have less impact in areas in which seasonal residents or transients greatly increase local expenditures.

3. Local officials may be corrupt or incompetent.

4. Local assessors may exercise discretion in their decisions on property valuation. Sometimes this discretion is influenced by local policies or politics which favor higher or lower assessments for particular kinds of property.

5. Population density and patterns of development are very important as far as the cost of services is concerned. For example, municipal services can generally be much more economically provided when development is clustered in particular areas rather than widely scattered.[4]

6. Circumstances in surrounding jurisdictions have bearing on a locality's tax situation. In particular, conditions in those areas which fall within shared school districts have a direct effect on school tax rates.

7. Local preference or problems may dictate high expenditures for a large police force or other public service.

8. Local preference or ability to pay may demand a broad scope

and/or a high quality of municipal services (e.g., frequent garbage collection, rapid snow removal, elaborate traffic controls).

9. Some of a jurisdiction's land may be held for special purposes by the state, the federal government, or a public utility. For example, in New York State several million acres in the Adirondacks and the Catskills comprise the state forest preserve and large areas of land in the Catskill region and in Westchester County are owned by the New York City Board of Water Supply. State forest preserve lands are removed from local tax rolls, but the state makes payments to the local government in lieu of taxes. In the case of both state forest preserve lands and New York City water supply property, virtually no local expenditures for services are required.

10. In general, property owned by the state or federal government and many non-profit organizations is exempted from property taxes. [The state payments made for state forest preserve lands, discussed in (9) above, are an exception to this rule.] The total amount of such exempt property across the state is substantial, and great variations in the amount of acreage involved exist from jurisdiction to jurisdiction.

Kinds of Costs Which Development Projects May Involve

The full costs of a development project to a community include both direct economic costs and more indirect or subtle economic, social, environmental, and esthetic costs. The following are some of the areas in which new developments can bring increased direct community expenditures:[5]

1. Road construction and/or maintenance, including snow removal. Developers often bear the costs of road construction, and then dedicate the roads to the local government, which becomes responsible for maintenance. As pointed out above, road maintenance is a major local government expense, in 1969 representing 33 percent of all current expenditures in towns in New York State and 21 percent in villages.

2. Schools. Theoretically, second home developments and administrative, office, or industrial development do not place demands on schools. In practice, second homes may become primary residences and office or industrial development may bring new families into the area, increasing the cost of this single most expensive public function.

3. Sewerage and water supply construction as well as other capital improvements.

4. Solid waste collection and disposal.

5. Fire protection and other emergency services.

6. Police services.

7. Traffic control.

8. Health services and hospitals.

9. Parks and recreation. An increased population requires a community to develop new recreational facilities and/or increase maintenance costs for existing facilities. In some instances, developers may be required or may choose to dedicate parks to the local government, which then becomes responsible for maintenance.

10. Local government administrative costs, including needs for additional personnel, space, and other expenditures.

Another problem some communities have had to face is the necessity of completing improvements begun by a developer who has gone bankrupt in the midst of a project.

Areas in which economic burdens are more subtle or long-range and/or in which other types of costs are incurred include:

1. Air pollution.

2. Water pollution.

3. Decreased water supply.

4. Traffic congestion.

5. Noise.

6. Esthetic blight.

7. Loss of open space.

8. Loss of local character, traditions, or values.

9. Attraction of new commercial concerns which compete with existing merchants.

There are other ways as well in which new developments can affect the basic revenue/expenditure patterns in a community. For example, since state and federal aid programs are often based on the permanent population of a locality, new second home or resort developments may increase municipal expenditures without increasing eligibility for such aid. An influx of city people into a rural area, moreover, may result in the demand for a scope and quality of municipal service beyond that expected by existing residents of the area.

In addition to the costs to a community which are associated with any particular development project, there are costs which accrue from the cumulative effect of new development. For example, up to a point residences may utilize septic tanks and individual wells; but as density of development in an area increases, sewerage facilities and a public water supply may be required. Thus, in assessing the costs of a proposed project, long-term thinking is required.

Recent Studies

Although real estate developers and local politicians are still using the tax benefits argument in many areas, the problems and complications associated with real estate development and the growth of communities are becoming much better known and public naïveté is diminishing at a rapid rate.

A recent front-page article in *The New York Times,* entitled "Nation's Cities Fighting to Stem Growth," reported the following:

> While some surveys sponsored by real estate people have indicated that big new developments can be an economic plus, many communities have made contradictory findings, and either blocked developments or concocted heavy surcharges on developers to defray costs of facilities such as streets, water, sewer, and electric lines, schools, and parks.
>
> A 1972 Denver study indicated that each new residence would cost taxpayers $21,000 for community services. A Stanford University study at Half Moon Bay, near San Francisco, indicated that a 1,262 unit subdivision would cost the community $400,000 a year by 1982 in indirect subsidies for public services.[6]

A study prepared for the city of Palo Alto in California, which combined cost-revenue with social and environmental criteria, considered the various development options open to the city. It explored different combinations of cluster residential development, professional-administrative office development, and open space. The findings indicated that:

> Of the 22 different development patterns studied, except in a few years none yielded a positive net cash flow to the city. The cost of municipal facilities and services generally exceeded revenue from property tax, sales tax, utilities (gas and electricity) sales, and other sources. Not surprisingly, cash flow to the School District was consistently negative;

and because its budget is substantially larger than the city's, there proved to be a total net cost to the taxpayer in all years. Even though two-thirds of each property tax dollar is paid by non-residential development in Palo Alto, it was found that $45,000 homes would have to be priced at $62,000 and $80,000 homes at $116,500 if they were to pay their way.[7]

After this study was completed, Palo Alto zoned ten square miles of land into ten-acre parcels to retard development.

Citizen Action

Citizens who are faced with claims by developers and local politicians that proposed development projects will bring great tax benefits to their community should, first of all, not accept such claims at face value. Recognizing that property taxes are determined by the interaction of many different factors, they should explore the facts of the particular situation and be ready to point out complications. Wherever possible, experiences of other communities in similar circumstances should be brought up for discussion. Determined efforts should be made to assess the full costs the proposed project would impose on the community.

Communities may also take advantage of powers available to them through state enabling legislation and home rule to adopt regulations requiring developers to provide many of the improvements necessary for developments and to post performance bonds to assure completion. Such powers have been discussed in Chapters 3 and 4.

In all, citizens should be as informed as possible about matters relating to property taxes and municipal expenditures in their locality so that they will not be at a loss to answer developers' claims. When these claims can be put into a realistic perspective, much more consideration can be directed toward environmental concerns and the impact of the proposed development on the esthetic, political, and economic characteristics of the community.

NOTES

1. This chapter is indebted to a study prepared for the Natural Resources Defense Council by William R. Ginsberg, Associate Professor of Law, Hofstra University.

Chapter 15 also discusses topics involving the property tax, including the special property tax provisions established for agricultural and productive forest lands in New York State.

2. A booklet entitled *Special Districts and the Alternatives,* published by the New York State Office for Local Government, explains and assesses the different kinds of special districts which exist in the state. *See* note 52 of Chapter 3 for comments regarding the availability of Office for Local Government publications.

3. Except in New York City, where the city government, which includes five counties or boroughs, pays the local share.

4. Studies show that clustering of development allows both the preservation of open space and considerable savings in service costs. *See* Task Force on Land Use and Urban Growth, *The Use of Land: A Citizen's Policy Guide to Urban Growth,* ed. William K. Reilly, a Task Force report sponsored by the Rockefeller Brothers Fund (New York: Thomas Y. Crowell Company, 1973), pp. 232–234; and Council on Environmental Quality, *Environmental Quality: The Fifth Annual Report of the Council on Environmental Quality* (1974). The land use section of the latter is available separately and at no charge as "Land Use Reprint from the Fifth Annual Report of the Council on Environmental Quality," from the Council on Environmental Quality, 722 Jackson Place, N.W., Washington, D.C. 2006.

5. Chapters 3 and 4 discuss state enabling legislation authorizing local governments to enact land use controls, some of which can require developers to bear costs associated with a development which might otherwise fall on the community.

6. July 28, 1974.

7. Lawrence Livingston and John Blayney, "Open Space vs. Development" (final report to the city of Palo Alto, California, Foothills Environmental Design Study, 1971), p.4, as quoted in Task Force on Land Use and Urban Growth, *The Use of Land,* p. 229.

CHAPTER 15

Preservation of Open Space

T HE FOCUS OF this book is on existing laws which mandate or permit various types of land use controls. Closely related to this concern is the question of how such resources as open space and historic sites can be preserved through property tax relief or through purchases by and/or donations to governments and charitable organizations. It is not possible here to treat this broad topic in full detail, but some perspectives on more recent ideas and methods can be provided and specific New York State laws concerned with preservation of open space can be described.

The approach taken by many conservationists to the problem of preserving open space has become much more pragmatic in recent years. While never abandoning the position that open space is vital to our society for reasons of ecology, public health and well-being, and esthetics, attention has been more and more focused on practical and economic means of encouraging and effecting such preservation. The need or desire of individual citizens to obtain tax benefits from gifts of land is now recognized as a basic factor in donations, and one that is entirely compatible with the desire to bring about benefits to the community. Rather than disparaging such motives, environmentalists are seeking to find ways in which individual tax needs and public open space needs can be dovetailed.

Far more research is being conducted to determine the economic and fiscal impact of open space in a community. First, it is now essentially clear that residential growth frequently involves fiscal penalties to a community because the costs of services required outweigh the increase in tax revenues received.[1] Documentation of this is being found in the experiences and studies of more and more communities each year. Thus, open space uses of land which require minimal services, if any, can be less costly to a municipality than residential development of the land. For example, the Foothills Environmental Design Study discussed in Chapter 14 found that acquisition of certain parcels of open space by the city of Palo Alto would be less costly to the city overall than many other alternative development patterns, particularly those with heavy emphasis on residential housing. In particular circumstances, complaints are still raised that preservation of open space takes land which could be used for development off the tax rolls, but there is a growing awareness that such complaints are often misguided.

Secondly, it has been demonstrated that open lands increase the valuation of adjacent property. People simply are willing to pay more for property that enjoys the amenity of open space. Thus, houses bordering on golf courses are assessed at high rates, even if their owners have no rights to the use of the course, and it is common practice throughout the country for FHA appraisers to place a higher valuation on lots if a development includes a park or is near a public park.

There is also new emphasis on encouraging uses of land which have commercial value but are consistent with maintenance of open space. Thus, viable farming and forestry operations can be sustained while at the same time open space is preserved for communities. The encouragement of such uses usually takes the form of some type of property tax relief. In New York State land is assessed not on the basis of its current use, but on the basis of its "highest and best use." Thus a farm on the fringes of suburbia is generally not assessed in terms of its agricultural value, but in terms of its potential for subdivision development. This has meant that many farmers have seen their property taxes steadily rise and have come under increasing pressure to sell out to developers. Likewise, federal and state inheritance taxes are also based on assessments of the "highest and best use" of land and thus families are often forced to sell land to pay such taxes. Under an agricultural tax relief system, variations of which have been adopted in many states, special agricultural districts may be set up, or farmers may make an agreement to use their land only for agricultural and related purposes in return for a reduction in property taxes on their farms. An Agricultural Districts Law, establishing such an agricultural tax relief system, was enacted in New York State in 1971. Another state law provides tax relief for certified forest lands. Both of these laws will be discussed in detail below.

It should be noted that the granting of tax relief for open space uses of land can raise land speculation problems. Under the New York State Agricultural Districts Law, for example, agricultural districts may be terminated by a county legislature after eight years. Thus, if a district were terminated, a farmer who had received property tax relief for eight years would then be able to sell his land to developers at market prices. Obviously, the profits which might be made in such a situation could be very high. Even within this eight-year period, if a farmer who has been receiving tax relief decides to sell the land to developers, the profits he makes on the sale will probably be much greater than the rollback tax he is required to pay. In such cases as these, where speculation in land is encouraged as well as open space uses, communities should weigh whether the balance of the inducement is toward continuing to hold or to sell land.

Another realization that has become accepted in recent years is that full or fee title to land does not necessarily have to be purchased by or donated to a government or charitable organization in order for the land to be protected from development. Such preservation can be achieved through the donation or purchase only of "development rights," i.e., the rights which entitle the landowner to develop his land, or of a negative or conservation easement whereby the landowner makes a covenant not to develop the land. In such cases, the landowner retains the rights to use the land in other ways, but it is no longer legally possible for him to develop the land or to sell it for development purposes.

Section 247 of the General Municipal Law, which is discussed on page 56 of Chapter 3, enables municipalities in New York State to acquire any type of interest in real property for the purposes of preserving open space within its jurisdiction. The statute states that:

> any county, city, town, or village after due notice and a public hearing may acquire, by purchase, gift, grant, bequest, devise, lease, or otherwise, the fee or any lesser interest, development right, easement, covenant, or other contractual right necessary to achieve the purposes of this [statute], to land within such municipality.[2]

Thus, local governments in New York State have been granted the legal flexibility to meet their individual open space needs in the best way possible. The law specifies that agricultural lands qualify as open lands under its provisions, so municipalities are authorized to obtain less than fee title to lands that can continue to be used for farming or forestry purposes. It should be pointed out, however, that in areas where there is very high development potential, the cost of development rights to farmland may be very high and only marginally less than the cost of fee title.

Once development rights or open space easements are acquired by a municipality, the assessment of the land for property tax purposes must reflect the limitations placed on its future use. This means a lower assessment and lower property taxes for the landowner.

No term of duration for restrictions on land use are established by Section 247. As far as the community is concerned, a restriction in perpetuity is probably the most desirable, but a period of at least five years should be established to prevent the provision from becoming simply a means of temporary tax relief.

The town of Ramapo in Rockland County has had an active open space easement program for more than five years and now has about 1,600 acres under restriction for development.[3] As is discussed below, Suffolk County has initiated a program in which it intends to buy both fee title and development rights to agricultural lands in the county. When it purchases fee title, it intends to strip the land of development rights and lease it back to farmers for agricultural purposes only.

It should be noted that the local environmental advisory conservation commissions and the county environmental management councils, discussed in Chapters 3 and 4, respectively, can serve as effective vehicles for the identification of open lands which ought to be preserved and the development of a plan for acquisition under Section 247 of the General Municipal Law.

There is currently much discussion and exploration around the country of a proposed system of land use regulation called "transfer of development rights" or TDR. Under this system development rights would be severed from other rights inherent in the ownership of land. Development would be prohibited in certain areas and allowed in others after the mandatory or voluntary purchase of development rights from the restricted land. Since the landowners in the restricted district would be able to sell the development rights from their land, such a system is not likely to be ruled a taking of private property, so long as there is an active market for the purchase of development rights.[4]

Basically, a TDR system would allow the owner of land devoted to low density use to transfer his unused development rights or development potential (i.e., the difference between the value of his land as it is now being used and as it could be used under current zoning) to an area that could or is already supporting high density use. In exchange, a property owner in the high density district would compensate the low density land owner for the transferred development rights. The proponents of TDR state that in this way low density resources can be saved and landowners can receive just compensation for restrictions on their property.

There is considerable interest in using TDR as a mechanism for saving urban landmarks and open space or lands of critical environmental concern which are in areas of present low density use but where the marketplace demands or urges high density use. For each of these purposes, an inventory should first be carried out to determine what land or landmarks the community desires to save. Then a "development rights transfer district," that is, the district into which development rights are to be transferred, must be selected and mapped out. A means of determining the value of development rights must also be worked out. Once this framework is established, the municipality can seek to facilitate the sale of development rights. Some proponents suggest that municipalities be given the right to condemn landmark buildings or their development rights if the owner refuses to negotiate a sale.[5]

Transfer of development rights systems have not yet been officially established for environmental protection, but exploration and experimentation are being carried out in Vermont, New Jersey, Pennsylvania, and Maryland. There are many features of TDR that must be further explored and delineated. For example, how should development rights be alloted within the restricted area? Should they be based on acreage, density, or the market value of the land? What should be the scope of the transfer district? How can an active market for the purchase of development rights be assured? Questions such as these must be answered before TDR becomes a workable zoning mechanism that can preserve open space.

The individual or family who wish to see land they own preserved as open space, have a number of different options, involving a wide range of tax benefits, including deductions from federal income tax, reduction of local property taxes, and reductions in state and federal inheritance taxes. The amount of a deduction from federal income tax for a charitable gift of land or a lesser interest in the land, as well as the value of this deduction to the taxpayer, will depend, among other things, on the nature of the gift, the size of the donor's income, and other deductions available to him. A tax counselor should be consulted regarding the best way to handle a proposed gift from a tax standpoint, just as legal counsel should be sought regarding the instrument of transfer used.

The federal income tax laws provide for a deduction from gross income of the present fair market value of land given to public charities, even if the land was purchased at a much lower value.[6] In general, a landowner may deduct up to 30 percent of his adjusted gross income for such a donation (corporations however, may only deduct 5 percent of their taxable income for such contributions), and any excess value over the 30 percent limitation (5 percent in the case of corporations) can be carried over and deducted in the next succeeding five years. Even if the total value of the land exceeds these broad limitations, or if the landowner wants to take deductions in particular years (perhaps because of fluctuations in his income), the problem can be solved easily by giving undivided interests in the land in the desired years. Such interests are fully deductible.[7] For example, a landowner could give an undivided quarter interest in the land in each of the years 1974, 1975, 1976, and 1977, and deduct a quarter of its value in each of those years.

In addition to the charitable deduction, a further benefit is obtained from the saving of capital gains taxes. Landowners who sell their land are required to pay a federal capital gains tax, which would not exceed 25 percent on the first $50,000 of net long-term gain[8] and a New York capital gains tax of up to 7.5 percent on the amount by which the sale price of the land exceeds its cost basis. If the land is given to a public charity, no capital gains taxes, federal or state, must be paid, regardless of how much the land has appreciated in value.

The savings in income and capital gains taxes resulting from a gift of land to a public charity can be illustrated by the following examples:

1. Assume that a forty-acre farm was purchased for $100 per acre, or a total of $4,000, and that it is now ripe for development and worth $1,000 per acre, or a total of $40,000. Assume further that the owner is single, and has federal taxable income of $22,000 per year.

He pays a federal income tax of $5,990 and a New York tax of $1,925.

If the farm were sold, there would be a capital gain of $36,000 on which the landowner would have to pay an additional federal tax of $8,400 and a New York tax of $2,689. He would realize a total cash return of $28,911.

If, however, the property were donated to a public charity, the landowner would pay no capital gains taxes, and would be able to deduct in each of six years 30 percent of his income, or $6,600. He would have to pay federal income tax of only $3,644 for a saving of $2,346 in the first year and annual savings of $2,086 in each of the next five years, a saving over the six-year period of $12,776. There would be an annual saving in New York taxes of $818, or a six-year total of $4,908.

The net result to the taxpayer from making a charitable contribution of his land rather than selling it is as follows:

Value of property	$40,000
Saving of federal capital gain tax	8,400
Saving of New York capital gain tax	2,689
Saving of federal income taxes	12,776
Saving of New York income taxes	4,908
Total tax saving	28,773

2. Consider the case of a wealthier taxpayer with federal taxable income of $70,000 per year, faced with the same choice of whether to sell land purchased for $4,000 but now worth $40,000, or to contribute it to a public charity.

This person pays annual federal income taxes of $32,790 and a New York tax of about $10,385. If he sold the land he would have to pay an additional federal capital gains tax of $12,040, plus an increase in New York tax of $2,700 (assuming that he has net long-term capital gains of at least $50,000).

If the property were contributed to a public charity, this landowner could deduct 30 percent of $70,000, or $21,000, in the year he makes the contribution, and the remainder of the value of the land, $19,000, in the following year. He would save $13,200 and $10,027, respectively, on his federal income tax. The saving in New York tax would be $3,150 and $2,850, respectively.

The net result to this taxpayer is as follows:

Value of property	$40,000
Saving of federal capital gain tax	12,040
Saving of New York capital gain tax	2,700
First year saving federal income tax	13,200
Second year saving federal income tax	10,027
New York tax saving	6,000
Total tax saving	43,967

An alternative method of deduction, Section 170(b)(1)(D)(iii) of the Internal Revenue Code, permits a taxpayer, at his election, to deduct up to 50 percent of his adjusted gross income in each year for a charitable contribution of appreciated property if he first reduces the value of the contribution to be deducted by one-half the amount of its capital gain—Section 170(e)(1)(A). The election of this alternative method would be advisable if the value of the property is substantial relative to income, if capital gains are relatively small, and if it is desired that maximum savings be obtained as soon as possible, or that deductions be concentrated in early years (for instance, because it might be expected that income will decline, or that other substantial contributions will soon be made).

In addition to the traditional means of donating land in its entirety to a local government, a government agency, or a charitable organization, the landowner has a number of other possible options.[9] He may prefer to donate an open space or conservation easement on his land, which will both provide open space for the community and allow him use of the land for purposes other than development. If the easement is donated to a local government in New York State, Section 247 of the General Municipal Law requires that a lower assessment based on the reduced value of the land be made for the owner's real property tax. If the easement is granted in perpetuity, the landowner is entitled to a federal income tax deduction of the fair market value of the interests in the land conveyed.

A third possibility is to donate the property, but retain possession and use of the property for one's own lifetime and/or the lifetimes of other members of one's immediate family. When a landowner establishes such a life estate, he can claim a tax deduction only if the property is a personal residence or a farm. The amount of this deduction will vary, depending on the age of the life tenants, in accordance with actuarial tables published by the Internal Revenue Service.

Another option is to convey property or a lesser interest therein in trust to a charitable organization that will carry out one's wishes regarding preservation and use. This is a very effective way of assuring perpetuation of desired restrictions. Due to the highly individualistic characteristics involved, however, great care will be required in establishing such a trust.

Gifts of land or interests in land may also be made in one's will. Provision may be made for an outright conveyance of land, with or without conditions, to a government agency or charitable organization; or for conveyance of a lesser interest, such as an open space easement; or for reservation of a life estate for one or more survivors. Such donations will reduce both federal and state inheritance taxes. Conveyance of an open space easement to a public or private agency will both reduce inheritance taxes and allow heirs to retain use of the property, which might not be possible if they had to pay full inheritance taxes on the land.

A landowner may also be able to provide an endowment for the maintenance of property donated. Such provision will make execution of the donor's special wishes more likely. In some cases, an agency may not be able to accept a gift of land unless it is accompanied by some type of endowment to provide for maintenance costs.

In addition to the different options that are available for making contributions to preserve open space, there are many different bodies to whom such gifts can be made. As pointed out in the discussion of Section 247 of the General Municipal Law, all municipal governments in the state are authorized to receive donations, after a public hearing, of land or interests in land for the preservation of open space. In addition, there are a number of state and federal government agencies which are authorized to accept donations of land and of lesser interests in land as part of their on-going programs. These include the Department of Environmental Conservation at the state level, and the Bureau of Fish and Wildlife in the Interior Department at the federal level. There are also many charitable organizations which can accept donations of land and lesser interests, as well as cash or securities to implement a land acquisition and preservation program. Perhaps the best known of these organizations is The Nature Conservancy, which is a national non-profit organization whose resources are solely devoted to the preservation of ecologically and environmentally significant natural land. The New York address of this organization is:

The Nature Conservancy
2 East 54th Street
New York, New York 10022

The address of the national office is:

The Nature Conservancy
National Office
1800 North Kent Street
Arlington, Virginia 22209

Another national organization that is very active in land preservation is the National Audubon Society, which has wildlife sanctuaries across the country. The address of this organization is:

National Audubon Society
950 Third Avenue
New York, New York 10022

In addition to these two well-known national organizations, there are many other national and local organizations which can accept gifts of land. The prospective donor may want to explore many different possibilities before determining which he feels will be the most effective use of the resources he wishes to contribute for public enjoyment.

One special legal provision with which prospective donors should be familiar is the possibility of including a "reverter" clause in the instrument effecting a transfer of land. This clause can specify that title to the land or interest in land will revert to its former owner or to a third party if it ceases to be used for the purpose defined in the instrument. For example, a parcel of land could be conveyed to the state government to be used as a nature preserve with the condition that it would revert to the Nature Conservancy if the land were used for purposes incompatible with this intent. A way to strengthen this provision is to make the original donation through an intermediate organization which can accept title from the donor and then transfer it to the recipient agency with a reverter clause in the instrument of transfer.

In some cases it is possible to donate land to programs for which there are federal matching funds available. Perhaps the best known of such programs is that operated by the Bureau of Outdoor Recreation of the U. S. Department of the Interior with resources from the

Land and Water Conservation Fund. Such possibilities should be researched for particular circumstances.

Of course, there are many other federal, state, and local activities which effect preservation of land through the establishment of parks, historical monuments, wildlife refuges, and environmental centers. In New York State, the Environmental Quality Bond Act of 1972 alone provided $175 million for land acquisition and protection by the New York State Department of Environmental Conservation (DEC), including

$59 million to acquire and protect forest preserve lands in the Adirondacks ($44 million) and in the Catskills ($15 million)

$18 million to acquire tidal wetlands and $5 million to acquire freshwater wetlands

$10 million to acquire unique areas outside of the forest preserves

$8 million to provide public access to currently inaccessible state-owned lands

$3 million to continue the state's fishing rights program

$9 million to preserve the public's right to access to New York's waterways

$59 million to acquire state parklands in urban areas, open spaces in or near urban areas and to complete the statewide trail network

This breakdown offers some insights into how major state funds for land acquisition and protection are being expended. It is not possible, however, to provide a full analysis here of how state, local, and federal programs and expenditures affect the problem of open space preservation.

It is possible, however, in the concluding section of this chapter to explain two important New York State laws which provide tax relief for preservation of open space that is used (1) for agricultural purposes; and (2) for reforestation. The first of these laws is the Agricultural Districts Law and the second, the forest tax law. Mention is also made of the special program instituted in Suffolk County for the protection of agricultural lands.

AGRICULTURAL DISTRICTS LAW

Although New York is not commonly regarded as a farming state, it ranks fourteenth in the nation in total value of farm products. In 1972 the state ranked second in the nation in cash receipts from dairying. Throughout the state about 200,000 people are employed in activities related to farming or the processing or marketing of farm products. One need only look at census figures, however, to find proof that the amount of farmland is dwindling. These figures show that in 1964 there were 66,510 farms in New York, comprising 12,275,500 acres. In 1969, there were only 51,909 farms, covering 10,148,349 acres; 14,601 farms, comprising over two million acres, had been lost in only five years.

In 1971 the New York State legislature passed the Agricultural Districts Law to encourage the development and improvement of the agricultural lands of the state for the production of food and other agricultural products, as well as to preserve open space:[10]

> It is also the declared policy of the state to conserve and protect agricultural lands as valued natural and ecological resources which provide needed open spaces for clean air sheds, as well as for aesthetic purposes.

In all, it is the purpose of the law:

> to provide a means by which agricultural land may be protected and enhanced as a viable segment of the state's economy and as an economic and environmental resource of major importance.

The law is intended to protect the state's agricultural lands from growing urban and suburban pressures. To implement this protection, it provides for the creation of "agricultural districts," special agricultural value assessments for property taxes, and certain restrictions to protect agriculture within established districts.

The property tax assessment provisions are the most important aspects of the law. In established districts and if certain conditions are met in agricultural lands outside these districts, farmers are eligible for an agricultural value assessment of their land. To qualify either within or without a district, a landowner must have "not less than ten acres of land used in agricultural production, which land had been used in the preceding two years for the production for sale of agricultural products of a gross average sales value of ten thousand dollars or more." The gross sales value of agricultural products produced on rented land may be added to the gross sales value of products produced on the farmer's own land in determining eligibility, provided that he owns at least ten acres of land. (Special provision is made for circumstances in which agricultural production is destroyed by "a natural disaster, an act of God, or continued adverse weather conditions.")

A qualified landowner must apply annually for an agricultural value assessment on forms prepared by the state Board of Equalization and Assessment. The following is the address of this board:

> The New York State Board of
> Equalization and Assessment
> Agency Building #4 Empire State Plaza
> Albany, New York 12223

A landowner outside an established district must make a commitment to continue to use his land exclusively for agricultural production for the next eight years. This commitment must be filed annually with the county clerk of the county in which the land is located. This filing entitles the land to be assessed on the basis of agricultural value as though it were in an agricultural district. In an established district, the landowner must file his annual applications with the assessor of the city, town, village, or county having the power to assess property for taxation. The law states that "[i]f the assessor is satisfied that the applicant is entitled to an agricultural value assessment, he shall approve the application and the land shall be assessed pursuant to this [law]."

Agricultural value per acre must be determined annually by the state Board of Equalization and Assessment, after consultation with the state Agricultural Resources Commission and consideration of data prepared by the U.S. Department of Agriculture and other appropriate data. Separate determinations are allowed for different regions of the state and for different types of farmland. In a particular instance then, an assessor will multiply the average value determined by the state by the number of acres of eligible land, apply the appropriate equalization rate, and arrive at an agricultural value ceiling for the lands concerned. No taxes may then be levied on that portion of the value of the land in excess of the agricultural value ceiling. This procedure, in theory, limits the real property tax of farmland to an assessment of its agricultural value only. There does exist some discontent, however, among lower Hudson Valley farmers, who question whether it is solely the agricultural value of their land which is being assessed. The tax ceiling in Dutchess County, for example, is much higher than it is in counties further north.

The law makes provision for the possibility that land assessed on an agricultural value basis may be converted to uses other than agricultural production. If such land is located within an established agricultural district, the owner is subject to a rollback tax on value in excess of the agricultural value assessment used for up to five years in the past, if he converts his land or a portion of it to non-agricultural uses. Outside of agricultural districts, landowners are subject to a tax penalty if they convert to other uses. If this landowner breaks the eight-year commitment which he has made, his land will be taxed at three times its assessed valuation in the year following the breach of commitment. Neither the rollback nor penalty provision applies if the conversion is the result of an eminent domain action or an otherwise involuntary proceeding, except for a tax sale.

The law sets out a detailed procedure to be followed in creating an agricultural district. It specifies that relevant considerations for determining whether a particular district ought to be established are (1) the viability of active farming in and adjacent to the proposed district, as well as the presence of viable farmlands that are not presently in active farming; (2) the nature and extent of non-farming land uses in the area; and (3) county developmental patterns and needs. The only inflexible condition set out by the statute requires that each proposed district be at least five hundred acres, and, as a general rule, large districts are preferred to smaller ones.

The process through which an agricultural district is established involves the following basic steps:

1. Landowners must prepare a proposal for a district and submit it to the county legislative body.

2. The county legislature must publish notice describing the proposal in a newspaper of general circulation within the proposed district and post this notice in five conspicuous places in the proposed district.

3. Any municipality whose territory encompasses the proposed district and any landowner who owns at least 10 percent of the land proposed for inclusion in a modification of the proposal may submit proposed modifications.

4. If it has not previously done so, the county legislative body must appoint an agricultural advisory committee, as authorized in the statute, consisting of four active farmers, four agribusinessmen, and one county legislator.

5. After a thirty-day period for the receipt of proposed modifications, the county legislature must refer the proposal and all proposed

modifications to the agricultural advisory committee and the county planning board for their recommendations.

6. The county legislature must then hold a public hearing on the proposal, providing notice of this hearing in a newspaper of general circulation.

7. Upon receipt of recommendations of the county planning board and the agricultural advisory committee, and after holding the public hearing, the county legislature must adopt, reject, or modify the proposal.

8. If the original or a modified plan is adopted, it is submitted to the commissioner of environmental conservation, who in turn sends a copy to the Agricultural Resources Commission.

9. If the commissioner of environmental conservation receives a report from this commission that the proposed district consists primarily of viable agricultural land, he may certify the plan or a modification thereof. (As originally written, the Agricultural Districts Law also required that the New York State Office of Planning Services review proposed districts to assess whether their creation would be consistent with the state's comprehensive plans, policies, and objectives. When the Office of Planning Services ceased operation in March 1975, the state legislature dropped this review procedure from the agricultural districts program.)

10. After certification, the county legislature may hold another public hearing on the plan and *must* hold such a hearing if the plan was modified by the commissioner of environmental conservation.

11. The county legislature must approve a plan modified by the commissioner of environmental conservation and may formally approve an unmodified plan. An unmodified plan that is not formally approved becomes effective thirty days after the termination of the public hearing or, if there is no public hearing, ninety days after certification.

An agricultural district, once created, must be reviewed every eight years. A public hearing must be held during this review, during which the district is reexamined at county and state levels. At this time, a district may be terminated or its boundaries may be changed.

The law also provides for another method by which agricultural districts may be formed. Beginning in September 1975, the commissioner of environmental conservation may create districts of 2,000 acres or more which contain "unique and irreplaceable" agricultural land. The statute defines such land as that which is "uniquely suited for the production of high value crops, including, but not limited to fruits, vegetables, and horticultural specialties." This type of district formation is also subject to substantial review by other agencies.

The Agricultural Districts Law also set forth certain measures intended to protect and encourage agriculture within established districts. No local government may enact laws or ordinances unreasonably restricting farming structures or practices, unless such enactments bear a direct relationship to public health or safety. State agencies are instructed, moreover, to encourage viable farming within districts through their administrative regulations and procedures.

Another provision of the law limits the exercise of eminent domain in agricultural districts, as well as the use of public funds for non-farm development. Any agency of the state, public benefit corporation, or local government which intends to acquire land or any interest in land or to advance a grant, loan, interest subsidy, or other funds within a district for non-farm purposes must file a notice of intent with the commissioner of environmental conservation at least thirty days in advance. The commissioner, in conjunction with the Agricultural Resources Commission, must review the proposed action to determine what its effect would be upon the preservation and enhancement of agriculture and agricultural resources within the district, and upon state environmental plans, policies, and objectives. If the commissioner finds that the proposed action might have an unreasonably adverse effect on such factors, he must issue an order to the agency, corporation, or government involved not to take action for an additional sixty-day period, during which time a public hearing must be held. After this hearing and a full review, the commissioner must report his findings to the body proposing the action in question and to all public agencies having review power over the action, and must also widely disseminate these findings to the public.

The commissioner may also ask the state attorney general to bring an action to enjoin anybody from violating any of the provisions of the Agricultural Districts Law.

It is too early to assess either the success or the impact of the agricultural district program, but it is clear that New York State farmers are taking advantage of the opportunity to create districts. Neither the paperwork, the time, nor the organizing involved in creating a district has discouraged the state's farmers. As of April 1, 1975, some 220 districts, comprising approximately 2.5 million acres, had been certified by the commissioner of environmental conservation. These districts are located in forty-four counties of the state, and include a sizable portion of the state's best farmland. It should be noted that counties near metropolitan areas where development pressures are greatest have been especially active in organizing agricultural districts. In Orange County, for example, which is only fifty miles from Manhattan, 21 agricultural districts had been established by the beginning of April 1975, providing protection for more than two-thirds of the county's farm acreage.

Suffolk County

Suffolk County, where a tremendous population growth is predicted in the next ten years and where land speculators have already bought up over half of the existing farm acreage, has instituted its own program of protection for agricultural lands. Under its farmlands preservation program, the county plans either to buy the development rights of farm acreage or to purchase the land outright and then lease it back to farmers stripped of development rights. A system of sealed bids will be used in these transactions. Thus, farmers will be able to continue farming, will receive payment for the development potential of their land, and will be relieved of substantial pressure to sell to developers.

In mid-1974 the Suffolk County legislature authorized a $60 million capital budget item to enable the county to make such purchases over the next three to four years. The first purchase under the program was made in August 1974 when the county purchased fee title to sixty-eight acres in the village of Bridgehampton. The county has now moved ahead with plans to purchase development rights from farmers. Sealed bids involving almost 18,000 acres were submitted to the county in February 1975, and the question of which of these rights to purchase was still under consideration in mid-April 1975.

FOREST TAX LAWS

New York State presently has on the books two statutes that establish tax relief programs for forest lands in which qualified tracts are assessed on the basis of their present use rather than their development potential. As a result of recent legislative action, however, no new lands may currently be accepted for such relief under either of these laws. The so-called Fisher Forest Act was passed in 1926 and reclassified as Section 480 of the Real Property Tax Law in 1959. This law was sharply criticized by forest property owners, and eventually was amended in Section 480-a of the Real Property Tax Law, which originally became effective on September 1, 1974. In May 1975, however, a bill was passed that postponed the implementation of Section 480-a until May 1977. Thus, since no new classifications of forest land can now be made either under the old Fisher Forest Act or the new Section 480-a, there is presently no means in New York State of obtaining tax relief for forest lands which have not already been classified.

The basic reason behind the state legislature's action to postpone the implementation of Section 480-a was a dissatisfaction with the effect this new forest tax law was having on local tax revenues. During the two-year postponement period, the New York State Department of Environmental Conservation (DEC) will study the law to assess its overall impact and to determine how it might be amended. The provisions of the law as it stands now are discussed below. Concerned citizens should be aware that amendments are likely before the law becomes effective once more in May 1977.

Under Section 480-a assessment of forest land can be made on the basis of present use rather than development potential. Each year the New York State Board of Equalization and Assessment must determine "the average value per acre of lands used in forest crop production in New York State . . ." Separate determinations may be made for different regions of the state and for different types of forest lands. The assessment of a given eligible tract of forest land is then determined by multiplying the average value per acre by the number of acres in the tract and adjusting the result by the latest state equalization rate or special equalization rate for the jurisdiction involved, if such a special rate has been established by the state Board of Equalization and Assessment.

Application for certification of forest lands under this act must be made with the New York State Department of Environmental Conservation (DEC). If DEC finds the tract to be eligible, it will file certificates of approval with local assessors and the county clerk of the county in which the land is located.

An eligible tract of land must be twenty-five or more acres in size (in contrast to the fifteen acres required under Section 480) and must be suitable for commercial forest growth, whether through seeding, planting, or the natural stand. Any land entered under this law must remain in forest production for eight years. If it is converted to another use during this time, the owner must pay a five-year rollback tax which represents the difference between the forest land assessment and the assessment of the same land at the alternate use. If the certified land is taken by eminent domain, the owner is not required to pay this penalty tax.

When in the judgment of DEC a certified tract contains 15,000 board-feet of merchantable timber per acre, either as sawtimber or pulpwood, hardwood, or softwood, the department must notify the owner that he must harvest this timber according to recommended forestry practices within two years. Six percent of the stumpage price must be paid to the town, whose supervisor must distribute the revenues between the town and the school district(s) in the same ratio as real property taxes were distributed in the same year. If the owner does not harvest within two years, he must pay the five-year rollback tax, and the land will be withdrawn from certification under Section 480-a.

The provisions of this law enable forest owners to preserve the open space character of their land while realizing an economic return on its natural resource. The older Section 480 also promoted open space preservation, but did not have stringent requirements for forest production. One could pay six percent of the estimated stumpage without actually harvesting and still retain Section 480 classification for the land.

Citizen Action

The range of possible citizen action to preserve open space is very broad and has been widely discussed in many quarters. Citizens may serve on local environmental conservation commissions which inventory the open lands in their community; they may form a citizens' group to work for the preservation of certain special areas; they may press their local governments to develop an open space plan and to take advantage of Section 247 of the General Municipal Law, which authorizes considerable flexibility in carrying out open space acquisition; as individuals, they can donate land or interests in land to make preservation of open space possible; they can conduct citizen education programs to inform the public of the growing vulnerability of remaining open space as well as of existing means of preservation. Indeed, the whole problem of preserving open space is such a far-reaching one that there are no clear limits to the range of citizen action and involvement.

344 /LAND USE CONTROLS IN NEW YORK STATE

NOTES

1. *See* Chapter 14.

2. This statute has been interpreted to permit acquisition by condemnation. *See* 18 Op. State Compt. 422 (1963).

3. *See* Chapters 2 and 3 for further discussion of Ramapo.

4. *See* Chapter 2 for discussion of the takings issue.

5. Professor John J. Costonis of the University of Illinois Law School has developed a TDR system designed to preserve landmark buildings. His three works on the subject are "The Chicago Plan: Incentive Zoning and the Preservation of Urban Landmarks," 85 *Harv. L. Rev.* 574 (1972); "Development Rights Transfer: An Exploratory Essay," 83 *Yale L. J.* 75 (1973); and *Space Adrift: Landmark Preservation and the Marketplace* (Urbana, Chicago, London: University of Illinois Press, 1974).

6. The following information on income and capital gains taxes, adjusted to reflect New York State law, is from a pamphlet entitled *Gifts of Land for Conservation,* which is available for $1 from the Conservation Law Foundation of New England, 506 Statler Office Building, Boston, Mass. 02116.

7. *See* Internal Revenue Code §170(f) (3) (B) (ii).

8. *See* Internal Revenue Code §1201(d) (3).

9. A publication of the Connecticut Department of Environmental Protection entitled, *Land: The Most Enduring Gift,* describes a number of the different options discussed here.

10. N.Y. Agriculture and Markets Law, Article 25AA, §300 *et seq.*

Addresses of Federal and State Agencies and Private Organizations Discussed in the Text

THE ADDRESSES AND telephone numbers of federal and state agencies and private organizations discussed in the text are provided in this appendix. For an annotated list of environmental organizations as well as of federal and state government environmental agencies, readers should consult *Environment U.S.A.: A Guide to Agencies, People, and Resources* (New York and London: R.R. Bowker Company, 1974). This reference work also provides a glossary of environmental terms and much other helpful information.

FEDERAL AGENCIES

Federal Insurance Administration
U.S. Department of Housing and Urban Development (HUD)
Washington, D.C. 20410
(202) 755–6770

Office of Interstate Land Sales Registration
U.S. Department of Housing and Urban Development (HUD)
451 Seventh Street, S.W.
Washington, D.C. 20410
(202) 755–5860

U.S. Environmental Protection Agency (EPA)
Waterside Mall
401 M Street, S.W.
Washington, D.C. 20460
(202) 755–2673

Region II
U.S. Environmental Protection Agency (EPA)
26 Federal Plaza, Room 1009
New York, N.Y. 10007
(212) 264–2525

UNITED STATES ATTORNEY

Northern District
Federal P.O. Building
Clinton Square
Syracuse, N.Y. 13201
(315) 473–6660

Southern District
40 Centre Street
New York, N.Y. 10007
(212) 791–0055

Western District
502 U.S. Court House
Niagara Square
Buffalo, N.Y. 14204
(716) 842–3479

Eastern District
225 Cadman Plaza East
Brooklyn, N.Y. 11201
(212) 596–5700

U.S. Securities and Exchange Commission
Division of Corporation Finance
500 North Capitol Street
Washington, D.C. 20549
(202) 755–1200

NEW YORK STATE AGENCIES

NEW YORK STATE DEPARTMENT OF ENVIRONMENTAL
CONSERVATION (DEC)

Central Office:

50 Wolf Road
Albany, N.Y. 12233
(518) 474–2121

*Regional Offices:**

Region 1:
NYS/EC Building #40
SUNY, Stony Brook, N.Y. 11794
(516) 751–7900

*See Map 2 on p. 348.

Region 2:
2 World Trade Center
61st Floor
New York, N.Y. 10047
(212) 488–2755

Region 3:
21 South Putt Corners Road
New Paltz, N.Y. 12561
(914) 255–5453

Region 4:
50 Wolf Road
Albany, N.Y. 12233
(518) 474–2121
and
Jefferson Road
Stamford, N.Y. 12167
(607) 652–7364

Region 5:
Route 86
Ray Brook, N.Y. 12977
(518) 891–1370

Region 6:
317 Washington Street
Watertown, N.Y. 13601
(315) 782–0100

Region 7:
100 Elwood Davis Road
North Syracuse, N.Y. 13212
(315) 473–8301

Region 8:
P.O. Box 57
Route 20
Avon, N.Y. 14414
(716) 926–2466

Region 9:
584 Delaware Avenue
Buffalo, N.Y. 14202
(716) 842–5824

NEW YORK STATE DEPARTMENT OF HEALTH (DH)

Central Office:
84 Holland Avenue
Albany, N.Y. 12237
(518) 474–2121

Office for New York City Affairs:
2 World Trade Center
49th Floor
New York, N.Y. 10047
(212) 488–2748

Regional Offices:
Building #9, Campus Site
Washington Avenue
Albany, N.Y. 12206
(518) 457–5150

584 Delaware Avenue
Buffalo, N.Y. 14202
(716) 842–4580

1475 Winton Road North
Rochester, N.Y. 14609
(716) 482–9711

677 South Salina Street
Syracuse, N.Y. 13202
(315) 473–8392

901 North Broadway
White Plains, N.Y. 10603
(914) 761–7900

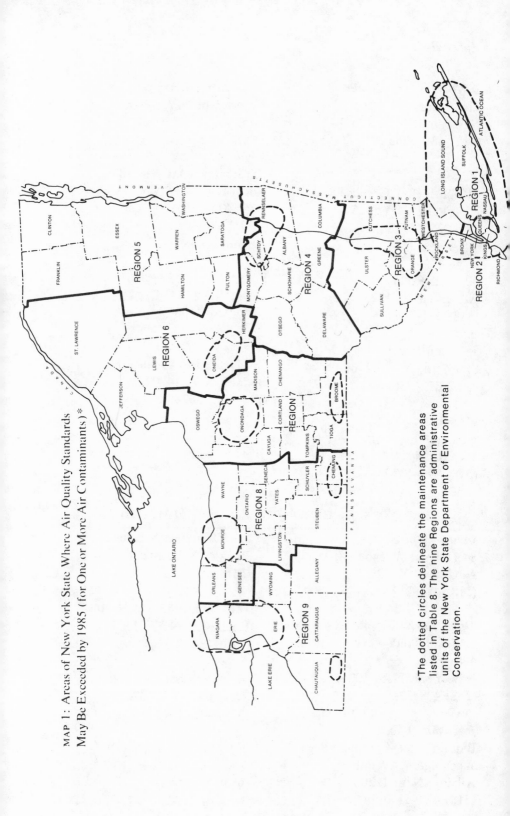

MAP 1: Areas of New York State Where Air Quality Standards
May Be Exceeded by 1985 (for One or More Air Contaminants) *

*The dotted circles delineate the maintenance areas
listed in Table 8. The nine Regions are administrative
units of the New York State Department of Environmental
Conservation.

District Offices:
81 North Street
Geneva, N.Y. 14456
(315) 789-3030

Quaker Village
Bay and Quaker Roads
Glens Falls, N.Y. 12801
(518) 793-3893

282 Canisteo Street
Hornell, N.Y. 14843
(607) 324-5120

19 North Williams Street
Johnstown, N.Y. 12095
(518) 762-3189

10 Water Street
Massena, N.Y. 13662
(315) 769-2870

6 Prince Street
Monticello, N.Y. 12701
(914) 794-2045

P.O. Box 459
Upper West Street
Oneonta, N.Y. 13820
(607) 432-3911

11-15 St. Bernard Street
Saranac Lake, N.Y. 12983
(518) 891-1800

207 Genesee Street
Utica, N.Y. 13502
(315) 797-6120

317 Washington Avenue
Watertown, N.Y. 13061
(315) 782-0100

OTHER NEW YORK STATE AGENCIES

Adirondack Park Agency
P.O. Box 99
Ray Brook, N.Y. 12977
(518) 891-4050

New York State Board of Equalization and Assessment
Agency Building #4
Empire State Plaza
Albany, N.Y. 12223
(518) 474-2121

New York State Department of Law
Bureau of Securities and Public Financing
2 World Trade Center
New York, N.Y. 10047
(212) 488-3310

New York State Department of State
Division of Community Affairs
162 Washington Avenue
Albany, N.Y. 12225
(518) 474–2121

New York State Department of State
Land Subdivisions
270 Broadway
New York, N.Y. 10007
(212) 488–3696

New York State Department of State
Licensing Services
162 Washington Avenue
Albany, N.Y. 12225
(518) 474–2121

Temporary State Commission to Study the Catskills
Rexmere Park
Stamford, N.Y. 12167
(607) 652–7511

PRIVATE ORGANIZATIONS

The Adirondack Mountain Club
172 Ridge Street
Glens Falls, N.Y. 12801
(518) 793–7737

The Catskill Center for Conservation and Development
Hobart, N.Y. 13788
(607) 538–3581

The Association for the Protection of the Adirondacks
21 East 40th Street, Room 704
New York, N.Y. 10016
(212) LE 2–4880
and
P.O. Box 951
Schenectady, N.Y.12301

Environmental Planning Lobby (EPL)
109 State Street
Albany, N.Y. 12207
(518) 462–5526

National Audubon Society
950 Third Avenue
New York, N.Y. 10022
(212) 832–3200

The Nature Conservancy
2 East 54th Street
New York, N.Y. 10022
(212) 751–2190

The Nature Conservancy
National Office
1800 North Kent Street
Arlington, Virginia 22209
(703) 524–3151

Sierra Club
Atlantic Chapter
50 West 40th Street
New York, N.Y. 10018
(212) 354–9624

The Conservation Foundation
1717 Massachusetts Avenue, N.W.
Washington, D.C. 20036
(202) 265–8882

GLOSSARY

Selected Legal Terms and Procedures

AMICUS CURIAE: Literally, a "friend of the court." In its discretion, a court may allow a party to present a brief or argument on an issue before the court as an *amicus curiae*. An *amicus* does not have the full rights of a party to the suit and should look at the issues before the court in a broad and fair-minded manner rather than adopting a partisan stance. Frequently an *amicus* seeks to provide special expertise or information that is helpful to the court.

"ARBITRARY" OR "CAPRICIOUS": Virtually synonymous words which constitute one of the standards by which courts judge the decisions of administrative agencies. Those decisions or orders of an agency which are arbitrary or capricious will be set aside. A decision or order will be found arbitrary or capricious if it is without rational foundation in logic or in the evidence.

ARTICLE 78 PROCEEDING: A legal action under Article 78 of the Civil Practice Law and Rules of New York State, which is the basic means of obtaining judicial review of administrative action (or non-action) by public officers or agencies. Typical circumstances which may prompt the initiation of such a lawsuit include the issuance of a decision by an agency, such as a zoning board of appeals or a planning board, or by an administrative officer, such as the commissioner of health or environmental conservation, which is felt to be arbitrary, discriminatory, or otherwise in violation of law; the refusal of a public officer or agency to take some particular (and nondiscretionary) action required by law; or the issuance of a license or permit, after a full-scale hearing, by such an officer or agency. Specifically, a proceeding under Article 78 may raise the following questions:

(1) whether the body or officer failed to perform a duty enjoined upon it by law; or
(2) whether the body or officer proceeded, is proceeding or is about to proceed without or in excess of jurisdiction; or
(3) whether a determination was made in violation of lawful procedure, was affected by an error of law or was arbitrary and capricious or an abuse of discretion, including abuse of discretion as to the measure or mode of penalty or discipline imposed; or
(4) whether a determination made as a result of a hearing held, and at which evidence was taken, pursuant to direction by law is, on the entire record, supported by substantial evidence.

In general, an Article 78 proceeding cannot be used to challenge a non-final decision or an action that is reviewable by normal appeal procedures, and it cannot be maintained where the action in question is legislative (e.g., the adoption of a zoning ordinance, as distinct from its enforcement). However, essentially all *administrative* action, whether by an individual officer or by a full agency, is reviewable under Article 78. In any such case, the court may annul or confirm the determination that has been made in whole or in part, or may modify it; and where non-action is the problem, the court may direct the responsible officer or body to take the action required by law.

An Article 78 proceeding is usually brought at a special term of the Supreme Court, but where there has been a full hearing on the record, the action may in some cases be brought in, or transferred to, the Appellate Division of the Supreme Court. The question of who may bring such a proceeding is a matter requiring the advice of an attorney. Generally, property owners and lessees who are or will be directly affected by the action or inaction involved may do so, but others may also qualify, depending on the particular circumstances.

Article 78 proceedings are intended to provide fast resolution of the matters they are designed to review. Thus a time limit is established requiring that, unless a shorter time is specified in a statute authorizing such a proceeding under particular conditions, an Article 78 proceeding must commence within four months after the determination to be reviewed becomes final and binding on the petitioner or after the respondent's refusal, upon the demand of the petitioner, to perform a duty. Shorter time limits are, for example, set for challenges to a decision by a zoning board of appeals (30 days)[1] and by the Adirondack Park Agency (60 days).[2] Citizens who are considering the possibility of bringing an Article 78 proceeding, therefore, should move quickly after the decision or default they wish to challenge to discuss the possibility with an attorney.

CITIZEN SUITS UNDER THE CLEAN AIR ACT OF 1970 AND THE FEDERAL WATER POLLUTION CONTROL ACT AMENDMENTS OF 1972: Under the Clean Air Act of 1970 any person has the right to sue in federal district court to enjoin violations of the act or the state implementation plans under it.[3] This broad right is limited in the following ways: (1) A citizen may not sue for damages, but only to enjoin an illegal act or to force the performance of a nondiscretionary duty. (2) If the administrator of the U.S. Environmental Protection Agency (EPA) or the state is diligently prosecuting a suit in the federal courts, a citizen may not institute a separate suit, but he may intervene and become a party to the suit. The act also provides for the payment of litigation costs, including attorney and expert witness fees, at the discretion of the court.[4]

The Federal Water Pollution Control Act Amendments of 1972 provide for citizen suits on essentially the same terms as the Clean Air Act, except that suits are limited to persons "having an interest which is or may be adversely affected."[5] Thus, a general, but unaffected interest in water pollution control would not be a sufficient basis for a lawsuit.

CRIMINAL PROSECUTION: Prosecution by the government (local, state, or federal) under a criminal statute usually resulting in liability for fine or imprisonment upon conviction.

DECLARATORY JUDGMENT: A decision of a court which declares the rights of the parties or expresses the opinion of the court on a question of law, without ordering anything to be done.

EXHAUSTION OF ADMINISTRATIVE REMEDIES: The doctrine that one must exhaust all remedies offered by an administrative agency before seeking court review of the agency's action. If the administrative remedies have not been exhausted by the plaintiff, many courts will dismiss on that ground a suit brought in the court.

INJUNCTION: A form of order issued by a court forbidding the party to whom the order is directed to perform certain acts. Injunctions are issued to stop or prevent actions which are or would be in violation of the law.

A *preliminary injunction* is an injunction issued at the beginning of a lawsuit to prevent a defendant from committing or continuing to commit an action which is disputed in the lawsuit. Preliminary injunctions are issued on a showing that the plaintiff is likely to suffer serious injury if the injunction is not issued and that the plaintiff is likely to prevail on the merits of the suit. At the close of the suit, the court decides the issues in dispute and either dissolves the preliminary injunction, allowing the defendant to undertake the prohibited action, or makes the injunction permanent or permanent until the defendant complies with particular legal requirements.

A *restraining order* is an order in the nature of an injunction. Temporary restraining orders are similar to preliminary injunctions in effect, but are issued in situations of emergency on the showing by the plaintiff that if the court does not act immediately, often without hearing the defendant, the plaintiff will suffer substantial injury to his interests.

INTERVENTION: An action taken by a party not originally part of a legal proceeding to become a party to the proceeding. For instance, agencies typically hold proceedings on applications for licenses and permits to which the agency and the applicant are automatically parties. Groups or members of the public may intervene in many of these proceedings by showing that they meet the agency's rules for intervention, and thus become parties to the licensing proceeding. Both the method of intervention and the rights of those allowed to intervene in agency proceedings vary markedly from one type of proceeding to another.

PRIVATE SUIT FOR DAMAGES OR RESTITUTION: A lawsuit brought by a private party against another in which the plaintiff asks the court to award him damages or restitution against the defendant on the basis of the defendant's invasion of the plaintiff's legal rights.

STANDING TO SUE: The doctrine that cases presented to the courts must be concrete controversies between parties with a real stake in the dispute presented. Parties bringing suits who do not have the necessary legally protected stake in the dispute do not have standing to sue, and the suit will be dismissed by the court. It is impossible to set out the exact bounds of the necessary stake, but financial injury certainly is sufficient to give standing, while only a generalized interest in an area never visited by the plaintiff and to which he has no economic ties is insufficient. Interests between these extremes are measured on a case-by-case basis, but generally in recent years the standards for standing have been relaxed and recreational and esthetic interests have been found sufficient to sustain a suit.

SUBSTANTIAL EVIDENCE: The U.S. Supreme Court has defined substantial evidence as "such relevant evidence as a reasonable mind might accept as adequate to support a conclusion."[6] In another case the Court has held that substantial evidence is "something less than the weight of the evidence, and the possibility of drawing two inconsistent conclusions from the evidence does not prevent an administrative agency's finding from being supported by substantial evidence."[7] The phrasing of the definition of this term thus varies in different cases, but the two above Supreme Court holdings cover its essential core meaning.

WRIT OF MANDAMUS: A form of order issued by a court which is usually directed to a government official or a lower court and commands the performance of a particular act pertaining to the public or official duty of the party to whom the order is directed.

NOTES

1. N.Y. Town Law §267(7); N.Y. Village Law §7–712(3); N.Y. General City Law §82(1).
2. N.Y. Executive Law §27–817(1).

3. 42 U.S.C. §1857h–2.
4. *Ibid.*
5. 33 U.S.C. §1365.
6. Consolidated Edison Co. v. National Labor Relations Board, 305 U.S. 197, 229 (1938).
7. Consolo v. Federal Maritime Commission, 383 U.S. 607, 620 (1966).

NOTE ON LEGAL CITATIONS

THE LEGAL CITATIONS which appear in some of the footnotes in this book, while readily understandable to attorneys, may appear somewhat perplexing to the general reader. The following explanations, therefore, offer some basic clarifying assistance:

1. *Federal Courts.* There are three levels of federal courts: the federal district courts, the circuit courts of appeals, and the U.S. Supreme Court. The district courts are the courts of first instance; appeals are taken from the district court to the circuit court of appeals. The circuit courts also review many decisions of federal administrative agencies which come to them directly without review by the district courts. The United States Supreme Court has the discretion to hear such appeals as it chooses from the circuit courts. The request for an appeal to be heard is made through a petition for a writ of certiorari. The Supreme Court also has discretion to hear cases appealed from the state courts where the cases raise federal constitutional questions.

The system of citations for the federal court system reflects the name of the case decided, the series in which the decisions are collected, the year and the court in which the decision was made, and sometimes the history of the case. The volume of the series always precedes the abbreviated title of the entire series cited and the page on which the case begins always follows the title of the series. The system is best understood by examples:

a. *District Courts:* Bass v. Richardson, 338 F. Supp. 478, 481 (S.D.N.Y. 1971). Bass is the plaintiff in the case and Richardson the defendant. The opinion in the case is found in volume 338 of the *Federal Supplement* ("F. Supp.") which collects the decisions of the district courts. The case begins on page 478 and the particular passage cited is on page 481. The decision was rendered by the District Court for the Southern District of New York in 1971. There are district courts for each state and the District of Columbia, many states being divided into more than one district.

b. *Circuit Courts of Appeals:* Gantt v. Mobil Chemical Co., 463 F.2d 691 (5th Cir. 1972). As with all citations, the names of the plaintiff and defendant give the case its title. The decisions of the circuit courts of appeals are collected in the *Federal Reporter,* which is now in the second numbered series ("F.2d"). The "2d" in the abbreviated title indicates the second series, as it does throughout the citation system. The court rendering the decision is indicated just before the date, here the Court of Appeals for the Fifth Circuit. There are eleven circuit courts of appeals, ten simply numbered and one for the District of Columbia Circuit. New York is in the geographic area of the Second Circuit.

c. *Supreme Court:* SEC v. Chenery Corp., 318 U.S. 80 (1943). The decisions of the Supreme Court are collected in the *United States Reports* ("U.S."). Since this series contains only the decisions of the Supreme Court there is no need to indicate the court of decision before the date in the citation.

In addition to these standard compilations of cases, there are two specialized reporter systems in the environmental field which record cases of all the federal, as well as state, court systems. These are the *Environment Reporter Cases* ("ERC") and the *Environmental Law Reporter* ("ELR"). They are cited in the same manner as the official reporters, e.g., Doe v. Roe. 6 ERC 1345, 1347 (S.D.N.Y. 1972).

2. *New York State Courts.* There are also three levels of state courts: the Supreme Court, the Appellate Division of the Supreme

Court, and the Court of Appeals, which is the state's highest court. The following examples indicate how the decisions of these courts are cited:

a. *Supreme Court:* Barnes v. Peat, Marwick, Mitchell & Co., 69 Misc. 2d 1068, 332 N.Y.S. 2d 281. (Sup. Ct. 1972). The *Miscellaneous Reports* ("Misc") in New York record the decisions of the Supreme Court. The *New York Supplement* series ("N.Y.S.") records cases from all New York courts; thus a double system of citation is used. The level of court, here the Supreme Court, is indicated just before the date of the decision.

b. *Appellate Division:* James v. Smith, 12 App. Div. 2d 120, 28 NYS 2d 95 (3rd Dept. 1968). *The Appellate Division Reports* ("App. Div.") record the decisions of the Appellate Division. The Appellate Division is divided on a geographical basis into a number of departments, and the department may be indicated just before the date in the citation.

c. *Court of Appeals:* Charles H. Greenthal & Co. Inc. v. Lefkowitz, 32 N.Y. 2d 457, 229 N.E. 2d 657, 346 N.Y.S. 2d 234 (1973). The decisions of the Court of Appeals are recorded in three series: the *New York Reports* ("N.Y."), the *Northeastern Reports* ("N.E."), and the *New York Supplement.* The *Northeastern Reports* include the decisions of the highest courts of the states in the northeastern part of the country. Because the *New York Reports* contain only the decisions of the New York Court of Appeals, the name of the court is not indicated before the date of decision in the citation.

3. *Federal statutes* are codified in the *United States Code* ("U.S.C."). In citations, the volume number precedes U.S.C. and the section number of the statute follows. For example, 33 U.S.C. §1251 *et seq.* (the citation for the Federal Water Pollution Control Act) indicates that the statute can be found at section 1251, and following, in volume 33 of the *United States Code.*

4. *Federal regulations* which are adopted pursuant to federal legislation are first published in the *Federal Register,* along with other official notices and information, and are then codified in the *Code of Federal Regulations,* which is cited as "CFR." Again, the volume number precedes the abbreviated series title and the part or section number follows.

5. *New York State statutes* are compiled in *McKinney's Consolidated Laws of New York.* Laws governing the same general subject matter are gathered under a topical title (such as Environmental Conservation Law and Real Property Law), and are published in separate volumes in an alphabetical series.

6. *New York State regulations* adopted pursuant to state legislation are codified in the *New York Code of Rules and Regulations,* which is cited as "NYCRR," with volume number preceding and part or section number following this abbreviation.

INDEX

United States Department of Transportation, 170

United States Environmental Protection Agency (EPA), 83, 84, 181–210, 212, 219, 295

United States Nuclear Regulatory Commission, 171, 295

United States Properties Corporation, 172

United States Supreme Court, 62, 190
basic Constitutional issues, 14–15, 16, 18–19
on zoning, 15

Utility transmission facilities, siting of, 303–307

Village Law, 26, 39, 46
Village level. *See* Town, city, or village level

Water Pollution Control Act Amendments of 1972, 10, 80, 85, 155, 160–161, 172, 211–232, 295
Army Corps of Engineers permits and, 224–227
citizen action, 227–230
land use planning provisions, 215–224
overview of, 212–215

Water Resources Commission, 73, 74, 76

Westwood Forest Estates, Inc. v. *Village of South Nyack*, 18

Wetlands, tidal and fresh water, 145–166
acreage (1967), 148
citizen action, 164–165
destruction of, 147–148
federal laws on, 156–163
importance of, 145–147

kinds of, 145
organic matter produced in, 146
other state laws on, 153–156
State Wetlands Act, 148–153
enforcement, 153
inventory, 150
land use regulations, 151–152
moratorium, 149–150
program and cooperative agreements for, 153

Wild, Scenic, and Recreational Rivers System, 287
citizen action, 293–294
management objectives, 288–289

Wild and Scenic Rivers Act, 281–287

Wisconsin Supreme Court, 17

Zoning ordinances, 26, 27, 28
Catskill region, 136
meaning of, 29
permit system for residential development (Ramapo, N.Y.), 18–19
"Petaluma Plan" (California), 18
Supreme Court on, 15

Zoning ordinances (local level), 29–40
adoption of, 29–31
implementation of, 31–32
site plan approval, 33
special provisions that may affect subdivisions, 33–34
innovative zoning, 33–34
planned unit developments (PUDs), 34
plats filed prior to adoption of (or amendments to), 33